CONSTITUTIONAL REASONING IN THE NORDIC SUPREME COURTS

This book explores the argumentative style of the supreme courts in the Nordic countries (Denmark, Iceland, Finland, Norway and Sweden).

Its findings are based on empirical research involving 280 leading constitutional cases which demonstrate that the impact of a constitutional ruling often extends far beyond the cases actually adjudicated by the courts and that it is crucial to understand how judges justify their decisions in constitutional cases.

In the cases researched, the authors identify and explain the common features of the Nordic constitutional reasoning, situating the Nordic experience within a broader comparative framework. The book compares these practices with those of non-Nordic jurisdictions, analysing whether and how the approaches of Nordic supreme courts align with each other and with global trends. This is made possible through the use of a well-established conceptual and methodological framework, adapted to the Nordic context. Key aspects of judicial reasoning are examined, including the emphasis placed on specific constitutional concepts, the use of non-legal arguments, the reliance on precedents, and the types of sources typically referenced – such as preparatory works, foreign legal materials, and academic writings. The book is aimed at anyone interested in the constitutional culture of the Nordic countries and informs normative debates on constitutional law, both in scientific and political discourse. It contributes to the global academic discourse on constitutional reasoning with a unique perspective from the Nordic countries, which have often been overlooked in comparative research.

Volume 35 in the series Hart Studies in Comparative Public Law

Hart Studies in Comparative Public Law

Recent titles in this series:

Australian Constitutional Values
Edited by Rosalind Dixon

Human Rights in the UK and the Influence of Foreign Jurisprudence
Hélène Tyrrell

The Nordic Constitutions
Edited by Helle Krunke and Björg Thorarensen

Regulation in India
Design, Capacity, Performance
Edited by Devesh Kapur and Madhav Khosla

New Media and Freedom of Expression
Rethinking the Constitutional Foundations of the Public Sphere
András Koltay

Why Religious Freedom Matters for Democracy
Comparative Reflections from Britain and France for a Democratic 'Vivre Ensemble'
Myriam Hunter-Henin

The Role of Monarchy in the Modern Democracy:
European Monarchies Compared
Edited by Robert Hazell and Bob Morris

Responsible Government and the Australian Constitution:
A Government for a Sovereign People
Benjamin B Saunders

Federalism and the Rights of Persons with Disabilities: The Implementation of the CRPD in Federal Systems and its Implications
Edited by Delia Ferri, Francesco Palermo and Giuseppe Martinico

Constitutional Courts, Media and Public Opinion
Angioletta Sperti

Judicial Review and Electoral Law in a Global Perspective
Edited by Cristina Fasone, Edmondo Mostacci and Graziella Romeo

Judicial Bricolage: The Use of Foreign Precedents by Constitutional Judges in the 21st Century
Edited by Tania Groppi, Marie-Claire Ponthoreau and Irene Spigno

Automation in Governance: Theory, Practice and Problems
Edited by Yee-Fui Ng and Matthew Groves

Federal Impartiality: Navigating Divisive Rights in the EU and the US
Mohamed Moussa

Constitutional Reasoning in the Nordic Supreme Courts

An Empirical and Comparative Legal Perspective

Edited by
Katalin Kelemen

•HART•
OXFORD • LONDON • NEW YORK • NEW DELHI • SYDNEY

HART PUBLISHING

Bloomsbury Publishing Plc

Kemp House, Chawley Park, Cumnor Hill, Oxford, OX2 9PH, UK

1385 Broadway, New York, NY 10018, USA

Bloomsbury Publishing Ireland Limited, 29 Earlsfort Terrace, Dublin 2, D02 AY28, Ireland

HART PUBLISHING, the Hart/Stag logo, BLOOMSBURY and the Diana logo are trademarks of Bloomsbury Publishing Plc

First published in Great Britain 2026

A catalogue record for this book is available from the British Library.

A catalogue record for this book is available from the Library of Congress.

Library of Congress Control Number: 2026935996

ISBN: HB: 978-1-50999-154-9
ePDF: 978-1-50999-152-5
ePub: 978-1-50999-153-2

Typeset by Compuscript Ltd, Shannon
Printed and bound in Great Britain

For product safety related questions contact productsafety@bloomsbury.com

To find out more about our authors and books visit www.hartpublishing.co.uk. Here you will find extracts, author information, details of forthcoming events and the option to sign up for our newsletters.

ACKNOWLEDGEMENTS

This book is the result of more than three years of collective effort by eight enthusiastic researchers, as well as a research project generously funded by the Swedish Riksbankens Jubileumsfond, an independent foundation that promotes and supports research in the humanities and social sciences (grant no. P20-0110). It would not have been possible without the dedication and curiosity of many people, first and foremost the other members of the research team: Maija Dahlberg, Morten Nadim, Haukur Logi Karlsson, Helle Krunke, Mikael Kenno Fogde, Åsa Elmerot, and Nicklas Pettersson. Working with them has been both intellectually stimulating and personally enriching. Their commitment, insight, and enthusiasm made leading this research not merely manageable, but joyful. I have learned an immense amount from every exchange.

We are especially indebted to the original creators of the CONREASON methodology, whose pioneering work laid the foundation for our analysis of the Nordic supreme courts. Their scientific vision lit the path we followed. Their conceptual clarity not only inspired our research design but also made this project possible. Among them, particular thanks are due to András Jakab, who sparked my interest in empirical legal research, provided invaluable assistance in formulating the project and later served on its Advisory Board.

We also owe a great deal to the many scholars who contributed to our academic conversations, challenged our interpretations and helped us refine our arguments. These include Jørn Øyrehagen Sunde, Johanna Fröhlich, Joakim Nergelius, Mila Versteeg, Tamás Győrfi, Jaakko Husa and Eoin Carolan. We are also grateful to all those who attended our seminars, commented on manuscripts, engaged in our webinar series, or otherwise supported our work. Finally, a special word of appreciation is owed to Anna Carlberg, research administrator, as well as economists Augin Acar and Urim Morina, all at Örebro University, who supported the practical dimensions of the project by arranging logistics and helping us navigate institutional procedures.

Katalin Kelemen

TABLE OF CONTENTS

Acknowledgements .... *v*
List of Contributors .... *ix*

1. *Exploring Constitutional Reasoning in the Nordic Supreme Courts Empirically: An Introduction* *1*
   Katalin Kelemen, Maija Dahlberg, Åsa Elmerot, Mikael Kenno Fogde, Haukur Logi Karlsson, Helle Krunke, Morten Nadim and Nicklas Pettersson

2. *About the Methodology: A Quantitative Approach to Comparing Constitutional Reasoning in the Nordic Supreme Courts* *23*
   Nicklas Pettersson and Katalin Kelemen

3. *Constitutional Reasoning at the Supreme Court of Denmark – In Front of and Behind the Scenes* *51*
   Helle Krunke and Mikael Kenno Fogde

4. *The Culture of Constitutional Reasoning in Iceland* *75*
   Haukur Logi Karlsson

5. *A Constitutional Culture in Transition? An Empirical Study on Finnish Supreme Courts' Constitutional Reasoning* *97*
   Maija Dahlberg

6. *International Constitutionalism: The Impact of International Law on Constitutional Reasoning in the Norwegian Supreme Court* *125*
   Morten Nadim

7. *Constitutional Reasoning in the Swedish Supreme Courts* *151*
   Åsa Elmerot

8. *Conclusions: Is there a Nordic Constitutional Culture?* *185*
   Katalin Kelemen

Appendix: Nordic CONREASON Project Codebook *209*

Complete List of Cases Used in the Nordic CONREASON Project *233*

Index *243*

LIST OF CONTRIBUTORS

Maija Dahlberg is Associate Professor of Public Law at the University of Eastern Finland Law School.

Mikael Kenno Fogde is Teaching Associate Professor at the University of Copenhagen, Denmark.

Åsa Elmerot is Senior Lecturer in Law at Uppsala University, Sweden.

Haukur Logi Karlsson is Associate Professor and Dean of Law Faculty at Bifröst University, Iceland.

Katalin Kelemen is Associate Professor in Law at Örebro University, Sweden.

Helle Krunke is Professor of Law at the University of Copenhagen, Denmark, head of the Centre for European, Comparative, and Constitutional Legal Studies, and the President of the International Association of Constitutional Law.

Morten Nadim is Associate Professor at the Department of Public and International Law at the University of Oslo (UiO), Norway.

Nicklas Pettersson is Senior Lecturer in Statistics at Örebro University, Sweden.

1

Exploring Constitutional Reasoning in the Nordic Supreme Courts Empirically: An Introduction

KATALIN KELEMEN, MAIJA DAHLBERG, ÅSA ELMEROT, MIKAEL KENNO FOGDE, HAUKUR LOGI KARLSSON, HELLE KRUNKE, MORTEN NADIM AND NICKLAS PETTERSSON

I. Judicial Power and Constitutional Reasoning in the Nordic Countries

The rise of judicial power has been a widely discussed global trend over the past three decades. Supreme and constitutional courts have been playing an increasingly influential role in defining the direction, shape and content of public policies in many countries.[1] The Nordic countries' supreme courts have not been an exception.[2] Somewhat unexpectedly, contrary to the general perception in comparative legal scholarship,[3] Nordic courts have started to take a firm stand on constitutional issues,[4] determining the fundamental questions of politics. In some cases, their decisions even provoked accusations of excessive judicial activism.[5] The impact of a constitutional ruling often goes well beyond the cases actually adjudicated by the courts. For that reason, it is of increasing importance to understand how Nordic judges justify their decisions in constitutional cases. The purpose of this book is to present the main findings of the Nordic CONREASON

[1] R Hirschl, 'The Judicialization of Politics' in R Goodin (ed), *The Oxford Handbook of Political Science* (Oxford, Oxford University Press, 2011).

[2] PH Lindblom, 'The Growing Role of the Courts and the New Functions of Judicial Process – Fact or Flummery?' (2007) 51 *Scandinavian Studies in Law* 281.

[3] M Wind and A Follesdal, 'Nordic Reluctance towards Judicial Review under Siege' (2009) 27 *Nordic Journal of Human Rights* 131; P Letto-Vanamo, 'Courts and Proceedings: Some Nordic Characteristics' in L Ervo, P Letto-Vanamo and A Nylund (eds), *Rethinking Nordic Courts* (Cham, Springer, 2021).

[4] M Sunnqvist, *Konstitutionellt kritiskt dömande: förändringen av nordiska domares attityder under två sekel. Vol. 1* (2. rev. uppl., Institutet för rättshistorisk forskning, 2014).

[5] F Wersäll, 'En Offensiv Högsta Domstol. Några Reflektioner Kring HD:S Rättsbildning' (2014) *Svensk Juristtidning* 1.

project, which examines constitutional reasoning in the Supreme Courts of the five Nordic countries, Denmark, Finland, Iceland, Norway, and Sweden.

Judicial reasoning can be understood in different ways. Our research does not delve into the causal-psychological process by which judges arrive at their decisions (known as motivational or motivating reasons). Judicial behaviour, as most political scientists define and use the term, falls outside the scope of this project. Instead, we focus on the written official justifications that the judges publicly provide for their decisions, which is commonly referred to as justificatory reasoning.[6] Of course, motives and justifications can sometimes overlap, but our primary focus is on those reasons that judges acknowledge as legitimate justifications for a judicial decision within their legal culture. We examine these justifications by considering both argumentation (examining different types of arguments, such as literal, teleological, systematic, etc) and conceptualisation (such as democracy, the rule of law, proportionality, etc) in judicial reasoning.[7] A conceptual system can vary in sophistication but is present in every legal system with an independent judiciary and an autonomous legal profession. It is not always solely based on the text of the constitution but often goes beyond that. Given that this conceptual system is built partly by courts, analysing the key constitutional concepts utilised by the courts in their reasoning provides valuable insights into a constitutional culture.[8]

While constitutional reasoning is not fundamentally different from legal reasoning based on statutory law,[9] what makes reasoning specifically 'constitutional' is that it is based on grounds that are commonly viewed as constitutional. Such grounds may vary among the Nordic countries. They primarily adhere to a formal definition of constitution, which refers to the rule (or body of rules) enjoying the highest rank in a legal order, with some material elements. For example, supranational norms and unwritten constitutional conventions may be encompassed if widely acknowledged as binding sources of law forming part of the constitution. All Nordic countries adopt a dualist approach to international law,[10] but the status of international law is rather complex and lacks detailed regulation in the domestic constitutions. While the Swedish Constitution explicitly prohibits the adoption of any act of law that contravenes Sweden's obligations under the European Convention for the Protection of Human Rights and Fundamental Freedoms (ECHR),[11] this provision formally does not elevate the ECHR to a constitutional

[6] A Jakab, A Dyevre and G Itzcovich, 'Introduction: Comparing Constitutional Reasoning with Quantitative and Qualitative Methods' in A Jakab, A Dyevre and G Itzcovich (eds), *Comparative Constitutional Reasoning* (Cambridge, Cambridge University Press, 2017).

[7] A Jakab, 'The Reasoning of Constitutional Courts in Europe' in A von Bogdandy, H Peter M and C Grabenwarter (eds), *The Max Planck Handbooks in European Public Law* (Oxford, Oxford University Press, 2023).

[8] ibid. For a more in-depth discussion of constitutional culture see the final chapter of this book.

[9] A Jakab, 'Judicial Reasoning in Constitutional Courts: A European Perspective' (2013) 14 *German Law Journal* 1215, 1224–26.

[10] T Ojanen, 'Human Rights in Nordic Constitutions and the Impact of International Obligations' in H Krunke and B Thorarensen (eds), *The Nordic Constitutions: A Comparative and Contextual Study* (Oxford, Hart Publishing, 2018).

[11] Chapter 2, Article 19 of the Instrument of Government (*Regeringsformen*) of 1974, which is the central component of the Swedish constitution.

level.[12] Nevertheless, there is a common understanding among Swedish scholars that the ECHR has a *de facto* semi-constitutional status.[13] A similar regulation is found in Norway. The Human Rights Act, which was passed as an ordinary piece of statutory legislation with a simple majority in Parliament, incorporates selected human rights conventions into Norwegian law,[14] and states that the rules in these conventions prevail if in conflict with other Norwegian law. However, they are not incorporated in the Norwegian Constitution. Still, the human rights conventions are considered to have the same *de facto* semi-constitutional status as in Sweden.[15]

Constitutional reasoning is not confined solely to the constitutional review of legislative and executive acts. The constitution is applied and interpreted by courts even in cases where no norm conflict arises between the constitution and lower norms, as exemplified by the well-known Danish *Tvind* case. This case concerned the scope of legislative power.[16] In its judgment, the Danish Supreme Court held that the principle of separation of powers, enshrined in Article 3 of the Constitution, sets certain limits on the extent to which the legislature may determine the legal relationships of individual persons. Based on our results, however, it is more likely that those cases become landmark constitutional cases where a norm conflict is at stake. In fact, cases of norm conflict make up the vast majority of our sample, which consists of the 40 leading constitutional cases from each of the examined supreme courts.[17]

In line with the CONREASON methodological framework that we have adopted,[18] the approach we take to constitutional reasoning draws on a realist account of judicial decision-making. Most constitutional comparativists do not accept the orthodox view of the legal profession, which advocates a formalist account of judicial behaviour.[19] The formalist (or legalist) account is built on the assumption that judges are primarily concerned with correctly applying legal rules and doctrines.[20] In this view, if judicial practices exhibit similarities, it is because

[12] J Nergelius, 'Judicial Review in Swedish Law – A Critical Analysis' (2009) 27 *Nordic Journal of Human Rights* 142, 152.

[13] Nergelius (n 12); Ojanen (n 10) 155.

[14] Currently, five conventions are incorporated by this law: UN Convention on the Rights of the Child 1989; UN Convention on the Elimination of All Forms of Discrimination against Women 1979; UN International Covenant on Economic, Social and Cultural Rights 1966; UN International Covenant on Civil and Political Rights 1966; The European Convention of Human Rights 1950.

[15] J Aall, 'Rettsstat og menneskerettigheter' (Fagbokforlaget, 2022) 115; E Smith, *Konstitusjonelt demokrati. Statsforfatningsretten i prinsipielt og komparativt lys*, 7th edn (Fagbokforlaget, 2024) 122; JEA Skoghøy, *Tvisteløsning*, 4th edn (Oslo, Universitetsforlaget, 2022) 538; R Aarli, '§ 92' in O Mestad and D Michalsen (eds), *Grunnloven* (Oslo, Universitetsforlaget, 2021) 898; J Fridthjof Bernt, '§ 113' in O Mestad and D Michalsen (eds), *Grunnloven* (Oslo, Universitetsforlaget, 2021) 1254. Also in Denmark, Jens Elo Rytter qualifies the relationship between the ECHR and Danish law as 'quasi-constitutional'. See JE Rytter, *Individets grundlæggende rettigheder*, 5th edn (Copenhagen, Karnov Group, 2024) 60.

[16] Højesteret Judgment 1999.841H of 19 February 1999.

[17] 258 of our 280 cases (ie 92.14% of our sample) are judicial review cases.

[18] See section III below on the methodological design.

[19] T Gyorfi, 'The Politics of Constitutional Interpretation' in M Tushnet and D Kochenov (eds), *Research handbook on the politics of constitutional law* (Cheltenham, Edward Elgar Publishing, 2023) 199.

[20] F Schauer, 'Formalism' (1988) 97 *Yale Law Journal* 509.

judges must apply similar rules, and if they diverge, it is because the rules they apply differ. Judicial decisions 'follow' from the rules, and if judicial decisions applying the same rules differ from each other, then one of them must be legally 'wrong'. Conversely, the realist model, associated with American legal realism, posits that judicial decision-making is determined by considerations that are not purely legal,[21] such as economic and social mechanisms as well as inherited institutional structures and cultural attitudes.[22] There is overwhelming empirical evidence demonstrating that constitutional adjudication is influenced by the policy preferences of individual judges as well as by institutional and strategic considerations that are not strictly 'legal' in nature.[23] Consequently, we recognise that a judicial decision does not necessarily fully reflect the decision-maker's actual reasoning. Nevertheless, it still provides a valuable picture of the (primarily legal) reasons that are considered legitimate within the given legal system.

In the Nordic context, however, a distinct form of legal realism shaped legal thinking. Scandinavian legal realism, unlike American legal realism, was a branch of analytical legal philosophy, or even a version of legal positivism,[24] opposing both natural law and 'legal idealism'. It aimed to establish a clear separation between law, as well as between politics and law and morality.[25] The Swede Vilhelm Lundstedt, a prominent figure of this school of thought, argued that abstract concepts such as 'rights' and 'interests' are pure metaphysics. He emphasised the power of the state as a constant presence in the background of and an indispensable precondition for private legal relations.[26] Alf Ross, a prominent and internationally well-known Danish legal realist, argued that justice cannot serve as a legal-political standard or a supreme criterion for determining which rule should be preferred over another. However, he maintained that rationality and predictability are closely linked to justice. Ross also argued that to establish the state of the law, one must predict how a case would turn out in the courts. He did not view judges at an individual level but rather as a group. He believed in the existence of a judges' ideology – a normative ideology – not driven by arbitrariness or waywardness of individual judges. Furthermore, Ross adopted a formal understanding of democracy, emphasising the importance of democratic procedures, which has had a great impact on how democracy is viewed in the Nordics.[27]

Scandinavian legal realists viewed legal formalism as a tool to challenge the dominance of the Historical School and the Conceptualist School (*Begriffsjurisprudenz*)

[21] OW Holmes, 'The Path of the Law' (1998) 78 *Boston University Law Review* 699.

[22] Jakab, Dyevre and Itzcovich, 'Introduction' (n 6) 15.

[23] JA Segal and HJ Spaeth, *The Supreme Court and the Attitudinal Model Revisited* (Cambridge, Cambridge University Press, 2002); L Epstein, WM Landes and RA Posner, *The Behavior of Federal Judges a Theoretical and Empirical Study of Rational Choice* (Cambridge, MA, Harvard University Press, 2013).

[24] GS Alexander, 'Comparing the Two Legal Realisms-American and Scandinavian' (2002) 50 *American Journal of Comparative Law* 131, 132.

[25] ibid.

[26] V Lundstedt, *Legal Thinking Revised: My Views on Law* (Stockholm, Almquist & Wiksell, 1956).

[27] A Ross, *Dansk Statsforfatningsret 1*, 3rd edn (Nyt Nordisk Forlag, 1983) 128–48.

in Nordic legal thought. By doing so, they hoped to create more room for the manifestation of popular sovereignty through legislation.[28] The popularity of this school of thought brought a perception of the law as an expression of the popular will and, therefore, a product of the legislature. This school of thought consequently favoured the government and the Parliament over the courts, allowing little room for judicial activism.[29] Even in Norway, Torstein Eckhoff, a leading legal scholar of the twentieth century, expressed scepticism about the power of judicial review.[30] This sets a very different scene from other European legal systems where the power of judicial review has been received with more enthusiasm.

Against this backdrop, this book aims to provide a more nuanced understanding of Nordic constitutionalism by examining constitutional reasoning in the Nordic supreme courts empirically. By comparing our findings with those from other jurisdictions, we highlight the ways in which Nordic constitutionalism both aligns with and diverges from global trends. These insights also aim to enrich comparative constitutional scholarship by emphasising the importance of adapting methodologies to specific contexts while ensuring cross-jurisdictional comparability. Ultimately, we seek to deepen our understanding of Nordic constitutional reasoning and contribute to the ongoing global discourse on constitutional law. To achieve this, we must first consider the key specificities of the Nordic context and choose an appropriate methodological approach.

II. Specificities of the Nordic Context

A. The Power of Judicial Review in the Nordic Countries

Today, all Nordic courts possess the power of judicial review. Therefore, the Nordic systems of judicial review can unequivocally be classified as belonging to the decentralised model. However, the Nordic supreme courts began to exercise this power during different historical periods and use it to varying degrees. While judicial review of legislative acts was, at least occasionally, exercised as a constitutional convention by the supreme courts of Norway, Denmark, Iceland and Sweden without an explicit basis in the constitutional text, in Finland a provision of the then constitution was interpreted *e contrario* as implying a strict prohibition of judicial review of legislative acts.[31] When the current Finnish Constitution came into force

[28] Alexander (n 24) 167.

[29] S Schaumburg-Müller, 'Parliamentary Precedence in Denmark – A Jurisprudential Assessment' (2009) 27 *Nordic Journal of Human Rights* 170, 182.

[30] T Eckhoff, 'Høyesterett som Grunnlovens vokter' [The Supreme Court as the Guardian of the Constitution] (1976) 10 *Jussens Venner* 1.

[31] J Husa, *The Constitution of Finland: A Contextual Analysis* (Oxford, Bloomsbury Publishing, 2011) 159–60.

in 2000, this implicit prohibition was replaced by an explicit permission.[32] Since then, the Finnish courts have also been able to review legislative acts.

In Sweden, judicial review was codified in 1979.[33] However, the existence of judicial review as a constitutional convention was acknowledged before codification, in parliamentary inquiries and preparatory works during the constitutional reforms from the 1960s and onwards.[34] At the time of codification, the Committee on the Constitution (*Konstitutionsutskottet*), a standing parliamentary committee, emphasised that the codification of judicial review was not intended to make it a routine aspect of daily court proceedings. Instead, the previously cautious approach should continue to guide its application.[35] It was thus not expected that the courts should actively make use of the power of judicial review.

In Norway, judicial review was codified in 2015,[36] while in Iceland and Denmark it is still exercised as an uncodified constitutional convention. The Norwegian system of judicial review is arguably the oldest in Europe, and the first case where a legislative act set aside by judicial review was decided in 1866. In contrast, as Finland was the last Nordic state to allow its judges to review the constitutionality of legislation, the Finnish journey into judicial review of such acts began much later than the other Nordic countries. However, as is shown in the table below, it did not take long before the first Finnish judgment where a law was set aside by judicial review (2004).

After a period of inactivity during much of the twentieth century, judicial review was revived in Norway with the *Kløfta* case in 1976. The Norwegian system of judicial review is not only the oldest but also the most active among the Nordic countries,[37] with the Icelandic system being the second most active.[38] The first case in which a legislative act was set aside in Iceland dates back to 1943.[39] However, the Supreme Court of Iceland had previously exercised the power of judicial review, but without finding a violation of the Constitution.[40]

Similarly in Sweden, the courts exercised judicial review as a constitutional convention before the first case of finding an actual violation. A Supreme Court judgment from 1964 is considered as the case establishing judicial review of legislative acts, although the act in question was not set aside as unconstitutional.[41]

[32] Article 106 of the Finnish Constitution. See, eg, K Tuori, 'Judicial Constitutional Review as a Last Resort' in *The Legal Protection of Human Rights: Sceptical Essays* (Oxford, Oxford University Press, 2011) 381.

[33] Chapter 11, Article 14 of the Instrument of Government.

[34] SOU 1963:17, 155–56.

[35] Konstitutionsutskottets betänkande 1978/79:KU39 [Parliamentary committee report] 13.

[36] Article 89 of the Norwegian Constitution.

[37] R Helgadóttir, *The Influence of American Theories on Judicial Review in Nordic Constitutional Law* (Brill | Nijhoff, 2006); K á Rógvi, *West-Nordic Constitutional Judicial Review: A Comparative Study of Scandinavian Judicial Review and Judicial Reasoning* (Copenhagen, DJØF Publishing, 2013).

[38] E Smith, 'Judicial Review of Legislation' in H Krunke and B Thorarensen (eds), *The Nordic constitutions: a comparative and contextual study* (Oxford, Hart Publishing, 2018) 113.

[39] R Helgadóttir, 'Status Presens – Judicial Review in Iceland' (2009) 27 *Nordic Journal of Human Rights* 185, 185.

[40] ibid.

[41] Nergelius (n 12) 145.

Interestingly, there is no general consensus as to which case was the first case where a legislative act was set aside by judicial review. The first case after the codification of judicial review in 1979 is a case from the courts of appeals of Western Sweden from the 1990s, which never even made it to the Supreme court.[42]

In Denmark, the first case where a law was set aside as unconstitutional was the *Tvind* case in 1999, although the Supreme Court of Denmark had considered itself competent to review the constitutionality of legislation well before that. Not only is this the first case where a Danish court set aside a law due to it being contrary to the Constitution, it is also the only such case to date, setting the Danish Supreme Court apart from its Nordic counterparts.[43]

The following Table summarises the most significant facts regarding the historical development and legal basis of (constitutional) judicial review in the Nordic countries:

Table 1 Significant facts regarding the historical development and legal basis of (constitutional) judicial review in the Nordic countries

	Denmark	Finland	Iceland	Norway	Sweden
Year of the constitution currently in force / last major constitutional reform(s)	1849 / 1953	2000	1944	1814 / 1905 / 2014	1974 / 2010
First case when a piece of legislation was found to be unconstitutional	U 1999.841 H (Tvind case)	KKO 2004:26 (ordinary Supreme Court)	10 L&H 601 (1943)	UfL 1866, p 165 (Wedel Jarlsberg case)	See main text.
Constitutional provision on the power of judicial review	no written provision, constitutional convention	Section 106 of the Constitution	no written provision, constitutional convention	constitutional convention until 2015, Art. 89 Const.since then	Accepted by doctrine since the 1930s.[44] Since 1979, enshrined in Chapter 11, Article 14 of the Instrument of Government

[42] RH 1997:47 (Hovrätten för Västra Sverige). J Nergelius, 'Om grundlagstolkning, grundlagsvänlig lagtolkning och åsidosättande av grundlagsstridig lag' (1996) *Svensk Juristtidning* 835.

[43] See also ch 3.

[44] Nergelius (n 12).

B. The Role of Non-judicial Bodies and Preparatory Works

The Nordic countries offer a unique setting for the study of constitutional reasoning in courts for several reasons. First, there are other, non-judicial bodies that play an important role in interpreting the constitution. These non-judicial bodies are either formally part of the legislature, such as the constitutional law committees of the Finnish Parliament (*Perustuslakivaliokunta*) and of the Swedish Riksdag (*Konstitutionsutskottet*), or they are independent bodies, such as the Council on Legislation (*Lagrådet*) in Sweden. Indeed, in the Nordic context it is particularly evident that not all constitutional reasoning takes place in courts. Even the parliamentary ombudsmen and other public authorities, such as the Chancellor of Justice (*Justitiekanslern*) in Sweden and Finland, engage in constitutional reasoning. Nevertheless, our focus is on constitutional reasoning in courts, which provide an important forum for discussing constitutional matters even in the Nordic context.

In addition to acknowledging the existence of significant constitutional interpreters outside the courts, it is also important to understand the role of preparatory works in legal reasoning in the Nordic courts when studying constitutional reasoning in greater depth. In order to understand the unique role of preparatory works in Nordic legal interpretation, it is necessary to acknowledge the peculiarities of Nordic legal culture in general, which ranks the legislature, as an expression of popular sovereignty, at the top.[45] Consequently, the preparatory works of legislation are given high status in the Nordic sources of law doctrine and are considered to be an independent source of law. The independence of the preparatory works from legislative texts means that such works contain, for example, statements about the meaning of the provision that go beyond what is explicitly stated in the text of the provision itself.[46]

In the Nordic context, preparatory works typically include material produced both before and during the legislative or constitution-making process. In the Nordic tradition, there are typically no preambles to legislative texts. Instead, the government's proposals describe the general objectives and purpose of the new enactment, as well as its relationship to existing legislation. Government proposals also contain detailed explanatory memoranda for each section and subsection. Preparatory works include government proposals, reports from parliamentary committees that have dealt with the proposal, and statements and suggestions made during the plenary session of Parliament. The preparation leading to the drafting of government bills varies. Important or politically sensitive bills are often

[45] M Lundström, 'Value Relativism, Procedural Democracy and Opinion Representation – Reflections on Three Conceptual Underpinnings of Swedish Anti-Constitutionalism' (2009) 27 *Nordic Journal of Human Rights* 242; Jaakko Husa, 'Constitutional Mentality' in P Letto-Vanamo, D Tamm and BOG Mortensen (eds), *Nordic Law in European Context*, vol 73 (Cham, Springer, 2019); M Wind, 'Do Scandinavians Care about International Law? A Study of Scandinavian Judges' Citation Practice to International Law and Courts' (2016) 85 *Nordic Journal of International Law* 281.

[46] L Björne, *Nordisk rättskälleläa: studier i rättkälleläran på 1800-talet* (Institutet för rättshistorisk forskning, 1991) 222.

prepared by various committees and task groups. As such, the deliberations of these committees are considered part of the preparatory works and are used in the same way by lawyers, prosecutors, judges, and legal scholars when interpreting the legislation.[47]

In contrast to the Nordic use of preparatory works in adjudication, other European legal systems recognise that preparatory material and legislative intent serve more as aids to interpretation, helping to establish the objectives of the written law. Moreover, some jurisdictions only allow the use of legislative history in cases where a provision is unclear or ambiguous.[48] Consequently, although legislative intent is recognised as a type of legal argument in all legal systems and is one of the types of argument we consider in our empirical analysis of leading constitutional cases in and outside the Nordics, it is employed as an independent argument in the Nordic countries. In addition, in the US context, for example, original intent – an interpretative method favoured by conservative interpreters of the US Constitution – requires the courts to interpret the Constitution in accordance with the understanding of its framers.[49] However, outside the Nordics, the framing documents or preparatory works are not considered to be an independent source of law. From a legal theoretical point of view, the use of legislative intent as a method of legal interpretation is highly criticised.[50] Taking all this into account, as we will demonstrate in the following chapters, the constitutional reasoning of the Nordic courts exhibits peculiarities compared to constitutional reasoning in Europe and beyond.

C. A Legislature-centred Approach to Constitutionalism

A unique feature of Nordic constitutionalism closely related to the ones discussed above is that the primary interpreter of the constitution in these countries has traditionally been the legislature. This places an expectation on the judges that they should give priority to the views of the present majority and only set them aside in cases where the conflict with the constitution is glaringly evident. The Nordic courts have typically exercised considerable restraint in using the power of constitutional review, often deferring to the legislature.[51] Indeed, their system of judicial review has been labelled as 'weak-form review'.[52]

[47] Husa, *The Constitution of Finland* (n 31) 29.
[48] M Florczak-Wątor (ed), *Constitutional Law and Precedent: International Perspectives on Case-Based Reasoning* (Abingdon, Routledge, 2022).
[49] K Whittington, *Constitutional Interpretation: Textual Meaning, Original Intent, and Judicial Review* (Lawrence, University Press of Kansas, 1999) 47–61.
[50] M Aalto-Heinilä, 'Intentionalism' in M Sellers and S Kirste (eds), *Encyclopedia of the Philosophy of Law and Social Philosophy* (Dordrecht, Springer Netherlands, 2023).
[51] Wind and Follesdal (n 3).
[52] ibid 131; R Hirschl, 'The Nordic Counternarrative: Democracy, Human Development, and Judicial Review' (2011) 9 *International Journal of Constitutional Law* 449, 451; I Nguyên Duy, 'New Trends in Scandinavian Constitutional Review' (2015) 61 *Scandinavian Studies in Law* 11, 13.

In the years around the turn of the eighteenth century, many Western states developed constitutions. Some, but not all, of the Nordic countries also adopted constitutions during this period. The Norwegian Constitution, adopted in 1814 and still in force, was a direct consequence of the end of the Napoleonic wars. Sweden (1809, in force until 1974) and Denmark (1849, still in force) also introduced constitutions in the wake of absolutism.[53] However, the Nordic constitutions were not revolutionary documents in the same sense as, for instance, the French and US constitutions. In these constitutions, the monarchy prevailed, but as one of the three branches of government established on the basis of Montesquieu's theory.

In *De l'esprit des lois*, Charles Montesquieu argued for a separation of powers into the legislative, executive and judicial branches. However, he emphasised the legislative branch as the most important of the three. The Nordic constitutions implemented this idea, and thus parliaments became important institutions. He envisioned courts as impartial and independent from political influence, with judges objectively applying laws, not making them. This view of the courts as more passive branches of government is illustrated by the process by which the Norwegian Constitution was created. The courts' role as active branches of government was hardly discussed at all.[54]

This emphasis on the parliament and the monarchy, and the downplaying of the role of the courts, may explain why Nordic courts have traditionally exercised restraint in judicial review. The history of how judicial review has been practised is obviously not the same for all Nordic courts, but they share these features from their constitutional history. In one jurisdiction, Norway, judicial review has been heavily discussed since the Constitution of 1814, and the way in which the court has reviewed the constitutionality of legislation has varied over time. However, in all judicial review cases, the Norwegian Supreme Court has, in one way or another, emphasised that Parliament's view on constitutionality should be a factor. The weight given to Parliament's views has varied. This shows a consistent deference to the legislature, but it also shows that the degree of deference has varied.

All Nordic countries have doctrines of deference to the legislature. The constitutional convention of judicial review, as developed in both Denmark and Sweden, revolves around the requirement of 'manifest unconstitutionality'. A requirement of 'manifest error' was formally incorporated into the Swedish Constitution between the 1979 and 2010 revisions, and it remains explicitly included in the Finnish Constitution, according to which judicial review is still limited to cases where the conflict with the constitution is evident.[55] In Denmark, although the

[53] Iceland became independent from Denmark in 1918/1944 and Finland gained independence from Russia in 1917.

[54] A Tverberg in O Mestad and D Michalsen (eds), *Grunnloven* (Oslo, Universitetsforlaget, 2021) 855–83, 861.

[55] See Article 106 of the Finnish Constitution, and Chapter 11, Article 14 of the Swedish Instrument of Government.

requirement has not been formally incorporated into the Constitution, it has been repeatedly confirmed by the Supreme Court.[56]

In Sweden, when judicial review was codified, there was a statement in the preparatory works of the constitutional amendment that the courts must respect the Parliament's assessment that a piece of legislation was compatible with the constitution, as long as it remained within the framework of a possible constitutional interpretation.[57] In other words, the preparatory works instructed the courts to show deference to Parliament. Although the requirement of manifest error was removed in the constitutional amendments of 2010, the current wording of the Swedish Constitution still reflects the traditional approach. After granting courts the authority to set aside a provision that conflicts with a fundamental law or another higher-ranking statute, Chapter 11, Article 14 of the Instrument of Government now stipulates that in exercising judicial review judges shall 'pay particular attention to the fact that the Riksdag, the Swedish Parliament, is the foremost representative of the people' and that 'the fundamental law takes precedence over the statute'. According to the preparatory works, this serves as a reminder that Parliament is regarded as the primary interpreter of the Constitution, while at the same time making it clear that political decision-making is confined within certain boundaries.[58]

In the Norwegian *Kløfta* case, the Court added that the Parliament's view on the constitutionality of a piece of legislation should 'clearly' be given 'considerable' weight and that the Court should be 'careful' not to prefer its own view to that of the legislature.[59] Norway differs from its Nordic counterparts, however, in its use of what might be called a Norwegian version of the American preferred position principle.[60] The principle, which originated in the *Kløfta* case, implies that the level of scrutiny applied by the courts should vary according to the nature of the constitutional provisions with which a statute is alleged to conflict.

Indeed, a similar line of reasoning can be seen in the preparatory works for the 2010 revision of the Swedish Instrument of Government. After emphasising the importance of judicial review of legislation in a way that clearly differs from the earlier preparatory works, rights and freedoms (including freedom of the press and the ECHR) are singled out as areas where it is especially crucial for constitutional provisions (and judicial review) to have an impact (*genomslag* in Swedish). As regards the working methods and division of functions of the state

[56] See, eg, Judgment no. U2008.378H. See also ch 3.

[57] Konstitutionsutskottets betänkande KU 1978/79:39 [Parliamentary committee report], 13.

[58] Prop. 2009/10:80, 148, Konstitutionsutskottets betänkande 2009/10:KU19 [Parliamentary committee report], 39.

[59] Rt. 1976 p 1 (*Kløfta*) 6.

[60] Tverberg (n 54) 877; G Brun Nissen et al, *Den dømmende makt: domstolene og rettsutviklingen 1814–1964* [The Judiciary: The Courts and the Development of the Law] (Copenhagen, Universitetsforlaget, 1967); F Backer, '"The Preferred Position Principle" i amerikansk og norsk rett' ["The Preferred Position Principle" in American and Norwegian law], in P Lødrup (ed), *Rettsteori og rettsliv: festskrift til Carsten Smith til 70-årsdagen 13. juli 2002* [Festschrift to Carsten Smith] (Copenhagen, Universitetsforlaget, 2002).

institutions, these are mentioned as areas where a more limited use of judicial review is justified.[61]

This legislature-centred approach to constitutionalism has significant institutional consequences too. First, none of the Nordic countries has a specialised constitutional court. Moreover, in Sweden and Finland there are two supreme courts: one for civil and criminal cases and another one for administrative cases, both with the power of judicial review. Indeed, the Swedish and Finnish legislatures did not anticipate that the courts would exercise their power of constitutional review actively, and they did not even introduce a mechanism to resolve conflicts between the two supreme courts, as that was not deemed necessary.[62]

D. The Position of International Law in the Nordic Legal Systems

However, the Nordic model has been under stress during the past three decades. Some scholars have started to claim that the Nordic countries, all five of them, are today slowly moving from the weak form of constitutional review to a relatively stronger one.[63] The most common explanation provided for this development is that, since the 1990s, there has been a 'progressive subordination' to both branches of European law (European Union law and the ECHR).[64] This led to a stronger emphasis on human rights and general principles, departing from the approach dictated by Scandinavian legal realism that dominated Nordic legal thinking during the twentieth century.[65]

The Nordic approach to international law within the domestic constitutional systems was during the second half of the twentieth century influenced by the dualist doctrine on the relations of international law and domestic law. Traditionally, all Nordic countries have been perceived as dualist, meaning that international law would need to be transposed or validated by the domestic legislator to have relevance within their domestic systems.[66] By the mid-1990s, this approach to international law within the domestic systems had become somewhat impractical. By then, the two great legal projects of European integration had granted Nordic citizens access to justice beyond the boundaries of the nation state. This in practice made the dualist approach towards these two systems of international law obsolete. Scrambling to adapt, through different means, the Nordics elevated the ECHR to a semi-constitutional status within each of the domestic systems during the 1990s.[67]

[61] Prop. 2009/10:80 p. 147.
[62] Smith (n 38) 116.
[63] ibid 23; Husa, 'Constitutional Mentality' (n 45) 41.
[64] Nguyên Duy (n 52) 44.
[65] Wind and Follesdal (n 3) 139.
[66] Ojanen (n 10) 133.
[67] M Dahlberg, HL Karlsson and K Kelemen, 'The Nordic Courts: An Example of Cooperation and Dialogue' in K Pócza (ed), *Constitutional Review in Western Europe: Judicial-Legislative Relations in Comparative Perspective* (Abingdon, Routledge, 2024) 294–95.

This gradually solidified the status of deference to ECHR-based human rights as a semi-constitutional adjudicative argument in domestic contexts, while also implicitly requiring domestic courts to consider the European Court of Human Rights' (ECtHR) case-law when interpreting domestic legislation. Although the domestic courts are not explicitly required to follow the Strasbourg court's jurisprudence, refusing to do so risks being humbled by a subsequent finding of the ECtHR.[68]

Similar developments occurred around the same time with regards to the legal system which later would become the European Union (EU). Three of the Nordic countries – Sweden, Norway and Denmark – had been among the founders of the European Free Trade Association (EFTA), the rival trade block to the European Economic Community (EEC, now the EU). Finland and Iceland later joined.[69] Denmark followed the UK into the EC in 1973, but a referendum blocked Norway from doing the same. By the late 1980s negotiations were initiated between the remaining EFTA states and the EEC regarding mutual market access, which resulted in the agreement on the European Economic Area (EEA Agreement), signed in 1992. One of the key issues during these negotiations was the status of EEA law within the national systems of the EFTA states. The EFTA states were reluctant to submit to the legislative, judicial and executive powers of the EEC institutions, while the EEC was unwilling to extend the internal market to the EFTA states unless the rules of the market would be homogeneous and homogeneously applied, meaning that EEA law should be homogeneous with respect to relevant EEC law.

The compromise was the two-pillar institutional system of the EEA Agreement, which allowed the EFTA states to find their own domestic constitutional solutions for granting effect and supremacy to EEA law, while maintaining the legislative prerogative firmly within the European Community (EC) pillar of the EU (established by the Maastricht Treaty in 1993) and solidifying the leading role of the European Court of Justice in interpreting both EC and EEA law.[70] Soon after the entering into force of the EEA agreement, three out of the remaining four EFTA Nordic countries decided to apply for full EU membership. Sweden and Finland joined on 1 January 1995, but the plans of the Norwegian government were again thwarted in a referendum in 1994. Thus, since 1995 Danmark, Sweden and Finland have been part of the EU, while Norway and Iceland remain closely aligned with the EU through the EFTA pillar of the EEA Agreement.[71]

[68] The political fallout from ECtHR judgments can be significant. See discussion on the fallout from the *Ástráðsson* case in HL Karlsson, 'The Emergence of the Established "By Law" Criterion for Reviewing European Judicial Appointments' (2022) 23 *German Law Journal* 1051, 1061.

[69] Finland became an associate member in 1961 and a full member in 1986. Iceland joined in 1970.

[70] The institutional arrangement of the EEA Agreement is prescribed in Part VII of the Agreement, ie Articles 89–114, OJ No L 1, 3.1.1994, p 3. The institutional arrangements EFTA pillar is further regulated by the Agreement between the EFTA States on the Establishment of a Surveillance Authority and a Court of Justice (Surveillance and Court Agreement), OJ L 344, 31.1.1994, p 3.

[71] Iceland applied for EU membership in 2009 following the financial crisis of 2008, but a few years later withdrew its application. Dahlberg, Karlsson and Kelemen (n 67) 295.

The different status of the Nordic countries with regards to the EU means that its laws are perceived differently. As EU member states, Denmark, Sweden, and Finland are explicitly subject to the EU's fundamental constitutional principles of direct effect, supremacy and state liability. This means that EU laws can hardly be considered external in terms of the dualism doctrine. However, due to the intricacies of the institutional design of the EEA Agreement, it can be argued that, with regards to Norway and Iceland, EEA law is still considered external in terms of the dualism doctrine. This remains the official view on the status of EEA law in Norway and Iceland. This argument, however, is undermined by the practical function of the EEA Agreement.[72]

Shortly after it came into force, it became clear that the Francovich doctrine of state liability, as well as a slightly softer form of supremacy, extended to the EFTA pillar of the EEA Agreement.[73] Norway and Iceland are thus required to grant EEA law supremacy within their domestic legal orders, and their citizens can take legal action for damages if their respective states fail to give proper effect to EU law that has been incorporated into the EEA Agreement. This practical nature of the EEA Agreement was poorly understood outside of academic circles in Iceland until recently.[74] Part of it stems from how cryptically Iceland's obligation under Protocol 35 of the EEA Agreement was incorporated into domestic legislation in 1993.[75] Part of it also stems from the Supreme Court's resistance and ambivalence towards the legal and institutional system of the EEA Agreement.[76] In Norway, Protocol 35 was from the start incorporated correctly, although various tactics have been used by Norwegian state organs to impede the effectiveness of

[72] Academic commentators noted this function of the EEA Agreement early on. See eg W van Gerven, 'The Genesis of EEA law and the principles of primacy and direct effect' (1992) 16 *Fordham International Law Journal* 955; L Sevon, 'The EEA judicial system and the supreme courts of the EFTA States' (1992) 3 *European Journal of International Law* 329.

[73] The Francovich state liability doctrine, based on joined Cases C-6/90 and 9/90 *Francovich and Bonifaci* EU:C:1991:428, [1991] ECR I-5357, was confirmed by the EFTA Court in Case E 9/97 *Sveinbjörnsdóttir* [1998]. A somewhat softer form of EU's supremacy doctrine was agreed on through Protocol 35 to the EEA Agreement in 1992.

[74] Einarsson wrote about this in an article in 2007 and since then many academic commentators have expressed the same view. ÓJ Einarsson, 'Bókun 35 og staða EES-samningsins að íslenskum rétti' (2007) 57 *Tímarit lögfræðinga* 371. See also ME Méndez Pinedo, *EC and EEA Law: A Comparative Study of the Effectiveness of European Law* (Europa Law Publ, 2009) 145–50; M Einarsdóttir, 'Forgangsáhrif EES-réttar í íslenskum rétti' (2014) *Tímarit Lögréttu* 75; GÞ Pétursson, 'Forgangur EES-reglan: Hvað er að frétta af bókun 35?' in S Ísfeld Ólafsdóttir (ed), *Fullveldi í 99 ár* (Hið íslenska bókmenntafélag, 2017) 201; GÞ Pétursson and ÓB Rúnarsson,' Consistent interpretation in the case-law of the Icelandic Supreme Court 1994–2016' in CNK Franklin (ed), *The effectiveness and application of EU and EEA law in national courts – Principle of consistent interpretation* (Intersentia, 2018) 363.

[75] The government planned to amend the implementing act to clarify the obligation under Protocol 35 during the Parliamentary session of 2022-23 but has not yet passed. See: Frumvarp til laga um breytingu á lögum um Evrópska efnahagssvæðið, nr. 2/1993 (bókun 35), mál nr. 890, þingskjal 1392, 153. löggjafarþing.

[76] See eg the recent judgment of the Icelandic Supreme Court in case H:24/2023 *Anna Bryndís Einarsdóttir*, where a woman was denied full maternity leave benefits in violation to her rights under the EEA Agreement, as interpreted by the EFTA Court in its advisory opinion in Case E-5/21 *Einarsdóttir*.

the EFTA pillar of the EEA Agreement and thus the influence of EEA law on the domestic legal order.[77]

E. Why Study the Nordic Countries Separately?

The four points discussed in detail in the previous subsections aim to highlight the key specificities of the Nordic context. However, the list is by no means exhaustive. Examining constitutional reasoning in Nordic courts also reveals additional distinctive developments, each contributing to the understanding of the unique path in constitutional law taken by the Nordic countries. Recent comparative research, for instance, has found that judicial expansion in the Nordic countries coincided with institutional changes that enhanced judicial autonomy. These institutional reforms may have played a larger part in this expansion than previously assumed.[78] This aligns with the fact that the Nordic Supreme Courts have generally been considered or came to be considered precedent courts (*prejudikatinstanser* in Swedish), meaning courts whose decisions are intended to create legal unity and clarity by adjudicating cases of general and significant social importance.[79] This may also have contributed to an expanded role.

Additionally, the accelerating pace of legislation and the adoption of a new approach to enacting framework laws and general statutes – previously foreign to Nordic legislation – have also contributed to a greater openness toward the judicial process.[80] These distinctive features of the Nordic context will serve as explanatory factors for our cross-cultural comparative findings, ie when we compare our findings with those from non-Nordic countries.[81]

In summary, the contours of a common Nordic approach to constitutional issues by the Nordic Supreme Courts appear to suggest that judicial review of constitutional matters is inherent in the Nordic constitutions, whether explicitly written or not. Furthermore, judicial review by the Nordic Supreme Courts is almost always conducted with considerable respect for the intentions and interpretations of the legislature, reflecting deference to its democratic mandate, while balancing this with international obligations, such as legal commitments to the ECHR and the EU/EEA. These two main characteristics have expanded the roles

[77] Undermining the independence of the EFTA Court through the appointment process of the Norwegian judge is a notable example. See the discussion on EFTA Court Case E-21/16 *Nobile* in Karlsson (n 68) 1057–58; and C Baudenbacher, *Judicial Independence: Memoirs of a European Judge* (Cham, Springer, 2019) 385–86.

[78] A Wallerman Ghavanini, G Grendstad and J Karlsson Schaffer, 'Institutions That Define the Policymaking Role of Courts: A Comparative Analysis of the Supreme Courts of Scandinavia' (2023) *International Journal of Constitutional Law* 1.

[79] A Bårdsen, 'De nordiske høyesterettene som prejudikatdomstoler – et perspektiv fra Norges Høyesterett' [The Nordic supreme courts as courts of precedent – a perspective from the Supreme Court of Norway] (2016) 55 *Lov og Rett* 259.

[80] Lindblom (n 2) 287–88.

[81] J Husa, *Introduction to Comparative Law*, 2nd edn (Oxford, Hart Publishing, 2023) 187.

of the Nordic Supreme Courts but have yet to result in a significant increase in the number of cases in which a breach of constitutional norms is found. One goal of this project is to analyse the reasoning for achieving this overall common approach, as employed by the various supreme courts.

This unique context prompted us to dedicate a separate research project to the Nordic countries, while still applying a pre-existing methodological framework – namely, that of the CONREASON project, which is explained in greater detail below. As with any comparative effort, we had to be aware of the differences and similarities among the legal systems being compared. This awareness occasionally required minor adjustments to the methodological framework. A persistent challenge was maintaining comparability of our data with data collected in other jurisdictions while adapting the variables to the specific features of the Nordic context.

First, to ensure that Nordic judgments could be coded in a manner consistent with the data from non-Nordic jurisdictions, it was necessary to adjust and add clarifications to many variable definitions. For instance, when looking for domestic harmonising arguments (variable N17), which seek to conciliate different constitutional requirements with one another, we specified that harmonising with international law should be excluded (as that is captured under another separate variable), even if the source of international law in question has been incorporated into national law. Also, while the same variable was treated as a binary variable ('yes' or 'no', indicating the presence or absence of the argument) in the other two projects that used the same methodology, we transformed it into a categorical variable by introducing an additional 'N/A' ('not applicable') option. This was necessary for cases where the domestic constitution was not applied at all because reasoning relied solely on the ECHR or general constitutional principles.

Second, an in-depth understanding of the Nordic context enabled us to enrich the original methodological framework by incorporating additional variables and creating subcategories within many existing variables. For instance, when coding arguments that establish or discuss the text of the constitution (variable N13), we made a distinction between arguments that discuss whether the ECHR is considered part of the constitution – a particularly relevant question in the Nordic context, as mentioned above – and arguments that consider whether other sources of written law, tradition, or custom are part of the constitution. This refinement enabled a more nuanced analysis of the cases in our sample.

III. Methodological Design

Our research adopts the conceptual and methodological framework elaborated on by the CONREASON project, conducted between 2011 and 2016. This project developed a groundbreaking conceptual and methodological framework for a comprehensive and systematic analysis of constitutional reasoning in 18 supreme jurisdictions,[82] without, however, extending its geographical reach to Northern Europe. We utilise their freely available dataset to facilitate comparisons between the Nordic countries and the rest of the world. A follow-up of the CONREASON project, known as the CORE Latam project, has recently concluded in Latin America.[83] This project involved constitutional and supreme courts from 16 jurisdictions in the region, thereby enriching the available data and expanding the range of jurisdictions for comparison with our findings.

Our research aims to conduct a twofold comparative analysis: first, among Nordic countries, and second, between Nordic countries and other countries globally. One of the findings of the CONREASON project was that labelling countries such as Australia and the United States as being committed to 'constitutional exceptionalism' can be misleading, as every court can be exceptional in certain aspects. Indeed, the federal supreme courts of these two countries were found to be outliers in some respects but not in others.[84] Therefore, our primary research question can be formulated as follows: In what aspects is the constitutional reasoning of Nordic supreme courts exceptional? In other words, to what extent does the style of reasoning of Nordic supreme courts resemble that of other supreme courts around the world? To address this primary question, we employ a combination of qualitative and quantitative methods. The results of the quantitative analysis control and complement the results of the qualitative analysis and vice versa (this is known as triangulation). Both methods contribute to the identification of various argumentation patterns, and to achieving a high degree of comparability across jurisdictions.

Due to the extensive number of cases in the long history of all Nordic supreme courts, conducting a comprehensive analysis of all constitutional decisions is not feasible. Therefore, a selection process was required. Following the CONREASON method,[85] we document the reasoning practices of each court based on its 40 leading cases. By 'leading cases' we mean those cases where the rulings are deemed the most important in the legal community, without any restrictions regarding the year of the judgments. Selecting 40 cases from each court (as in the two related projects) represents a balanced approach, which allows for a thorough examination of every judgment, while still providing a meaningful basis for comparison.

Leading or landmark cases often shape a court's jurisprudence, serving as a lens through which observers recognise the defining traits of a court's approach to constitutional argumentation.[86] At the same time, the systematic analysis of

[82] A Jakab, A Dyevre and G Itzcovich (eds), *Comparative Constitutional Reasoning* (Cambridge, Cambridge University Press, 2017).

[83] Their first results have been published in October 2023, in a Special Issue in Volume 78 of the *Austrian Journal of Public Law*. The main findings are published in J Fröhlich, *Constitutional Reasoning in Latin America and the Caribbean* (Oxford, Hart Publishing, 2024).

[84] A Jakab, A Dyevre and G Itzcovich, 'Conclusion' in A Jakab, A Dyevre and G Itzcovich (eds), *Comparative Constitutional Reasoning* (Cambridge, Cambridge University Press, 2017) 791.

[85] Jakab, Dyevre and Itzcovich, 'Introduction' (n 6) 27.

[86] ibid.

non-salient cases may reveal different patterns. Consequently, the implications of our choice to focus on leading cases must be carefully reflected upon: our results show the style of constitutional reasoning in leading cases and not the 'average' patterns in the analysed courts. For the selection of the 40 leading cases, we utilised a method commonly employed in social sciences: expert opinion. The selection was carried out by constitutional scholars from the five Nordic countries, who were later also responsible for the quantitative and qualitative analysis of the selected cases.

We operated under the assumption that there is generally a relative consensus within the scholarly community regarding which decisions are considered leading judgments. To validate this assumption, each scholar was asked to designate five other constitutional law experts from their jurisdiction to review their choice of cases. These experts were then individually requested to express their agreement with the selections made. In the letter sent to all 25 experts, we included the instructions that the project participants received for selecting the leading cases. These instructions outlined the criteria for choosing the 'canon of cases' that they consider to be the 'most well-known' or 'most important' within the legal (scholarly and/or judicial) community. In essence, they were expected to guess the general (mainstream) scholarly opinion on the list of 40 leading judgments. Possible proxies for the selection included: (1) cases typically found in textbooks on domestic constitutional law, (2) cases frequently cited in scholarly literature, and (3) cases that are often relied upon as precedents by the analysed court itself. However, it was specified that none of these three proxies alone would be decisive. The selection process was to carefully consider a combination of all three factors.[87]

Most scholars who agreed to be our experts submitted their opinions (23 out of the 25). The experts unanimously ratified 89 per cent (246) of the cases on the proposed lists of leading judgments and only 0.7 per cent (two) were ratified by a minority. Gwet's AC_1[88] (which is a chance corrected agreement coefficient ranging from -1 to 1, where a value around 0 is expected by chance and the range 0.8–1.0 is considered to be 'almost perfect') also averaged 0.94 for the seven courts with the minimum as high as 0.86 (for Iceland). The highest level of consensus is observed in Finland (0.98 for the ordinary Supreme Court and 1 for the Supreme Administrative Court), which might not be surprising, given the short time frame of the Finnish cases, all of which were decided under the new Constitution adopted in 2000. This limited time frame constrained the selection of cases that could be classified as 'leading constitutional cases'. Nonetheless, even though we

[87] The instructions also mandated disregarding the specific issues covered by the cases when preparing the leading cases. The sole requirement was that all cases must contain constitutional reasoning. This implies that the project participants should not attempt to make the list representative of constitutional cases in general. For example, they should not focus on including a certain number of fundamental rights cases or ensuring that the list covers diverse constitutional matters, concepts or argumentation styles. Doing so would have introduced a bias in our dataset.

[88] KL Gwet, 'Computing Inter-Rater Reliability and Its Variance in the Presence of High Agreement' (2008) 61 *British Journal of Mathematical and Statistical Psychology* 29.

employed the same method and were exposed to the risk of a framing effect,[89] our results revealed a significantly higher level of consensus among the experts regarding the leading cases in the Nordic countries compared to other jurisdictions. In our parent project, only 63 per cent of all cases were unanimously ratified by all the experts.[90] This can be attributed to two factors. First, the total number of cases containing constitutional reasoning is much more limited in the Nordic countries, with the possible exception of Norway, than in other parts of the Western world. Indeed, out of 2,308 published judgments in civil and criminal cases from the Swedish ordinary Supreme Court between 1991 and 2016, only 227 can be classified as 'constitutional' in the broad sense, as they contain references to the basic laws.[91] Second, the Nordic countries have small legal and scholarly communities,[92] which leads to a more homogeneous national legal culture.

As regards the qualitative element of the research, we organised two webinar series to discuss the legal, political, and social context of constitutional reasoning in each of the five Nordic countries. As to the quantitative pillar, all data were collected in Excel sheets and then imported into R[93] where the statistical analysis was conducted. We encoded information on a number of general and argumentative characteristics, repeating this for every leading case. Our dataset therefore consists of a summary of the characteristics of 280 landmark Nordic constitutional cases. We conducted pilot research to test our methodology in the Nordic context and refine our variables and the instructions for coding. The pilot included an inter-coder-reliability analysis, in which 42 cases were pairwise coded by six project participants. The analysis indicated that 72 per cent (64 out of 89) nominal variables were coded 'almost perfectly' (Gwet's AC_1), while a few variables posed challenges. Specifically, the inter-coder reliability for the variable measuring the frequency of arguments invoking a concept or principle not mentioned in the constitution (N20) was only 'fair' (0.2–0.4). This outcome was hardly surprising, given that the reliability tests were conducted by constitutional scholars from different jurisdictions who lacked in-depth knowledge of each other's constitutional systems. Additionally, the inter-coder reliability was found to be 'moderate' (0.4–0.6) in relation to seven variables, including the structure of argument variable, three types of arguments, and three key concepts. These findings were thoroughly discussed by all project participants during a two-day workshop held in Örebro (Sweden) in order to refine the instructions provided in the Codebook. Furthermore, during the analysis, the distinctive characteristics of the Nordic constitutional systems, as discussed in the previous section, were

[89] A Tversky and D Kahneman, 'Rational Choice and the Framing of Decisions' in K Schweers Cook and M Levi (eds), *The Limits of Rationality* (Chicago, University of Chicago Press, 1990) 60.

[90] Jakab, Dyevre and Itzcovich, 'Introduction' (n 6) 29.

[91] This data has been obtained from Johan Lindholm, Mattias Derlén and Daniel Naurin in the Swedish High Court Database (version 0.9.1, 1 May 2023).

[92] U Kischel, *Comparative Law* (Oxford, Oxford University Press, 2019) 565.

[93] R Core Team, *R: A Language and Environment for Statistical Computing. R Foundation for Statistical Computing* (2023) www.R-project.org.

identified. These features led us to introduce new variables and create subcategories for existing binary ones.[94]

The variables are grouped into four broad categories. They encompass not only argument types and key concepts but also 11 general characteristics of each case, which can be used as independent variables, see Table 2 below.

Table 2 Categorisation of coded variables with examples

Categories of variables:	**Examples of variables:**
(1) general characteristics of the case (11 in total)	• year • dissenting or concurring opinions • general topic • type of dispute • panel formation
(2) arguments used in the case (20 in total)	• structure of argument • non-interpretative arguments, such as establishing or discussing the text of the constitution and analogical reasoning • interpretative arguments, such as literal, systematic, teleological reasoning, harmonising with international law, precedent-based arguments, non-legal arguments, reference to scholarly work and foreign law, etc.
(3) key concepts and generic constitutional doctrines used in the case (21 in total)	• rule of law • democracy • sovereignty • government form • proportionality • human dignity • equality • freedom of expression • transparency
(4) measurement variables (2)	• overall weight of arguments • implicit use of concepts

We study univariate distributions (typically proportions) and bivariate correlations both within or in comparison to Nordic courts (or countries). The analyses are employed on a within or between subgroups (typically administrative and non-administrative cases) level, or is undertaken with regards to the subgroup (eg, controlling for country or differences between administrative and non-administrative cases).

[94] See our Codebook and dataset at doi.org/10.60689/zmk7-0z14. In total, we used 53 variables (56 for the two Swedish Supreme Courts), to compare with the 37 variables used in the CONREASON Project. Of our variables, 27 are binary, while the rest are categorical, most of which can be collapsed into binary maintaining comparability with datasets from the two related projects.

Comparisons are also made between the Nordic courts/countries/regions and other international courts or legal systems and several of the analyses are based on various types of regression models. Part of the analysis is undertaken on an aggregate court data level (eg, the average proportions of argumentation vs conceptualisation between international courts) and potential underlying patterns in the data are explored, for example, via dimensional reduction and clustering techniques.

Trends over time are also analysed. The most recent Nordic cases are from 2022, while the oldest (Danish) case dates back to 1920.[95] However, the distribution – as observed in the CONREASON and CORE Latam projects – is highly skewed, with only eight cases from before 1970. Therefore, in our statistical analysis, we usually approximate the growth of the number of leading cases as exponential over time and employ a log-transformed scale[96] but always interpret the results in terms of the back-transformed actual year. The next chapter provides a detailed overview of the undertaken descriptive and inferential statistical analyses, including power calculations.

IV. Structure of the Book

Following the general introduction to the theoretical and methodological foundations of our research in this chapter, the second chapter – authored by Nicklas Pettersson and Katalin Kelemen, the statistician and the principal investigator of the project, respectively – provides a more detailed, technical explanation of the quantitative pillar of our methodological design. A separate chapter is then devoted to each of the five Nordic countries, all of which follow a similar structure. First, they provide context by focusing on the historical, political and institutional idiosyncrasies of the jurisdiction under examination. Then, they present the most relevant findings from our empirical research. Finally, they conclude with some closing reflections.

In chapter three, Helle Krunke and Mikael Kenno Fogde present findings related to the Supreme Court of Denmark. When interpreting the quantitative data, the authors also rely on the deliberation protocols of three important cases from our sample. The Court has only recently made these protocols available to researchers upon request. In chapter four, Haukur Logi Karlsson discusses the findings relating to the Icelandic Supreme Court in light of the tension between doctrines of defensiveness and openness which have dominated Icelandic constitutional scholarship. Chapter five, authored by Maija Dahlberg, provides an analysis of the constitutional reasoning of Finland's two Supreme Courts, both

[95] Case U1921.148H decided by the Danish Supreme Court on 11 December 1920.

[96] Typically we use -log(age of case since 2023), or similarly -log(2023-year of case), to measure the year of a case. The appropriateness is confirmed in modelling by estimates of the Box-Cox lambda parameter being about 0, see also GEP Box and DR Cox, 'An analysis of transformations'(1964) 26 *Journal of the Royal Statistical Society, Series B* 211.

of which have only more recently been granted the power of judicial review, and therefore covers a shorter time period. When interpreting the data, the author reflects extensively on the continuing significant role of the Constitutional Law Committee of the Finnish Parliament in Finnish constitutional culture. In chapter six, Morten Nadim examines how international law and US legal culture have shaped constitutional reasoning in the Norwegian Supreme Court. He argues that Norwegian constitutional reasoning has developed a character distinct from that of its Nordic counterparts, challenging the idea of a uniquely Nordic style. In chapter seven, Åsa Elmerot analyses the argumentative practices of the two Swedish Supreme Courts, showing how Sweden's decentralised, consensus-driven constitutional review – shaped by four separate 'fundamental laws' rather than a single constitution – differs from that of its Nordic neighbours. She concludes that the Parliament's status as the primary authority on the Constitution remains a defining feature of Sweden's constitutional culture, where constitutional evolution is mainly achieved through frequent constitutional amendments and cautious, deferential judicial interpretation rather than bold precedent-setting. In chapter eight, Katalin Kelemen reviews the aims of the study and its analytical framework, explaining how the authors used the CONREASON methodology to examine constitutional reasoning in the Nordic supreme courts through a cultural-comparative lens, as well as Kaarlo Tuori's theory on the law's multiple levels. This final chapter contextualises the findings, which cover the historical roots of Nordic legal culture, patterns of argumentation and concept use, Europeanisation, and intra-Nordic variation, within broader debates on whether a distinctive Nordic constitutional culture exists.

2

About the Methodology: A Quantitative Approach to Comparing Constitutional Reasoning in the Nordic Supreme Courts

NICKLAS PETTERSSON AND KATALIN KELEMEN

I. Introduction

In this chapter we present a systematic quantitative approach analysing the reasons that judges in Nordic countries publicly adduce as justifications for their decisions in constitutional matters, as implemented in the Nordic CONREASON Project.[1] Based on encodings of 40 (per court) purposively selected landmark cases, common traits and patterns of constitutional argumentative practices in each of the Nordic supreme courts were identified and international comparisons were made to courts from related studies. Our results provided strong reasons why, regarding specific aspects (on a univariate level), within the Nordic countries, one or more courts typically tended to deviate from the other Nordic courts. Also, in a worldwide comparison there were variations between the Nordic supreme courts. However, although not detached from other supreme courts (on both univariate and multivariate levels) the Nordic supreme courts clearly seemed to occupy an area of their own on the international map of constitutional reasoning.

[1] These methodological reflections and explanations were previously presented in a working paper: N Pettersson and K Kelemen, 'Yet Another Case of Nordic Exceptionalism?: A Quantitative Approach to an Intra-Nordic and an International Comparison of Supreme Courts' Constitutional Reasoning' (Örebro University School of Business, 2024) Working Paper (Statistics) 7/2024, swopec.hhs.se/oruesi/abs/oruesi2024_007.htm.

II. Background and Purpose

The aim of the Nordic CONREASON Project was a twofold comparative analysis of argumentative practices of supreme courts in constitutional cases: (1) among the Nordic countries, and (2) between Nordic countries and other countries worldwide. The focus in (1) was to discover common traits and trends among the Nordic countries, and in (2) to compare the Nordic region to other countries worldwide. This aim was intended to be accomplished by systematically documenting the argumentative practice of the Nordic supreme courts in their leading constitutional cases, and through incorporating the methodology of and the data collected within previous similar projects.

The primary research question may be phrased as: In what aspects is the constitutional reasoning of Nordic supreme courts exceptional? In other words, to what extent does the style of reasoning of Nordic supreme courts resemble that of other supreme courts around the world? To address the question, a combination of qualitative and quantitative methods is employed. Through triangulation, the results from the quantitative and the qualitative analysis control and complement each other, increasing the comparability across the jurisdictions and contributing to the identification of various argumentation patterns. The following chapter documents the quantitative methodology used in the project and provides some of the main results and scopes for further research.

III. Design and Data Collection

The Nordic CONREASON project collected data on the reasoning-practice of the supreme courts of the five Nordic countries: the Swedish Högsta domstolen, the Norwegian Høgsterett, the Icelandic Hæstiréttur, the Danish Højesteret, and the Finnish Korkein oikeus. Two of the Nordic countries also have a supreme administrative court (the Swedish Högsta förvaltningsdomstolen and the Finnish Korkein hallinto-oikeus), which were also included in the analysis. Their inclusion was motivated by the fact that administrative courts also have the power to review the constitutionality of the laws they apply, thus engaging in constitutional reasoning. The inclusion of administrative supreme courts in the study also allows us to compare argumentative practices of these courts with those of the ordinary supreme courts.

In order to compare the reason-giving practices of the Nordic countries with supreme and constitutional courts in other parts of the world, the project used the methodology of the CONREASON-project (2011–2016), adapting it to the Nordic context. The CONREASON-project, led by András Jakab, developed a groundbreaking conceptual and methodological framework to enable a comprehensive and systematic analysis of constitutional reasoning in 18 supreme jurisdictions,[2] without, however, extending its geographical reach to Northern Europe.

The first regional follow-up of the CONREASON project, the CORE Latam Project, was launched in Latin America in 2018, headed by Johanna Fröhlich at the Pontifical Catholic University of Chile. This project examined the reason-giving practice of 15 Latin American jurisdictions, including the Inter-American Court of Human Rights and the Caribbean Commonwealth. The CORE Latam project also relied on the methodology of the first CONREASON project, while adapting it to the Latin American constitutional context.

In line with the two related projects, our analysis of the reasoning practices of a court was based on landmark (or leading) cases, that is, cases where the rulings were deemed the most important in the legal community, with no time limit as to the year of the delivery of the judgments. Such cases tend to set the tone of a court's jurisprudence, as they often provide the lens through which court watchers recognise the defining traits of a court's approach to constitutional argumentation.

A. Expert Consensus and Inter-coder Reliability

The selection of 40 leading cases within each Nordic high court was based on the expert opinion of the project participant responsible for the given jurisdiction, as accompanied by five constitutional law scholars of their own jurisdiction to review the choice of cases.

We employed Gwet's AC1 agreement coefficient among multiple raters[3] to evaluate consensus and inter-coder reliability. An important property of this estimator is that the correction for pure agreement by chance is adjusted consistently to the prevalence of the underlying phenomenon (as measured by the observed ratings). In the first situation, we evaluated the agreement among experts in the proposal of cases, and found it on average to be very high (0.94), smallest (but still high) in Iceland (0.86) and in Finland the agreement was perfect (1.00). Second, we compared ratings of 89 variables among the coders made during their pilot phase training and classified the estimates according to a common benchmark.[4] Initially, the outcome was fairly decent, where 64 variables were found to be almost perfect(0.8-1.0), 17 substantial(0.6-0.8), 7 moderate(0.4-0.6), 1 fair(0.2-0.4) and

[2] G Itzcovich, 'The European Court of Justice' in A Jakab, A Dyevre, and G Itzcovich (eds), *Comparative Constitutional Reasoning* (Cambridge, Cambridge University Press, 2017).

[3] KL Gwet, 'Computing inter-rater reliability and its variance in the presence of high agreement' (2008) 61 *British Journal of Mathematical and Statistical Psychology* 29, 29–48.

[4] See JR Landis and G Koch, 'The measurement of observer agreement for categorical data' (1977) 33 *Biometrics* 159, 164–65.

none slight(0-0.2) or poor(<0). The results were then used as a basis for additional training in order to improve the agreement of the final coding, focusing mostly on creating consensus in the coding of the variables that were found to have the lowest agreement.

B. Variables Collected in the Nordic CONREASON Project

The court and country indicators were coded as unique variables. A complete description of the variables that were coded from the cases may be found in the Nordic CONREASON Project Codebook.[5] Variables labels were noted by a capital letter 'N' followed by a variable number, sometimes with the addition '_#' for subcategory #. For example, variable N3_6 refers to the sixth subcategory of variable N3.

The variables coded from cases were sorted, based on their topic, into the following four groups:

- Variables related to the characteristics of the case (N1-N11)
- Variables related to the arguments used in the case (N12-N30)
- Variables related to the conceptualisation (N31-N51)
- Conclusive measurement variables (N52-N53).

Two variables only contained text (N1, N6), four were multinomial (N4, N7, N17, N53), four were continuous (N2, N8, N9 and N9__8 = N9/N8, the length (in words) of the majority reasoning relative to the length of the judgment), one included voting counts (N10), and two were ordinal (N12, N52). All other variables were coded as binary (YES/NO) including those with multiple separated subcategories (N3, N5, N13, N14, N16, N18, N23, N24, N25, N26, N31, N34, N38, N41, N45, N50) and/or aggregated subcategories (N3, N25, N26). The only exceptions were N10 (unanimous/non-unanimous decision-making panel) and N11 (ordinary/strengthened panel). Two variables had the same value recorded on all 280 cases: the fourth subcategory of N25, N25_4 (only 'NO' answers); and N52 (only 'M=majority of the arguments mentioned in the opinion were *ratio decidendi* or *obiter dictum* arguments' answers') and were therefore later disregarded in the quantitative analysis.

[5] Data is available at: K Kelemen, 'Nordic CONREASON kollektion av data om konstitutionellt resonemang i de nordiska högsta domstolarna (Version 1), 15 Maj 2024' (Örebro University, 2024) doi.org/10.60689/zmk7-0z14.

C. Set of Variables after Merging with Other Projects

Since both the CORE Latam and the Nordic CONREASON projects adapted their methodology and variable definitions from the CONREASON project, in combination with mutual exchange and collaboration between the principal investigators of all three projects, it was reasonable to assume a high comparability among them. However, some adaptations to regional conditions were still made in both the CORE Latam and the Nordic CONREASON projects, such as the addition of extra variables or subcategories of existent variables.

One example of the latter were the categorisations of law system. In our international comparison, the classification of legal systems from the CONREASON project were adapted. A first classification (CIV_COM) stated whether the legal system was Civil, Common, Mix of civil and common, Regional(international), or Nordic. The second classification (CEN_DIF) captured whether the model of judicial review was Centralised, Diffused, a Hybrid of centralised and diffused, or Regional. An extra variable (CEN_DIF2) with subcategories of Diffused(Nordic) and Diffused(Other) were also added, enabling comparisons between Nordic versus other countries, all applying a diffused judicial review model. In all classifications the European Court of Human Rights (ECHR), the European Court of Justice (ECJ) and the Inter-American Court of Human Rights (IAC) were classified as Regional. In the Nordic CONREASON project, we did not include any regional court.

The case variable labels in the merged dataset kept the same numbering as in Nordic CONREASON, but replaced the initial letter 'N' with 'R'. The merged dataset included all the 37 original variables from CONREASON. Extra subcategories in CORE Latam and Nordic CONREASON were suppressed through merging into the form used in the CONREASON project (for example in R26). Variables that were included in only CORE Latam and Nordic CONREASON were also included (R28, R32, R47-R52) and thus had missing values on the courts in CONREASON. More details on the specific variable codings in the merged dataset are given in Table A1 in the Appendix below.

D. Linking to Other External Datasets

To our knowledge, external data for the whole population of cases in (primarily Nordic) countries were limited. A majority (26 out of 40) of the cases in our sample from the Swedish Supreme Court were linked to a database containing a partial population (of 2,482 civil and criminal cases) from the Swedish Supreme Court (*Högsta domstolen*).[6] This subset of our sample deviated in various aspects

[6] Data is available at J Lindholm, M Derlén and D Naurin, 'Swedish High Court Database (version 1.0.0, 7 June 2024)' (Umeå University, 2024) doi.org/10.5281/zenodo.11516266.

from the partial population, being on average more recent (2005 vs 1999), had a higher proportion of criminal cases (73 per cent vs 45 per cent), and had cases classified as covering more types of legal areas (on average 1.61 vs 1.23) out of the 24 types that were categorised under traditional domestic law in the partial population.

The merged dataset (see section III(C) above) was also linked to datasets concerning constitution rankings,[7] and national estimates of values,[8] culture[9] and public opinion.[10]

IV. Inference and Methods

The output of our quantitative approach consisted of sample descriptions and inferential statistics in accordance with the project aims. In order to make generalisable statements, we aimed for translating the research objectives into tractable statistical models. However, the use of (by experts) purposively selected cases has implications for the interpretation of the inference, see section IV(B) below.

We studied univariate distributions (typically proportions) and bivariate correlations, both within or in comparison with Nordic courts (or countries). The analysis was often employed on a within or between subgroup level (typically Administrative versus Non-administrative) or was undertaken with regards to subgroups (for example, to better comprehend how the Administrative cases differ from the Non-administrative cases in the Nordic region, we controlled for Country).

Comparisons were also made between the Nordic courts/countries/region and other international courts or legal systems, with several of the analyses based on regression models. Part of the analyses were undertaken on an aggregate court data level (for example the average proportions of argumentation vs conceptualisation between international courts) and potential underlying structures and patterns in the data were explored via dimensional reduction, clustering and other multivariate techniques, and our inference also included multivariate hypotheses tests.

[7] Data is available at Z Elkins and T Ginsburg, 'Characteristics of National Constitutions, Version 4.0' (Comparative Constitutions Project, 2022) comparativeconstitutionsproject.org/ccp-rankings.

[8] Data is available at R Inglehart, C Haerpfer, A Moreno, C Welzel, K Kizilova, J Diez-Medrano, M Lagos, P Norris, E Ponarin and B Puranen et al (eds), 'World Values Survey: All Rounds – Country-Pooled Datafile' (Madrid, JD Systems Institute, 2014) www.worldvaluessurvey.org/WVSDocumentationWVL.jsp.

[9] Data is available at Geert Hofstede, 'National cultural dimensions', geerthofstede.com/research-and-vsm/dimension-data-matrix.

[10] Data is available at European Commission, Brussels (2022). Eurobarometer 95.3 (2021) (ZA7783; Version 1.0.0) [Data set]. GESIS, Cologne, doi.org/10.4232/1.13826.

Trends over time were also analysed, and when found to be relevant, accounted for in the analysis. The most recent Nordic cases were from the year 2022, while the oldest (Danish) case dated back to 1920. However, among Nordic cases the distribution over time, as observed also in the CONREASON and CORE Latam projects, was highly skewed, with only eight cases predating 1970. Therefore, in our statistical analysis, we usually approximated the growth of the number of leading cases as exponential over time and employed a log-transformed scale. However, for ease of interpretation, afterwards we always back-transformed the results to the original (yearly) scale, see Figure 1 below.

Figure 1 Histogram of leading cases by year in the Nordic countries and the Nordic region as a whole

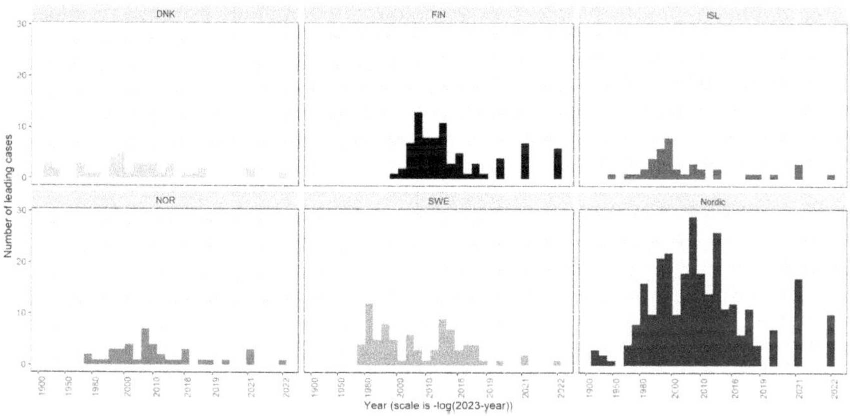

A. Descriptives

Tables, graphs and summary statistics were used for description and exploration. When described, most variables were presented as proportions with accompanying confidence intervals estimated using Wilson scores,[11] which do not suffer from the problems of ordinary normal approximation intervals. Since we have fairly few observations, and proportions quite often are low (close to 0) or high (close to 1), we also employed a Yate's continuity correction.[12]

[11] EB Wilson, 'Probable inference, the law of succession, and statistical inference' (1927) 22 *Journal of the American Statistical Association* 209, 209–12.

[12] F Yates, 'Contingency tables involving small numbers and the χ^2 test' (1934) *Supplement to the Journal of the Royal Statistical Society* 217, 217–35.

For nominal variables with more than two categories (N4, N7, N17, N53) we employed simultaneous confidence intervals for multinomial probabilities.[13] Estimated means (with confidence intervals based on normal approximations) and medians (with non-parametric confidence intervals) were used with the continuous variables (N2, N8, N9, N8_9).

B. Inference

The inference relied on the assumption that there exists a data generating process (governed by a set of parameters) from which our set of observations constitutes one, out of an infinite number of possible, outcomes. The data generating process was thus an abstraction of how the supreme courts' leading constitutional cases came about, and our inference thus refers to this abstraction, or more specifically, the parameters by which it was governed.

Inference may take the form of point estimation where for example a parameter might be: the proportion of cases with 'arguments from silence' (*argumentum ex silentio*) in a court, as measured by variable N21; in interval estimation it could be a confidence interval for the same proportion; and in hypothesis testing it could be whether there was support against (or not) the assumption that the proportion parameters of the data generating process were the same among different (Nordic) courts.

In null hypothesis testing, we consistently used a significance level (that is, the type I error) of $\alpha=0.05$. Whenever possible, we opted for two-tailed alternative hypotheses. Similarly, when utilising confidence intervals, we always employed double-sided intervals with a confidence level of $1-\alpha=95$ per cent. (Viewed from a perspective of repeated sampling, given that the null hypothesis would be true, we expect that 1 in 20 (that is, 5 per cent) of the realisations would result in the false decision to reject the null hypothesis.)

Similarly, given that the null hypothesis was false the type II error (one minus the power of the test) of β per cent (conditional on the specific test, effect, and sample size) represents the amount of repeated realisations where the conclusion of the test incorrectly would be that the null hypothesis should be rejected. As an example, in a test situation with a two-sample t-test of difference in proportion (or correspondingly a chi-square test of independence given a two-by-two contingency table) where the null hypothesis was that the proportions of a binary variable in two courts (each with 40 observed cases) were the same, the type II error of the test would depend on both the two true underlying proportions, see Table 1 below. For example, assume that the true proportions (in the abstraction

[13] CP Sison and J Glaz, 'Simultaneous confidence intervals and sample size determination for multinomial proportions' (1995) 90 *Journal of the American Statistical Association* 366, 366–69.

given by the data generating process) differ between two courts. Then the more extreme (that is, close to 0 per cent or 100 per cent) the true proportion of one of the courts is, the lower the likelihood would be of drawing the false conclusion from the hypothesis test that the true proportion does not differ between the courts.

Table 1 The type II error of a chi-square test of independence between two binary variables, one depicting the question of interest and the other the two courts (each with n=40 cases)

Type II error of chi-square test		**Proportion in first court (n=40)**										
		0	*10*	*20*	*30*	*40*	*50*	*60*	*70*	*80*	*90*	*100*
Proportion in second court (n=40)	*0*		0.46	0.15	0.04	0.01	0.00	0.00	0.00	0.00	0.00	0.00
	10	0.46		0.76	0.39	0.13	0.03	0.00	0.00	0.00	0.00	0.00
	20	0.15	0.76		0.82	0.50	0.20	0.05	0.01	0.00	0.00	0.00
	30	0.04	0.39	0.82		0.84	0.55	0.23	0.05	0.01	0.00	0.00
	40	0.01	0.13	0.50	0.84		0.85	0.57	0.23	0.05	0.00	0.00
	50	0.00	0.03	0.20	0.55	0.85		0.85	0.55	0.20	0.03	0.00
	60	0.00	0.00	0.05	0.23	0.57	0.85		0.84	0.50	0.13	0.01
	70	0.00	0.00	0.01	0.05	0.23	0.55	0.84		0.82	0.39	0.04
	80	0.00	0.00	0.00	0.01	0.05	0.20	0.50	0.82		0.76	0.15
	90	0.00	0.00	0.00	0.00	0.00	0.03	0.13	0.39	0.76		0.46
	100	0.00	0.00	0.00	0.00	0.00	0.00	0.01	0.04	0.15	0.46	

Aside from the risk of drawing the wrong conclusion in null hypothesis testing, although a rejection of the null hypothesis would be correct (when the p-value was smaller than the chosen significance level), a practical significance was not automatically assumed but the estimated size was considered on factual grounds. A substantial reduction of an observed p-value (below the chosen significance level) did not automatically imply a significant change in the belief regarding the underlying parameter(s) of the data generating process.

Although our explicit inferential claims were limited to the specific setting of leading constitutional cases in high courts, given a model based on well-considered assumptions one could potentially increase the external validity of inference to parameters of data generating processes regarding higher court or constitutional cases in general, but this is less likely regarding lower courts or court cases in general. However, to make any such claims one would need to carefully consider the situation at hand in detail.

While inference is related to the question of *why* statistical analysis is undertaken, there is a preceding need for statistical methods (based on underlying algorithmic techniques) on *how* to perform the analysis. The choices of inferential methods are presented and motivated in sections V–VIII of this chapter, including some relevant examples from the main results. An overview of the data and analysis are also given in Figure 2 (sections V–VII) and Figure 3 (section VIII).

Figure 2 Overview of data and analysis in sections 4–6

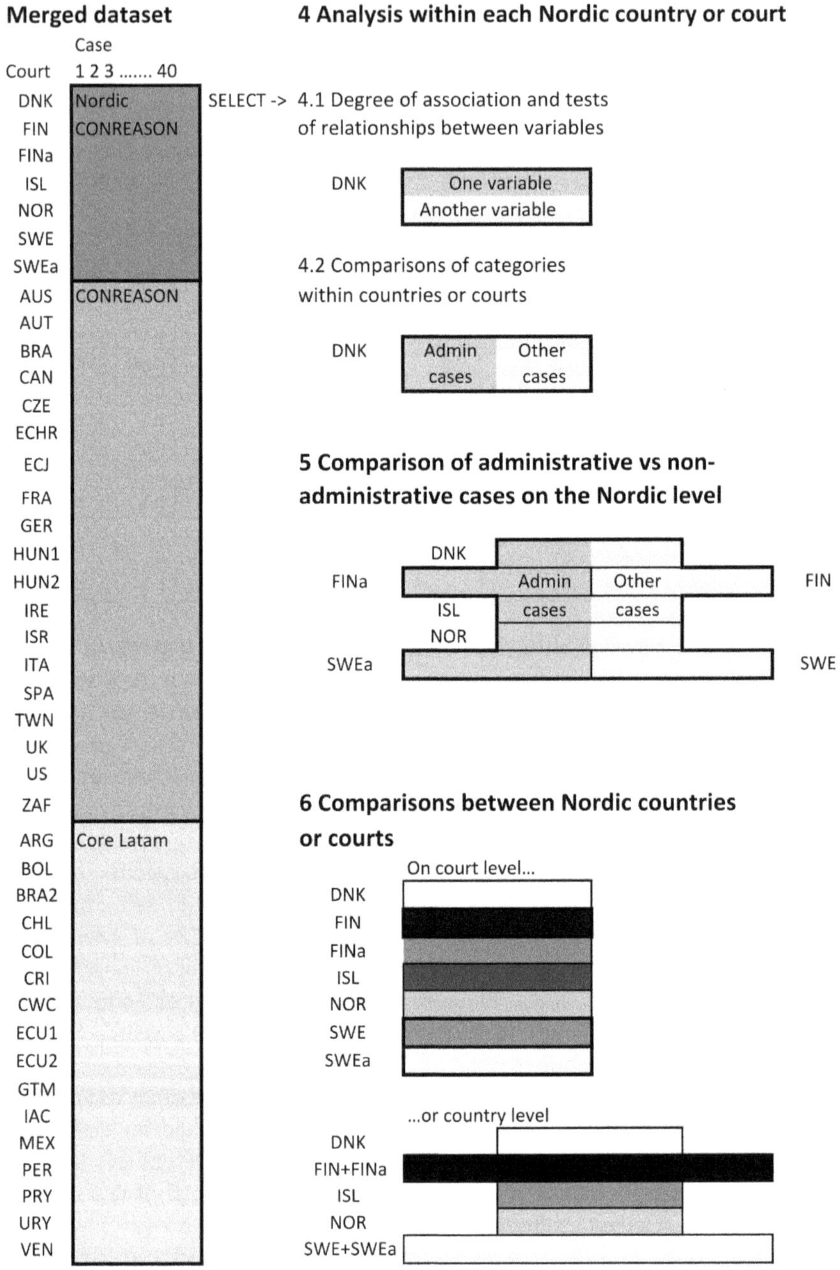

Figure 3 Overview of data and analysis in section 7

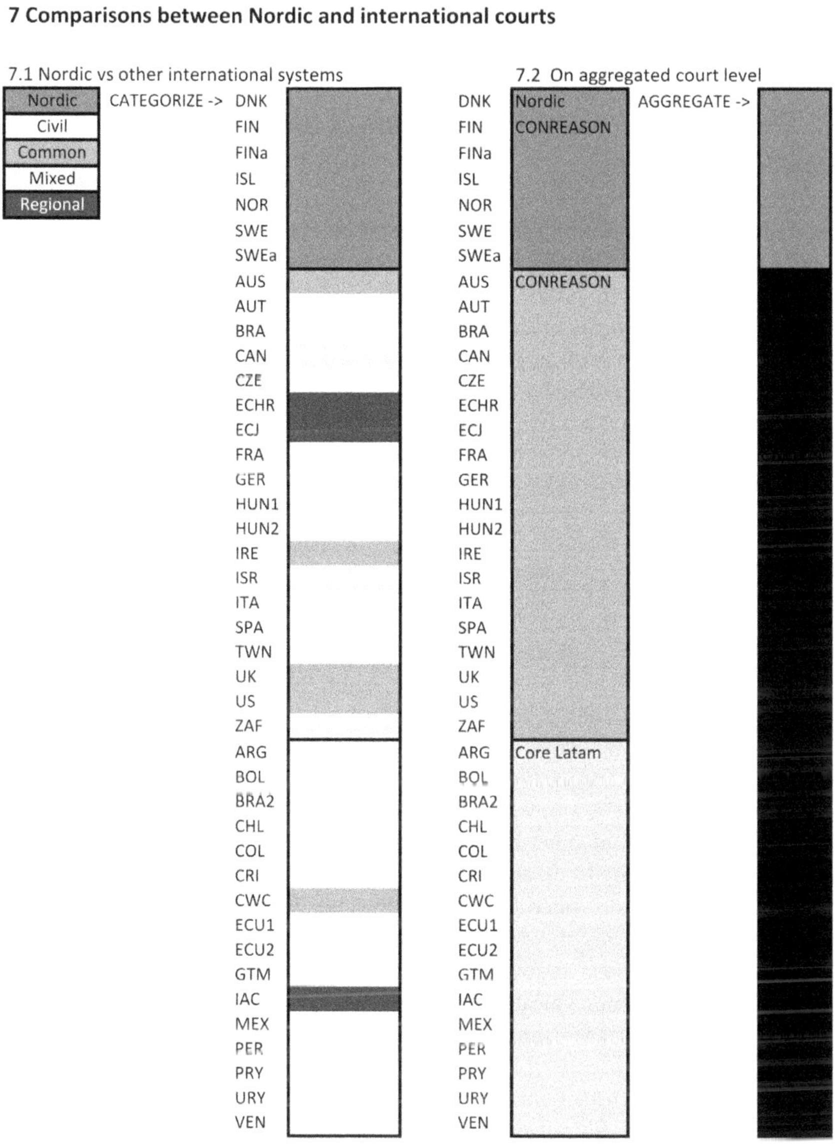

V. Analysis within Each Nordic Country or Court

The purpose of the analysis in this section was to understand the relationship between variables within a country. In Finland and Sweden, where there were two courts, we also studied the relationships within each of the two courts. In addition, we also compared whether there were differences between subgroups of cases (for example administrative vs non-administrative) within countries/courts.

A. Degree of Association and Tests of Relationships between Variables

The degree of linear association was measured by Pearson's correlation coefficient *r*, or in the case of two binary variables the equivalent *Phi* correlation coefficient, see Table 2. Asymptotic confidence intervals were calculated by use of a Fisher transformation. When the ordinal variable (N12) was involved, we used Tau-c to measure the degree of ordinal association, since this measure is suitable when the other variable is measured by a different scale. Confidence intervals were then found by Monte Carlo simulation.

Table 2 Correlation measure by scale of variables

	1st variable is:		
2nd variable is:	*binary*	*ordinal*	*continuous*
binary	Phi	Tau-c	Pearson's r
continuous	Pearson's r	Tau-c	Pearson's r

Within each Nordic country, we also estimated partial (conditional) correlations between variables,[14] controlling for the influence of administrative vs non-administrative cases. The partial correlations try to equalise the conditions in the Nordic countries. For example, if the correlation between two variables among all the countries would have been stronger among Administrative cases, then we expect the estimated correlation to be stronger within a country if it had a high proportion of Administrative cases. However, in the partial correlation, the difference in proportions of Administrative cases is controlled for. A partial correlation was found by first regressing each of the two variables of interest on an Administrative indicator variable. The correlation was then calculated between the two resulting sets of residuals. Values of the Administrative indicator variable were deducted directly for Sweden and Finland (since Administrative and Non-administrative cases belonged to different high courts). In the remaining Nordic countries, the values were deducted from variable N7.

When at least one nominal variable (with more than two categories) is involved the concept of correlation is not applicable. However, we undertook chi-square tests of independence between a nominal and another (nominal, binary or ordinal)

[14] K Baba, R Shibata and M Sibuya, 'Partial correlation and conditional correlation as measures of conditional independence' (2004) 46 *Australian and New Zealand Journal of Statistics* 657, 657–64.

variable. The p-values were then simulated[15] from 10,000 Monte Carlo replicates so as to always avoid the unreliable chi-square approximation when pairwise outcomes of variables have low expected counts.

By regressing a continuous variable on a nominal variable, we also undertook a null hypothesis test of no significant difference among all categories (through an F-test) or of no significant difference between individual categories (via t-tests).

B. Comparisons of Categories within Countries or Courts

We tested whether there was a difference between pairs of groups of cases based on types of disputes (N7) within Nordic countries, and case disposition (N4) and general topic (N5) in Nordic high courts. The groups were thus:

- N4: whether the court found (at least partially) against the law/decision/act (of the government) challenged (all three pairwise sets: Yes vs No; Yes vs Not applicable; No vs Not applicable).
- N5: the general topic (all six pairwise sets based on the four topics: Fundamental rights; State organisation; Procedural; Other). However, there were no Procedural cases in the Finnish administrative court, and no State organisation cases in either of the two Swedish courts.
- N7: administrative vs non-administrative cases.

For two of the variables (N4 and N7), the equality of means of continuous variables between two categories were tested by Welch's (unequal variances) t-tests. To test the equal location null hypothesis between two groups for the ordinal variable (N12) we employed a Wilcoxon-Mann-Whitney test. The equality of binary variable proportions between two groups were tested using a chi-square test (with monte-carlo based p-values). A chi-square test was also employed to test the equality between two groups of proportions for nominal (with more than two categories) variables. Fairly few observations were involved in these comparisons, and we seldom found any significant or substantial differences.

Each of the four general topics (N5) may be applicable to the same case so they were not mutually exclusive. In order to test if the impact of a variable was equal among two such topics, we first regressed our variable of interest on indicator variables of the four general topics. Then we used a general linear hypothesis test[16] of the equivalence of the regression parameters for the two topic indicators.

[15] ACA Hope, 'A simplified Monte Carlo significance test procedure' (1968) 30 *Journal of the Royal Statistical Society Series B* 582, 582–98.

[16] F Bretz, T Hothorn and P Westfall, *Multiple Comparisons Using R*, 1st edn (Boca Raton, CRC Press, 2010).

VI. Comparison of Administrative vs Non-administrative Cases on the Nordic Level

In order to test whether location (parameters) or proportions were equal between Administrative and Non-administrative cases on a Nordic level, we employed all the Nordic cases and then regressed the variable of interest on the Administrative indicator, while adding a set of indicator variables representing the Nordic countries as controls. For

- continuous variables we used linear regression.
- binary variables we used logistic regression.
- the ordinal variable (N12) we used ordinal regression.
- nominal variables we used multinomial regression.

Then, we tested the significance of the Administrative indicator parameter in linear regression (t-test), logistic regression (Wald test), and ordinal or multinomial regression (by profile likelihood-based confidence intervals). We found there to be reasonable substantial and significant differences in several situations, such as fewer opinions invoking freedom of expression rights (N45) among the Administrative cases.

VII. Comparisons between Nordic Countries or Courts

In a comparison of the Nordic countries, we started with an unconditional view (without accounting for differences in either time or Administrative cases) and tested null hypotheses that the Nordic countries had equal:

- means among continuous variables, via F-tests in an ANOVA.
- medians among ordinal variables and the continuous variables, using Kruskall-Wallis-test.
- proportions among binary or ordinal variables, using chi-square tests.

The reason to also apply the Kruskall-Wallis-test of (median) location to continuous variables was its robustness to non-normal underlying data generation processes, since some distributions were somewhat skewed.

The null hypothesis of equality was rejected in almost every case. The only exceptions were the case disposition (N4) and some of the conceptual variables (N38, N39, N42, N45, N50). Typically, one or two countries (most often Denmark and/or Norway) differed from the others. This was also seen in tests of equality (pairwisely) of proportions (using chi-square test) between the Nordic courts.

Occasionally (in selected situations for a specific country and variable of interest), estimates of the (logistic) regressions in section V were used to estimate country proportions conditional on having the same proportion of administrative cases as the selected country. We then also tested whether each of the other Nordic countries' proportions differed significantly from the chosen country's, using robust estimators[17] when needed to undertake the test.

In order to test if trends over time differed between courts, we regressed the binary variables on a random court intercept (as control), a court indicator, a time variable, and their interaction. In this way, we simultaneously tested whether a court had a different level or trend over time compared to other courts. Each court was found to have a few (four variables on average) significantly different levels or trends compared to the other courts. Deviations were more common for Norway, and also among the argumentative variables.

VIII. Comparisons between Nordic and International Courts

The purpose of employing the methods in this section was to explore whether the Nordic higher courts, in terms of constitutional reasoning, distinguished themselves from other constitutional and international courts. We thus made use of the merged data from the Nordic CONREASON, the CONREASON, and the CORE Latam projects, as described in section III(C) above.

A. The Nordic System vs Other International Systems

In order to make comparisons between the Nordic and other constitutional systems, we employed the legal system categorisations described in section III(C) above, Nordic; Civil; Common; Mixed and Regional (CIV_COM) and Diffused(Nordic); Diffused(Other); Centralised; Hybrid and Regional (CEN_DIFF2).

Depending on which projects a variable was measured in, see Table A.1 in the Appendix below, we had at most 42 courts, each with 40 cases. These courts may not be considered as a random sample of all potential courts, not least since both the CORE Latam and the Nordic CONREASON project included high courts in specific geographical regions. We therefore assumed a model where we conceptualised a level effect of each court to be a random draw from a much larger set of potential levels emanating from a common underlying data generating process.

[17] E Cantoni and E Ronchetti, 'Robust Inference for Generalized Linear Models' (2001) 96 *Journal of the American Statistical Association* 1022, 1022–30.

At the same time, we treated the potential differences between the legal systems of interest as structural.

We then regressed the variable we investigate on (indicators of) the court systems of interest (with Nordic as the reference category) but also included a random intercept for each of the courts in our model. In this way we tried to control for the dependence between cases within the same court.

When the variable of interest was continuous, we estimated a generalised linear mixed model. We choose to transform the nominal variables to sets of binomial variables, so that when the variable was not continuous, we estimated binomial generalised linear mixed models. We then chose to use the Nordic or Diffused(Nordic) category as reference, and then we tested whether the (fixed) effects of each of all the other systems, that is, either Civil; Common; Mixed; Regional, or Diffused(Other); Centralised; Hybrid; Regional, differed significantly from the Nordic reference.

In order to visually study the development over time, given each variable of interest, we first fitted LOESS[18] curves (including confidence intervals) on an accumulated 'global' level, and then did the same for each constitutional system (but without accounting for court). In this way we could visually get an idea of any potential trends, although without performing any formal tests. As a way of trying to control for any overall trends, we added natural cubic splines[19] to the previously fitted regression models.

We also tested whether the Nordic countries differed in level and/or in the linear trend over time compared to other countries, through a binomial generalised linear mixed model, in a similar way to that described in section VII above among Nordic courts. Thus, we regressed the variable of interest on an indicator of the Nordic courts, a time variable, and their interaction. As previously, we included a random intercept for each of the courts. In addition to these formal tests, we visualised the predicted model outcomes with confidence intervals. We found about the same number of significant differences as among the Nordic courts, and a third of them were exactly the same.

B. Nordic vs International Courts on Aggregated Court Level

In this section of the analysis, we aggregated data on court level. The analyses focused on the argumentative (R12-R26, R28-R29) and conceptual (R31-R50) variables. All variables were thus aggregated into binary proportions on court level. Some of the variables were missing from all the courts in the CONREASON project (see Table A.1 in the Appendix below), and also from one court (ECU1)

[18] WS Cleveland, E Grosse and WM Shyu, 'Local regression models' in JM Chambers and TJ Hastie (eds), *Statistical Models in S* (Pacific Grove, Wadsworth & Brooks/Cole, 1992).

[19] TJ Hastie, 'Generalized additive models' in JM Chambers and TJ Hastie (eds), *Statistical Models in S* (Pacific Grove, Wadsworth & Brooks/Cole, 1992).

in the CORE Latam project. The ECU1 court was therefore excluded from this analysis.

The available variables, conditional on the projects included, are presented in Table 3 below. Since variable R12 was ordinal with three mutually exclusive categories, it was represented by two binary variables. Unless anything else is stated, we choose to proceed with all of the projects (that is, 41 court observations excluding ECU1) and thus in total with 32 (17 argumentative and 15 conceptual) variables.

Table 3 Available variables conditional on courts/projects included

Dataset includes	All projects	Two projects	One project
Projects included			
Nordic CONREASON	X	X	X
CORE Latam	X	X	
CONREASON	X		
Number of courts	41	22	7
Argumentative variables			
Names	R12-R26, R29	R12-R26, R28-R29	N12-N30
Number of variables	17	18	20
Conceptual variables			
Names	R31, R33-R46	R31-R50	N31-N51
Number of variables	15	20	21

We then compared proportions of all the courts for each variable at a time. We also calculated the average proportion among argumentative and conceptual variables and compared these two averages among all the courts.

The Nordic courts did not stick out particularly on either of the scales compared to other courts, irrespective of whether we compared to all courts with fewer (32) variables, or only CORE Latam courts including more (38) variables.

i. Pairwise and Canonical Correlations

In order to better understand the relations both within the two sets of (argumentative and conceptual) variables we studied the pairwise (Pearson's r) correlations between all pairs of variables, considering them by the sets. Correlations were on average slightly stronger among conceptual (mean=0.24, median=0.22, sd=0.18) than argumentative (mean=0.18, median=0.22, sd=0.21) variables, and on average (although only) somewhat weaker between the sets (mean=0.16, median=0.15, sd=0.19).

Due to the small number of observations (41) relative to the number of variables (32), it was sometimes hard to directly extract reliable multivariate results. Such a small dataset may principally be framed as likely to be facing the 'curse of dimensionality'. In other words, if dimensions (that is, variables) are added (linearly) the observations get sparser (since the volume of the space spanned up by the variables grows exponentially) and each observation thus seems to become more distant from the other observations. When fitting a statistical model in such a situation (with very few observations), the risk of overfitting to the data is a potential problem. (On the other hand, given that the variables to a high degree are relevant to the phenomena studied, that would help out in, for example, discrimination of groups).

To investigate the overall correlation between argumentative and conceptual sets, we applied canonical correlation analysis (where one constructs canonical variates, that is, linear combinations in each of the variable sets, such that the correlations between the canonical variate pairs are maximised under the constraint that the canonical variate within a set is orthogonal to other variates of the same set). However, the results strongly suggested overfitting to the data.

We therefore choose a more robust approach and repeated the analysis, using only a random draw of three variables in each of the two sets. On average, we had one out of three canonical variates being significantly different from zero, thus lending some support for a correlational structure between the two sets of variables.

However, considering both the pairwise and the canonical correlations, it was suggested that the structural distinction between argumentative and conceptual variables were not necessarily that strong. Although the matter could be further investigated, the availability of data was still a major limitation. In the further analysis, initially we therefore did not distinguish between the two sets of variables, although we still looked for any anomalous differences between them.

ii. Dimensionality Reduction and Multiple Factor Analysis

One way of dealing with the sparsity was to reduce the dimensionality of the data while trying to extract the relevant information, that is, to try and 'increase the amount of signal relative to noise' in our chosen set of variables.

In practice this typically means that we projected (all, or many of) our variables onto a (much) smaller set of new (latent) variables in such a way that they still captured a lot of the information held within the original variables. Calculating average number of occurrences, as we did for the argumentative and conceptual variables, reduced the dimension to two (potentially correlated) variables, and might thus not be an efficient way of preserving the information in the variables.

Instead, first we tried out non-linear dimensionality reduction techniques. The similarity between observations were modelled either (in a Euclidean space) using t-distributed stochastic neighbour embedding (t-SNE),[20] or (in a Riemann space) with Uniform manifold approximation and projection (UMAP).[21] The results were then visualised in two dimensions.

While UMAP focuses more on preserving global structures, the t-SNE leans more towards local aspects but the results are more variable (and therefore repetitions of the procedure are needed to ensure that the results are reliable). However, the outcome of both methods was still highly dependent on the choice of hyperparameters and exploration of these are therefore also needed. Although, given a set of hyperparameters, it might have seemed that different groups of observations would be clustered, the distances between groups were not directly interpretable and specific outcomes should mainly be used as suggestions. However, after a thorough exploration, both methods seemed to suggest that all the Nordic courts, perhaps together with the IAC court, might form a group of observations on their own.

In contrast, linear dimensional reduction methods[22] such as principal component analysis (PCA) do have interpretable distances.[23] The method is based on finding linear combinations of the original variables, such that the linear combinations explain as much of the variance in the original variables as possible. At the same time, the linear combinations are themselves orthogonal to each other and are thus not correlated. The direction of the first principal component will therefore fall along that in which the observations vary the most, and so on for the following principal components.

Since PCA is scale dependent, all variables were standardised to have the same mean (0) and standard deviation (1) ahead of PCA. The first principal component explained 24 per cent of the variation, the second 11 per cent, the third 8 per cent and so on in descending order. When the scores of the six first components (comprising 62 per cent of the variation) were compared, we noticed that, except for components four and five, most of the Nordic courts tend to either have only positive (or negative) scores, indicating that they, as a group, tended to deviate from the overall mean of all the courts, see Figure 4 below.

[20] LJP van der Maaten and GE Hinton, 'Visualizing High-Dimensional Data Using t-SNE' (2008) 9 *Journal of Machine Learning Research* 2579, 2579–605.

[21] J Healy and L McInnes, 'Uniform manifold approximation and projection' (2024) 4 *Nature Reviews Methods Primers*, doi.org/10.1038/s43586-024-00363-x.

[22] JC Gower 'Some distance properties of latent root and vector methods used in multivariate analysis' (1966) 53 *Biometrika* 325, 325–28.

[23] KV Mardia, JT Kent and JM Bibby, *Multivariate Analysis* (London, Academic Press, 1979).

Figure 4 Dotplot of court scores for each of the six first principal components extracted from argumentative and conceptual variables

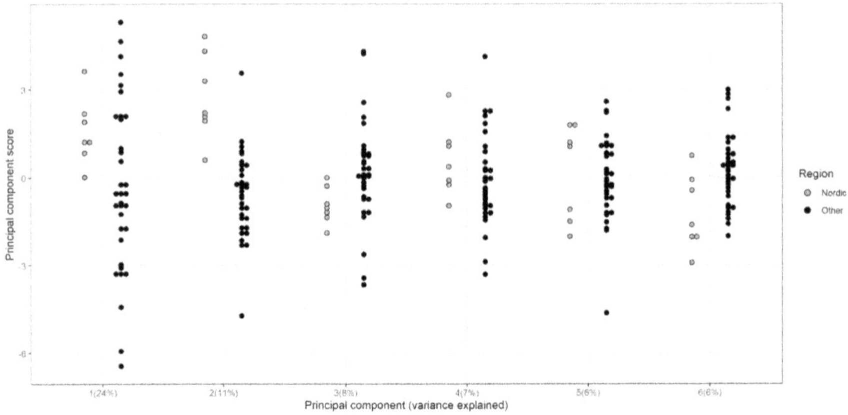

A scatterplot of the first two components' scores showed results similar to those of the non-linear dimensional reductions techniques, largely confirming that the Nordic supreme courts tended to deviate from other courts, see Figure 5 below.

The Nordic courts seemed to take a fringe position, although SWEa was a bit further away (primarily along the first dimension) from the others. Now IAC lay on its own, with ECHR as its nearest neighbour, but at the same level as the Nordic countries on the second dimensions. AUS also lay on its own, but on the opposite side of the second dimension. As was indicated in Figure 4, the third component also contributed to discriminating between the Nordic and the other courts.

Figure 5 Court scores on principal components extracted from argumentative(R12-R26,R29) and conceptual(R31,R33-R46) variables

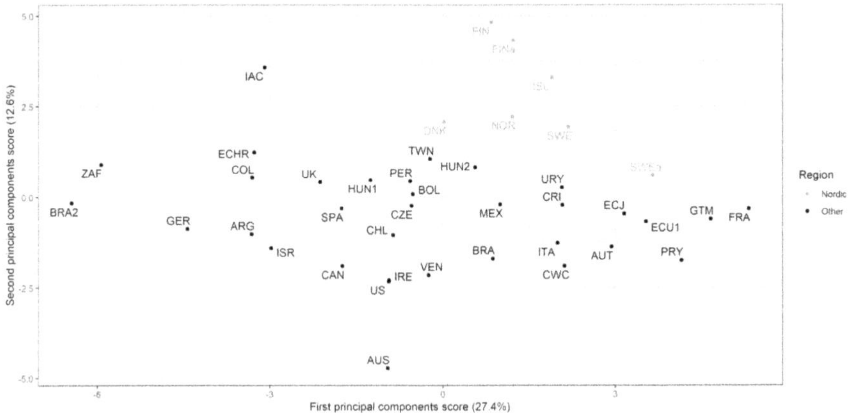

None of the (conceptual or argumentative) variables seemed to have a dominant impact on the principal components, and there was no clear pattern among the variable loadings on the principal components regarding the argumentative vs conceptual sets of variables. On average the absolute loadings on the first (mean=0.17, median=0.17, sd=0.06), the second (mean=0.15, median=0.15, sd=0.09) and the third (mean=0.15, median=0.12, sd=0.10) component were also fairly similar. It was therefore hard to interpret the principal components, beyond their ability to extract variation in the data.

In order to further investigate the influence of the two sets (of argumentative and conceptual) variables we undertook a multiple factor analysis, similar to a PCA, accounting (via weights) for the fact that the two sets of variables had a different number of variables. The argumentative and conceptual sets of variables essentially had the same impact (50 per cent) on the first dimension, and a very similar impact on the second (54 per cent and 46 per cent) and third (53 per cent and 47 per cent), although slightly less evenly on the fourth (41 per cent and 59 per cent). As with the similarity among loadings, this provides further support that there was not so much of an argumentative vs conceptual structure observable in the data.

iii. Cluster Analysis

Although the Nordic courts, regarding the projection unto fewer dimensions, seemed to lie along the boundary of the data, it was not clear whether any separation into well-defined groups or clusters of courts seemed reasonable. In order to investigate whether one could find such a separation, we employed clustering techniques on (at least two) of the principal components.

Clustering is to a large extent used as an exploratory methodology, so we choose to utilise a broad spectrum of clustering techniques including:

- k-means clustering;
- PAM (partitioning around mediods) – a more robust alternative to k-means clustering;
- hierarchical clustering (using various linkages and similarity measures);
- SOTA (self-organising tree algorithm) clustering;
- DBSCAN (density-based spatial clustering of applications with noise);
- FANNY (fuzzy analysis clustering) allowing observations to belong to more than one cluster;
- model-based expectation-maximisation (EM) clustering.

However, none of these methods gave any strong additional insights and there was never any clear separation into clusters. We also transposed the data and undertook principal component analysis using variables as observations and courts as variables, followed by similar clustering attempts, but without any new substantial insights.

iv. Discriminatory Power

An alternative approach to investigate whether there was anything distinct from Nordic vs other courts was to apply supervised (statistical) learning techniques and test the discriminatory power of fitting such a model to the data. As in clustering, there are a plethora of methods available.

For a small dataset with many variables in relation to the number of observations, a partial-least-squares[24] discriminatory-analysis (PLS-DA) would likely perform reasonably well. PLS resembles PCA, but does not only focus on explaining the variance of the other variables but also accounts for the variable of interest in the chosen projection (while PCA is unsupervised, PLS involves supervised dimensional reduction). In PLS-DA, the variable of interest was qualitative, that is, the Nordic court indicator variable. (As an alternative method, we also tried out support vector machines[25] combined with PCA and various configurations, but the results were always almost similar or worse.)

The modelling was performed in the following way:

1. We randomly selected 35 (that is, 85 per cent of all) courts, conditional on six of them being Nordic and 29 not (that is, a stratified train-test split). In this way, we ensured that the proportion of Nordic cases was the same (17 per cent) both among the selected and the non-selected courts. (One could allow for more variation in the number of Nordic vs non-Nordic cases, but this balance was chosen for its pragmatism here.)
2. Based on the 35 selected courts, utilising both the variables and the Nordic indicator variable, we estimated a model which was calibrated to have good discriminatory power. The model depended on the selection of a hyperparameter (namely the number of components to be used, analogous to the number of principal components selected in PCA) automatically chosen through a leave-one-out cross-validation (LOOCV) procedure.
3. Based on the estimated model and the variable values of the six excluded (including one Nordic) court observations, we then predicted the class (Nordic or not) among each of them.
4. In order to evaluate the discriminatory power, we then compared the predictions to the true values (Nordic or not) which had been held out during the prediction phase.

[24] G James, D Witten, T Hastie, and R Tibshirani, *An introduction to statistical learning*, 2nd edn (New York, Springer, 2021).

[25] ibid.

The above procedure was repeated many (10,000) times, such that each of the Nordic courts on average would be predicted 10,000/7≈1429 times each (and the other courts (6-1)*10,000/34≈1471 times each). We then evaluated the average discriminatory power, that is, how often the classifications were correct. Almost all Nordic countries were always classified correctly, except for NOR (which was classified falsely 14.3 per cent of the time). Among the other courts, HUN2 were falsely classified as Nordic 12.7 per cent of the time, and IAC 0.6 per cent of the time, while all the other courts were always classified correctly. With regards to some of the previous (non-linear) results this did not seem conspicuous since HUN2 lay fairly adjacent to the Nordic courts, and NOR sometimes lay fairly close to IAC. In total the misclassification rate was thus only 0.7 per cent. The average Area Under the Curve (AUC), a measure which better accounts for the category imbalance, was 0.85, so the discriminatory ability might be considered to be 'Excellent'.[26]

Although other setups were attempted, for example balancing the dataset through oversampling, the results turned out to be robust to several alternative specifications. This lends even more support to the fact that there was something measured in the data which made the Nordic courts distinct from the other courts. Still, it was hard to interpret exactly why we observed the discrimination, and there is of course scope for examining how the individual variables enter such a prediction model.

Regarding the hyperparameter, three components were selected 80.0 per cent of the time, two components 19.7 per cent of the time, and four components 0.3 per cent of the time. This seemed to be consistent with the previous results. A discriminatory model such as the one used is more likely to select a (too) large than a (too) small model. Notably, from the PCA it also seemed that the two (or perhaps three) first components were a reasonable representation.

v. *Multivariate Hypothesis Testing of Differences in Means*

Another approach to compare the Nordic courts to other courts was to formally test whether there was a significant difference in means between them. Such tests may be undertaken directly on variables, and would primarily align with the results in section VIII(A) above where the Nordic system was compared to other international systems. In eight of those cases (involving variables R19, R21, R22, R26, R31, R34, R35, and R42) it was generally recognised that the Nordic system differed significantly from the other legal systems.

[26] See the rule of thumb in DW Hosmer and S Lemeshow, *Applied Logistic Regression*, 3rd edn (Hoboken, John Wiley & Sons, 2013) 143.

In order to take on a more comprehensive approach, we applied a multivariate test. Due to the data sparsity, and the nature of the principal components (which had relatively symmetrical and bell-shaped distributions), we choose to use the Hotelling's t-squared distribution as a reference. Then we stated a null hypothesis that the multivariate mean of the difference in principal components (extracted in section VIII(B)(ii)) between Nordic and other courts was zero, before we undertook the test.[27]

It turned out that the null hypothesis was rejected irrespective of the number of components included. However, tests of skewness and kurtosis (under normality) were both rejected with more than four components. (When components were tested individually, the null hypothesis of no difference were rejected for the first three and the sixth and seventh principal components.) Considering the small number of observations and previous results, this still lends huge support in favour of the Nordic courts (as a group) being different from the other courts.

IX. Concluding Remarks

The availability of the data from the Nordic CONREASON project, including the merging with data from previous similar projects worldwide, opened up entirely new possibilities for studying and generalising on constitutional reasoning in supreme courts, both on a Nordic and on an international level.

Since the field was largely unexplored, we applied a systematic approach where we carefully analysed the data using different selections, conditionings and levels of analysis. In addition, through applying a wide range of relevant methods, hopefully we did not miss out essential structures or fail to explain variation based on the factors that were available.

However, it cannot be ruled out that, in particular, part of the observed differences between the Nordic and other supreme courts may be due to systematic differences in the measurement process of the Nordic courts compared to the other projects. Such an investigation was beyond the scope of this analysis and would rather demand qualitative validations, in addition to those that we have already been undertaken.

Variable codings used when merging the projects

[27] H Hotelling, 'The generalization of Student's ratio' (1931) 2 *Annals of Mathematical Statistics* 360, 360–78.

Table A1 Variable coding when merging the three CONREASON projects into one dataset

Variable	Variable in the Nordic CONREASON Project		Variable in the CONREASON Project		Variable in the Core Latam Project	
Name:	*Name:*	*Coded as:*	*Name:*	*Coded as:*	*Name:*	*Coded as:*
Project		NC		CR		CL
Country	Country		Country		CODE	'BRA' as 'BRA2'
Court	Court		Country		CODE	
civ_com	*	Nordic	*	Civil; Common; Mixed; Regional	*	Civil; Common; Regional
cen_dif	*	Diffused	*	Centralize; Diffuse; Hybrid; Regional	*	Diffuse; Hybrid; Regional
cen_dif2	*	Diffused(N)	*	Centralize; Diffuse(O); Hybrid; Regional	*	Diffuse(O); Hybrid; Regional
R1	N1		Q1		Q1	
R2	N2		Q2		Q2	
R3	N3	1 = 'any is 1'; 0 = 'none is 1'	Q3		Q3	
R4	N4	NaN = 'if N/A', NA = 'if blank'	Q4	NaN = 'if N/A or NA', NA = 'if blank or 99'	Q4	NaN = 'if n.a', NA = 'if blank'
R5_F	N5_F		Q5A		Q5_F	
R5_S	N5_S		Q5B		Q5_S	
R5_O	N5_O	1 = 'N5_P or N5_O is 1'	Q5C		Q5_O	
R6	N6		Q6		Q6	

(continued)

Table A1 *(Continued)*

Variable	Variable in the Nordic CONREASON Project		Variable in the CONREASON Project		Variable in the Core Latam Project	
R12_C	N12_C	1 = 'none or only C is 1'; 0 = 'other'	Q7	1 = 'none or only C is 1'; 0 = 'other'	Q9	1 = 'none or only C is 1'; 0 = 'other'
R12_L	N12_L	1 = 'only L, or C and L is 1'; 0 = 'other'		1 = 'only L, or C and L is 1'; 0 = 'other'		1 = 'only L, or C and L is 1'; 0 = 'other'
R12_D	N12_D	0 ='none, or only C or L is l'; 1 = 'other'		0 = 'none, or only C or L is 1'; 1 = 'other'		0 = 'none, or only C or L is 1'; 1 = 'other'
R13	N13	1 = 'any is 1'; 0 = 'none is 1'	Q8		Q10	
R14	N14	1 = 'any is l'; 0 = 'none is 1'	Q9		Qll	
R15	N15		Q10		Q12	
R16	N16	1 = 'any is 1'; 0 = 'none is 1'	Qll		Q13	
R17	N17		Q12		Q14	
R18	N18	1 = 'any is 1'; 0 = 'none is 1'	Q13		Q15	
R19	N19		Q14		Q16	
R20	N20		Q15		Q17	
R21	N21		Q16		Q18	
R22	N22		Q17		Q19	

R23	N23	1 = 'any is 1'; 0 = 'none is 1'	Q18		Q20	
R24	N24	1 = 'any is 1'; 0 = 'none is 1'	Q19		Q21	
R25	N25	1 = 'any is 1'; 0 = 'none is 1'	Q20		Q22	
R26	N26	1 = 'any is 1'; 0 = 'none is 1'	Q21		Q23	1 = 'any is 1'; 0 = 'none is 1'
R28	N28			NA	Q24	
R29	N29		Q22		Q25	
R31	N31	1 = 'any is 1'; 0 = 'none is 1'	Q23		Q26	1 = 'any is 1'; 0 = 'none is 1'
R32	N32			NA	Q27	
R33	N33		Q24		Q28	
R34	N34		Q25		Q29	
R35	N35		Q26		Q30	
R36	N36		Q27		Q31	1 = 'any is 1'; 0 = 'none is 1'
R37	N37		Q28		Q33	
R38	N38		Q29		Q34	
R39	N39		Q30		Q32	
R40	N40		Q31		Q35	

(continued)

Table A1 *(Continued)*

Variable	Variable in the Nordic CONREASON Project		Variable in the CONREASON Project		Variable in the Core Latam Project	
R41	N41	1 = 'any is 1'; 0 = 'none is 1'	Q32		Q36	
R42	N42		Q33		Q37	
R43	N43		Q34		Q38	
R44	N44		Q35		Q39	
R45	N45	1 = 'any is 1'; 0 = 'none is 1'	Q36		Q40	
R46	N46		Q37		Q41	
R47	N47			NA	Q43	
R48	N48			NA	Q44	
R49	N49			NA	Q45	
R50	N50	1 = 'any is 1'; 0 = 'none is 1'		NA	Q47	
R52_M	N52_M			NA	Q50A	
R52_E	N52_E			NA	Q50B	
R52_R	N52_R			NA	Q50C	

* For all explanation, see the CONREASON project documentation.

3

Constitutional Reasoning at the Supreme Court of Denmark – In Front of and Behind the Scenes

HELLE KRUNKE AND MIKAEL KENNO FOGDE

I. Introduction

Like the other Nordic countries, Denmark does not have a constitutional court. However, the Danish Supreme Court has the competence to review the constitutionality of legislation. This competence has its legal basis in judgments from 1921, and a constitutional convention. However, it was not until 1999 that the Supreme Court actually found that a piece of legislation violated the Constitution in the so-called '*Tvind* judgment'. The Danish Supreme Court has adopted the manifestly ill doctrine, and today the mentioned judgment from 1999 is still the only example of the Supreme Court ruling that a piece of legislation has violated the Constitution. This makes the Danish Supreme Court stand out, not only in a global and European context but also in a Nordic context.

In this chapter, we will shed light on judicial reasoning at the Danish Supreme Court through quantitative empirical studies combined with qualitative studies. In the following, we will focus on the most interesting findings in the empirical study of the 40 leading Danish Supreme Court judgments. We will include a qualitative method when analysing the empirical data in order to provide a deeper understanding and explanation of the outcome and significance of the quantitative data. In this regard, we will draw on literature on constitutional law, and on protocols of the deliberations among the judges in three of the most important Danish judgments. U1999.841H (*Tvind*), U1996.1300H (*Maastricht formality*), and U1998.800H (*Maastricht reality*). The deliberation protocols of the Supreme Court are in essence extended minutes of the Court's meetings where the legal aspects of the case are discussed among the judges appointed to the case. The judges comment on the legal issues of the case one by one, in the order of their appointment to the Supreme Court, and starting with the judge who joined the Court most recently. A clerk at the Supreme Court takes minutes of the comments made by each judge. The minutes do not show how the Supreme Court reached the final judgment. Deliberation protocols are sealed from the public for 20 years after the decision. When that period elapses, the President of the Supreme Court can grant access to specific protocols if a research purpose is proven to the Court. For this research project, the President of the Supreme Court granted access to the deliberation protocols of three of the most important of the 40 chosen cases, at the request of the authors. These were the cases U1996.1300H (*Maastricht formality*), U1998.800H (*Maastricht reality*) and U1999.841 (the *Tvind* case). The deliberation protocols can be viewed as empirics, which we base our analysis on. However, they also contribute to a better qualitative understanding of the empirical data from the coding of the 40 judgments.

II. Legal, Political, Institutional, and Academic Context

In this section, we will provide the reader with a short introduction to the Danish constitutional system and context. As an illustration, we will include empirical findings from the 40 coded judgments and the deliberation protocols.

The Danish Constitution was introduced in 1849. It has been revised four times since then, and the last revision took place in 1953. The Nordic constitutional systems are often viewed as sharing many characteristics. However, the Danish constitutional system differs from the other Nordic constitutions in a few significant ways. First, the other Nordic constitutions are amended more often than the Danish Constitution. In light of this, their human rights catalogues are more extensive and more inspired by the European Convention of Human rights (ECHR) and other human rights conventions. At Danish courts, the ECHR plays an increasingly important role in legal reasoning on issues of human rights since the human rights provisions in the Constitution have not been revised since 1953. The ECHR is however not a formal part of the Danish Constitution. Furthermore, 'green rights', gender equality, and digital rights are emphasised in some other Nordic constitutions. In Denmark, such matters are regulated by ordinary legislation.[1] In the Finnish and Swedish Constitutions, the European Union (EU) is mentioned. While Denmark entered the European Community (EC, now EU) in 1973 – more than 20 years before Sweden and Finland – the EU is not mentioned in its Constitution. Important constitutional principles such as democracy, rule of law, human dignity and human rights are

[1] See H Krunke and B Thorarensen (eds), *The Nordic Constitutions. A Comparative and Contextual Study* (Oxford, Hart Publishing, 2018) 204.

now mentioned in the first Articles in most of the other Nordic Constitutions. This is not the case in the Danish Constitution, which still reflects the old Nordic tradition of not mentioning general principles in the first Article of the Constitution.[2]

We then turn to some of the most important principles and competences of the courts in the Danish constitutional setting, starting with the principle of separation of powers in Article 3 of the Danish Constitution:

> Legislative authority shall be vested in the King and the Parliament conjointly. Executive authority shall be vested in the King. Judicial authority shall be vested in the courts of justice.

Article 3 was introduced with the 1849 Constitution. Today, 'the King' is broadly interpreted as the government. The independence of the judges is underlined in Article 64:

> In the performance of their duties, the judges shall be governed solely by the law. Judges shall not be dismissed except by judgement, nor shall they be transferred against their will, except in cases in which a rearrangement of the courts of justice is made. A judge who has completed his sixty-fifth year may, however, be retired, but without loss of income up to the time when he is due for retirement on account of age.

The competence of the courts to review the constitutionality of legislation does not have a legal basis in the constitutional text. However, it is considered to be a constitutional norm based on a legally binding constitutional convention. At least since 1921, the Supreme Court has considered itself competent to review the constitutionality of legislation.[3] However, it was not until 1999 that the Supreme Court in the so-called *Tvind* judgment found that a legislative Act violated the Constitution.[4] The legislator then took immediate action to amend the law in light of the judgment. Today, the *Tvind* judgment is still the only case in which the Supreme Court has judged a legislative Act to be unconstitutional.[5] This means that, while the courts clearly have the competence to review the constitutionality of legislation, they are very reluctant to conclude that an Act violates the Constitution, including the Supreme Court. There must be a manifest violation

[2] H Krunke, 'Global Values, International Organisations and Constitutional Change' in X Contiades and A Fotiadou (eds), *Handbook of Comparative Constitutional Change* (Oxfordshire, Routledge, 2020); and H Krunke, 'Constitutional Identity in the Nordic Countries 1950–2015' in P Slotte, N Gregersen and H Årsheim (eds), *Internationalization and Re-Confessionalization: Law and Religion in the Nordic Realm 1945–2017* (Odense, Syddansk Universitetsforlag, 2022) 339–62.

[3] Ugeskrift for retsvæsen (U) (weekly law reports) 1921.148 H (Den.) and U 1921.153 H (Den.) followed by U 1921.168 H (Den.) and U 1921.169 H (Den.).

[4] U 1999.841 H (Den.).

[5] Administrative acts and decisions have however been subject of constitutionality review at the Supreme Court a number of times, and in some cases, they were ruled unlawful or unconstitutional. Examples are U 1994.536 H (Den.), U 1996.1300 H (Den.), U 2004.382 H (Den.) and U 2013.3328 H (Den.) as mentioned later in this section.

of the Constitution in order for the courts to declare legislation unconstitutional. The courts' reluctance is a result of a judge-made criterion inducing self-restraint through the case law of the Supreme Court.

This context explains why the case law of the Danish Supreme Court stands out in a global comparison with case law from other Supreme Courts and Constitutional Courts in the other two CONREASON projects (see Figure 1 below).

Figure 1 Proportion of cases in which the court found a constitutional violation

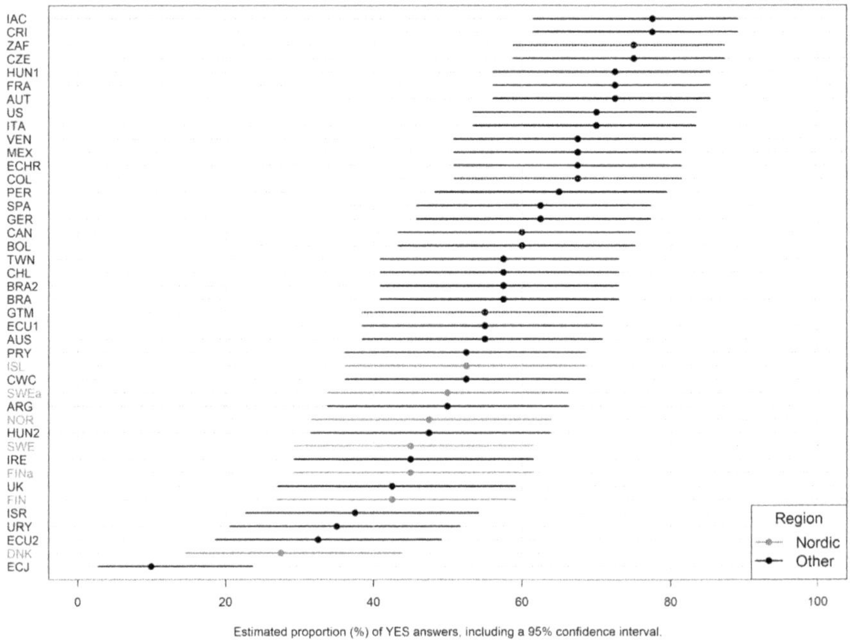

Denmark, together with Uruguay, has the highest proportion of leading constitutional cases in which the Supreme Court did not find a constitutional violation globally, and the second lowest proportion of cases in which it found against the political branches of government, after the Court of Justice of the European Union (CJEU).[6]

[6] This variable had two additional values: it was left blank if the judgment prescribed a binding interpretation of a statute or constitutional provision, and it was not applicable (N/A), if the legal dispute took place between private individuals or organisations and did not involve judicial review (see the instructions for variable N4 in the Codebook in the Appendix). Three cases in the Danish sample fell into the latter category (U 1980.1037/2 H, U 1986.898/3 H, and U 2017.824 H), and none fell into the former.

Another interesting observation is that Denmark is placed highest on applicability of the Constitution globally in the empirical material (see Figure 2 below).

Figure 2 Proportion of cases discussing the applicability of the Constitution

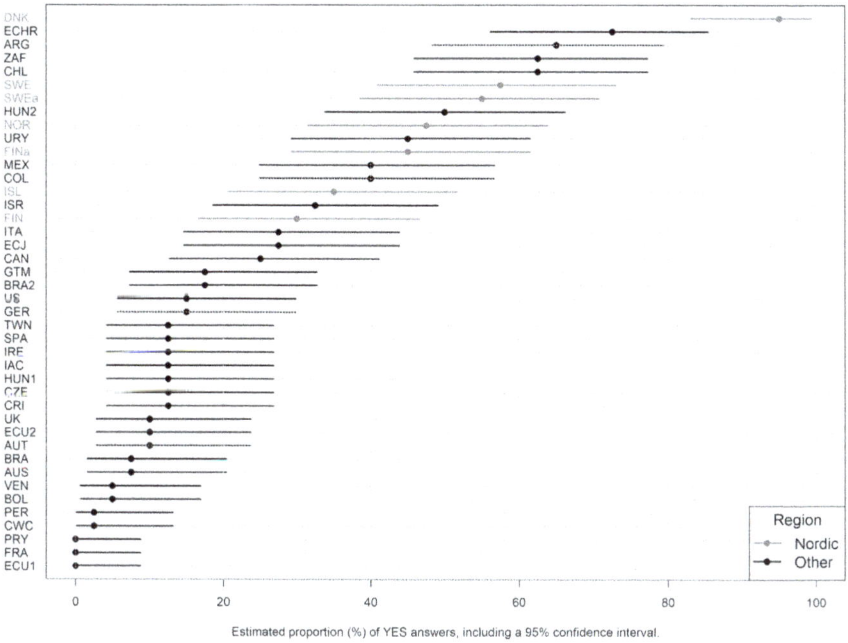

This may reflect that the state attorney or both parties to the case alerted the Supreme Court to the fact that it is overall reluctant to thoroughly review the constitutionality of legislation as far as it is seen as within proximity of legislative discretion.

Danish courts also have the competence to review administrative decisions and administrative acts. This follows directly from Article 63(1) of the Constitution:

> The courts of justice shall be empowered to decide any question relating to the scope of the executive's authority; though any person wishing to question such authority shall not, by taking the case to the courts of justice, avoid temporary compliance with orders given by the executive authority.

Based solely on the ordinary meaning of the wording of Article 63, the Supreme Court should have a wide competence to review the constitutionality of administrative acts and decisions. In reality Article 63 has undergone different textual interpretations through time from an originally very limited right of the courts to review administrative acts to an almost full competence to review administrative acts and decisions today. This means that the courts have expanded their competence in this field over time. Many of the 40 leading cases are regarding judicial review of administrative acts and decisions.[7]

An exemption to the right to full review is the use of so-called finality clauses, which allow the legislative branch to limit the scope of the court's review, if this is done through a clear finality clause in the relevant legislation. In U1997.1157H, through somewhat questionable due process arguments, the Supreme Court confirmed that the historical right for the legislative branch to use finality clauses was in accordance with Article 63. In essence this means that the courts are limited in their ability to review the factual basis of the administrative acts or decisions but not the legal assessments, and therefore not the constitutionality of the decisions.

In Denmark, democracy is traditionally understood as providing the legislature with a wide competence because of the legislature's popular legitimacy. Courts do not enjoy such popular legitimacy, and therefore they should not be 'activist'. Judges in Denmark are appointed through the Independent Appointment Council. Members of the Council are formally appointed by the Minister of Justice but half the appointees are to be judges, and the Council is always to be chaired by the appointed Supreme Court Justice. Nevertheless, as mentioned, the Danish courts have over time to some extent expanded their review competence as regards constitutional review of legislation by the introduction of a constitutional convention at constitutional level, and as regards review of administrative review by an expanded interpretation of Article 63.

In constitutional literature, democracy is traditionally interpreted as 'formal democracy' with emphasis on procedures which support elections and democratic decision making in Parliament.[8] This is reflected in constitutional interpretation and interpretation of ordinary legislation. In Denmark, and the Nordic countries in general, preparatory legislative material (*travaux préparatoires*) is said to play an important role when interpreting the Constitution and legislation.[9] The will of the legislator is considered very important, just as legal certainty is. This might explain why rule of law is often invoked as an argument in the Danish Supreme Court (and other Nordic supreme courts) compared to other supreme and constitutional courts globally (see Figure 3).

[7] 29 out of the 40 judgments are cases against the executive/administration (which we measured with variable N7). This includes appeal cases of administrative decisions, where the main legal question in reality is constitutionality of legislation or legality in relation to the ECHR. An example of this is U 1997.1157 H. Out of the 29 judgments, 11 judgments have an administrative decision as the main focus. An example is U 2013.3328 H on citizenship.

[8] Among others, the legal scholar Alf Ross has had great impact on how democracy is understood in Danish constitutional thinking. Ross represents a formal understanding of democracy. See A Ross, *Dansk Statsforfatningsret 1* (Copenhagen, Nyt Nordisk Forlag, 1983) 128–48, and A Ross, *Hvorfor demokrati* (Copenhagen, Nyt Nordisk Forlag, 1999).

[9] Whereas the European Court of Justice of the European Union is sceptical as regards putting too much weight on preparatory works, see 71/02 *Bjørnkulla* and C-611/14 *Canal Digital Danmark*, the Danish Supreme Court does not share this scepticism in its practice.

Figure 3 Proportion of cases in which the concept of rule of law is invoked

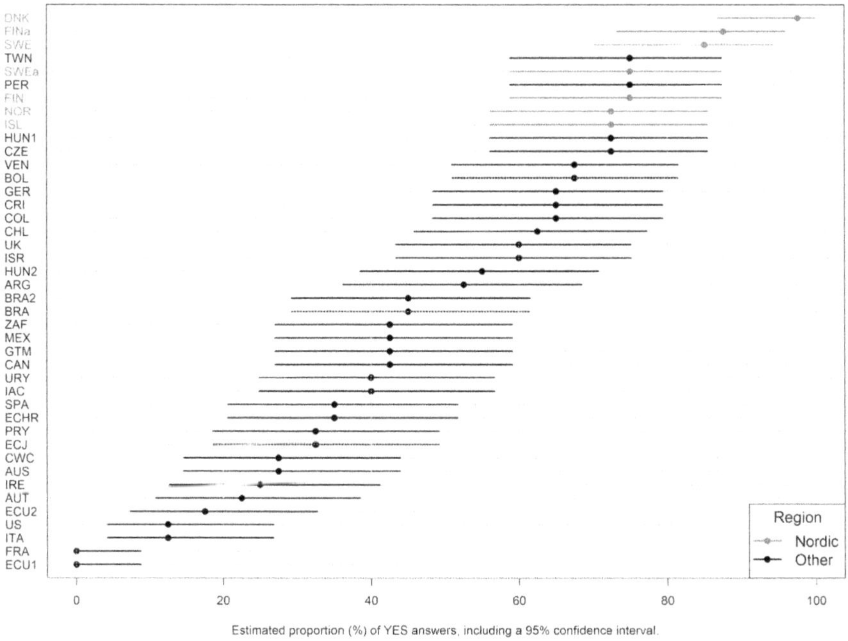

An important observation is that since *travaux préparatoires* play such an important role when interpreting the Constitution, such sources are quoted extensively in some of the 40 judgments. U1998.800H is a clear example of this. As a consequence, arguments by political actors become part of the judicial reasoning at the Supreme Court in our study. This is a general observation in relation to the project design of the CONREASON project, and it seems that it has a special significance in the Nordic constitutional setting, and that the results of the coding of the judgments must be viewed and interpreted in light of this.

Furthermore, all-embracing principles are said to play a more limited role in Nordic Law than in other legal systems such as French and German Law.[10] As mentioned, the Danish Constitution does not emphasise important constitutional principles in the first Article as we see in some constitutions.[11] The Supreme Court is said to seldomly refer explicitly to general principles that do not have a written legal basis in the Constitution.[12] If we turn to our empirical data and compare it with the doctrine, we see that there are many references to especially the principle of legality.

[10] U Bernitz, 'What Is Scandinavian Law? Concept, Charateristics, Future' (2007) 50 *Scandinavian Studies in Law* 13, 14 and 28.

[11] Krunke, 'Global Values' (n 2).

[12] H Krunke, 'Constitutional Identity and Equality: The Challenge of the Nordic EU Member States' (2023) 1 *Comparative Constitutional Studies* 124; H Krunke, 'Constitutional Identity in Denmark: Extracting Constitutional Identity in the Context of a Restrained Supreme Court and a Strong Legislature' in C Calliess and G van der Schyff (eds), *Constitutional Identity in a Europe of Multilevel*

The principle of legality is a well-established principle, which is often said to have a legal basis in Article 3 of the Constitution. Furthermore, there are references to separation of powers (N31_4), which also has its legal basis in Article 3, and to judicial independence (N32), which has a legal basis in Article 64. An interesting empirical observation is that democracy is referred to in four judgments (N33). The term 'democracy' is not directly mentioned in the Constitution, but it is reflected in many provisions that Denmark is a democracy. Interestingly, 'democracy' is understood as a democratic form of government in U1998.800H, which fits well with a formal concept of democracy.[13] Inspired by the ECHR, U1999.1798H reflects a more substantial understanding of democracy, where freedom of expression, assembly, and association are a necessary precondition for democracy.

Traditionally, influential legal scholarship has separated the concept of 'justice' from the concept of 'law'.[14] Therefore, there is no strong tradition at the courts for referring to 'justice' in its own right. This might also explain why the Danish Supreme Court (together with the Swedish Administrative Supreme Court) turn out lowest as regards references to 'justice' in comparison with Latin America (CORE Latam project) (see Figure 4 below). We return to key concepts later in this chapter.

Figure 4 Proportion of cases in which the concept of justice is invoked

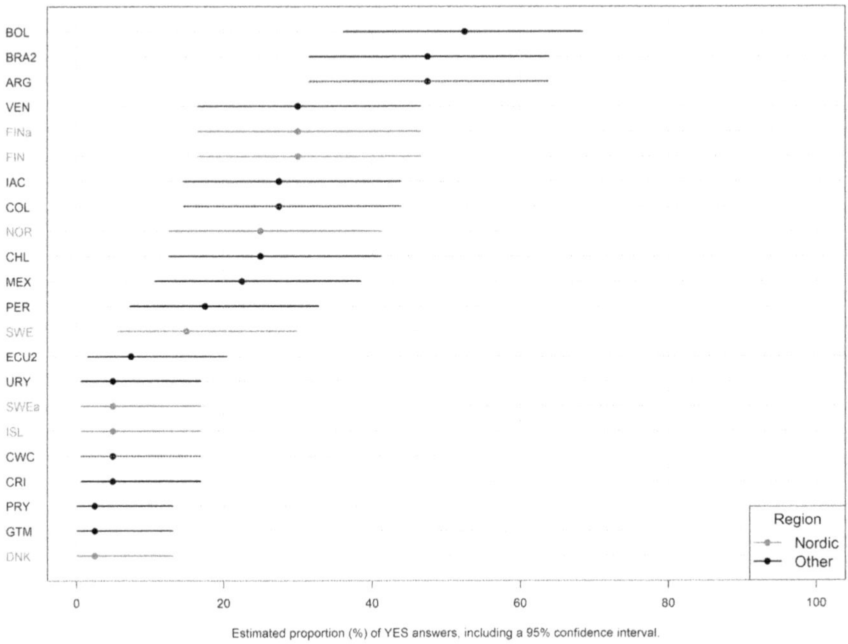

Constitutionalism (Cambridge, Cambridge University Press, 2019) 114–33; and Krunke, 'Constitutional Identity in the Nordic Countries 1950–2015' (n 2).

[13] See above.

[14] A Ross, *Ret og Retfærdighed* (Copenhagen, Nyt Nordisk Forlag Arnold Busck, 1953).

Furthermore, the Court is said to be reluctant in defining constitutional principles and constitutional identity.[15] An interesting observation in this regard is found in the deliberations among the Supreme Court judges in the *Tvind* judgment (U1999.841H). They show that it is discussed whether an unwritten principle of equality should be mentioned as legal basis in the judicial reasoning of the judgment. However, several judges express that since the case can be referred to Article 3 of the Constitution, they prefer not to mention an unwritten principle of equality as legal basis. Since such a principle is not mentioned in the Constitution, and it has been debated in constitutional literature whether such an unwritten constitutional principle exists, it would have had great impact if the Supreme Court had chosen to also refer to such a principle. The deliberations in the *Tvind* judgment this way confirm what follows from existing literature. Furthermore, there are no references to national identity (N38_1) in the 40 judgments, also confirming existing research in this field.

Another characteristic of judicial reasoning in the Nordic legal systems, which is often mentioned in legal literature, is the frequent use of analogies, particularly within the law of obligations.[16] One might ask whether this also applies to constitutional law? We shall return to this question in light of the empirical material in the Nordic CONREASON project below.

Case law plays a role in legal reasoning, and in interpreting the Constitution. Normally, the Supreme Court will follow its own judgments, though precedence is not formally binding for the court. However, in seldom cases the Supreme Court may introduce a new interpretation. An example is the judgment on the formality (admissibility) of the *Maastricht* case. After thorough consideration,[17] the Supreme Court decided to widen the existing access to court, which had been introduced and consequently followed in earlier judgments. This meant that a group of citizens with no concrete legal interest in the ratification of the Maastricht Treaty were able to sue the Danish State regarding the procedure applied for accession to the Treaty. This at the same time meant that the Supreme Court's competence to review constitutionality was widened. Another example is the *Ajos* judgment (U2017. 824H), where the minority judge expresses that she is applying the precedence of the Supreme Court in the Maastricht judgment, and therefore reaches a different conclusion to the other judges.

A key finding of our research into the deliberation protocols was that the Supreme Court used the deliberation protocols from older judgments when they deliberated on new cases. This was the case in the deliberations on the *Tvind* judgment (U1999.841H) where the deliberation protocol from the so-called *HT* judgment (U1986.898/3H) was studied and discussed in relation to whether the Supreme Court should refer to an unwritten principle of equality in the *Tvind*

[15] Krunke, 'Constitutional Identity and Equality' (n 11); Krunke, 'Constitutional Identity in Denmark' (n 11); and Krunke, 'Constitutional Identity in the Nordic Countries 1950–2015' (n 2).

[16] Bernitz (n 10) 28.

[17] This follows from the protocol on the deliberations among the Supreme Court Judges on U 1996.1300 H (Den.).

judgment. Also, in the deliberations on the formality of the *Maastricht* judgment, deliberation protocols from older cases were studied and discussed. There seems to be a contrast between the often quite short judicial reasoning of the Supreme Court in its judgments, and the fact that the Court uses its own much more extensive deliberations from older cases, when discussing how judicial reasoning should be in a new case. One might say that this practice is not ideal for transparency and the protection of legal certainty and rule of law, since citizens and attorneys have no access to the deliberation protocols, even though they seem to be a source that contributes to the judicial reasoning of the Supreme Court and how the Court interprets its former judgments. Deliberation protocols are not mentioned in traditional legal literature on legal reasoning. However, they are an important source for gaining a deeper understanding of the Supreme Court's judicial reasoning and add another dimension to our empirical analysis of the coded judgments.

Foreign case law is normally not considered a source for interpreting the Constitution. However, the Supreme Court may study and consider foreign case law in alike cases. In the deliberations on the *Maastricht* case (U1998.800H), the German *Maastricht* judgment was discussed among the Supreme Court judges and seems to have been a source of inspiration. Literature on constitutional law is often said to play a more important role as regards interpreting the Constitution than it plays in other legal fields.[18] In the 40 landmark cases, 15 have references to scholarly work, often cited by the parties. The Supreme Court sometimes makes reference to relevant (though not exhaustive) literature concerning the topic of the case in a footnote in the beginning of the judgment. This way, it is not possible to (directly) see which parts of literature have affected which parts of the legal reasoning in the judgment. However, if one studies the deliberation protocols in for instance the *Maastricht* judgment (U1998.800 H) and the *Tvind* judgment (U1999.841H), it is clear that the judges have studied, considered, and discussed constitutional literature extensively, and to a larger degree than mentioned in the decisions. International literature on the topic has also been studied to some extent.

III. Argumentative Patterns in Case Law: The Most Interesting Findings

In this section we focus on the most interesting findings, among others in a comparative perspective, in the empirical study of the 40 leading Supreme Court judgments.

[18] H Zahle, *Dansk forfatningsret. Studieudgave* (Copenhagen, Christian Ejler's Forlag, 2006) 50.

As mentioned above, a special feature of the Nordic legal systems is normally said to be the frequent use of analogies, particularly within the law of obligations. Our empirical data shows that analogical reasoning appears frequently in Danish judgments (see Figure 5 below).

Figure 5 Proportion of cases in which analogical reasoning is applied (N15)

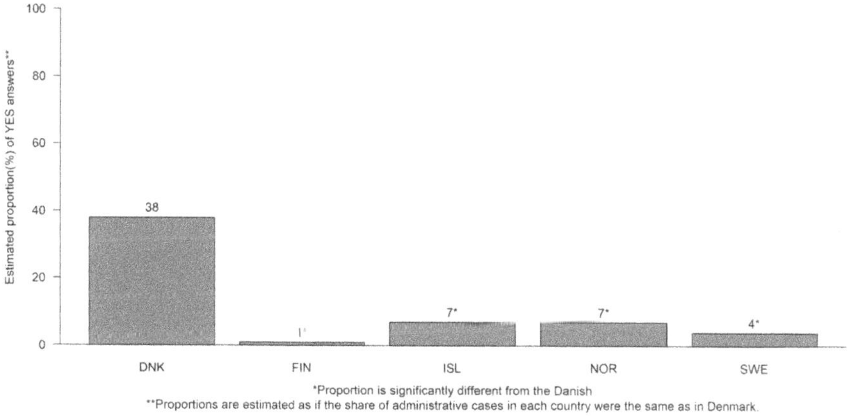

Importantly, this is not only the case as regards the law of obligations. Analogical reasoning is also applied in legal reasoning in constitutional law cases. This is a new finding considering existing comparative literature on the Nordic legal systems. At a closer look at our data, it turns out that the argument is normally introduced by the parties.[19] Danish courts are quite reluctant when it comes to free legal reasoning. However, analogical reasoning is seen as an accepted way of handling cases that do not fit neatly into formal legal reasoning. Since the last revision of the Danish Constitution was in 1953, and some constitutional provisions date all the way back to 1849, there might be more need for a tool such as analogical reasoning, when the parties to a case argue on how to interpret the Danish Constitution in a modern-day society, than is the case in the other Nordic countries, where the constitutions have been revised more recently.

Denmark has the highest rate, more than 50 per cent, also as regards teleological (textual) arguments (see Figure 6 below).

[19] An example is U 1998.800 H (Den.), where the parties argued for and against the idea that reluctance to consider a piece of legislation as unconstitutional should follow precedents from case law on the right to property.

Figure 6 Proportion of cases in which a teleological (textual) argument is used (N22)

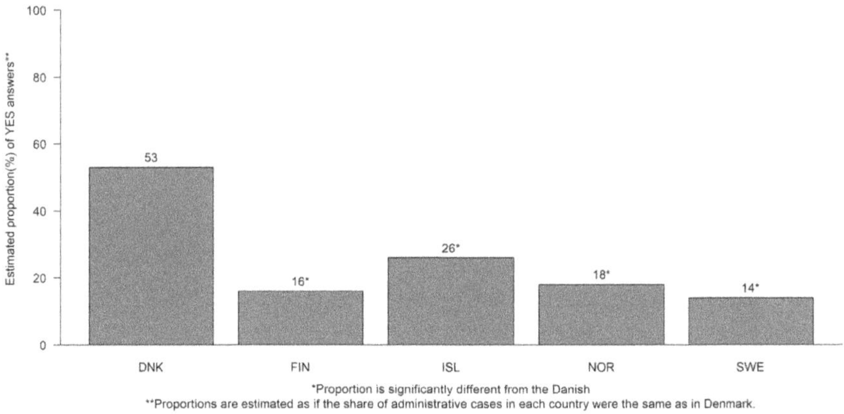

This might seem a little surprising in light of the fact that these types of teleological arguments do not include references to preparatory work.[20] Teleological (textual) arguments are objective teleological arguments referring to the purpose of the text. However, since the constitutional text is normally the first source to consider and the first argument in legal reasoning, maybe it is not so surprising after all. Starting with the constitutional text and moving on to the preparatory works would be in accordance with the way constitutional literature traditionally describes constitutional interpretation.[21] This means that objective teleological reasoning is applied first, followed by subjective teleological reasoning. The parties seem to follow this pattern of argumentation in cases before the Supreme Court. In some cases, such as U2013.1451H and U2021.4999H, the judicial reasoning of the Supreme Court also reflects such a tandem of interpretation styles, while other cases seem to reflect a choice between them. A prime example of exclusively using an objective teleological interpretation of Article 3 in the Constitution is U1999.841H. Seen in a time perspective, it is interesting that objective teleological reasoning apparently has become more common during the last approximately 20–30 years, especially during the mid- to late 1990s and from 2010 to 2022.[22] Objective teleological reasoning will generally provide the interpreter with more room for interpretation than subjective teleological reasoning where the interpreter relies heavily on the intention of the legislator. This could perhaps indicate a slight turn towards a freer judicial reasoning style over the past 20 years, which is an interesting observation.

[20] References to preparatory works were measured under a separate variable (N23 subjective teleological arguments).

[21] JP Christensen a.o., *Dansk Statsret* (Århus, DJØF Forlag, 2020).

[22] In 22 judgments we find teleological (textual) arguments: eight judgments from 2010–22, three from 2000–10, six from 1990–99 (all from 1994–99), one from 1980–89, one from 1970–79, one from 1960–69, one from 1930–39, and one from 1920–29. This must of course be seen in light of the fact that we overall have selected few judgments from before 1945 (only four).

The extent of such a turn would, however, depend on how far the interpreter goes into objective teleological interpretation, and on whether an indicator of the intention of the legislator exists in the respective cases, and how clear it is. This might not always be the case. A lack of clarity may also lead to the Supreme Court allowing for an expanded competence for the legislator based on democratic legitimacy considerations.

As a starting point, literature on foreign legal systems is not seen as a formal source of interpretation when interpreting the Danish Constitution. The Nordic constitutions are not similar, though the Icelandic Constitution builds on an earlier version of the Danish Constitution and therefore still has some provisions which are close to the text of the Danish Constitution. While the empirical data stemming from the 40 judgments show that references to scholarly work from other Nordic countries is not part of legal reasoning at the Supreme Court, a closer look at the deliberation protocols show that the judges actually read and discuss scholarly work from other Nordic countries. This is for instance the case in the *Maastricht* case (U1999.800H) and especially the *Tvind* case (U1999.841H), where one judge discusses a Norwegian scholarly work on the premise that Norwegian legal culture closely resembles Danish legal culture. Interestingly, literature on non-Nordic foreign law is also read and discussed by the judges during the deliberations.[23] However, since the Maastricht Treaty was an EU Treaty which applied to all EU member states and had to be ratified in all member states maybe this is not so surprising. Obviously, questions such as national courts' competence to review the constitutionality of EU law, the *Kompetenz-Kompetenz* doctrine, and supremacy of EU Law, are questions which are common to all the member states. Therefore, judgments from other Supreme Courts and Constitutional Courts, not least the German Constitutional Court, and foreign literature on such judgments, can be a source of inspiration. In fact, during the deliberations on the *Maastricht* case U1998.800H, some judges expressed a desire to look at even more comparative material. In the Danish context, while foreign literature is studied and discussed by Supreme Court judges during deliberations, they are not directly referred to in the legal reasoning of the judgment itself. The parties are more likely to include foreign legal material in their legal reasoning at the Supreme Court. See for instance U1994.536H, where the parties refer to Danish and foreign literature and to case law from other Nordic countries.

At the Danish Supreme Court, references to Nordic case law are almost always references to Norwegian case-law (N26). The Norwegian legal system and legal culture is generally viewed as quite similar to the Danish legal system and legal culture though there are of course also differences. Here the data seems to fit quite well with the traditional East-West division among the constitutional systems of the Nordic countries. Though the East-West division does not apply in all

[23] Denmark has the highest proportion of N26_4 among the Nordic countries (40%).

dimensions, there are still traces to be found in some fields.[24] The reason why it is primarily Norwegian case law and not Icelandic case law, could be that the Norwegian language is much closer to the Danish language than the Icelandic language. Therefore, Norwegian case law is more easily accessible to the Danish judges and the parties to the cases.

Yet, another interesting perspective when studying the empirical material is that Denmark has the highest rate among the Nordic countries (seven cases = 17.5 per cent) when it comes to 'external sovereignty' understood as state sovereignty in legal reasoning at the Supreme Court. This might be explained by the fact that a number of judgments are related to Denmark's membership of the EC/EU. Denmark is the 'oldest' Nordic member of the EC/EU and has been a member of the EC/EU since 1973. In light of this, it may seem natural that Denmark has many judgments regarding transfer of sovereignty to the EC/EU. Some of the most well-known Danish landmark cases are the judgments on the Danish accession to the EC (formality), the *Maastricht* judgments (formality and substance), the *Lisbon* judgment, and the *Ajos* judgment. Interestingly, both the *Maastricht* judgments and the *Lisbon* judgment also contain references to internal sovereignty understood as parliamentary sovereignty. The reason for this is that external and internal sovereignty normally go hand in hand in cases concerning transfer of national sovereignty to the EU. In the Danish Constitution there is also a procedural question regarding how much Parliament must be involved when Denmark enters into treaties, Article 20, Part 2. Parliament's ongoing control of the government in the EU legislative process is also a common theme in such cases.[25] Furthermore, Denmark's military interventions abroad in the past decades are also reflected in the subject matters of the 40 judgments.

Denmark stands out in the Nordic context when 'state form' is mentioned as an argument in three judgments. Maybe not surprisingly, two of these judgments are related to Denmark's membership of the EU (U 1998.800H, and U2017.824H). Arguments related to government form appear in eight of the Danish judgments (20 per cent) which is the highest rate in a Nordic context. While the *Maastricht* case is among the judgments, the other judgments concern mostly rights, and a few of them legality and judicial independence, and as such concern different topics usually seen as core constitutional subjects on government form. U1993.757H regards the boundaries of taxation as indirect taxation, ie through government acts, which are constitutionally prohibited. In U2017.1795H, the Supreme Court had to consider whether a government enforced right to same sex marriages breached the Constitution's rules on the relationship between state church and government.

[24] H Krunke and B Thorarensen, 'Concluding Thoughts' in Krunke and Thorarensen (n 1) 207–10.

[25] H Krunke and S Klinge, 'The Danish Ajos-case – the missing case from Maastricht and Lisbon' (2018) 3 *European Papers* 157, 164, doi.org/10.15166/2499-8249/204.

A last interesting observation is that it is quite common in the selected Danish judgments to refer to the core of constitutional rights or competences. Denmark displays the highest rate even in global comparison (see Figure 7 below).

Figure 7 Proportion of cases in which the concept of the core of constitutional rights or competences is invoked

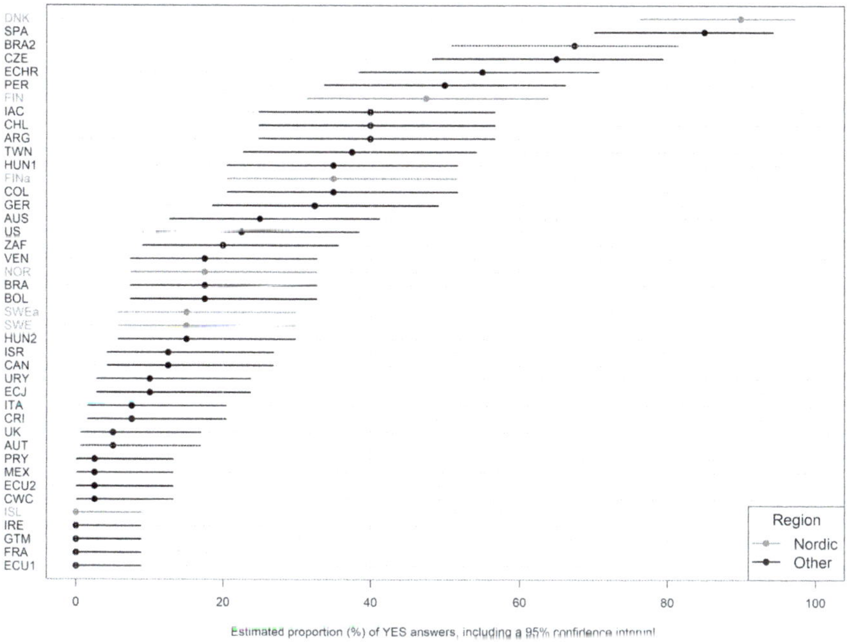

The concept of core content is not used in the Danish Constitution. One might wonder whether the Danish context with a reluctant Supreme Court with little willingness to enter into dynamic interpretations – in respect of the legislator – could provide an explanation. In such a context, the parties might refer to the core of constitutional rights and competences in order to convince the Supreme Court that it is a qualified violation of the Constitution. In Iceland, on the other hand, which is also part of the Western Nordic tradition, and which shares some overlaps in the constitutional text, we find no such references. However, there are some differences between the constitutional systems of Denmark and Iceland, which may contribute to explain this. Iceland revised its human rights charter in the 1990s in light of the ECHR and international human rights conventions, while the human rights catalogue of the Danish Constitution dates back to 1953 and reflects the original human rights catalogue in the 1849 Constitution. In this way, the human rights protection in the Icelandic constitution is more modern and more impacted by European and international trends and in such a context, the parties might not need to refer so much to the core of human rights. The Supreme

Court of Iceland is normally said to be the most active as regards reviewing the constitutionality of legislation together with Norway, and especially since 1995.[26] The 'threshold' for entering into judicial review is lower in Iceland and Norway than in Denmark, and therefore there is no need to refer to 'core arguments'.

IV. Length of Decisions and Separate Decisions

As regards the length of the full judgments, we find the highest variance among the Danish judgments compared to the other Nordic countries. In one end of the scale, we find judgments of 676,323 words (U2022.3378H) and 186,693 words (U2004.382). At the other end of the scale, we find judgments of 307 (U1941.1070H), 758 (U1921.148H), 1066 (U1921.644H), and 1226 words (U1925.277H). These are all rather old judgments from respectively 1941, 1925 and 1921. This indicates that the older judgments are typically shorter and the parties to the case in recent years are more inclined to introduce more material arguments to the case. However, there are exceptions, such as a judgment from 1997, which is only 1,603 words long (U1997.1157H).

Interestingly, some of the old judgments concern very important constitutional topics such as the competence of the courts to review constitutionality, state of emergency, right to property, right of association, and right of liberty. The development in the length of judgments somewhat corresponds with the fact that the legal reasoning of the judges in Supreme Court judgments is traditionally not very long but might be slightly rising in length, as the total case material dictates longer reasoning (the longest full judgment U2022.3378H also has the longest majority reasoning).[27] The legal reasoning is however usually linked closely to the result of the concrete case and the legal culture of only expressing the reasoning that a majority of judges sees as most relevant to the case. This is probably due to the complexity of the cases, but also the ease with which the parties can include data, documents etc. compared to 30–40 years ago.[28] In general, our statistical analysis also shows that in the average proportion between total length and length of the majority reasoning (N9/N8), Denmark stands out with the lowest proportions.[29]

The empirical material shows that the Supreme Court has a low rate of dissenting opinions compared to the other Nordic countries (N3). Out of the 40 judgments, only in six cases do we find dissenting opinions on constitutional issues, and in four judgments dissenting opinions on other issues. Furthermore,

[26] Krunke and Thorarensen (n 1) chs 5 and 8.

[27] See also JS Christensen, 'Domsskrivning i Højesteret' in H Udsen et al (eds), *Festskrift til Mads Bryde Andersen* (Copenhagen, DJØF Forlag, 2018).

[28] U 2021.4999 H (Den.) is a prime example of this. In that case the government decided to include vast amounts of evidence and data and therefore generated a lot more material for the judges to consider.

[29] Iceland comes out with the second lowest proportions (N9/N8).

there are no concurring opinions in the 40 judgments. Altogether, this shows that not only do the judges not often dissent they almost never offer alternative reasoning that would lead to the same outcome of the case. In general, the judges formulate legal reasoning and outcome in a way which all the judges can agree on. This might also explain why the reasoning of judgments is normally rather short. Furthermore, the fact that judgments are normally focused on the concrete case and its circumstances might be seen in this context. Again, we might turn to the deliberation protocols in order to understand what goes on during the deliberations before the final judgment is written and made public. In U1996.1300H, one judge reserves the right to dissent in the deliberation protocol. However, the final judgment is unanimous. In the deliberations of U1998.800H, the judges agree on the outcome of the case, but we find nuances regarding the legal reasoning. In the final judgment, these are not all visible. During the deliberations of case U1999.841H, some judges consider whether a general but unwritten constitutional principle of equality is a preferable legal ground for striking down the legislative act as unconstitutional, but they agree with the majority of judges, that a breach of separation of powers, Article 3 of the Constitution, is also an acceptable choice of legal ground and should be preferred to an unwritten constitutional principle. This is not mentioned in the final decision as a possible concurrent opinion. All in all, the deliberation reports confirm a strong legal culture of as short a legal reasoning as possible and a strong sense of finding common ground among all judges on the concrete legal issues.

V. Key Concepts

In existing legal literature, it is assumed that key concepts are rarely applied directly in Danish judgments.[30] In the cited source, this conclusion is based on a study of how often rule of law in the form of '*retsstat*' (*Rechtsstaat*) and '*retssikkerhed*' (*Rechtssicherheit*) directly appear in Danish judgments (not only judgments on constitutional law). However, this does not necessarily mean that the substance of such concepts is not important in Danish case law. Danish judges attach importance to key concepts such as rule of law and legal certainty, however they may not always refer directly to such concepts in the judgments.[31]

[30] See H Krunke and T Baumbach, 'The Role of the Danish Constitution in European and Transnational Governance' in S Bardutzky and A Albi (eds), *The Role and Future of National Constitutions in European and Global Governance: National Constitutions in European and Global Governance: Democracy, Rights, the Rule of Law National Reports* (New York, Springer, 2019) 269–313, 278–86.

[31] ibid. See also B Dahl, 'Keynote Speech' in U Neergaard and C Jacqueson (eds), *Proceedings: Speeches from the XXVI FIDE Congress, FIDE 2014* (Copenhagen, DJØF Publishing, 2014) 26–30, where former President of the Supreme Court, Børge Dahl, expresses concern for legal certainty and rule of law in light of dynamic interpretations by the CJEU. However, in the Danish *Ajos* judgment there were no direct references to principles of legal certainty and rule of law.

Turning to the outcome of the coding of the 40 landmark judgments, it appears that in constitutional cases key concepts appear explicitly in the judgments. This is an interesting observation when compared to the outcome of the cited study above, though not a contradiction since that study also refers to some of the 40 constitutional law judgments as regards references to '*retssikkerhed*' (*Rechtssicherheit*). When we look closer at the 40 coded judgments, we see that rule of law in the form of '*retsstat*' (*Rechtsstaat*) only appears explicitly in one case (U1999.841H). In this judgment, the Supreme Court refers to the Danish term '*retssikkerhed*' as an underlying principle behind Article 3 of the Constitution on separation of powers. One might discuss whether the Danish term '*retssikkerhed*' should be interpreted as a *Rechtsstaat* argument or as a legal certainty argument. In the Nordic CONREASON project, it was coded as a *Rechtsstaat* argument.[32] However, even so, just one judgment which refers to *Rechtsstaat* is very little.[33] This confirms the former study of case law mentioned above.

Rule of law in the form of 'principle of legality' on the other hand appears in 33 of the 40 Danish judgments. Actually, Denmark has the highest rate of references to the principle of legality among the Nordic countries (80 per cent) (see Figure 3 above). Furthermore, according to our data, the principle of legality is the preferred 'rule of law' argument in Danish Supreme Court cases. First, some cases directly concern whether the principle of legality has been upheld. In judgments, which concern a review of the legality of administrative acts and administrative decisions, it is natural to refer to the principle of legality as an argument. In cases which concern the ECHR it is also natural to discuss the principle of legality. Therefore, the composition of cases can play a role for the outcome of the data analysis. Second, the principle of legality is an established legal principle in the Danish legal system, with legal basis in Article 3 of the Constitution, while an explicit rule of law argument ('*Rechtsstaat*' argument) is less well defined in the Danish legal system. The Danish Constitution does not explicitly mention rule of law as a constitutional principle. Therefore, if the Supreme Court based a judgment on an explicit rule of law argument rather than on a principle of legality argument, it would have to apply a freer legal reasoning style. This would, of course, also affect the arguments put forward by the parties.[34] In some of the other Nordic constitutions, 'rule of law' is directly mentioned as a constitutional principle. Therefore, maybe this could play a role for the outcome of our study. A general observation is that this variable may reflect how much the legal reasoning style of the supreme

[32] See the instructions for the coding of variable N31 in the Codebook in the Appendix.

[33] As mentioned above, a clear reference to the *Rechtsstaat* ('*retsstat*') appears in the Danish impeachment judgment, U 2022.653 R (Den.), in relation to the settlement of the penalty in the case.

[34] Interestingly, a reference to the rechtstaat – in the form of 'the ground rules of the *Rechtsstaat*' – is made by the Danish Impeachment Court in an impeachment case against the former minister, Inger Støjberg, in regard to settling the penalty for the offence, see U 2022.653 R (Den.). The *Rechtsstaat* argument was applied in favour of choosing unconditional imprisonment as a penalty for a breach of the ministerial code. The Impeachment Court consists of (up to) 15 Supreme Court Judges and 15 members appointed by the Parliament.

courts in the Nordic countries have been affected by the more dynamic interpretation and reasoning style of the CJEU and the ECtHR, which also draw more on general legal principles. In other comparative studies of Nordic constitutional law, it has been pointed out that the Danish Supreme Court – compared to the other Nordic countries (as regards the EU especially Finland and Sweden) – has apparently been less affected.[35]

Furthermore, the coding of the 40 judgments shows that rule of law arguments in the form of legal certainty appear in six judgments. Legal certainty is an underlying value behind several constitutional provisions, including Article 64 on judicial independence and Article 3 on separation of powers.[36] However, contrary to separation of powers, legal certainty is not directly expressed in a provision. Maybe that is the reason why legal certainty does not appear very often in the 40 judgments.

Arguments based on separation of powers, which we also considered a component of the rule of law, appear in 14 judgments. Apparently, this is also seen as a quite strong argument. The reason may be that the principle of separation of powers follows directly from Article 3 of the Constitution, though without specifically using that term.

Access to justice appears in 13 judgments. For instance, in judgments regarding legal standing this argument is applied quite often by the government's lawyer and probably as a strategy to get proceedings halted before the courts can assess the material questions in the case.

The fact that only one judgment appears under the other implicit rule of law argument shows that the other rule of law concepts established as subcategories of the rule of law variable in our project (namely: principle of legality, legal certainty, separation of powers, and access to justice) cover the reasoning at the Danish Supreme Court very well.

Judicial independence appears in six judgments. Though the term is not directly applied in the constitutional text, Article 64 clearly expresses the principle when providing that 'in the performance of their duties the judges shall be governed solely by the law'. Therefore, the judicial independence of courts must be seen as a quite strong argument. Not that many cases concern judicial independence, but comparatively Denmark exhibits a quite high proportion of judgments, which refer to judicial independence (see Figure 8).[37]

[35] Krunke and Thorarensen (n 1).

[36] As mentioned, in the so called '*Tvind* judgment' (U 1999.841 H) the Supreme Court referred to the Danish term '*retssikkerhed*' as an underlying principle behind Article 3 of the Constitution. This term could be interpreted as legal certainty or as *Rechtsstaat*. It was coded as the latter in the Nordic CONREASON project.

[37] In this context it should be mentioned that two of the six coded Danish judgments (U 1935.1 H (Den.) and U 1994.536 H (Den.)) are quite special cases concerning changes in the pension rights of judges (U 1935.1 H) and the common use of temporary judges who simultaneously are on leave from their jobs at the Ministry of Justice (U 1994.536 H).

Figure 8 Proportion of cases in which the concept of judicial independence is invoked (N32)

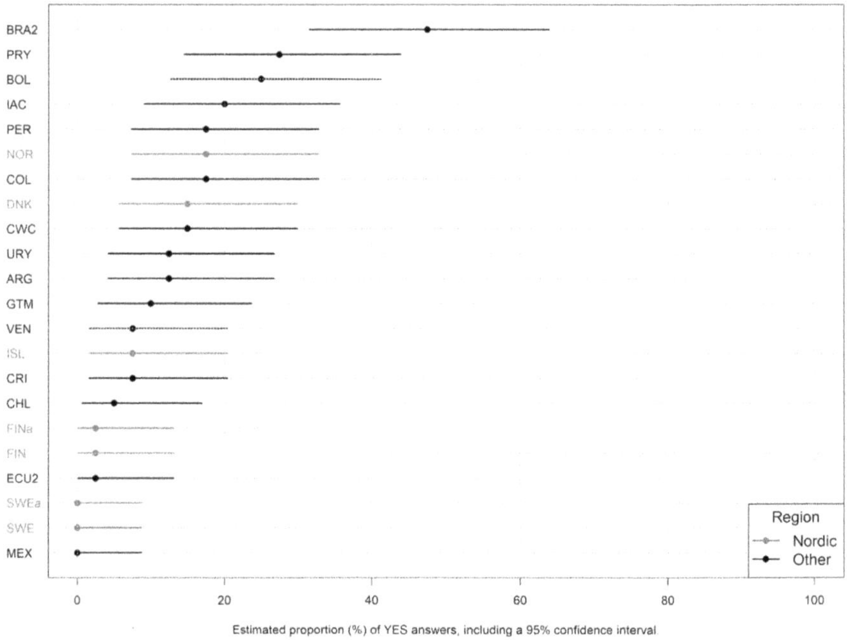

The concept of democracy does not appear directly in the Danish Constitution. However, as it has been pointed out, several provisions express democratic values, and furthermore it follows from the *Maastricht* judgment (U1998.800H) that 'Denmark has a democratic form of government'. The empirical study shows that four judgments refer to democracy.

National identity in a Nordic context has been studied in constitutional literature.[38] It has been stated that Nordic Supreme Courts do not apply the term 'national identity' and they do not define national identity.[39] This plays a special role in relation to EU law and judicial dialogue between Nordic Supreme Courts and the CJEU.[40] The empirical study of 40 Danish judgments confirms that only one judgment refers to 'the nation state or national identity' and in this case it is the 'nation state'. As pointed out in legal literature, the reluctance of the Nordic courts to define and apply the concept of national identity in their judgments seems to go hand in hand with their general reluctance of Nordic courts to engage

[38] See, for instance, Krunke, 'Constitutional Identity and Equality' (n 11); Krunke, 'Constitutional Identity in Nordic Countries 1950–2015' (n 2); Krunke, 'Constitutional Identity in Denmark' (n 12); and J Salminen (eds), 'Special Issue in Constitutional Identity' (2014) 37 *Retfaerd: Nordisk Juridisk Tidsskrift* 147.

[39] See Krunke, 'Constitutional Identity and Equality' (n 12).

[40] ibid.

in very dynamic interpretations of their constitutions. This reluctance is a characteristic of the Nordic legal systems in general as a legal family, which, among other things, attach importance to preparatory material when interpreting the constitution and in which all-encompassing principles play a more limited role.[41] Restrained courts, bound by preparatory works, have very little room for entering into a freer definition of national identity, and this may weaken the impact of the Nordic constitutional systems on the EU legal system.

VI. Final Reflections and Conclusion

In this chapter, we have supplemented the analysis of the 40 selected Danish landmark judgments with a study of the deliberations among the Supreme Court judges that eventually led to the judgments of the Supreme Court in three important cases: the *Maastricht* case (formality, U1998.800H), the *Maastricht* case (reality, U1996.1300H), and the *Tvind* case (U1999.841). By comparing the judgments with the deliberations among the judges, it becomes clear that this is an important period in the Supreme Court as regards court activism. The judgments indicate that the Supreme Court steps into a role as a third state power by extending the definition of legal interest and thereby *de facto* extending its competence to review the constitutionality of legislation (U1996.1300H), underlining that the Court has a final saying regarding review of whether an EU Act or a judgment by the CJEU extends the competence which has been transferred to the EU and violates the Danish Constitution (U1998.800H), and by declaring an Act as unconstitutional for the first time (U1999.841H).[42] This indication is strengthened by the deliberations among the Supreme Court judges. As regards the *Maastricht* judgments on the substance and the formality, the deliberations indicate a wish to enter into a dialogue with other constitutional and supreme courts and with the CJEU. The German Constitutional Court and its *Maastricht* judgment is clearly an important focus point.

Furthermore, emphasising the Supreme Court's competence to review the constitutionality of legislation is a focus point. At this point in the history of the Supreme Court there seems to be self-consciousness, self-confidence, and a desire to emphasise the role of the Supreme Court as a third state power and as a court that can enter into a dialogue with European constitutional courts, supreme courts, and the CJEU. It has been put forward in constitutional literature that it is more difficult for the Nordic countries to define and communicate their constitutional identity to the EU including the CJEU than it is for example for the German Constitutional Court.[43] However, when studying the deliberations among

[41] ibid.
[42] Krunke and Klinge (n 25).
[43] Krunke, 'Constitutional Identity and Equality' (n 12).

the Supreme Court judges in combination with the judgments, it is clear that the Supreme Court had an ambition in the 1990s of stepping into a more active role. The Danish Supreme Court has to some extent followed this line in the *Lisbon* judgment (U2013.1451 H) and in the *Ajos* judgment (U2017.824 H) as regards the EU.[44]

The bold *Tvind* judgment (U1999.841H), in which the Supreme Court for the first time found a piece of legislation to be unconstitutional, has not been followed by other judgments that have declared legislation to be unconstitutional.[45] One might ask what the reason for that can be. One possibility is that there have not been any violations by the legislator since the *Tvind* case, or at least that no one with legal interest has brought such a case to the Supreme Court since then. The fact that Denmark has quite healthy political institutions, which normally respect principles of good governance, democratic decision-making, and human rights, combined with a longstanding professional civil servant tradition and the lowest corruption rate in the World could perhaps speak in favour of such a thesis. Another possibility could be that there has been a shift over time in how the Supreme Court views its own role. Such a development could for instance be linked to the fact that the composition of the Court in the 1990s changed over time. Unfortunately, it is not possible for researchers to study the deliberations among the Supreme Court judges until 20 years after a judgment was handed down. This makes it more difficult to qualitatively study possible developments over time in the way the Supreme Court judges view the role of the Supreme Court. In other words, such studies can only be based on the legal reasoning directly mentioned in the judgments. A number of recent verdicts by the Supreme Court, such as the one delivered on 23 October 2023 in a criminal case against a former Minister of Defence for sharing confidential information regarding the Danish Defence Intelligence Service, could perhaps indicate that the current Supreme Court is ready to step up as the third state power when needed.[46] The case is not included in the coded judgments.

An important outcome of the coding of the 40 judgments is that, according to our empirics, there has been an increase in objective teleological interpretation in the constitutional reasoning at the Supreme Court during the past 20–30 years. Objective teleological reasoning will generally provide the interpreter with more room for interpretation than subjective teleological reasoning where the interpreter relies heavily on the intention of the legislator. This could perhaps indicate a slight turn towards a freer judicial reasoning style, which is an interesting observation.

[44] Krunke and Klinge (n 25); and H Krunke, 'The Danish Lisbon Judgment: Danish Supreme Court, Case 199/2012, Judgment of 20 February 2013' (2014) 10 *European Constitutional Law Review* 542.

[45] With the possible exemption of right to property cases, where the Supreme Court frequently dissents on a violation. A recent example of this is U 2008.378 H (Den.) where a 5–4 majority ruled a compulsory sale of social housing not to be a violation of right to property.

[46] See among others U 2024.384 H (Den.).

Another important observation is that when the actual judgments are read in light of the protocol on the deliberations among the judges it becomes clear that the judges – at least in the three selected judgments – attach much more weight to reading literature (including foreign) and foreign legislation and judgments than is visible in the judgments. Especially in the deliberations on the *Maastricht* case (substance) it is reflected that the judges show interest in comparative material. Importantly, this does not mean that this material is considered binding in any way but serves more as an inspiration.

A third observation is that the judgments read in light of the deliberations among the judges confirm that the Supreme Court considers its role as deferential in relation to the legislator, and that the Court can only set aside legislation as unconstitutional if there is a manifest violation of the Constitution. The traditional Danish understanding of democracy as described above in this chapter is also confirmed in the *Maastricht* case (substance), where the Supreme Court judges discuss a passage in a book by the constitutional scholar Henrik Zahle, where he writes that it must be taken into consideration that so many Danes have voted in favour of membership of the EC in 1972 and at later referendums on the EC treaties including the Maastricht Treaty, and that more than five-sixths of Parliament (according to Article 20 of the Danish Constitution) has supported these treaties. The idea is that this must be taken into consideration when the Supreme Court reviews a possible violation of Article 20 on transfer of sovereignty. The legislator must be provided with quite extensive discretion, and the courts must be reluctant as regards the intensity of the review of constitutionality. This is a very interesting observation.

As it appears from the qualitative and quantitative empirical studies of the length of the 40 selected judgments, the legal reasoning of the Supreme Court judges – as reflected in the judgments – is often rather short, formulated in a way which relates to the concrete case at hand, with very few dissenting opinions, no concurring opinions, and no direct references to legal literature and foreign material (though there might be a generic footnote which lists some relevant literature in the beginning of the judgment). According to a statistical analysis of the average proportion between total length and length of the majority reasoning, Denmark stands out with the lowest proportions. This is a remarkable finding. The study of the protocols on the deliberations among the judges in three selected cases shows that the short legal reasoning in the judgments does not reflect the actual deep and nuanced reflections that take place among the judges. Maybe that is why the judges draw on deliberations in former cases during deliberations of new cases. While a short judgment that all judges can agree on might strengthen the legitimacy of the judgments of the Supreme Court, one might ask whether it would be desirable for the Supreme Court to show its academic capacity more. This could be another way of strengthening the legitimacy of the Supreme Court based on its competences, while promoting transparency, legal certainty and the rule of law in the legal system.

One last important finding is that, since *travaux préparatoires* play an important role when interpreting the Constitution, such sources are quoted extensively in some of the 40 judgments. This is especially significant in cases concerning transfer of sovereignty to the EU, such as the *Maastricht* judgment. A consequence is that arguments by the political branches are present in the judgments. Our results project therefore must be seen in light of this.

4

The Culture of Constitutional Reasoning in Iceland

HAUKUR LOGI KARLSSON

I. Introduction

The aim of this chapter is to report on several of the main findings of the Icelandic part of the Nordic CONREASON Project.[1] They reflect constitutional reasoning found in the text of 40 leading constitutional cases decided by the Icelandic Supreme Court. The oldest case is from 1943 and the latest from 2022.[2]

Several of the findings that I want to highlight in this chapter contribute to interesting domestic academic discussions about the constitutional status of legal norms derived from instruments of international law. Notable instruments in that regard are the European Convention on Human Rights (ECHR) and the Agreement on the European Economic Area (EEA Agreement).[3] These discussions mirror similar debates in the other Nordics. The empirical findings from this project reflect an increasingly unsustainable legacy of the dualist view of domestic and international law, which has dominated doctrinal writings about Icelandic constitutional law for several decades. Other empirical findings are noted due to how oddly they stick out in comparison with the other Nordic countries. Before engaging with the data, the societal and institutional context within which constitutional reasoning in Iceland occurs is briefly outlined.

[1] See the project's website hosted under Örebro University website: www.oru.se/nordic-conreason/.

[2] About the methodology see ch 2 in this book. The dataset is available at K Kelemen, 'Nordic CONREASON kollektion av data om konstitutionellt resonemang i de nordiska högsta domstolarna (Version 1), 15 Maj 2024' (Örebro University, 2024) doi.org/10.60689/zmk7-0z14.

[3] The EEA Agreement extends the European Union's internal market to the EFTA States Iceland, Norway, and Liechtenstein.

II. Legal and Political Context

The legal and political context of Icelandic constitutional reasoning is shaped by two competing narratives about the origins, being, and the necessary conditions for the survival of Icelandic statehood.[4] On the one hand, there is a traditional school of thought that interprets the historical experience of the Icelandic people in such a way that it is imperative to be suspicious of external influences, specifically with regards to core constitutional structures of the State involving the three branches of government.[5] On the other hand, a competing progressive school of thought interprets the historical experience of the Icelandic people in the opposite way, emphasising the benefits of embracing external influences for advancing cultural and economic progress.[6]

The foundational myth of the Icelandic State describes how Iceland was colonised by Norwegian settlers and the members of their households, some of which were from the British Isles, during the times of the great Viking raids and migration of the ninth and tenth centuries.[7] By 930 the island had been fully colonised, and the leading settlers had decided to establish a commonwealth centred on a legislative and judicial institution, referred to as *Alþingi*. Ultimately the commonwealth failed due to internal strife of the leading chieftains and was absorbed by the Norwegian kingdom in 1262–64.[8] The old commonwealth institution *Alþingi* continued to exist as a judicial institution, but the legislative prerogative had been absorbed by the king.[9] The foundational myth was created and romanticised during the revolutionary period in Europe during the nineteenth century.[10]

The alleged golden age of the commonwealth between 930 and 1264 was central to arguments about the existence of Icelandic people, separate and distinct from other peoples of the Danish empire.[11] When the Danish king relinquished some of his powers to the new Danish Parliament in 1849, in line with the new Danish

[4] These narratives correspond to different academic schools within the study of history. See further G Hálfdanarson, *Íslenska þjóðríkið* (Reykjavik, Hið íslenska bókmenntafélag, 2001) 25–28.

[5] Key authors and advocates of the traditional school in the early 20th century were historian Jón Jónsson Aðils (1869–1920) and educator and politician Jónas Jónsson frá Hriflu (1885–1968).

[6] See for example Hálfdanarson (n 4); A Kristinsson, *Hnignun, hvaða hningnun?* (Reykjavik, Sögufélag, 2018).

[7] J Benediktsson, 'Landnám og upphaf allsherjarríkis' in S Líndal (ed), *Saga Íslands I* (Reykjavik, Hið íslenska bókmenntafélag, 1974) 153, 155–65.

[8] G Karlsson, 'Frá þjóðveldi til konungsríkis' in S Líndal (ed), *Saga Íslands II* (Reykjavik, Hið íslenska bókmenntafélag, 1975) 1, 31–33. For the history of the civil war see also S Jakobsson, *Auðnaróðal* (Reykjavik, Sögufélag, 2016). The Norwegian takeover allegedly happened through a special agreement referred to as 'Gamli sáttmáli 1262–64' (The Old Convention of 1262–64). B Þorsteinsson and S Líndal, 'Lögfesting konungsvalds' in S Líndal (ed), *Saga Íslands III* (Reykjavik, Hið íslenska bókmenntafélag, 1978) 17, 34–40.

[9] Þorsteinsson and Líndal (n 9) 43–48 and 60–70.

[10] Hálfdanarson (n 4) 179–81; Kristinsson (n 6) 61–67.

[11] A key text in this regard is an essay by Jón Sigurðsson (1811–79). J Sigurðsson, 'Hugvekja til Íslendinga' (1848) 8 *Ný félagsrit* 1. Norway was eventually absorbed the Danish kingdom and Iceland thus became part of the Danish empire.

Constitution, Icelanders refused to participate in the new Danish parliamentary institution, instead demanding that the king relinquish his powers directly back to the Icelandic people and granting them their own constitution.[12] This request was refused by the representatives of the Danish monarch at a constitutional assembly in Reykjavik in the summer of 1851.[13] A political standoff ensued, which eventually resulted in the sovereignty of Iceland in 1918, and full independence in 1944. A key constitutional moment during this standoff was the unilateral decision of the Danish king to grant the Icelandic people with a special constitution in 1874.[14] The current Constitution of the Republic of Iceland from 1944 is a modified and modernised version of the Constitution of 1874, as revised in 1920.[15] The current Constitution has been amended several times, most significantly in 1995 when the human rights chapter was modernised.[16]

The myths about the golden age and the legacy of the struggle for independence still shape how the domestic political and legal elites view their role as defenders of Iceland's sovereignty. The prevalent sentiment is that all is well when Icelanders can determine their own political and economic fortunes, undisturbed by the agenda of ruling elites in foreign capitals. A central element of this narrative is the uniform category of *we* Icelanders, versus *them* foreigners.[17] This nationalistic perception however neglects the plurality of interests within the *we* category. While the Icelandic elites were during earlier times undoubtedly restrained by the Danish elites, the wider Icelandic population was largely powerless against both elites and without any meaningful political agency.[18]

A revisionist view on the history of Iceland suggests a competing narrative, highlighting the role of the domestic elites in Iceland's greatest misfortunes through cartelisation of the political and the economic spheres, thus stifling economic and political reforms liable to disrupt their power monopolies in a socioeconomic sense. On the revisionist view, the principal source of reforms are foreign political, legal, and cultural influences that the ruling domestic elites are unable to deny the domestic population from enjoying.[19]

The British and American occupation of Iceland during World War II was an event that catalysed the arrival of modernity in Iceland. Iceland became a part

[12] ibid 14–16.

[13] M Suksi, 'Common roots of Nordic constitutional law? Some observations on legal-historical development and relations between the constitutional systems of five Nordic countries' in H Krunke and B Thorarensen (eds), *The Nordic Constitutions – A Comparative and Contextual Study* (Oxford, Hart Publishing, 2018) 31.

[14] Stjórnarskrá um hin sjerstaklegu málefni Íslands, 5. janúar 1874.

[15] Stjórnarskrá lýðveldisins Íslands, nr. 33/1944.

[16] Lög nr. 97/1995 um breyting á stjórnarskrá lýðveldisins Íslands, nr. 33/1944, með síðari breytingum.

[17] This is a representation of the nationalistic political ideology of the 19th and the early 20th centuries, which nowadays has the negative connotation of populistic political ideology. See discussion of this in a Nordic Context in E Bergmann, *Nordic Nationalism and Right-Wing Populist Politics: Imperial Relationships and National Sentiments* (London, Palgrave Macmillan, 2017).

[18] Hálfdanarson (n 4) 138–43.

[19] Kristinsson (n 6).

of the Western Alliance as a founding member of NATO and an Atlantic frontier territory in the Cold War against the Eastern Block.[20] This required economic cooperation with allies, which meant joining the European Free Trade Agreement (EFTA) in 1970 and gaining access to the European Union's (EU) internal market through the EEA Agreement in 1994.[21] This also meant adhering to the value system of the Western Alliance, which preordained becoming signatory of the European Convention of Human Rights (ECHR) in 1950, the United Nation's (UN) International Covenant on Economic, Social and Cultural Rights in 1968, and the UN's International Covenant on Civil and Political Rights in 1968.

These progresses were imposed on the domestic elites. Developments beyond their control required them to relinquish their exclusive power over the domestic marketplace and over domestic legal norms. Iceland was simply too insignificant to defy European and global developments of internationalisation of trade, politics, and philosophical values. For the domestic population at large, these were positive changes. Prosperity increased with increased trade and less trade barriers, while resourceful litigators began, on behalf of their clients, to exploit the opportunities presented by the foreign legal norms that the Icelandic State was obliged to respect, resulting in positive institutional reforms in the public sector and a more liberal approach to market regulation.[22]

These two narratives are of course not mutually exclusive. They tell the same story from alternative perspectives. The reclamation of external sovereignty and internal self-determination did save Icelandic elites from having to adhere to the power of Danish elites, while the subsequent opening of international trade and the joining of supranational political alliances somewhat unchained the average member of the public from the domestic cartel arrangement of the domestic elites. In terms of constitutional reasoning a struggle between these different views is however a persistent theme. Citizens start court proceedings to claim rights protected by the ECHR or the EEA Agreement, while the State apparatus argues for the irrelevance of such sources. In such cases, the courts are in a state of limbo regarding having to decide on the extent of influence of foreign legal norms within the domestic context.

III. Institutional and Academic Context

The primary venue of Icelandic constitutional reasoning is the Supreme Court. It is a court of last instance for any kind of legal issues that fall within the jurisdiction of the general courts, including both private law issues and public law issues, and

[20] Þátttaka Íslands í Norður-Atlantshafssamningi, 177. mál, þingskj. 499, 68. löggjþ. (1948–49).

[21] The EFTA Convention and the Agreement on the European Economic Area (OJ No L 1, 3.1.1994, p 3).

[22] According to IMF's statistics Iceland's GDP per capita was 25,000 USD in 1990 but had risen to 87,000 USD in 2023, www.imf.org/en/Countries/ISL#countrydata.

it routinely addresses constitutional questions.[23] Constitutional judicial review has been exercised in Iceland since before the entering into force of the current Constitution of 1944, with the first judgment finding legislation incompatible with the constitution in 1943 and earlier cases where the court implies wielding such powers without finding an incompatibility in those cases.[24]

Recent institutional reforms within the Icelandic judicial system have the potential to alter the approach to constitutional reasoning of the Supreme Court. The change, implemented in 2018, involved the establishment of a new appellate court at a tier below the Supreme Court, which now handles most appeal cases from the district courts.[25] Cases now reach the Supreme Court upon application subject to a rigorous selection process, following the judgment of the new appellate court.[26] This was a change from the previous system, where almost all judgments of the district courts would be granted with leave of an appeal to the Supreme Court upon application. The introduction of a dock control has enabled the Supreme Court to focus its work efforts on fewer cases and thus supposedly on cases deemed important and worthy of a careful deliberation. The effect of this change on the caseload of the Supreme Court and on the workload of individual judges is significant, but it is yet to be seen if this will over time alter the reasoning style of the Court and the length of judgments.

Table 1 *Workload of the Icelandic Supreme Court 2015–23*

Year	**2015**	**2016**	**2017**	**2018**	**2019**	**2020**	**2021**	**2022**	**2023**
Applications	862	869	857	69	166	138	156	172	160
Judgments	761	762	690	18	50	38	55	60	51
Ratio % (J/A)	88%	87%	80%	26%	30%	28%	35%	35%	32%
Number of Judges	10	10	10	8	8	7	7	7	7
Judgments per Judge	76.1	76.2	69.0	2.3	6.3	5.4	7.9	8.6	7.2

New appellate court est.

Source: Annual Reports of the ICE Supreme Court 2015–2023.

[23] R Helgadóttir, 'Nonproblematic judicial review: A case study' (2011) 9 *I-CON* 532, 536.

[24] R Helgadóttir, 'Status Presens – Judicial review in Iceland' (2009) 27 *Nordisk Tidskrift for Menneskerettigheter* 185, 185.

[25] Lög nr. 117/2016 um breytingu á ýmsum lögum vegna stofnunar millidómstigs.

[26] Exceptionally, it is possible to apply for a judgment of a district court to be reviewed directly by the Supreme Court, skipping one appellate stage. See provisions on dock control in the two main procedural law codes: lög nr. 91/1991 um meðferð einkamála, 167. gr. and 176. gr.; and lög nr. 88/2008 um meðferð sakamála, 211. gr. and 215. gr.

Since the reform of 2018, there should be seven judges at the Supreme Court. The normal composition of a panel in a case is five judges, with a possibility of a plenary composition in cases deemed important. Applications are initially screened by a panel of three judges.[27] Judgments are rendered by a majority of a case panel and separate opinions are allowed. The text of the judgments is drafted by the judges themselves, with one judge leading the drafting in each case. The identity of that judge is however not revealed to the public. Several legal clerks work at the Supreme Court. They are not assigned to individual judges, and they do not participate in the drafting of the judgments.

The appointment of Supreme Court judges has on numerous occasions caused political controversy. The current recruitment system, in place since 2010, consists of an open call for applications when vacancies arise, followed by the scrutiny of an independent vetting panel. The Minister of Justice selects a new judge from a list of candidates deemed most qualified by the vetting panel. The catch is that the Minister must follow the advice of the vetting panel, or alternatively suggest a different candidate to the parliament, which then must approve the selection. In the end the President, a largely ceremonial figure in the institutional structure of the Icelandic State, must sign off the appointment. The judiciary has managed to dominate the vetting panel by strategically nominating three out of its five members, which means that the elite of incumbent judges controls the recruitment options of the Minister of Justice. In theory the Minister could suggest a different candidate to the Parliament, but this option currently is a political impossibility following the appointment scandal that culminated in the Grand Chamber Judgment of 2020 in *Ástráðsson v Iceland* of the European Court of Human Rights (ECtHR). The *Ástráðsson* case concerned a conflict between the Icelandic judicial and political elites over the appointment of 15 judges on a new appellate court. The judicial elites tried to force the hand of the responsible Minister, who responded by discarding their list of picks. This unravelled into a legal and political dispute that cumulated in a condemnation from the Strasbourg Court and the resignation of the responsible Minister.[28]

Historically, academia in Iceland has consisted of a single public university appropriately named the University of Iceland. It was established in 1911 in parallel with other efforts to establish key institutions domestically during the process of separation from Danish rule.[29] Law was among the initial subjects taught at the University. Prior to this, most lawyers in Iceland were educated at the University of Copenhagen and during much of the twentieth century Danish legal culture

[27] Lög nr. 50/2016 um dómstóla, 16. gr.

[28] *Ástráðsson v Iceland*, Application no. 26374/18, Grand Chamber Judgment of 1 December 2020. See also HL Karlsson, 'The Emergence of the Established "By Law" Criterion for Reviewing European Judicial Appointments' (2022) 23 *German Law Journal* 1051, 1060–64.

[29] G Jónsson, *Saga Háskóla Íslands – Yfirlit um hálfrar aldar starf* (Reykjavik, Háskóli Íslands, 1961) 15–25.

continued to influence Icelandic legal academia. These influences still somewhat remain, but with a new generation of scholars with a more varied education and with the increasing influence of European law, they are diminishing. At the turn of the twenty-first century the academic environment changed in Iceland. Numerous new universities were established, both in private and public institutional forms. By 2003, four universities were offering law programmes and continue to do so to this day.[30] The constitutional law curriculum in Iceland centres on a single textbook that has periodically been updated by the incumbent professor of constitutional law at the University of Iceland.[31]

A distinguishing aspect of legal academia in Iceland is its close connection and dependence on the judiciary and the executive. Salaries of legal academics are low compared to equally skilled legal professionals working in the private or the public sectors.[32] This makes it tempting for academics to accept contracts from the executive to write reports or legislative bills as side projects to boost their university salaries and to sit on various public boards and committees. In turn this makes them hesitant to criticise the executive, which has the discretion to provide or deny them extra work. The relationship with the judiciary is more complex and varies between dependence and interdependence. As mentioned before, the judiciary dominates the recruitment of new judges at all three levels of the court system. Due to the prestige of the position of the judge and the comparatively generous salary, many in legal academia aspire to migrate to the judiciary during the latter half of their working careers, or occasionally as soon as they reach the position of full professor within the academic system. This is however not a one-way relationship. Some within the judiciary also aspire to the intellectual prestige of holding an academic title and being affiliated to a university. The result is that many legal academics get promoted to the courts in due course, many judges also hold part-time academic positions and academic titles, and many judges retire back into the universities, sitting on doctoral committees and recruitment and promotion panels. This is a classic revolving door scenario and has the potential to compromise academic scrutiny of the judicial branch of government.[33]

[30] These are University of Iceland, Bifröst University, Reykjavik University, and University of Akureyri.

[31] *Stjórnskipun Íslands* was authored by Ólafur Jóhannesson in 1960. Gunnar G Schram published a revised edition in 1997 under the name *Stjórnskipunarréttur* and Björg Thorarensen in 2015 published a revised edition under the name *Stjórnskipunarréttur – Undirstöður og handhafar ríkisvalds.*

[32] According to information from the Icelandic Statistical Office (statice.is) average total salaries in 2021 for academics was €6.733 per month, while judges made €11.893 per month (exchange rate in June 2024).

[33] Viðarsson wrote about the potential pitfalls when writing academically about his/her own work as a judge or decisionmaker within the executive branch. See O Þorri Viðarsson, 'Fræðileg umfjöllun um eigin úrlausnir' [Scholarship on one's own results in practice] (2022) 72 *Tímarit lögfræðinga* 315.

IV. Argumentative Patterns

With barely 400,000 citizens, a primary attribute of Icelandic statehood is size and vulnerability. It is a constant feature of Icelandic self-identity to worry about being absorbed by external political or cultural entities. There are conflicting views about how to best deal with this existential reality of the Icelandic State and the Icelandic people. As explained in section II above, one view holds that it is imperative to resist external influences as much as is possible, while an alternative view maintains that the external world should be embraced. These debates regarding defensiveness or openness towards the external world extend to Icelandic constitutional debates. Several variables coded in the Nordic CONREASON project from the 40 leading Icelandic constitutional cases reflect the tension between doctrines of defensiveness and openness in Icelandic constitutional literature. Arguments in the leading cases relating to how the supranational legal norms deriving from the EEA Agreement and the ECHR are used in constitutional reasoning before domestic courts provide evidence of a tension between an argumentative posture of defensiveness and openness towards external influences in the leading cases. References to these norms are occasionally used to anchor constitutional arguments, while intermittently their constitutional relevance is dismissed.

During the last few decades cohorts of Icelandic law students have learned by heart from the doctrinal literature that 'Iceland is a dualist country' when it comes to defining the nature of the relationship between national law and international law. The dualist view does not however have basis in the text of the Constitution, which is silent about the nature of this relation. Instead, the doctrinal literature supports this view with reference to 'long tradition' and an 'unwritten custom'.[34] Recent research however shows that this view is not consistent with how the Supreme Court argued in numerous cases from 1930 until a seminal judgment of 1975 in case H:23/1974.[35] Following the judgment of 1975, the Supreme Court maintained a dualist approach in several high-profile cases in the 1980s, including cases H:81/1983 and H:239/1987. By the late 1980s and the early 1990s the Supreme Court again at times showed monist tendencies in its approach to the status of the ECHR, for example in Case H:120/1989 and Case H:31/1990, both of which were handed down before the Convention was incorporated into domestic legislation in 1994.[36] This development in the case law of the Supreme Court in the early 1990s, regarding a departure from the dualist view, was noted in the

[34] GG Schram, *Stjórnskipunarréttur*, 2nd edn (Reykjavik, Háskólaútgáfan, 1999) 40; B Thorarensen, *Stjórnskipunarréttur – Undirstöður og handhafar ríkisvalds*, 2nd edn (Reykjavik, Codex, 2021) 27, 129.

[35] B Torfadóttir and B Már Magnússon, 'Eineðli lands- og þjóðaréttar í dómum Hæstaréttar til 1975' (2022) 72 *Tímarit lögfræðinga* 167, 219–21; See also T Ingadottir, *The relationship between international and national law: Re-visiting concepts of dualism and monism* (PhD Thesis – University of Helsinki, 2022) 82–83.

[36] DT Björvinsson, *The intersection of international law and domestic law* (Cheltenham, Edward Elgar, 2015) 121–27; D Þór Björgvinsson, 'Þjóðaréttur og landsréttur í dómum Hæstaréttar Íslands' in Þorgeir Örlygsson et al (eds), *Hæstiréttur í hundrað ár – Ritgerðir* (Reykjavik, Hið íslenska bókmenntafélag, 2020) 95, 103–12; Schram (n 34) 41.

1999 edition of the main textbook on constitutional law.[37] In the 2021 edition of the textbook, these cases are however considered exceptional and it is noted that they did not mark a permanent departure from the dualist view on behalf of the Supreme Court.[38]

The 1995 revision of the human rights chapter of the Constitution fell short of elevating the status of the ECHR to a constitutional level. Instead, similar provisions were written into the Icelandic Constitution while also considering other international human rights instruments.[39] This leaves a possibility of discrepancies between how corresponding provisions of the ECHR and the Constitution are understood. On the one hand, the interpretation of the ECtHR with respect to the former, and on the other hand the interpretation of the Supreme Court with respect to the latter. To further complicate the issue, a special provision was inserted into the legislative act that incorporated the ECHR into national legislation stating that the judgments of the ECtHR were not binding precedents for domestic courts.[40] In the preparatory materials accompanying the incorporating legislation it is explicitly acknowledged that in numerous cases during the early 1990s the Supreme Court had directly applied the ECHR for reviewing the validity of domestic legislation and administrative actions.[41] This was often disguised by the Supreme Court as a harmonisation argument, instead of explicitly recognising the constitutional relevance of the ECHR.[42] For the purposes of the Nordic CONREASON study it should be noted that two of the cases mentioned in the preparatory works as examples of the Supreme Court directly applying the ECHR, were coded as harmonisation arguments in the study.[43] The text of these two judgments is relatively explicit in that the argument is a harmonisation argument. In the opinion of the authors of the preparatory works, the Supreme Court had however, in practical terms, clearly gone beyond what could be described as the interpretive method of harmonisation with international law obligations.[44]

With this context in mind, it is of interest to see the prevalence of two types of arguments in the Nordic CONREASON study. The first type comprises arguments mentioning harmonisation with international law requirements of the ECHR (variable N18-2):

[37] Schram (n 34) 41.

[38] Thorarensen (n 34) 178–79.

[39] Frumvarp til stjórnarskipunarlaga, mál 297, þingskj. 389, 118. löggjþ. (1994) sections IV and V.

[40] Lög nr. 64/1994 um mannréttindasáttmála Evrópu, 2. gr.

[41] Frumvarp til laga um mannréttindasáttmála Evrópu, mál 102, þingskj. 105, 117. löggjþ. (1993) section V.

[42] The basis for this approach is the interpretive maxim that domestic law should be interpreted in harmony with international law obligations, but this maxim falls short of *contra legem* interpretations.

[43] Cases H:120/1989 (1990) and H:31/1990 (1990).

[44] Members of the committee that wrote the bill were prominent members of Icelandic legal society. These were Ragnhildur Helgadóttir (former Minister), Björn Bjarnason (MP), Eiríkur Tómasson (Supreme Court Attorney, later became Professor and Supreme Court Judge), and Markús Sigurbjörnsson (Professor, later became president of the Supreme Court). Ragnar Aðalsteinsson (Supreme Court Attorney) was also on the committee but did not support the legislative approach of the majority.

Figure 1 Estimated proportion among leading constitutional cases in the Nordic countries with an interpretation of constitutional law in light of ECHR

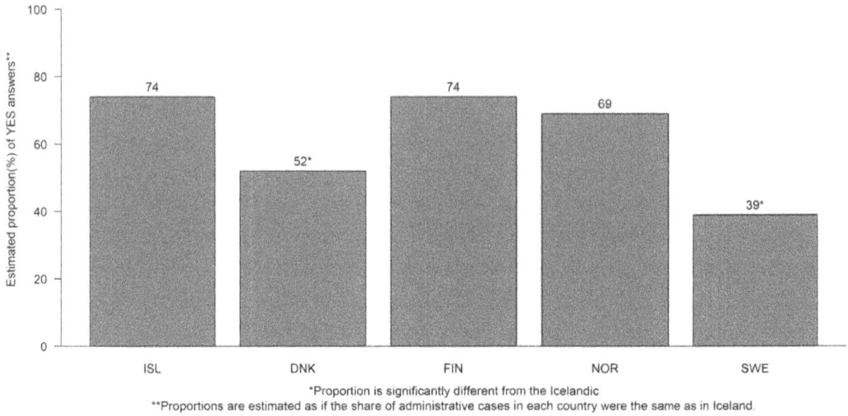

Figure 1 shows that an ECHR harmonisation argument is highest in Iceland and Finland (74 per cent), and significantly higher than in Denmark (52 per cent) and Sweden (39 per cent). Cases registering arguments on this variable suggest a dualist approach to the status of the ECHR within the domestic systems, where courts and parties to cases try to apply it by harmonising it with domestic laws. The second type of argument of interest is the one establishing the text of the constitution with reference to the ECHR (variable N13-1, see Figure 2), which would indicate a more monist approach and an acknowledgment of the constitutional nature of the ECHR within the domestic systems:

Figure 2 Estimated proportion among leading constitutional cases in the Nordic countries discussing whether the ECHR is considered part of the national constitution/constitutional law

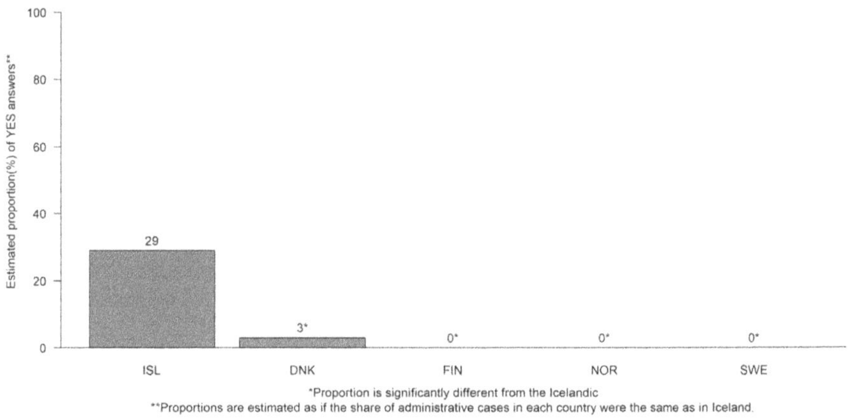

Although less prevalent than harmonisation arguments, Iceland stands out. All other Nordic countries are significantly lower (0–3 per cent) regarding cases which include an argument that establishes the text of the constitution with reference to the ECHR (29 per cent). The oldest such case is from 1975 and the most recent is from 2021.[45] Interestingly, 9 out the 18 most recent judgments include such an argument, and these are judgments delivered between 2000 and 2022. This shows that despite emphasis in the traditional doctrinal literature on the adherence of the Icelandic legal system to a dualist view on the nature of the relation of domestic law and international law obligations, it is a relatively common argument in leading constitutional cases to treat the ECHR not only as being part of the domestic legal sources, but as having a constitutional status in the hierarchal sense, when reviewing the constitutional compliance of domestic legal acts and actions of administrative nature. This does however not mean that such arguments have always determined the result of the respective cases. Quite the opposite, they have often been unsuccessfully asserted by lower courts or the parties, or if accepted in substance by the majority of the Supreme Court, the argument could be reformulated to fit the harmonisation reasoning style.[46] But a closer look nonetheless shows that during different periods such arguments have been explicitly accepted by the Supreme Court, which undermines the orthodox view about Iceland being a dualist state and contests the scope of the concept of a constitution as described in the Icelandic doctrinal literature.[47]

A recent case study shows that during the period 1920–75 the Icelandic Supreme Court used a monist reasoning modality in 18 cases, while no example was found of a dualist reasoning modality, which contradicts the leading doctrinal literature from the same period.[48] Between 1975 and 1990 the Supreme Court delivered several key rulings using a dualist reasoning modality. This changes with respect to the ECHR in 1990, when the Supreme Court starts to use the Convention to set aside incompatible domestic legislation and administrative practice. This again changes by the early 2000s, when the Court reverts to a more dualistic approach, only applying the ECHR in conjunction with the Constitution and with reference to the incorporating act. Plain references to the ECHR and the judgments of the ECtHR as constitutional arguments continue to appear in the sample of the 40 leading cases during this period, and increasingly after 2010. Another shift in the approach of the Supreme Court was triggered by the Court's treatment of Case H:10/2018 (2018), which showed in plain view the shortcomings of a dualist approach to the interpretation of the ECHR, anchored in the special interpretative provision of the incorporating act (Article 2) that instructed the domestic court to

[45] Case H.23/1974 (1975) and Case H:34/2020 (2021).
[46] Example of the latter is Case H:31/1990 (1990).
[47] See, eg, Thorarensen (n 34) 178–79.
[48] Torfadóttir and Magnússon (n 35) 181–83; Ólafur Jóhannesson, *Stjórnskipun Íslands* (Reykjavik, Hlaðbúð 1960) 96–97.

disregard the precedents of the ECtHR.[49] The doctrinal problem revealed through the case was that it is not a tenable approach to allow substantial discrepancies in interpretation of provisions of the ECHR by domestic courts and the ECtHR, thus revisiting the problem of the early 1990s that supposedly had been solved by the incorporating act of 1994.

Following the initial section judgment condemnation by the ECtHR of the Supreme Court's approach in the *Ástráðsson* case, the Supreme Court refused to yield and insisted in strong terms on a dualist approach to the ECHR in Case H:12/2018 (2019). In explicit language it refused to abide by the precedents of the ECtHR if these would require the setting aside of domestic law, citing the dualism principle and Article 2 of the incorporating act. Few months later, on 1 December 2020, the Grand Chamber of the ECtHR confirmed the section judgment in *Ástráðsson v Iceland*. Following that result a shift occurred in the rhetoric of the Supreme Court in a judgment of 18 March 2021 in Case H:34/2020 (2021). Instead of a blanket refusal to abide by the interpretation of the ECHR by the ECtHR, the Supreme Court now acknowledged that it was long established in the case law of the Supreme Court that domestic courts should abide by the precedents of the ECtHR when interpreting the requirements of the ECHR in the context of domestic legislation. The Court then went on and cited numerous cases of the ECtHR to establish what Article 6 of the ECHR required in the context at hand and by analogy the corresponding Article 70 of the Icelandic Constitution.[50] There was no mention of the dualism principle or Article 2 of the incorporating act, which were forcefully invoked by the same Court in May 2019 during the initial fallout from the *Ástráðsson* case.

At least two contributing factors led to and enabled this sudden change of attitude towards the status of precedents of the ECtHR and thus to the constitutional status of the ECHR within the domestic legal order. One contributing factor was the untenable position of the Supreme Court to be both domestically and internationally seen as an inept facilitator of human rights following the high-profile condemnation by the ECtHR in the *Ástráðsson* case. A second contributing factor was the change in personnel within the Supreme Court. The judges that had been influential in the court from the late 1990s were retiring by the end of the 2010s and a new generation of judges were starting to make their mark on the Court's approach. Members of the old guard were prominent on the five-judge panel in the 2019 case, while a new court president, elected in 2020, and three new judges that were appointed in 2020 were on the five-judge panel of the 2021 case. Only one judge was on both panels.

[49] This judgment was the object of the ECtHR's decision in *Ástráðsson v Iceland*, Application no. 26374/18, Grand Chamber Judgment of 1 December 2020. See also Karlsson (n 28).

[50] Case H:34/2020 (2021) paras 18–19.

Table 2 *New generation on the Icelandic Supreme Court after 2020*

	Panel in Case H:12/2018 **(2019)**		Panel in Case H:34/2020 **(2021)**	
Judge #	Year born	Year appointed	Year born	Year appointed
1	1952	2011 (SC president)	1965	2012 (SC president)
2	1942	1992	1959	2020
3	1946	1994	1960	2020
4	1961	2003	1961	2003
5	1962	2015	1966	2020

The meaning of the shift in attitude from a defensive posture towards a posture of openness is subtle but important. The Supreme Court now clearly views precedents of the ECtHR as authoritative when reviewing compliance of domestic law with the requirements of the ECHR and by inference the Icelandic Constitution. This is of course not a radical approach and should be viewed as a normalisation and a departure from an untenable previous interpretive doctrine by the Supreme Court. This reformed view is consistent with how most members of the Icelandic legal system have been approaching constitutional reasoning since at least the 1990s with respect to precedents of the ECtHR, often doing so implicitly, but also explicitly. But this also means that constitutional normativity now emits from the ECHR and the ECtHR into the domestic constitutional order, irrespective of the supposed dualism barrier.

V. Judicial Style of Reasoning and Key Concepts

The judicial style of reasoning in Iceland tends to be concise and direct. An extreme example from the study of the leading cases was a judgment from 2002, where the majority reasoning (N9) comprised only eight words.[51] Starting in the 1970s and plateauing in 2008, judgments have become progressively longer over time. Despite the increased length of judgments, the majority's reasoning has consistently accounted for one-sixth of the text over time. The gradual increase in length could be explained with reference to the advent of computerised word processors and digital publication methods, which has significantly reduced the cost in material and effort to write and publish long texts. The high case load of the Supreme Court before the 2018 reforms meant that judges needed to wrap up judgments quickly to keep up with the workload, which discouraged them from spending time on writing long elaborate arguments, which may have factored as a

[51] Case H:167/2002 (2002). The court simply endorsed the approach of the lower court.

restraint on length. The exceptionally heavy caseload following the financial crisis of 2008 may also have contributed to the plateauing of the length around the same time. It is yet to be seen if judgments will on average become longer after the reduction in workload of the Supreme Court following the 2018 reforms. It is unusual for Icelandic judges to elaborate obiter dictum on issues that do not strictly need to be addressed through the text of a judgment. There are however exceptions, one notable being the majority opinion in Case H:12/2000 (2000), where an obiter dictum argument provided a blueprint for the legislator to solve a politically sensitive issue with regards to allocation of Icelandic fishing rights.[52]

The parties of a private law case have control over how the constitutional issue is framed in line with the party disposition principle and the court is expected to address the issue within that framework. Administrative law cases also generally reach the courts through the private law procedure and are thus subject to a corresponding restraint with regards to party control over the framing of a potential constitutional law issue. In theory, the party disposition principle does not apply to criminal cases, but normally a court would not address constitutional issues in a criminal case unless raised by the defence. Usually, the courts are cautious and try to limit their findings to the issue at hand and they are not keen on making sweeping statements, preferring a deference to the legislator. The approach of the Supreme Court towards addressing constitutional issues involving the other branches of government can be described as a policy of cooperation and dialogue.[53] It should, however, be noted that during the 1990s and early 2000s the Supreme Court handed down several judgments that could be classified as judicial activism, but by the mid-2000s following backlash from the conservative coalition government at the time, the Supreme Court backtracked and retreated to a more deferential stance towards policies and programmes of the other branches of government.[54] These were mostly cases involving the interpretation of the ECHR and other human rights obligations undertaken by the Icelandic State. Two lines of cases are usually cited as marking a turning point, both of which are represented on the list of the 40 leading cases. These are two cases concerning fishing rights and two cases involving rights to social security.[55]

While, as mentioned above, the doctrinal literature has advocated for a strict compartmentalisation of international and domestic law, which during intermittent

[52] M Dahlberg, HL Karlsson and K Kelemen, 'The Nordic courts – An example of cooperation and dialogue' in K Pócza (ed), *Constitutional Review in Western Europe – Judicial-Legislative Relations in Comparative Perspective* (Abingdon, Routledge, 2024) 288, 304.

[53] ibid 306–307.

[54] One subsequent result of the backlash were two controversial appointments of judges on the Supreme Court. See Karlsson (n 28) 1053–54.

[55] Cases H:145/1998 (1998) and H:12/2000 (2000) concerning fishing rights; and Cases H:125/2000 (2000) and H:549/2002 (2003) concerning right to social security. See also K Hólmar Ragnarsson, 'Falsvonir Öryrkjabandalagsdómsins? Nýleg dómaframkvæmd um félagsleg réttindi' (2017) 70 *Úlfljótur* 41.

periods has correlated with the decisional practice of the Supreme Court, Iceland nonetheless ranks at the top among Nordic countries in terms of the prevalence of the *harmonising with international law requirements* type of arguments (N18) in the Nordic CONREASON study (see Figure 3). Such an argument can be found in all but six of the 40 leading cases, including in every case after 1993 and in all but two cases after 1983. This indicates a constitutional culture that consistently views adjudicative arguments based on international law as being constitutionally relevant and part of a culture that is open to such arguments. The question is thus not *whether*, but *how* relevant such sources are in the hierarchy of constitutionally relevant legal norms.

Figure 3 Estimated proportion among leading constitutional cases in the Nordic countries interpreting constitutional law in light of international law

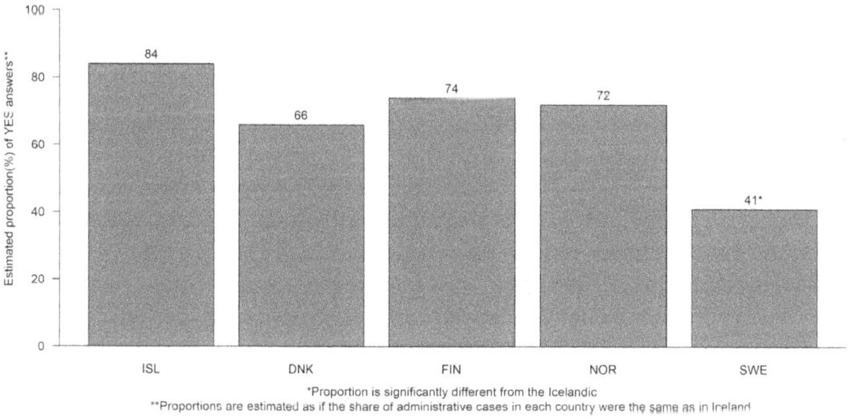

In their recent article, Torfadóttir and Magnússon identify a variance in how the doctrinal literature from the mid-twentieth century described the relation of international law and domestic law, and how the Supreme Court approached this relation in its judgments between 1920 and 1975. They concluded their study with a question about why this discrepancy had occurred.[56] One variable in our project could give a clue about why the courts have not been influenced more by the doctrinal literature. Variable N25 registered references to scholarly work as a constitutional argument (see Figure 4). In only four out of 40 cases (10 per cent) such references could be found in the Icelandic leading cases, and none of them appeared in the reasoning of the Supreme Court itself. This registered as the lowest in the Nordic comparison and all except Finland (20 per cent) were significantly higher.

[56] Torfadóttir and Magnússon (n 35) 220–21.

Figure 4 Estimated proportion among leading constitutional cases in the Nordic countries with reference to scholarly work

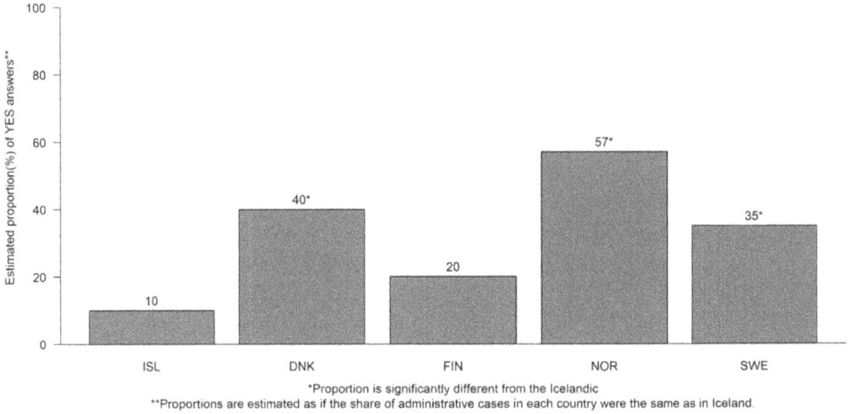

This could explain why the Supreme Court was not influenced by the doctrinal literature in its approach to cases during the period studied by Torfadóttir and Magnússon. It simply did not consider the literature as being relevant and did thus not engage with it. This does however not explain why the doctrinal literature was not influenced by the actual practice of the Supreme Court. This mid-twentieth century literature was primarily of a descriptive nature and supposedly should thus have reflected the actual practice. At the time, however, the domestic court practice was limited in volume, and it is thus probable that the authors were partly reflecting theories and court practices described in textbooks on the other Nordic legal systems, in particular the Danish and the Norwegian systems. This is, however, difficult to confirm, since modern scholarly citation practices were not applied rigorously during this period in Icelandic legal academic writings.[57]

More recent literature provides hints at the reason for the relative absences of references to scholarly work in the Icelandic cases. Apparently, there are two conflicting views in Iceland on the appropriateness of using scholarly work as a normative basis for legal argumentation in courts. The traditional view is that scholarly works are not part of the materials that can provide normative authority for an interpretation of a legal provision. This view prioritises the intent of the legislator, and thus references to materials that give evidence of that intent.[58] The alternative view makes a distinction between materials originating from the actual legislative process and other materials that judges can use for the interpretation of legislation. The former materials are what is normally referred to

[57] ibid 183.
[58] RR Spanó, *Túlkun lagaákvæða*, 2nd edn (Reykjavik, Codex, 2019) 103–105.

as preparatory works from the legislative process, while the latter can include scholarly works and various other materials that in practice influence legal interpretation.[59]

The traditional view is more formalistic in nature and indicates a narrow positivistic view, or rather a Scandinavian realist view on the stringent role of judges in legal interpretation and a refusal of the metaphysical. The alternative view gives judges more leeway for extracting a reasonable context specific meaning out of legal provisions, which is more in line with modern contextual or natural law based interpretive methods, revived during the post war period in continental Europe and exemplified in the interpretive practices of the ECtHR and the CJEU.[60] Both views acknowledge the reluctance of Icelandic courts to refer explicitly to scholarly works. The positivistic view however presents this as an expression of a proper interpretive methodology, while the natural law view explains that this obscures actual judicial practice in Iceland, suggesting that Icelandic judges routinely consult scholarly work, often however without explicitly citing their sources.[61]

Most likely both views incompletely explain the attitude among Icelandic judges towards the relevance of scholarly work as norms that can influence legal interpretation. Some judges may refrain from citing such work in their judgments due to the belief that it would represent an improper adjudicative methodology. Others probably use scholarly work extensively to inform their own approach to interpretive dilemmas, but due to drafting customs within the judiciary, such work is not explicitly referenced in the actual text of judgments. Different attitudes towards the relevance of scholarly work in judicial decision-making can also be seen to complement opposite attitudes towards the relevance of foreign legal materials. A narrow positivistic view on permissible legal materials complements a defensive attitude towards external influences, while a natural law view that accepts more types of legal materials would complement an open attitude towards external influences.

As for Icelandic constitutional interpretation, a heavy methodological focus on the legislative intent is a less credible approach than for other types of legislation. Much of the Constitution of 1944 is the same as the Constitution of 1920, which was an updated version of the constitution granted unilaterally by the Danish

[59] D Þór Björgvinsson, *Lögskýringar* (Reykjavik, JPV 2008) 49–50.

[60] See, eg, J Gerards, 'The European Court of Human Rights' in A Jakab, A Dyevre and G Itzcovich (eds), *Comparative Constitutional Reasoning* (Cambridge, Cambridge University Press, 2017) 255–56; G Itzcovich, 'The European Court of Justice' in A Jakab, A Dyevre and G Itzcovich (eds), *Comparative Constitutional Reasoning* (Cambridge, Cambridge University Press, 2017) 298–300; G Letsas, 'The ECHR as a living instrument: its meaning and legitimacy' in A Føllesdal, B Peters and G Ulfstein (eds), *Constituting Europe – The European Court of Human Rights in a National, European and Global Context* (Cambridge, Cambridge University Press, 2013) 106; C Moser and B Rittberger, 'The CJEU and EU (de-)constitutionalization: Unpacking jurisprudential responses' (2022) 20 *I-CON* 1038.

[61] Spanó (n 58) 104; Björgvinsson (n 59) 77–78.

Monarch in 1874, which again was influenced by the Danish Constitution of 1849. To extract a legislative intent would thus often require examining the intent of the Danish Monarch in the third quarter of the nineteenth century. Whether Icelandic courts in the twenty-first century *should* grant normative value to such a historical legislative intent is an open question. But as an empirical observation it can be seen from our study that *teleological (historical-intentional) arguments* (N23-1) have appeared in the majority opinion of the Icelandic Supreme Court in six out of 40 leading cases, which is the lowest frequency in the intra-Nordic comparison (see Figure 5).

Figure 5 Proportion of cases in which the majority opinion invokes a teleological (historical-intentional) argument

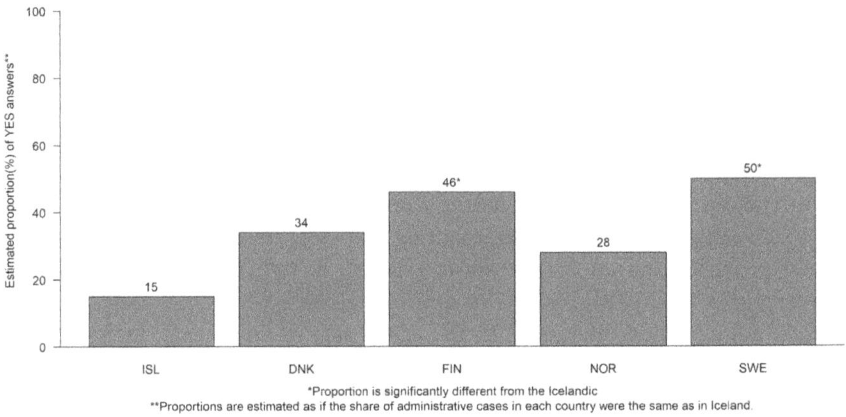

It should, however, be noted that five of these six cases were decided after the amendment of the human rights chapter of the Constitution in 1995 and relate to the intent of the domestic legislator during the 1995 amendment. In case H:239/1987 (1988) a reference was made to the legislative intent behind Article 92 of the Danish June Constitution of 1849, which corresponded to Article 55 of the Icelandic Constitution of 1874 and Article 73 of the present-day Constitution of 1944 as it stood in 1988.[62]

Our results also show that it is common in the constitutional reasoning culture of Iceland to refer to concepts or principles not contained in the text of the constitution (N20). Such references appeared in 28 out of 40 cases. This reasoning pattern matches with the prevalence of several concepts also registered in the results of the study. The first of these is the concept of equality (N43), where the

[62] Case H:239/1987 (1988) Bls. 1534.

frequency of 19 out of 40 cases registers the highest in the intra-Nordic comparison (see Figure 6).

Figure 6 Proportion of cases in which the concept of equality is invoked

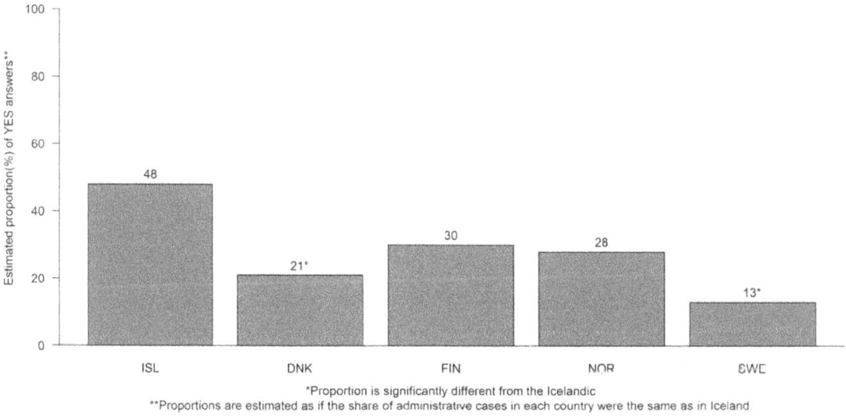

This concept was initially not included in the principles protected by the Constitution. This, however, changed in 1995 following amendments to the human rights chapter. In the 11 judgments delivered before the constitutional amendment, four nonetheless contained a reference to the principle of equality, which was by then recognised by the Supreme Court as a constitutional custom.

The principle of proportionality (N40) is not mentioned in the Icelandic Constitution, but it still registers as a constitutional argument in 14 out of the 40 leading cases.[63] This includes an early case from 1968, where the principle was used implicitly by the Supreme Court to balance the freedom of print with privacy rights, both of which had a basis in the written Constitution at the time.[64] A designated act describing the principles of good administration entered into force in 1994, which includes the proportionality principle and the equality principle.[65] This act is not considered to have a formal constitutional status in the doctrinal literature, although it restricts the actions of administrative bodies and officials in a comparable manner as the constitution and their actions are similarly subject to judicial review with regards to these principles.[66]

[63] Thorarensen (n 34) 210–12.
[64] Case H:159/1968 (1968).
[65] Stjórnsýslulög nr. 37/1993, 11. gr. and 12. gr.
[66] Thorarensen (n 34) 27–28; Jóhannesson (n 48) 2.

The concept of a custom (N48) as a constitutional argument appears in 12 out of 40 leading cases, which is a similar frequency as in Denmark and Norway, but more frequent than in Sweden and Finland (see Figure 7).

Figure 7 Proportion of cases in which the concept of custom is invoked

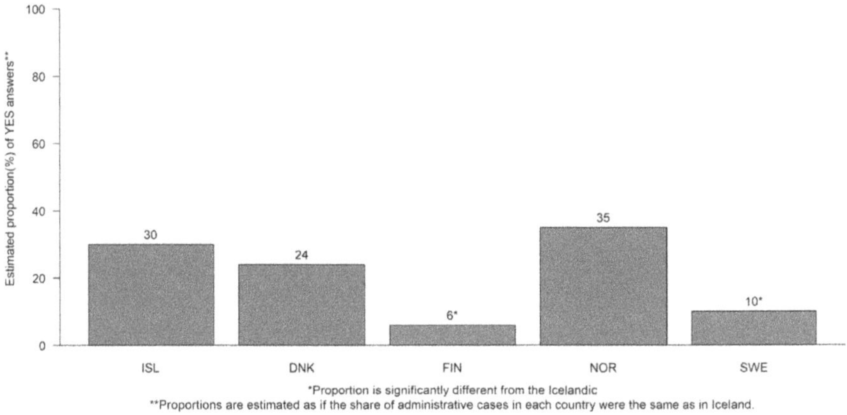

It has long been recognised in the doctrinal literature that customs are among the sources of constitutional law, and it has been argued that established constitutional customs need to be amended in the same way as normal provisions of the Constitution.[67] Important aspects of the Icelandic constitutional order are based on constitutional customs, such as the power of courts to perform judicial review of legislation and the governance system of parliamentarianism. Neither of these have an explicit basis in the written Constitution but are nonetheless considered fundamental constitutional maxims.

VI. Conclusions

The focus of this chapter on the Icelandic results of the Nordic CONREASON project has been on findings that contribute to debates about the role of external influences on the culture of constitutional reasoning in Iceland. We have seen how the constitutional debates of the nineteenth century about the secession from the Danish colonial empire reverberate in present-day debates about the status of ECHR legal norms within the domestic legal order. These historical debates provide an important context for understanding the world view of the actors that participate in the institutionalised form of constitutional reasoning that occurs before the Icelandic Supreme Court.

[67] Jóhannesson (n 48) 93–95; Thorarensen (n 34) 161–68.

Analysis of the argumentative patterns in the leading cases of the Icelandic Supreme Court reveals conflicting views on the relevance of external legal norms in Icelandic constitutional reasoning. Should they be kept at arm's length and gradually incorporated into the domestic system at the discretion of the political elites, or should they be internalised more proactively by the courts through viewing the internal and the external as being constitutive parts of an all-encompassing European legal system? This finding contradicts the one-sided emphasis in doctrinal literature on the dualist nature of the domestic legal system and international law. Recent academic writings suggest that this orthodoxy is becoming difficult to maintain in practice. The analysis of the leading cases shows that the dualist principle has long been a contested idea in Iceland and that there are signs that the Supreme Court is yet again in the process of softening its approach towards external influences, by embracing ideas and doctrinal approaches pioneered by the enforcement mechanisms of the ECHR. This highlights the position of the Court as being in limbo between the domestic ruling elites that emphasise defensiveness against foreign influences, and the average member of the public that sees opportunities in openly embracing external ideas, connections and constitutional norms.

The judicial style of reasoning in Iceland tends to be tight and to the point. Judges view their role strictly as interpreters of the law as decided by the legislator, and the normal interpretive methodology emphasises deference to the legislator and their intent as expressed in the legislative preparatory works. Due to the age of larger parts of the Constitution and its origin within the Danish government offices of the 1870s, this interpretive methodology is less relevant for constitutional reasoning. The Nordic CONREASON study shows that references to academic writings are very rare in constitutional reasoning in the leading cases. This finding is confirmed by comments in the academic literature. There are, however, opposing opinions about the relevance of academic writings in judicial decision-making. While one view argues that judges do frequently and justifiably use academic work as inspiration, another understanding sees academic work as an improper basis of judicial interpretation of legal statutes. The former facilitates a more open view on the proper sources of legal interpretation, including an open view on the role of external legal norms, while the latter seeks to limit the proper sources to a narrow list focused on the legislative intent, thus excluding external legal norms.

The concept of sovereignty has been brought up in the context of discussions in Iceland regarding Iceland's participation in international cooperation involving supranational enforcement and rulemaking mechanisms, the most prominent being participation in the ECHR and EEA legal regimes. It has been debated whether participation in such cooperation involves surrender of sovereignty incompatible with the Constitution. Some argue that the Constitution should be amended to allow for participation in such international legal regimes, while others claim that participation in such legal regimes is already compatible with the constitutional order with reference to a decades-old constitutional custom.[68] The former argument fits within the protective or defensive worldview of those who maintain that participation in the ECHR and the EEA means surrendering sovereignty, while the latter view is more open towards the external world, seeing international cooperation as an important aspect of exercising state sovereignty.[69]

Without rehearsing these arguments in full, a small contribution to these debates can be extracted from the Nordic CONREASON study. The data shows that constitutional arguments without an explicit basis in the Constitution appear in about two-thirds of the leading cases. Given that a constitutional argument is intrinsically made with reference to a norm containing constitutional properties in view of the provider of the argument, the Icelandic data thus indicates a culture of constitutional reasoning that accepts references to various constitutional norms that do not have explicit basis in the text of the Constitution. The Nordic CONREASON study thus confirms that Iceland's constitutional reasoning culture accepts arguments referring to a small 'c' constitution, as well as to the large 'C' written Constitution.[70] This lends weight to the argument of Björgvinsson and others that the exercise of sovereignty through international cooperation is already compatible with the Icelandic constitutional order thanks to constitutional custom.

[68] D Þór Björgvinsson, *EES-réttur og landsréttur* (Reykjavik, Codex, 2006) 478; Thorarensen (n 34) 145–47; B Thorarensen, 'Stjórnarskrárákvæði um framsal ríkisvalds' in S Ísfeld Ólafsdóttir, B Þórhallsson, G Hálfdanarson and Ó Ísleifsson (eds), *Fullveldi í 99 ár – Safn ritgerða til heiðurs dr. Davíð Þór Björgvinssyni sextugum* (Reykjavik, Hið íslenska bókmenntafélag, 2017) 113, 136–39; S Magnússon, 'Er þörf á stjórnarskrárákvæði um stöðu þjóðaréttar?' in S Ísfeld Ólafsdóttir, B Þórhallsson, G Hálfdanarson and Ó Ísleifsson (eds), *Fullveldi í 99 ár – Safn ritgerða til heiðurs dr. Davíð Þór Björgvinssyni sextugum* (Reykjavik, Hið íslenska bókmenntafélag, 2017) 143, 161–65; S Magnússon, 'Fullveldishugtakið í íslenskum rétti frá 1918 til samtímans' in G Jónsson et al (eds), *Frjálst og fullvalda ríki – Ísland 1918–2018* (Reykjavik, Sögufélag, 2018) 129, 162–63.

[69] B Þórhallsson, 'Fullveldi smáríkja' in S Ísfeld Ólafsdóttir, B Þórhallsson, G Hálfdanarson and Ó Ísleifsson (eds), *Fullveldi í 99 ár – Safn ritgerða til heiðurs dr. Davíð Þór Björgvinssyni sextugum* (Reykjavik, Hið íslenska bókmenntafélag, 2017) 73, 88–90.

[70] A Chilton and M Versteeg, 'Small-c constitutional rights' (2022) 20 *I-CON* 141, 146–48, ie, references to both the 'formal' and the 'material' constitution are accepted.

5

A Constitutional Culture in Transition? An Empirical Study on Finnish Supreme Courts' Constitutional Reasoning

MAIJA DAHLBERG

I. Introduction

In Finland, as in the other Nordic countries, courts play relatively modest roles in judicial review owing to the high level of respect for the Parliament and the legislature. Indeed, judicial review of legislative acts was strictly prohibited until the current Finnish Constitution entered into force in 2000, and judicial review is still limited to cases where there is an 'evident' conflict with the Constitution (section 106 of the Constitution).[1] Consequently, the legal threshold is set rather high for the courts to conclude that a legislative act is unconstitutional. All in all, section 106 of the Finnish Constitution also influences constitutional reasoning and the use of the Constitution in Finnish courts in general. In addition, since the Finnish constitutional mentality and legal culture do not support judicial activism, it is traditional for courts to refrain from challenging the legislature's choices.[2]

In this chapter, I point out the main characteristics and style of constitutional argumentation in the leading constitutional cases of the Finnish Supreme Courts.

[1] See eg K Tuori, 'Judicial Constitutional Review as a Last Resort' in T Campbell, KD Ewing and A Tomkins (eds), *The Legal Protection of Human Rights: Sceptical Essays* (Oxford, Oxford University Press, 2011) 365, 381; J Lavapuro, T Ojanen and M Scheinin, 'Intermediate Constitutional Review in Finland: Promising in Theory, Problematic in Practice' in J Bell and ML Paris (eds), *Rights Based Constitutional Review: Constitutional Courts in a Changing Landscape* (Cheltenham, Edward Elgar Publishing, 2016) 218, 227–28.

[2] See eg VP Hautamäki, 'Judicial Activism and "the Final Frontier" – Remarks on the Nordic Law' (2005) 21 *Rechtstheorie* 141, 151–52; Lavapuro, Ojanen and Scheinin (n 1).

Second, I outline similarities and differences compared to other Nordic countries. More importantly, I analyse and explain why such differences exist and the legal cultural specificities they may reveal. Third, I will point out some differences between the two Finnish Supreme Courts relating to constitutional interpretation. This chapter is based on the empirical findings of the Nordic CONREASON project.[3]

II. Background to Constitutional Reasoning

A. Legal, Institutional, and Academic Contexts

Finnish constitutional culture has the same roots as Swedish constitutional culture. For a long time, Finland was under Swedish rule, and it was allowed to keep its Swedish constitutional arrangements despite becoming an autonomous part of the Russian Empire in 1809. Both the Swedish and Finnish constitutional systems place a high value on the principle of parliamentary supremacy. This becomes clear when one analyses the role of the courts and the legal interpretative doctrines which emphasise the role of the Finnish Parliament (*Eduskunta*) and the intentions of the legislator (expressed in the preparatory works of legislation).[4]

The current Constitution of Finland (*Perustuslaki*) entered into force in 2000 and replaced the four constitutional acts previously in force. Besides including some new elements, the Constitution codified certain existing practices and doctrines. In essence, the 2000 Constitution sought to strengthen the parliamentary features of the Finnish political and constitutional system while decreasing the powers of the president. These parliamentary features were further strengthened in 2012 when the Constitution was amended, and the responsibilities of the president and the government were clarified. Therefore, the Finnish constitutional system can no longer be described mainly as semi-presidential; it is now primarily a parliamentary system.[5] However, the de facto role of the president may indirectly become more significant due to the country's NATO membership, which began in April 2023.

[3] Regarding the methodology of the Nordic CONREASON project, see ch 2 by N Pettersson and K Kelemen in this volume. In our country comparisons, all proportions are estimated as if half of the cases in each country were administrative, as they were in Finland. An asterisk (*) indicates that the country in question's proportion differs significantly from the Finnish proportion.

[4] See eg M Suksi, 'Finland' in D Oliver and C Fusaro (eds), *How Constitutions Change: A Comparative Study* (Oxford, Hart Publishing, 2011) 87, 88–90; T Ojanen, 'Constitutional Amendment in Finland' in X Contiades (ed), *Engineering Constitutional Change: A Comparative Perspective on Europe, Canada and the USA* (New York, Routledge, 2013) 93, 93–95.

[5] See eg J Husa, *The Constitution of Finland: A Contextual Analysis* (Oxford, Hart Publishing, 2011) 42–50; Suksi (n 4) 88; Ojanen (n 4) 100–103.

The importance of constitutional rights came to the fore in the 1990s, mainly due to international obligations (related to the European Convention on Human Rights (ECHR) and the European Union (EU)). The catalogue of constitutional rights was fully revised and entered into force in 1995 under the previous constitution. Since then, the Finnish Constitution has covered both traditional civil and political rights as well as social, economic, and cultural rights. In addition, the provisions of the fundamental rights were designed to lend themselves to direct application by courts and authorities. Today, in addition to its traditional emphasis on legalism and legislative supremacy, Finnish constitutional law also emphasises individual rights and any international obligations relating to them.[6]

Both the emphasis that the Finnish constitutional system places on the principle of parliamentary supremacy and the practical constitutional innovations that arose when Finland was an autonomous part of the Russian Empire are important in order to understand why the constitutional review is organised as it is in Finland.[7] Finland has always lacked a distinct constitutional court and, significantly, judicial review of legislative acts of Parliament only became permissible with the entry into force of the current Constitution in 2000 but only in cases where there is an 'evident' conflict with the Constitution (section 106 of the Constitution). According to the preparatory works of the Constitution, if a law was reviewed ex ante and the Constitutional Law Committee (CLC, *Perustuslakivaliokunta*) did not identify any constitutional issues in it, then courts are barred from finding such issues.[8] Overall, Finnish courts have been rather cautious in carrying out constitutional review. The primary review is done ex ante by one of the standing committees of the Parliament, namely the CLC.[9] Our empirical findings partly confirm this. We measured the outcome of the constitutional issues,[10] and the proportions of leading constitutional cases where the court found an act or decision unconstitutional were as follows: 44 per cent in Finland (FIN), 26 per cent in Denmark (DNK), 53 per cent in Iceland (ISL), and 48 per cent in both Norway (NOR) and Sweden (SWE). The global comparison confirms the cautious attitude of Finnish Supreme Courts in constitutional cases (see Figure 1).

[6] Lavapuro, Ojanen and Scheinin (n 1) 222–23.

[7] For an explanation of the context and background of Finnish ex ante constitutional review, see J Husa, 'Locking in Constitutionality Control in Finland' (2020) 16 *European Constitutional Law Review* 249.

[8] See CLC (PeVM) 10/1998 and Government Bill (HE) 1/1998.

[9] See eg the Finnish Supreme Court's judgment KKO 2004:26; Tuori (n 1); Lavapuro, Ojanen and Scheinin (n 1) 223 and 227–28; T Ojanen, 'From Constitutional Periphery toward the Center – Transformations of Judicial Review in Finland' (2009) 27 *Nordisk Tidsskrift for Menneskerettigheter* 197.

[10] See the instructions for the coding of variable N4 in our Codebook in the Appendix.

Figure 1 Proportion of cases where the court found an act or decision unconstitutional in a global comparison

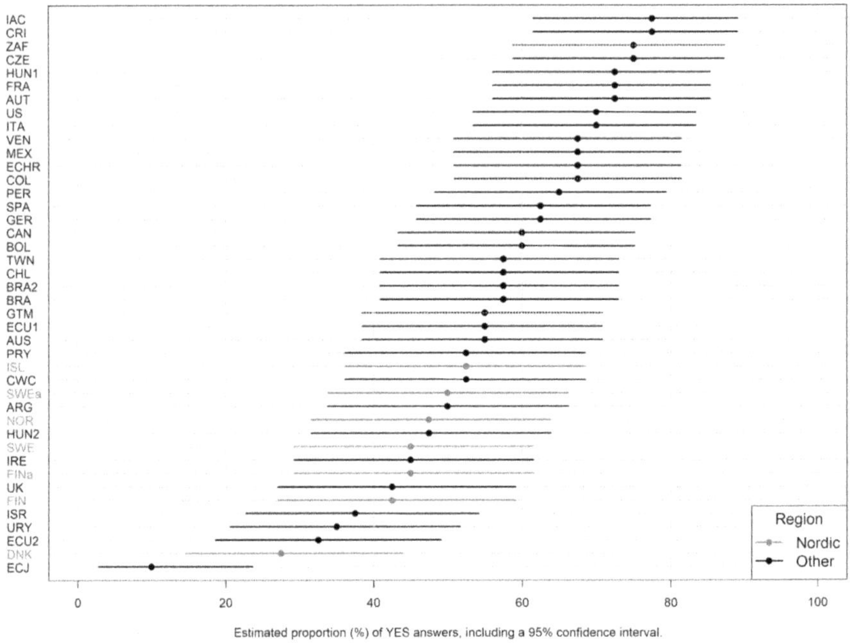

The Finnish Constitution (section 74) provides that the primary review mechanism for ensuring the constitutionality of draft legislation, including conformity with international obligations and EU law, is the ex ante review carried out by the CLC.[11] The CLC consists of 17 Members of Parliament (MPs) who come from all parliamentary parties and assess the constitutionality of proposed laws. In the international legal literature, the CLC has been compared to a typical constitutional court, since it carries out constitutional reviews using judicial techniques and methods.[12] However, Finnish legal scholars have described the CLC as a 'quasi-judicial' body rather than a constitutional court.[13]

The CLC's work has certain vital characteristics. First, even though the CLC is composed of politicians, the evaluation of the constitutionality of proposed legislation is carried out on a legal basis. Second, the CLC always consults external

[11] The President of the Republic, the Supreme Courts, and the Speaker of the Parliament also have a role in ex ante constitutional review. For further details, see eg K Tuori, 'Verfassungsgerichtsbarkeit in Finnland' in A von Bogdandy, C Grabenwarter and PM Huber (eds), *Handbuch Ius Publicum Europaeum. Band VI, Verfassungsgerichtsbarkeit in Europa: Institutionen* (Heidelberg, CF Müller, 2016) 198, 220 and 224–25.

[12] JL Requejo Pagés, 'The Decline of the Traditional Model of European Constitutional Jurisdiction' in A von Bogdandy, PM Huber and C Grabenwarter (eds), *The Max Planck Handbooks in European Public Law IV, Constitutional Adjudication: Common Themes and Challenges* (Oxford, Oxford University Press, 2023) 613, 620.

[13] See eg Husa (n 5) 83; Tuori (n 1) 380.

constitutional law experts and, as a rule, follows their opinions. Furthermore, the final statements the CLC makes regarding the constitutionality of draft legislation are de facto binding on Parliament. Significantly, when it detects a conflict with the Constitution, the CLC indicates how the bill should be amended in order to remove the conflict. This means that the CLC has a considerable impact on the content of forthcoming legislation.[14]

Besides the essential role of the CLC, the role of the judiciary is also growing in Finnish constitutional law. The independence of the judiciary is guaranteed by the Constitution (section 3(3)). Judicial cases are divided into three main types of procedures: civil, criminal, and administrative cases. In Finland, there are two separate court systems: general courts decide civil and criminal cases, whereas administrative courts decide administrative cases. Consequently, there are two supreme courts in Finland, namely, the Finnish Supreme Court (KKO, *Korkein oikeus*) and the Supreme Administrative Court (KHO, *Korkein hallinto-oikeus*).

Political and judicial deliberation must, in principle, be kept separated in Finnish judicial decision-making. According to section 2(2) of the Constitution, the exercise of public powers shall be based on a legislative act. In all public activity, the law should be strictly observed. Thus, in their judicial decision-making, Finnish courts are bound by the law, and this must be shown in their reasoning. The right to a fair trial, which is provided by the Constitution (section 21), acknowledges the right to receive a reasoned decision and the right to appeal.[15] More concretely, judicial reasoning must be based on the applied legal provisions and much explain which facts influence the decision and why.[16]

Even though the above-mentioned principal rules for how judicial interpretation must be carried out are found in written law, there are some important unwritten rules based on legal theory and custom. In this sense, the doctrine on sources of law defines limits for judicial adjudication. It draws a boundary between what is legal and what is not.[17] Sources of law refer to the material or content on which a legal interpretation must be based. The strongly binding sources on

[14] See eg T Ojanen and J Salminen, 'Finland: European Integration and International Human Rights Treaties as Sources of Domestic Constitutional Change and Dynamism' in A Albi and S Bardutzky (eds), *National Constitutions in European and Global Governance: Democracy, Rights, and the Rule of Law* (The Hague Springer Nature, 2019) 359, 360–62; M Dahlberg, 'Openness of Constitutional Review: A Comparative Analysis of How Transparency is Ensured in Ex Ante Constitutional Review' in J de Poorter, G van der Schyff, M Stremler and M De Visser (eds), *European Yearbook of Constitutional Law 2021: Constitutional Advice* (The Hague, Asser Press, 2021) 155; Husa (n 5) 226.

[15] Section 21(2) of the Finnish Constitution: 'Provisions concerning the publicity of proceedings, the right to be heard, the right to receive a reasoned decision and the right to appeal, as well as the other guarantees of a fair trial and good governance shall be laid down by an Act.'

[16] See Tuomioistuinlaki [Act on Courts], 673/2016, § 1, Ch. 9, Oikeudenkäymiskaari [Act of Justice], 4/1734, § 4, Ch. 24; Laki oikeudenkäynnistä rikosasioissa [Act on Trial in Criminal Cases], 689/1997, § 4, Ch. 11; Laki oikeudenkäynnistä hallintoasioissa [Act on Proceedings in Administrative Matters], 808/2019, § 87.

[17] See eg A Aarnio, 'On the Sources of Law' in K Nuotio, S Melander and M Huomo-Kettunen (eds), *Introduction to Finnish Law and Legal Culture* (Helsinki, Publications of the Faculty of Law, University of Helsinki, 2012) 51, 54; P Timonen, 'Sources of Law and Material on the Sources of Law' in J Pöyhönen (ed), *An Introduction to Finnish Law* (Helsinki, Kauppakaari, 2002) 22.

which legal decisions must be based are written law and established custom. Consequently, written law is always the primary and unconditionally binding source of law in legal interpretation. Weakly binding sources are legislative proposals, other documents produced in the parliamentary process, and previous court decisions. Importantly, it is generally acknowledged that the status of preparatory work is higher in the hierarchy of legal sources than of case law.[18] Non-legal arguments – for example, arguments relating to moral or factual circumstances – can be employed only if no other sources of law exist. Importantly, there are also forbidden sources of law, which contain arguments that go against the law or good practice or are openly political.

In sum, judicial and political deliberation are kept separated mainly through the legal doctrine on sources of law, which steers and limits legal interpretation and argumentation. However, as some scholars have pointed out, the Nordic style of argumentation is rather pragmatic, meaning that courts do not stick closely to the written statutory and constitutional text but seek a more general argumentative base for justification purposes.[19]

B. Style of Judicial Constitutional Reasoning

As is the case in a decentralised model of judicial review, all Finnish courts have the power to set aside unconstitutional laws that are in evident conflict with the Constitution. However, judicial review is de facto concentrated in the Supreme Courts. Importantly, Finnish courts regularly interpret constitutional and human rights in their cases but not constitutional provisions relating to, for example, institutions, democracy, and the separation of powers. Our dataset illustrates this well: 94 per cent of the leading constitutional cases in Finland concern fundamental rights (N5).[20] In addition, there is no case in the Finnish sample that contains arguments relating to state form (N35) or federalism/government system by power structure (N39), and only two of the 80 cases invoke government form (N36) as part of an argument.

The Nordic style of legal argumentation has been described as being not as 'heavy' as in Germany nor as cryptic as in France; instead, the argumentation is

[18] J Boucht, 'Introduction to Finnish and Swedish Legal Method' in I Helland and S Koch (eds), *Nordic and Germanic Legal Methods: Contributions to a Dialogue between Different Legal Cultures, with a Main Focus on Norway and Germany* (Tübingen, Mohr Siebeck, 2014) 165, 173; Ojanen (n 9) 196; J Husa, 'Nordic Constitutionalism and European Human Rights – Mixing Oil and Water?' (2010) 55 *Scandinavian Studies in Law* 101, 105–106.

[19] See eg J Husa, 'Panorama of World's Legal Systems – Focusing on Finland' in K Nuotio, S Melander and M Huomo-Kettunen (eds), *Introduction to Finnish Law and Legal Culture* (Helsinki, Publications of the Faculty of Law, University of Helsinki, 2012) 5, 14; D Tamm, 'The Nordic Legal Tradition in European Context – Roman Law and the Nordic Countries' in P Letto-Vanamo (ed), *Nordisk identitet: Nordisk rätt i europeisk gemenskap* (Helsingfors, Helsingfors universitet, 1998) 15, 17.

[20] We measured this with variable N5 (general topic of the case), which had four subcategories: fundamental rights, state organisation, procedural and due process aspect, and 'other'. A case could cover more than one topic. See the Codebook in the Appendix.

casuistic in nature.[21] In addition, many scholars have pointed out that the Nordic style of argumentation could be characterised as a legal positivistic style that is less formalistic than Germanic law. On the one hand, the essence of legal positivism in the Nordic context means that written statutory text is binding on the interpreter. On the other hand, Nordic legal thinking is rather pragmatic, meaning that courts do not stick exclusively to such text but seek a more general argumentative base for justification purposes.[22]

In recent studies, scholars have claimed that Finnish courts have adopted an active and dynamic legal reasoning style inspired by the Court of Justice of the European Union and the ECtHR. In addition, Finnish courts' behaviour has been described as close to that of activist courts and a value-oriented way of thinking.[23] Finnish courts have undoubtedly adopted the European perspective on constitutional rights interpretation by frequently referring to ECtHR case law. Furthermore, Finnish courts avoid conflicts between national and EU law in the sense that they frequently use harmonising arguments rather than admit that there could be conflicts between national law and EU law.[24] Despite Finnish courts' tendency to use European law as a source of inspiration or in an even more binding way, the constitution-makers and the interpretative praxis of the CLC play essential roles in judicial constitutional interpretation. In this sense, there is not much room for Finnish judges to develop their own vision of a norm's object and purpose. Accordingly, there are strict limits on Finnish judges' ability to exercise dynamic legal reasoning. Therefore, this chapter calls for caution in describing Finnish courts as activist, since the changes caused by Europeanisation have been gradual and the traditional mindscape of Finnish judges – which emphasises the key role of the legislature – does not change quickly.

The Finnish Supreme Courts' reasoning style in constitutional cases has occasionally been criticised. Critics have claimed that when the Supreme Courts refer to the interpretative praxis of the CLC, they are rather selective, meaning that they use this praxis only when a case concerns the application of section 106 of the Constitution and not generally when constitutional rights are interpreted.[25] However, the Supreme Courts' constitutional reasoning has sometimes been praised as comprehensive and as fully taking into account all sides of cases.[26] In addition, scholars have pointed out that the Supreme Courts generally seem to

[21] Husa (n 18) 109–10.

[22] See eg Husa (n 19); Tamm (n 19); J Elo Rytter, 'A Nordic Approach to the Interpretation of the European Convention on Human Rights?' in A Kjeldgaard-Pedersen (ed), *Nordic Approaches to International Law* (Leiden, Brill, 2017) 63, 65.

[23] H Krunke and B Thorarensen, 'Concluding Thoughts' in H Krunke and B Thorarensen (eds), *The Nordic Constitutions: A Comparative and Contextual Study* (Oxford, Hart Publishing, 2018) 203, 212 and 218.

[24] S Miettinen, 'The Principle of Consistent Interpretation in Finnish Courts' in CNK Franklin (ed), *The Effectiveness and Application of EU and EEA Law in National Courts: Principles of Consistent Interpretation* (Cambridge, Intersentia, 2018) 291, 297; Lavapuro, Ojanen and Scheinin (n 1) 241.

[25] Lavapuro, Ojanen and Scheinin (n 1) 233.

[26] J Lavapuro, 'Perusoikeusargumentaation kontrolloitavuudesta' in T Heinonen and J Lavapuro (eds), *Oikeuskulttuurin eurooppalaistuminen: Ihmisoikeuksien murroksesta kansainväliseen vuorovaikutukseen* (Helsinki, Suomalainen Lakimiesyhdistys, 2012) 143, 164–65.

settle for protecting the rights of individuals only to the standards set by international human rights treaties (mainly the ECHR), neglecting the fact that national constitutional rights may provide a higher level of protection.[27]

III. Constitutional Interpretation: Finnish Peculiarities

A. The Respect for the National Parliament

In the legal literature, it has been emphasised that the doctrine of 'political question' is found in all Nordic systems. In the Nordic legal system, the political question doctrine means that the politicisation of courts is not applauded since it is the national parliaments that play the role of legislator in each country.[28] The key question is whether the widespread use of the political question doctrine could reduce the tensions surrounding judicial review.[29] Regarding the legitimacy of state power and sovereignty questions, there are slight differences among the Nordic states. The Finnish and Swedish constitutional cultures, in particular, are based on parliamentary supremacy and popular sovereignty (*folksuveränitet*), while the Norwegian, Danish, and Icelandic constitutional cultures emphasise the separation of powers.[30]

Our empirical data demonstrate that all Nordic Supreme Courts use 'political question doctrine'-type arguments on a regular basis in constitutional landmark cases. In the Finnish Supreme Courts' cases, this argumentation is frequently found in cases dealing with the application of section 106 of the Constitution, which allows courts to set aside an act if it is in evident conflict with the Constitution. Courts regularly point out that the constitution-maker sets the threshold relatively high in cases where courts could conclude that laws are unconstitutional. For example, in the case 2007:77, the KHO argued that section 106 of the Constitution 'emphasises the position of the Parliament as the highest state body whose legislative solutions cannot, as the main rule, be challenged before the courts after the laws have entered into force.' The applicability of section 106 of the Constitution demonstrates the sensitive relationship between the legislature and courts in judicial review, since the Finnish legal system has great respect for the Parliament as the democratically chosen legislator.[31]

[27] T Ojanen, 'Human Rights in Nordic Constitutions and the Impact of International Obligations' in H Krunke and B Thorarensen (eds), *The Nordic Constitutions: A Comparative and Contextual Study* (Oxford, Hart Publishing, 2018) 133, 165.

[28] See eg Husa (n 18) 108; J Husa, 'The Stories We Tell Ourselves – About Nordic Law in Specific' (2010) *Isaidat Law Review* 1, 11.

[29] J Nergelius, 'Law and Politics. On Democracy and Judicial Review' in A Aarnio, R Alexy and G Bergholtz (eds), *Justice, Morality and Society: A Tribute to Aleksander Peczenik on the Occasion of his 60th Birthday 16 November* 1997 (Lund, Juristförlaget, 1997) 303, 305–306.

[30] See, eg, KÅ Modéer, 'Nordisk juristkultur en del av rättskulturen' in P Letto-Vanamo (ed), *Nordisk identitet: Nordisk rätt i europeisk gemenskap* (Helsingfors, Helsingfors universitet, 1998) 1, 12.

[31] See eg M Hidén, 'Övervakningen av lagarnas grundlagsenlighet i Finland' (1998) *Jussens Venner* 66, 76–77; Husa (n 18) 107.

Respect for the national Parliament and Nordic democracy are also concretised in the methods and arguments of constitutional interpretation. The starting point for legal argumentation is grammatical (ie, the literal meaning of a text), but the teleological and intentional argumentative style is frequently used, particularly in constitutional interpretation.[32] Our dataset confirms this: in leading constitutional law cases, the Finnish Supreme Courts mainly use subjective teleological arguments[33] and relatively rarely use arguments relating to precedents (N19) compared to other Nordic countries. In statistical terms, if we combine the two variables and consider cases in which there is no reference to precedents, but a subjective teleological argument is employed, Finland has the largest estimated proportion – a proportion that is significantly higher than in Iceland and Norway (FIN 34 per cent, DNK 20 per cent, ISL 13 per cent*, NOR 3 per cent*, and SWE 21 per cent).

Our empirical findings partly align with the general Finnish sources of law doctrine. The main distinction is the use of subjective teleological arguments in constitutional interpretation. In statutory interpretation in general, Finnish scholars have warned against allowing opinions in preparatory works to have a direct impact, as this would give too much power to the administrative machine that prepares the statutory provisions.[34] It has even been argued that there is a Finnish tradition whereby the intention of the lawmaker (subjective intention) has not been considered decisive. Instead, the objective purpose of the statutory provisions (*ratio legis*) has – first and foremost – been ascribed relevance.[35] However, our empirical results reveal that the Finnish Supreme Courts frequently use subjective teleological arguments and infrequently use objective teleological arguments (variable N22) in constitutional interpretation. This raises a question regarding whether there should be a separate doctrine of sources of law in constitutional law since the general doctrine of sources of law does not seem to fit fully in constitutional adjudication.[36]

In the interpretation of the Constitution, the most important sources of law – besides the text of the Constitution – are the preparatory works of the Constitution and the interpretative praxis of the CLC.[37] Formally, the statements of the CLC are only weakly binding sources of law, but in practice they have a much stronger position as de facto authoritative sources for constitutional law interpretation. Of course,

[32] Husa (n 18) 109–10.

[33] Finland and Sweden demonstrated the highest proportions of the use of subjective teleological arguments in leading constitutional cases (variable N23).

[34] See eg A Aarnio, 'Statutory Interpretation in Finland' in N MacCormick and RS Summers (eds), *Interpreting Statutes: A Comparative Study* (Aldershot, Dartmouth, 1991) 123.

[35] Boucht (n 18) 174.

[36] The Finnish sources of law doctrine has been developed mainly by private law scholars. Consequently, it has been pointed out that there is a need to consider the characteristics relating to public law and other fields of law in the doctrine of sources of law. See eg T Määttä, 'Soft law som rättskälla på nya rättsområden i den nationella rätten' (2006) *Tidskrift utgiven av Juridiska Föreningen i Finland* 553. In the context of constitutional law, see Husa (n 5) 28.

[37] See eg Husa (n 5) 28–32; J Husa, 'Guarding the Constitutionality of Laws in the Nordic Countries: A Comparative Perspective' (2000) 48 *American Journal of Comparative Law* 345, 380. Interestingly, it has been argued that Swedish courts and judges are generally more bound to preparatory works than their Finnish colleagues; see L Ervo, 'Culture and Mentality in East-Nordic Courts' in L Ervo, P Letto-Vanamo and A Nylund (eds), *Rethinking Nordic Courts* (Cham, Springer, 2021) 89, 100.

the age of a constitution is also a central factor when one analyses subjective teleological interpretation. The Finnish Constitution is relatively new (it was amended in full in 2000), so the subjective intention of the constitution-maker is not outdated compared to Norway, for example, where the Constitution is more than 200 years old.

B. The Use of Precedents

Our empirical data show that Finnish, Danish and Swedish supreme courts' use of precedents in leading constitutional law cases is relatively limited compared to other Nordic countries (see Figure 2).

Figure 2 Proportion of cases in which the opinion refers to a precedent

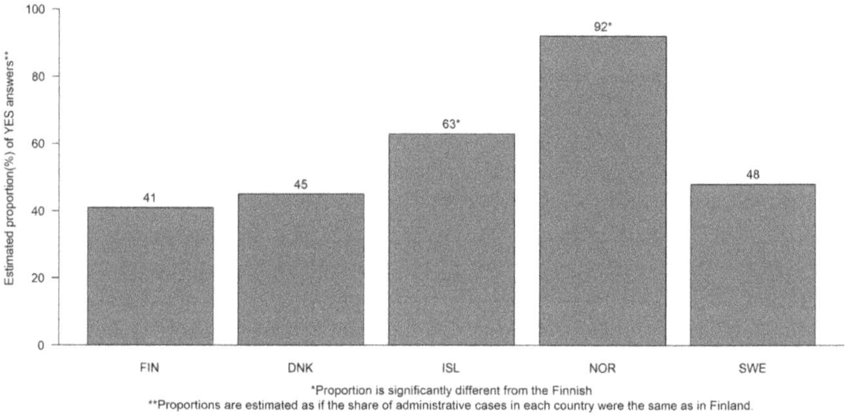

In the Nordic countries, there is no doctrine of binding precedent. In some of these countries (ie, Finland, Sweden, and Denmark), precedent has played a remarkably small role in the formal and doctrinal sense. One reason for this could be that according to the Finnish, Swedish, and Danish legal cultural attitude, moral and political questions should be left to national parliaments, not to courts of law.[38]

At the global level, there is a strong assumption that case-based reasoning is used by all courts and tribunals adjudicating constitutional cases, regardless of whether these bodies operate in common law or civil law systems. An argument based on a court's own authority is seen as one of the most significant and

[38] B Bengtsson, 'Den svenska grundlagen och domstolarna' (1998) *Jussens Venner* 56; I Cameron, 'The Influence of European Human Rights Law on National Law' in M Hemmo, EJ Hollo and P Letto-Vanamo (eds), *National Law and Europeanisation* (Helsinki, Suomalainen Lakimiesyhdistys, 2009) 63, 73; Husa (n 18) 106. Nergelius has, however, criticised the old idea of judges limiting themselves to legal interpretation and leaving all the political decision-making to the political, democratically elected bodies; see J Nergelius, 'Between Collectivism and Constitutionalism: The Nordic Countries and Constitutionalism – A "Final Frontier" or a Period of Transition?' in J Nergelius (ed), *Constitutionalism: New Challenges. European Law from a Nordic Perspective* (Leiden, Martinus Nijhoff Publishers, 2008) 119, 130.

persuasive modes of argumentation in current constitutional jurisprudence.[39] From a European perspective, European constitutional courts refer most often to their own previous case law. This way of arguing, based on a court's own authority, is particularly evident in the German Federal Constitutional Court.[40]

When analysing the role of precedents in Finnish constitutional law, one must remember that the number of court cases in the field of constitutional law is relatively small, and all these cases concern constitutional rights or the delegation of laws and have no connection to questions about the separation of powers or competences of the highest state organs. In our dataset, out of 80 leading cases, 75 cases concern fundamental rights, and 21 cases relate to the delegation of laws.[41] The supreme court cases are pedagogically important because they show how the highest courts apply legal norms but also, to an extent, that they create the rules in practice.[42]

Interestingly, due to the rise of the Finnish fundamental rights doctrine since the modern catalogue of fundamental rights was introduced and the country joined the European human rights system in the 1990s, there has been a tendency to argue that precedent, in a persuasive sense, should play a more important role than it did before. Arguably, this school of thought has created pressure to move towards a legal culture in which courts and the judiciary would be de facto in more significant positions than before. As a result, this way of thinking about law in general seems to advocate for an ever-greater role for constitutional law-related rulings of supreme courts, specifically in the area of constitutional rights.[43] In addition, some scholars have argued that the word 'evident' should be removed from section 106 of the Constitution, since the current threshold for judicial review is said to be too high. In contrast, other legal scholars have stated that the word 'evident' is an essential part of the Finnish judicial review system and removing the 'evident' criteria would upset the Finnish system of constitutional review.[44]

Traditionally, the Nordic mentality has emphasised the role of parliaments, and judges have seen themselves more as executors of the legislators. The public has also trusted the democratically chosen legislators in the field of fundamental rights. Against this backdrop, the Nordic courts have mainly practiced judicial self-restraint. From a Finnish perspective, the principle of democracy has been taken seriously and, for a long time, the ex ante parliamentary control by the CLC was seen as sufficient and judicial control was not considered necessary.[45]

[39] M Florczak-Wator, 'Introduction' in M Florczak-Wator (ed), *Constitutional Law and Precedent: International Perspectives on Case-Based Reasoning* (London, Taylor & Francis, 2022) 1, 1–2.

[40] This is also shown in our aggregated (global) dataset. Germany has 100% for R19. However, not all European constitutional courts rank high – the Spanish and Italian constitutional courts are exceptions. See our dataset, K Kelemen, 'Nordic CONREASON Collection of Data on Constitutional Reasoning in the Nordic Supreme Courts (Version 1)', doi.org/10.60689/zmk7-0z14.

[41] See also n 20 and accompanying text above.

[42] See eg Husa (n 5) 30–31.

[43] For more on the importance of judicial human rights protection, see eg Ojanen (n 27).

[44] For arguments in favour of removing 'evident' criteria, see eg Lavapuro, Ojanen and Scheinin (n 1) 228. For arguments against, see eg Tuori (n 1) 384 and 391.

[45] A Jyränki, 'Taking Democracy Seriously: The Problem of the Control of the Constitutionality of legislation: The Case of Finland' in M Sakslin (ed), *The Finnish Constitution in Transition* (Helsinki,

Norway is slightly different in terms of judicial self-restraint than other Nordic countries, but the Norwegian Supreme Court has also avoided open conflicts with the Parliament.[46] The rise of international human rights obligations and EU law have, however, increased the role of courts in all Nordic countries. Consequently, the judicial protection of human rights has become more central.[47]

C. Arguments Relating to the European Convention on Human Rights

When the use of arguments relating to the ECHR is analysed, Finland, Iceland, and Norway stand out, as they use ECHR-related arguments more than other Nordic supreme courts (see Figure 3).

Figure 3 Proportion of cases in which the opinion seeks to interpret constitutional law in light of the ECHR and ECtHR case-law

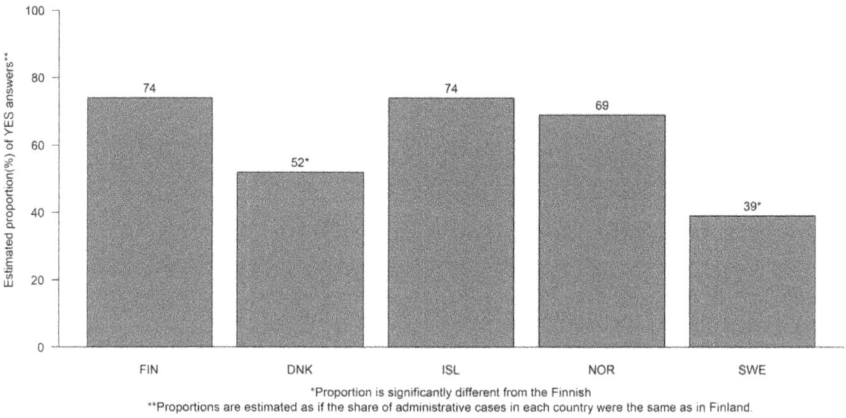

Regarding the formal incorporation of ECHR obligations, Finland and now also Sweden in 2024 are the only Nordic countries which have ratified the newest Protocol of the ECHR on advisory opinions (Protocol 16).[48] Ratifications of ECHR obligations affect the legal status of ECHR norms at the national level and, consequently, the use of international norms in court argumentation. Interestingly, according to our data, the Swedish Supreme Courts seem to be far behind their

Finnish Society of Constitutional Law, 1995) 6; T Pohjolainen and J Husa, 'Prospects of Reforming the Finnish Constitution' (1997) 3 *European Public Law* 45, 51.

[46] See eg M Wind, 'The Nordics, the EU and the Reluctance Towards Supranational Judicial Review' (2010) 48 *Journal of Common Market Studies* 1039; Hautamäki (n 2) 172; Husa (n 28) 12; Ervo (n 37) 101.

[47] See eg Ojanen (n 27) 140.

[48] Norway signed it in 2014 but has not ratified it yet. For the list of ratifications, see Council of Europe Treaty Office, Chart of Signatures and Ratifications of Treaty 214, www.coe.int/en/web/conventions/full-list?module=signatures-by-treaty&treatynum=214.

Finnish counterparts in this regard, even though the legal literature has emphasised that Finland and Sweden are more receptive to the ECHR's law than Denmark and Norway.[49] The difference may be related to how the leading cases in each country were selected. In the Finnish case selection, the ECHR cases were considered constitutional cases, whereas in the Swedish case selection, the researcher did not automatically classify ECHR cases as constitutional cases.[50]

The ECHR is not hierarchically superior to national law in any of the Nordic legal systems. The national legislator determines the status of an incorporated convention.[51] In Finland, the ECHR has the status of an ordinary statute. In addition, the ECHR and other human rights treaties binding on Finland have been described as having semi-constitutional status.[52] This is because constitutional and human rights are dealt with together in section 22 of the Constitution,[53] and the constitutionality control exercised by the CLC includes determining whether a legislative act conforms to international human rights obligations (section 74 of the Constitution).[54]

The role of the ECHR was evident when the Finnish fundamental rights catalogue was fully amended in 1995. For example, the right to a fair trial as protected in Article 6 of the ECHR was a clear role model for the Finnish constitution-makers when legal safeguards for individuals were drafted (section 21 of the Constitution).[55] Furthermore, constitutional pluralism is often highlighted, meaning that it is no longer possible or even meaningful to distinguish between constitutional, European, and international systems for the protection of human rights.[56] In the same vein, the Finnish Constitution emphasises the congruence of national fundamental rights protection and international human rights protection (sections 22 and 74 of the Constitution). In addition, legal scholars have highlighted how the case law of the European Court of Human Rights (ECtHR) is being cited often, even by district courts.[57] Consequently, our empirical data which show that the Finnish Supreme Courts regularly use the ECHR in their constitutional

[49] Husa (n 18) 110; L Ervo, 'Förhållandet mellan Europadomstolen och Nationella Domstolar – Finländska Perspektiv' (2006) 144 *Tidskrift utgiven av Juridiska Föreningen i Finland* 411; J Niemi-Kiesiläinen, 'Comparing Finland and Sweden: The Structure of Legal Argument' in J Husa, K Nuotio and H Pihlajamäki (eds), *Nordic Law: Between Tradition and Dynamism* (Antwerp, Intersentia, 2007) 89, 107.

[50] See Åsa Elmerot's analysis in ch 7, section I(C) in this volume.

[51] See, eg, DT Björgvinsson, 'The Effect of the Judgments of the ECtHR before the National Courts: A Nordic Approach?' (2016) 85 *Nordic Journal of International Law* 303.

[52] See ch 1, section II(D) in this volume.

[53] See section 22 of the Finnish Constitution: 'The public authorities shall guarantee the observance of basic rights and liberties and human rights.'

[54] See eg Ojanen (n 27) 155; Ojanen and Salminen (n 14) 378.

[55] See Government Bill (HE) 309/1993, at 21, 39, 73–4.

[56] See eg Ojanen (n 27) 165; cf Husa (n 5) 32, who argues that it would be going too far to state that the borders relating to national, European, and international systems for the protection of human rights have totally disappeared.

[57] T Tuominen, '"Common Constitutional Tradition" as Europeanization of Constitutional Culture: The Finnish Case' (2022) 14 *Italian Journal of Public Law* 11, 22.

interpretation align with the Finnish legal cultural mentality, which emphasises the role of the ECHR when national constitutional rights are interpreted.

In the Nordic countries, there have sometimes been voices critical of the ECtHR's human rights interpretations. There have been fewer critics in Finland than in other Nordic countries.[58] The reluctance to criticise the ECHR system might be an aspect of Finnish legalism. The general attitude of Finnish courts to both the ECHR system and EU law has been harmonising and loyal.[59] This might partly explain why Finland, Iceland, and Norway stand out from Sweden and Denmark when the use of the ECHR as an argument is measured.

Somewhat surprisingly, the Finnish Supreme Courts stand out from other Nordic countries when the use of the *pro homine* principle is measured.[60] This is true even in comparison with the Latin American countries (see Figure 4).

Figure 4 Proportion of cases invoking a *pro homine* or *pro persona* principle in Nordic and Latin American supreme and constitutional courts (N28)[61]

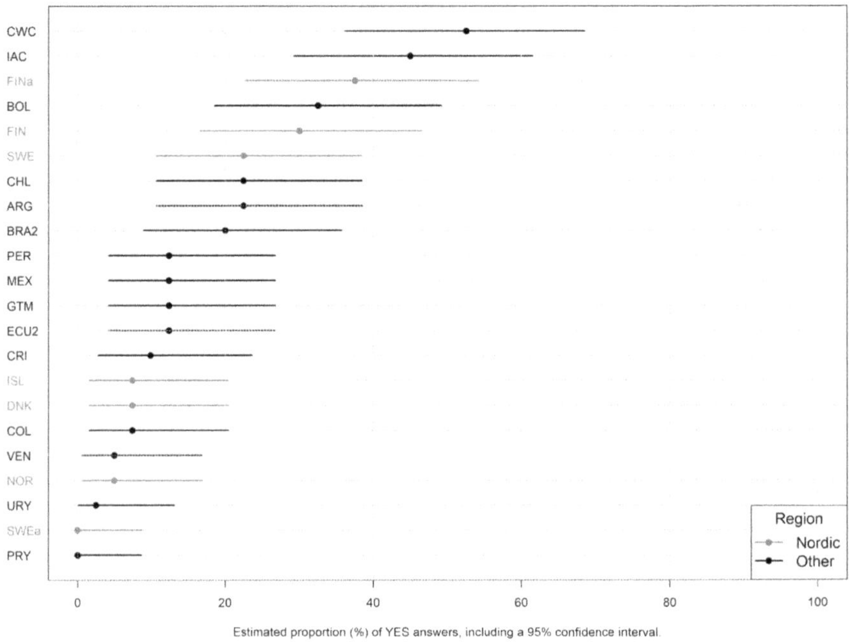

[58] See eg J Elo Rytter, 'Går Menneskerettighedsdomstolen for Vidt? Fortolkning og Retsskabelse i Strasbourg' (2006) *Juristen* 9; Ervo (n 49).

[59] See eg Lavapuro, Ojanen and Scheinin (n 1) 241; Miettinen (n 24); Ojanen and Salminen (n 14) 373.

[60] Proportions relating to N28 are: FIN 34%, DNK 8%*, ISL 7%*, NOR 5%*, and SWE 11%*.

[61] The table also includes the proportion for an international court: the Inter-American Court of Human Rights (IAC).

The other Nordic supreme courts seldom use arguments relating to the effectiveness of constitutional rights, whereas the Finnish Supreme Courts occasionally use the effectiveness of rights as an argument when the case concerns constitutional rights. The relatively frequent use of the *pro homine* principle is partly linked to the relatively common use of the ECHR (N18_2) in the Finnish leading constitutional law cases. Our statistical findings reveal that the statistical correlation between N28 and N18_2 is 0.28. Accordingly, there is a positive but weak correlation between variables N28 and N18_2. Traditionally, the ECtHR's interpretation of the ECHR has emphasised the practical and effective protection of Convention rights. Consequently, it should not be a surprise that the way in which the ECtHR has interpreted the ECHR influences the Finnish Supreme Courts' constitutional interpretation when the ECHR is used as an argument. The interpretative praxis of the ECtHR is an integral part of the national courts' reasoning when citing ECHR rights.[62] For example, in a case which concerned children's rights, the KKO pointed out that

> according to the ECHR, the state has a positive obligation to ensure that national legislation does not lead to conflicts with the rights protected under Article 8 ECHR. There is also a general principle in Section 22 of the Constitution according to which public authorities have an obligation to protect fundamental rights and human rights.[63]

Another explanation for the rather frequent use of the *pro homine* principle in Finland is the doctrine of effective protection of constitutional and human rights enshrined in section 22 of the Constitution. The preparatory works underline that public authorities are obliged, to a certain extent and in certain circumstances, to actively promote and protect the effective exercise of fundamental rights.[64] Interpretations of the effective protection of constitutional rights are closely linked to the well-established Finnish constitutional doctrine on constitutionally conforming interpretations, which requires that courts must choose the justifiable option for interpreting the law that best promotes constitutional rights.[65] In Finland, constitutionally conforming interpretations are important and arguably serve as the main vehicle for enforcing the Constitution, since the powers of judicial review are limited.[66] However, since our research focused on interpretations

[62] See eg E Bjorge, *Domestic Application of the ECHR: Courts as Faithful Trustees* (Oxford, Oxford University Press, 2015); H Keller and A Stone Sweet (eds), *A Europe of Rights. The Impact of the ECHR on National Legal Systems* (Oxford, Oxford University Press, 2008).

[63] KKO 2012:11, para 25.

[64] See Government Bill (HE) 309/1993, at 75: 'The effective exercise of fundamental rights often requires effective action by public authorities.'

[65] The CLC has developed the doctrine on constitutional-friendly interpretation; see CLC (PeVL) 6/1988.

[66] See eg M Klatt (ed), *Constitutionally Conforming Interpretation: Comparative Perspectives* (Oxford, Hart Publishing, 2023).

of constitutional provisions, we excluded constitutionally conforming interpretations of statutory law from the analysis.[67]

The CLC explicitly supported international human rights-friendly interpretation for the first time when Finland incorporated the ECHR in 1990.[68] According to that principle, there is a duty to interpret national law, including national constitutional rights, in a way that fulfils international human rights obligations. However, the Finnish doctrine emphasises that these obligations create only a minimum standard for the protection of human rights, so national constitutional rights protection can be at a higher level than international human rights obligations.[69]

Even though Finnish courts have generally adopted European standards in interpreting constitutional rights, there has been some resistance. The ECHR system relies heavily on the interpretations of the ECtHR and, therefore, puts less emphasis on the power and role of the democratically elected national legislators. The ECHR power balance between courts and the legislature fits Nordic constitutionalism rather poorly, particularly regarding the division of competences between courts and parliaments. The different role of courts in the ECHR system compared to the Finnish legal culture is concretised in some of the Finnish cases. In these cases, Finnish judges have shown some reluctance to follow the interpretations of the ECtHR in relation to Finnish law and have argued that the ECtHR has not fully understood national peculiarities in this respect. Our quantitative data (N18_2) have some limitations in this regard: they do not show whether a reference to the ECHR means that the court followed the ECtHR's line of interpretation or whether the court rejected the line of argumentation used by the ECtHR. Indeed, the aim of our research was to measure the openness to that type of argument. For example, the KHO did not fully accept the ECtHR's interpretations in the case *X v Finland* (2012),[70] which concerned the compatibility of the Finnish mental health legislation with requirements of Article 5(1) of the ECHR. The KHO pointed out that in the ECtHR's assessment of the procedure for continuing involuntary treatment, it did not take into account the adequacy of the remedies and procedure and other safeguards under national law when evaluating whether the system fulfils the conditions provided in the ECHR.[71]

D. References to Non-judicial Bodies

As explained above, one of the key features of the Finnish constitutional culture is the existence of the CLC and non-judicial ex ante review. Against this background,

[67] See A Jakab, A Dyevre and G Itzcovich (eds), *Comparative Constitutional Reasoning* (Cambridge, Cambridge University Press, 2017) and the introductory explanations in Section 2 of the Codebook in the Appendix.

[68] See CLC (PeVL) 2/1990.

[69] See eg Lavapuro, Ojanen and Scheinin (n 1) 228; Ojanen and Salminen (n 14) 376.

[70] *X v Finland*, App. No. 34806/04, ECHR 2012 (extracts).

[71] KHO 2012:75.

it is hardly surprising that the Finnish Supreme Courts stand out from other Nordic countries when one analyses the use of references to national non-judicial bodies in leading constitutional cases (see Figure 5).

Figure 5 Proportion of cases in which there is a reference to a domestic non-judicial body

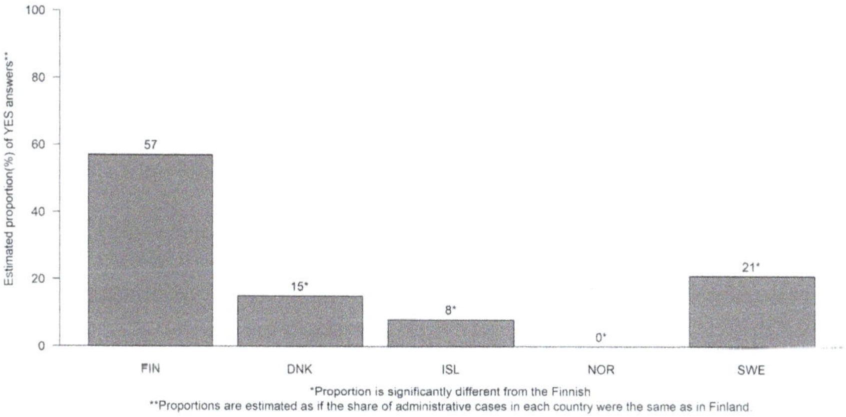

Legal scholars have, however, criticised the Finnish Supreme Courts for seemingly not taking judicial notice of the interpretative practice of the CLC.[72] Surprisingly, our empirical data show the contrary: the Finnish Supreme Courts rely rather frequently on the reasoning and praxis of the CLC in the leading constitutional cases. Frankly, to do otherwise would go against the Finnish constitutional mindset.[73] In previous studies, scholars have highlighted that the Finnish Supreme Courts base their constitutional reasoning more on the ECHR than the interpretative praxis of the CLC.[74]

There may, however, be some risks to rely so heavily on the interpretative practice of the CLC. Keeping in mind that the CLC is composed of MPs, the greatest challenge is undoubtedly disentangling the roles of politician and CLC member; that is, stepping outside of partisan politics to assume the neutral and independent role of guardian of the constitution. To be sure, this challenge is sometimes too great; in the present CLC (formed in 2023), there have been cases where party politics has arguably taken precedence over impartial constitutional interpretation.[75]

[72] Lavapuro, Ojanen and Scheinin (n 1) 233.

[73] As Husa put it, 'the practice of judges defying the will of democratically elected majority lawmakers has certainly not been a traditional part of Finnish constitutional morality'. See Husa (n 5) 159.

[74] See eg Lavapuro, Ojanen and Scheinin (n 1); J Lavapuro, 'Ihmisoikeuskulttuurin murrokset? Eräitä kvantitatiivisia havaintoja korkeimman oikeuden ratkaisukäytännössä tapahtuneista muutoksista v. 1976–2010' in T Hyttinen and K Weckström (eds), *Turun yliopiston oikeustieteellinen tiedekunta 50 vuotta* (Turku, Turun yliopisto) 357, 367–68.

[75] The most recent example is the legislative proposal concerning the pushback of migrants on the Russian border, which was introduced and accepted in summer 2024, even though the legislation is undisputably against the Constitution, the ECHR and EU law (especially the non-refoulement

In addition, the CLC frequently gives guidance how the law in question should be interpreted in courts. For example, the CLC gave the contested statement concerning the legislative proposal on the pushback of migrants on the Russian border, which was introduced and accepted in summer 2024. Besides many constitutional problems relating to the CLC statement, the CLC also gave guidance to courts if they are applying the law in concrete cases.[76] The CLC reminded that the section 106 of the Constitution is not applicable in parliamentary Acts which are legislated in constitutional order.[77] However, the CLC ignored the fact that constitutional doctrine recognises that in the application of section 106 of the Constitution and when reviewing the constitutionality of parliamentary Acts, the courts understand international human rights obligations in the same interpretative standing with constitutional rights.[78]

Consequently, there have been some concerns regarding backsliding in terms of the rule of law in Finland, and the credibility and legitimacy of the CLC have been questioned.[79] Finnish courts may face a new challenge in constitutional questions if the CLC abandons its role as a legal interpreter and its interpretations will be politicised. In this case the Finnish courts can no longer automatically rely on CLC interpretations in constitutional cases.

IV. Differences between the Supreme Court (KKO) and the Supreme Administrative Court (KHO) in Constitutional Interpretation

A. References to the ECHR

Legal scholars have pointed out that the KKO regularly refers to the decisions of international courts and tribunals in cases concerning fundamental and human rights.[80] Similarly, the KHO has been described as taking extensive account of

principle). This was the first time that the CLC decided to ignore the constitutional tradition (which was more than 100 years old) of following the unanimous opinion of external constitutional law experts.

[76] See M Sormunen, 'Legalising Illegality – Finland's Proposed Pushback Legislation' *Verfassungsblog* 2024, verfassungsblog.de/legalising-illegality/, DOI: 10.59704/62fce8d640d64d9b.

[77] CLC (PeVL) 29/2024.

[78] See eg KKO 2024:20.

[79] M Dahlberg and A Kantola, 'Tensions in Finland's Ex Ante Constitutional Review: The Interplay of Politics, Law, and Media' (2024) 22(2) *International Journal of Constitutional Law* 376; T Ojanen, 'Finnish Constitutional Exceptionalism: The Pluralist System of Constitutional Review Combining Ex-Ante and Ex-Post Functions of Review' in M Granat (ed), *Constitutionality of Law Without a Constitutional Court: A View from Europe* (Abingdon, Routledge, 2024) 219.

[80] H Pihlajamäki (ed), *Lainkäyttöä läpi vuosisadan: Näkökulmia korkeimman oikeuden historiaan 1918–2018* (Helsinki, Edita, 2018) 225; T Ojanen, 'Perusoikeuspluralismi kotimaisessa tuomioistuimessa' (2011) *Defensor Legis* 442, 448.

fundamental and human rights law as part of its reasoning.[81] However, it has been pointed out that fundamental and human rights law play a greater role in the KHO than the number of references alone would suggest. This means that even though the ECHR has been carefully studied in the legal question at hand, there might be no references to the ECHR in the KHO's judgment.[82]

In previous research, the scholars have emphasised some differences between the two Finnish Supreme Courts in terms of their constitutional reasoning. The main difference seems to be the use of the ECHR as an argument in constitutional cases. Scholars have claimed that the KKO is more active than the KHO in using the ECHR as an argument.[83] Our empirical research confirms that the KKO refers significantly more to the ECHR than the KHO in key constitutional decisions. The relative proportions are 84 per cent for the KKO and 62.5 per cent for the KHO. Moreover, a further analysis shows that in the last three years (2020–22), only four out of ten constitutional decisions of the KHO use the ECHR as a justification (25 per cent) which is less than half of the overall share (62.5 per cent).

One possible reason for the difference in reasoning between the KKO and the KHO may be, first of all, that in criminal cases decided by the KKO, the ECtHR tends to interpret the rights of the accused and of a fair trial rather broadly. Of the KKO decisions analysed in this study, the number of criminal and civil cases is almost equal (15 criminal cases, 17 civil cases, 8 petitions[84]). Looking more closely, 15 criminal cases form 37.5 per cent of all KKO-cases in the sample. This is a considerable number especially considering that there are no criminal cases at all in the sample of the KHO. However, issues of the right to a fair trial are also frequently raised in administrative proceedings, where an extensive body of ECtHR case law is available. In my view, the different types of disputes do not therefore fully explain the differences in ECHR-related reasoning between the KKO and the KHO. Of course, the decisions of the KHO may also concern constitutional issues other than those related to fundamental and human rights, such as the delegation of legislative powers and the self-government of municipalities. This may be one of the main reasons why the KKO refers in its constitutional cases more to the ECHR than the KHO.

B. References to the EU Law

As regards the references to the EU law, legal scholars have previously pointed out that the KHO refers to the EU Charter of Fundamental Rights and Freedoms

[81] Ojanen (n 80) 448.

[82] M Jokisipilä, 'Korkein hallinto-oikeus 1940–2018 – hallintolainkäyttö alati muuttuvassa maailmassa' in M Kari, J Kekkonen and M Jokisipilä (eds), *Oikeusvaltion rakentaja. Korkein hallinto-oikeus 100 vuotta* (Helsinki, Edita, 2018) 112, 131.

[83] Lavapuro, Ojanen and Scheinin (n 1) 243.

[84] Petitions concern usually extraordinary appeals where reversal of a final judgment is requested.

in its reasoning more than the KKO does.[85] It has also been stated quite directly that the work of administrative courts is influenced more by EU law than by international human rights treaties.[86] In our research, we did not measure references to the Charter specifically; we only measured references to sources of EU law in general (N18_1). The relative proportions are 7.5 per cent for the KKO and 17.5 per cent for the KHO. In our sample, the KKO refers less to EU law in constitutional reasoning than the KHO, which seems to confirm the assumption; in the leading constitutional cases, this is certainly the case, even though the difference is not statistically significant (pv=0.311).

The wider scope of EU law in administrative law matters is, in my view, one obvious reason why the KHO makes greater use of EU law sources in its constitutional argumentation than the KKO. EU law has traditionally been more concerned with public law – ie between the state and the individual – than, for example, with legal relations between individuals. The Treaty reforms have naturally changed the Union's competence, giving it a legal basis for regulating traditional civil and criminal law matters under Union law. On the other hand, there has been a strong tradition that EU law continues to regulate specifically administrative matters.[87]

Scholars can often give an over-optimistic picture of the reference to the EU Charter of Fundamental Rights as part of a judicial constitutional argument.[88] However, reference to EU law in the constitutional argumentation of Supreme Courts is, overall, quite limited, and the main international source of constitutional argumentation of Finnish Supreme Courts is the ECHR. This is not surprising, given the relatively slow legal development of the European Union in the field of fundamental rights. The EU Charter of Fundamental Rights only became legally binding in 2009, whereas the ECHR system has been developing since the 1950s. Of course, the Court of Justice of the European Union (CJEU) began to develop a system of fundamental rights protection at the EU level already in the 1970s. In addition, the ECHR incorporated into Finnish legal system in the 1990. Consequently, the picture is complex, and the age of the ECHR and EU Charter do not alone explain why the ECHR is more frequently used than the EU Charter in the Finnish Supreme Courts' constitutional cases.

[85] T Ojanen, 'Räppänä raollaan Eurooppaan – Euroopan unionin perusoikeudet Suomen oikeudessa' in T Heinonen and J Lavapuro (eds), *Oikeuskulttuurin eurooppalaistuminen: Ihmisoikeuksien murroksesta kansainväliseen vuorovaikutukseen* (Helsinki, Suomalainen Lakimiesyhdistys, 2012) 241, 259–62.

[86] P Hallberg, 'Korkein hallinto-oikeus oikeusvaltiota rakentamassa' in E Aalto, P Vihervuori, N Jääskinen and T Arolainen (eds), *Korkein hallinto-oikeus 90 vuotta* (Helsinki, Korkein hallinto-oikeus, 2008) 18, 26–27.

[87] See eg H Kanninen, 'EY-oikeuden soveltamisesta korkeimmassa hallinto-oikeudessa' (2003) *Lakimies* 1256.

[88] See eg Ojanen (n 27) 161–63.

C. References to the Constitutional Law Committee

Regarding other differences between the two Finnish Supreme Courts' reasoning styles, we found a higher proportion of references to the opinions of non-judicial bodies (N27) in the KHO, and the difference is statistically significant (pv=0.012). The relative proportions are 42.5 per cent for the KKO and 72.5 per cent for the KHO. Legal scholars have criticised the fact that the importance of what the CLC has said about the constitutionality of the relevant law at the stage of its enactment has sometimes been overemphasised, especially in the decisions of the KKO.[89]

This study shows that, as a rule, the Finnish Supreme Courts refer to the CLC whenever a question concerning the constitutionality of a parliamentary Act is under consideration. In doing so, the courts often reiterate the primacy of the role of the CLC in reviewing the constitutionality of laws. In the present data, the total number of decisions invoking section 106 of the Constitution (which obliges the courts to set aside a parliamentary Act if it is in evident conflict with the Constitution) was 17 in the KHO and 14 in the KKO. Thus, the difference between the KKO and the KHO in referring to the CLC cannot be explained by the fact that there would have been clearly more section 106-related decisions in the KHO than in the KKO.

One reason why the KHO makes more reference to the opinions of the CLC may be that its constitutional cases concern also issues other than fundamental and human rights. For example, in case KHO 2006:58, the KHO refers to the statement of the CLC when dealing with the relationship between municipal environmental protection regulations and section 80(2) of the Constitution which regulates how legislation can be delegated. In our data, the constitutional questions before the KKO always concern fundamental and human rights. An exception is the judgment KKO 2011:43, which concerned private parking control and its relation to the significant exercise of public power regulated by section 124 of the Constitution. All other decisions of the KKO in this study are related to fundamental and human rights, whereby reference to the ECHR and its case law may be more relevant than relying on the interpretations of the CLC.

D. References to Precedents

There is also a statistically significant difference between the two Finnish Supreme Courts in terms of the use of precedential arguments: the KKO has a higher

[89] T Ojanen, 'Eduskunnan perustuslakivaliokunta ja tuomioistuimet – kohti valtiosääntöistä dialogia?' in P Letto-Vanamo, O Mäenpää and T Ojanen (eds), *Juhlajulkaisu Mikael Hidén 1939–7/12–2009* (Helsinki, Suomalainen Lakimiesyhdistys, 2009) 239, 247–48.

proportion of arguments relating to precedents compared to the KHO (more than double; pv=0.001). The respective proportions are 60 per cent for the KKO and 22.5 per cent for the KHO. The result obtained in this study is in line with previous literature which has highlighted the fact that the KHO is more reluctant than the KKO to refer to its own previous decisions.[90]

The possible reasons for the differences may be related to the fact that the KKO had the first version of the leave to appeal system in 1922 and gradually became a full court of precedent in the 1980s, whereas the leave to appeal system in the KHO entered into force only in 2020. In addition, since the administrative court system is only two-tiered in Finland, the KHO has had a mixed function as a regular appellate court and a court providing significant case law. In this sense, the KHO's transformation from a court of appeal to a court of precedent is still in progress.[91] Against this background, it is understandable that since the KKO has a long tradition of setting precedents, it may be tempted to refer to its own case law instead of interpretations of the CLC.

E. Concluding Thoughts

Despite the slight differences, our empirical findings show that in general there are no significant differences in constitutional interpretation by the Finnish Supreme Courts. This is a positive finding, since the biggest challenge in a system with two Supreme Courts is undoubtedly ensuring consistent constitutional interpretations in both. Nor should the Supreme Courts find themselves in a situation where there is a kind of contest to see who has the last word on a particular constitutional question.[92]

Statistical analysis of the Supreme Courts' reference technique is useful in revealing key differences between different reasoning practices. It is clear, of course, that statistical analysis only provides a basis for a more in-depth analysis of the differences in reasoning and citation practices, as well as their possible causes and consequences.

[90] J Virolainen and P Martikainen, *Tuomion perusteleminen* (Helsinki, Talentum, 2010) 422.

[91] See eg A Nylund, 'An Introduction to Finnish Legal Culture' in S Koch and MM Kjølstad (eds), *Handbook on Legal Cultures: A Selection of the World's Legal Cultures* (Cham, Springer, 2023) 525, 536–37; P Letto-Vanamo, 'Finland' in JM Smits, J Husa, C Valcke and M Narciso (eds), *Elgar Encyclopedia of Comparative Law* (Edward Elgar Publishing, 2023) 130, 133.

[92] Surprisingly, in 2024 the KKO and KHO had an open dispute over the question relating to the interpretation of the Constitution (section 107). Both courts had a pending case concerning reasonable level of legal aid fee. First KKO gave its judgment (KKO 2024:71) where it concluded that the level of legal aid fee defined in a decree is too low and therefore does not meet the requirements set out in the act of the reasonableness of the level of legal aid fee. Since there is a conflict between the decree and the parliamentary act, the decree must not be applied (section 107 of the Constitution). Just after the KKO's judgment, the KHO gave a fully opposite interpretation (KHO 2024:129) on the same constitutional question. The saga ended in April 2025 when KKO made a U-turn in its constitutional interpretation (KKO 2025:38) and followed KHO's outcome in the constitutional question.

To avoid differences between the constitutional interpretations of the KKO and the KHO, it would be important that both courts use a similar legal source as the basis for their constitutional interpretation. I argue that the use of the international human rights' normative basis and its interpretative jurisprudence or the use of purely national constitutional sources of law when considering a constitutional case can lead to very different outcomes in constitutional interpretation. As constitutional interpretations are often politically, socially and morally charged, it would be important that both Finnish Supreme Courts are on an equal footing in resolving these issues.

V. Key Concepts in Constitutional Reasoning

Legalism and a strongly positivistic attitude to law and legal interpretation have been described as key features of the Finnish constitutional culture. The Russian Era (1809–1917) and the Russification (ie, when the Finnish system was made to adapt to Russian rules and procedures) were resisted using formal legal argumentation to back Finnish interpretations of constitutional documents.[93] Arguably, the legalistic tradition reflects the Finnish attitude to constitutional norms.

In the Nordic context, the Finnish legal culture has often been described as legalistic, unlike other Nordic countries. The fact that Finland was once an autonomous part of Russia while trying to defend the rights of the Grand Duchy of Finland may be one reason for the different attitude to law in Finland compared to other Nordic countries.[94] The alleged legalism refers traditionally to the position of statutory law as the supreme legal source. However, legalism in a wider sense represents an essential aspect of the attitude of Finnish civil servants and the judiciary towards the law.[95] Nevertheless, some scholars have stated that the notion that legality plays a greater role in Finland than in other Nordic countries is a myth. As a matter of fact, it has been also argued that legality is a basic tenet of Nordic law.[96]

Our empirical findings show that Denmark and Sweden use the concept of legality the most in their leading constitutional law cases. Finland and Iceland share second place, and Norway is in last place (see Figure 6).[97]

[93] M Hidén, 'Constitutional Rights in the Legislative Process: The Finnish System of Advance Control of Legislation' 17 (1973) *Scandinavian Studies in Law* 95, 104; Tuominen (n 57) 13–14.

[94] P Letto-Vanamo, 'Finland' (n 91) 130; A Aarnio, 'Precedent in Finland' in N MacCormick and RS Summers (eds), *Interpreting Precedents* (Aldershot, Ashgate, 1997) 65, 72.

[95] J Husa, K Nuotio and H Pihlajamäki, 'Nordic Law: Between Tradition and Dynamism' in J Husa, K Nuotio and H Pihlajamäki (eds), *Nordic Law: Between Tradition and Dynamism* (Antwerp, Intersentia, 2007) 1, 13; P Letto-Vanamo and D Tamm, 'Nordic Legal Mind' in P Letto-Vanamo and D Tamm (eds), *Nordic Law in European Context* (Cham, Springer, 2019) 1, 7–8.

[96] Ervo (n 37) 95.

[97] See Morten Nadim's analysis in ch 6 in this volume.

Figure 6 Proportion of the cases in which the principle of legality is invoked

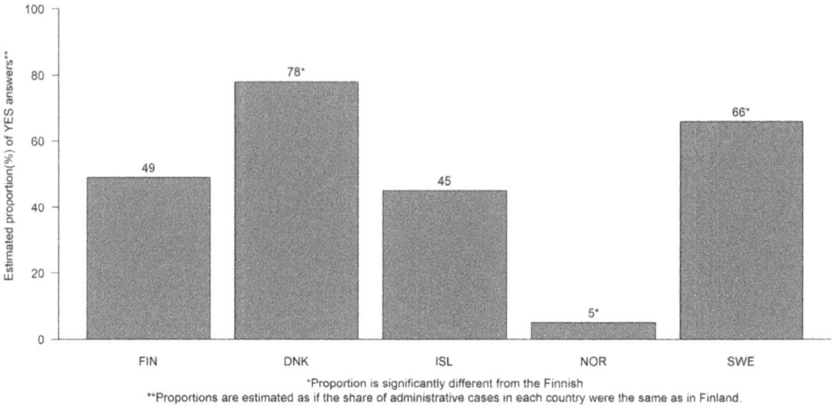

Legalism is of course a much wider concept than the principle of legality. However, I would claim that the emphasis on the principle of legality, lawfulness and the rule that certain matters must be regulated by Parliamentary Act (and not by lower degrees) indicates the same mentality and attitude which is also at the heart in legalism.[98] Consequently, our empirical findings do not exactly support the traditional view, which emphasises Finland as the most legalistic Nordic country. The case selection might have affected the number of references to the principle of legality: if the majority of the leading constitutional cases concern the delegation of laws, references to legality are more or less automatic. For example, there is a statistically significant difference between the KKO and the KHO. The KHO has a higher proportion of N31_2 and the explaining factor is that the KHO has several cases in the sample which concern the delegation of laws whereas the KKO has only one case in the sample where the main constitutional question was the use of public power and requirement of legislation (KKO 2011:43).

When it comes to the use of the principle of proportionality, the two Finnish Supreme Courts use a proportionality doctrine developed by other courts (mainly the ECtHR) and the CLC; they do not have their own doctrine on proportionality.[99] As pointed out previously, since Finnish courts frequently base their analyses on ECtHR case law, the principle of proportionality as emphasised in the ECHR system is included. Our empirical findings rank Finland in first place in terms of the use of proportionality argumentation (see Figure 7).

[98] See explanations of variable N31_2 of the Codebook in the Appendix.
[99] Tuominen (n 57) 21–22.

Figure 7 Proportions of the Nordic countries relating to the use of proportionality arguments in leading constitutional cases

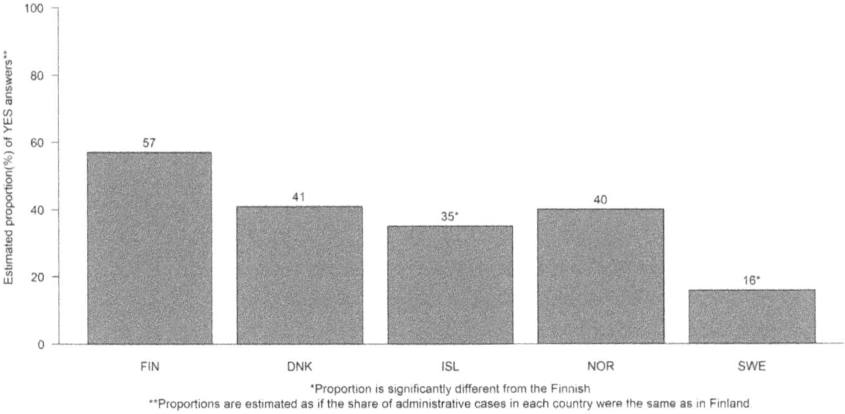

Denmark and Norway more or less share second place and Iceland is third, whereas Sweden is quite far behind the other Nordic countries. The previously mentioned finding which proves that the Finnish Supreme Courts use the ECHR in their constitutional interpretation quite frequently partly explains the frequent use of the proportionality principle in their argumentation. Furthermore, most of the constitutional cases decided by the Finnish Supreme Courts concern constitutional rights. In these cases, balancing different constitutional rights or constitutional rights and other interests of society is essential and brings proportionality to the fore. However, this was the case also in other Nordic countries. So, the sample's focus on constitutional rights does not explain why Finland stands out from other Nordic countries in this respect. One possible explanation may be the crucial role of the CLC in the Finnish Supreme Courts' constitutional interpretation as explained above. Indeed, the CLC has developed a constitutional doctrine relating to the restriction of constitutional rights which requires that limitations on constitutional rights are proportionate.[100]

VI. Conclusions

Overall, our study proves empirically that the key features of Finnish constitutionalism are: (1) a high level of respect for the democratically chosen legislator and a small role for the courts, (2) a relatively new and comprehensive catalogue of constitutional rights with a strong formal and substantive connection to the ECHR, and (3) a strong ex ante non-judicial constitutional review. The features

[100] See CLC (PeVM) 25/1994, at 5.

pull in slightly different directions when courts interpret constitutional provisions. By this I mean that the Finnish constitutional mentality regarding the legislature causes the courts to focus on the preparatory works and the praxis of the CLC, while exercising self-restraint in constitutional adjudication. By contrast, the strong formal and substantive connection to the ECHR leads courts to emphasise the judicial protection of constitutional rights and dynamic interpretations of rights.

In constitutional jurisprudence, an argument based on a court's own authority is seen as one of the most significant and persuasive modes of argumentation.[101] However, as this chapter has shown, the Finnish Supreme Courts do not frequently base their reasoning on their own authority. Instead, they base it on the authority of the Parliament by emphasising the constitution-maker's will and the authoritative interpretations of the CLC. The casuistic reasoning style of the Supreme Courts also partly explains why precedent-based reasoning does not prevail on a larger scale. Interestingly, however, our empirical analysis shows that the Finnish Supreme Courts have keenly adopted the ECHR as an argument in constitutional law cases as well as interpretative methods relating to the ECHR (*pro homine* and the principle of proportionality). In this sense, constitutional argumentation by the Finnish Supreme Courts mixes the traditional interpretative methods relating to respect for the legislature and trust in international human rights norms. The pragmatic form of interpretation combines the judicial self-restraint and dynamic views of the ECtHR.

Another peculiarity of Finnish constitutional law is that the CLC does not usually refer to case law by the domestic Supreme Courts. Even in cases involving interpretative tensions between the CLC and the Supreme Courts, the CLC has tended to disregard judicial interpretations.[102] In this sense, the constitutional dialogue goes only in one direction: the Finnish Supreme Courts refer to the interpretations of the CLC, but not the other way round.[103] However, a genuine dialogue between the CLC and Supreme Courts would be beneficial for the quality of constitutional argumentation and the overall development of constitutional interpretation in Finland. Instead of creating a dialogue between courts, the CLC has invoked a practice where it gives interpretative guidance towards courts when applying the law in concrete cases.[104]

Some scholars have argued that there are no analogies for the current form of Finnish constitutionalism to be found in the Nordic or German cultures, despite these being the systems that are otherwise closest to the Finnish legal system. Instead, the closest resemblance lies in the institutional solutions that

[101] Florczak-Wator, 'Introduction' (n 39).

[102] Lavapuro, Ojanen and Scheinin (n 1) 233.

[103] See more M Dahlberg, HL Karlsson and K Kelemen, 'The Nordic Courts: An Example of Cooperation and Dialogue' in K Pócza (ed), *Constitutional Review in Western Europe: Judicial-Legislative Relations in Comparative Perspective* (New York, Routledge, 2024) 288, 299–301.

[104] See section III(D) above.

have emerged in Commonwealth countries in recent decades.[105] Consequently, the central features of Finnish constitutionalism align with Stephen Gardbaum's presentation of new Commonwealth constitutionalism. Gardbaum argues that bills of rights in Canada, New Zealand, the United Kingdom and Australia revised or accepted in the twenty-first century are an experiment in a new third approach to structuring and institutionalising basic constitutional solutions. An essential feature of Commonwealth constitutionalism is the simultaneous presence of ex ante review and a weak form of judicial review.[106]

Political and moral questions are closely linked to constitutional rights, which have an influence on legal argumentation. Something might be left unsaid to avoid, for example, accusations of politicisation. All relevant arguments may not be openly stated, and constitutional argumentation might seek to conceal the political choices and evaluations made relating to constitutional rights. This is, of course, somewhat absurd since constitutional judges unavoidably create new laws and thereby produce policy outputs.[107] Bearing all this in mind, it is important to analyse the constitutional arguments explicitly mentioned by the courts, as we have done in this research. However, it is also important to study arguments in constitutional interpretation which are left unsaid. The latter should be studied with the help of qualitative empirical research methods, such as interviews.

[105] Lavapuro, Ojanen and Scheinin (n 1) 224.

[106] S Gardbaum, *The New Commonwealth Model of Constitutionalism: Theory and Practice* (Cambridge, Cambridge University Press, 2013) 21–46.

[107] See eg A Dyevre, 'The French Constitutional Council' in A Jakab, A Dyevre and G Itzcovich (eds), *Comparative Constitutional Reasoning* (Cambridge, Cambridge University Press, 2017) 323, 347.

6

International Constitutionalism: The Impact of International Law on Constitutional Reasoning in the Norwegian Supreme Court

MORTEN NADIM

I. Introduction

This chapter explores constitutional reasoning in the Norwegian Supreme Court. The analysis is based on the empirical findings of the Nordic CONREASON project,[1] in which 40 landmark cases from all seven Nordic Supreme Courts were coded using the categorisation of constitutional reasoning developed by the CONREASON project.[2] For the Norwegian Supreme Court, this means that 40 constitutional cases on which legal academics for the most part agree are landmark cases are coded with the intent to explore key constitutional concepts and argumentative patterns. Of the 40 cases, all but two cases are decided by strengthened panels, ie either grand chamber with 11 justices or *en banc*, as opposed to the normal five justice panels. The cases span from 1976 to 2022 and consist of multiple different legal topics within the scope of constitutional law.

The Nordic countries and their legal systems are often grouped together in comparative law as the 'Nordic legal family' because of the similarities between the five countries. In the Nordic CONREASON project, both the similarities and the differences in the constitutional reasoning of the countries' supreme courts are explored. In this chapter, I will focus on the Norwegian Supreme Court and

[1] Regarding the methodology of the Nordic CONREASON project, see N Pettersson and K Kelemen, ch 2 in this volume.

[2] See the A Jakab, A Dyevre and G Itzcovich, 'Introduction' in A Jakab, A Dyevre and G Itzcovich (eds), *Comparative Constitutional Reasoning* (Cambridge, Cambridge University Press, 2017) for a more detailed explanation.

highlight when the Court stands out from its Nordic counterparts.[3] To understand the particularities of the constitutional reasoning in landmark decisions of the Norwegian Supreme Court, it is necessary to provide legal, political, institutional, and academic context. Moreover, given the historical significance of the Norwegian Constitution, a brief overview of its constitutional history is essential to fully comprehend the constitutional reasoning in the Court.

II. Legal, Political, Institutional and Academic Context

A. Constitutional History

Norway's constitutional journey began in the early nineteenth century, during the tumultuous era of the Napoleonic Wars.[4] The Danish prince, Kristian Fredrik, who was sent to Norway as governor[5] in 1813 to protect the interests of the Danish crown against the threat from Sweden, initiated opposition against the Treaty of Kiel. To keep Norway independent, a Constituent Assembly convened at Eidsvoll in April 1814 to draft a constitution. On 16 May 1814, the Constituent Assembly agreed on a constitutional text and elected Prince Kristian Fredrik as King of Norway. He signed the Constitution on 17 May 1814, which still functions as the Constitution of Norway today, making it the second oldest written constitution in the world, and the oldest in Europe.[6] The drafters of the Norwegian Constitution were inspired by the enlightenment era, and they drew heavily on the US Federal Constitution from 1787 and the French constitutions from 1791 and 1795 when drafting the constitutional provisions.[7]

However, in November 1814, just months after the adoption of the Eidsvoll Constitution, the signatory states to the Treaty of Kiel forced Norway to uphold the treaty, thus forcing Norway into a union with Sweden, and consequently, Kristian Fredrik abdicated and returned to Denmark where he later became king. Norway's independence was short-lived. To accommodate the new political situation that the union represented, the newly formed Parliament had to amend the Constitution. The Parliament managed to preserve most of the Eidsvoll Constitution, but some amendments were necessary to reflect the compromises needed to realise

[3] In comparisons on country level, all proportions are estimated as if the share of administrative cases in each country would have been the same.

[4] The short historical overview is based on E Holmøyvik, D Michalsen and O Mestad, *Lærebok i forfatningsrett,* (Oslo, Pax, 2015) 15–39. See also O Mestad, 'Grunnlovshistoria – eit oversyn' in O Mestad and D Michalsen (eds), *Grunnloven: Historisk kommentarutgave 1814-2020* (Oslo, Universitetsforlaget, 2021) 39–52.

[5] '*Stattholder*' in Norwegian.

[6] F Sejersted, 'Grunnlovens funksjon i de nordiske land' (2014) 127 *Tidsskrift for Rettsvitenskap* 535, 536.

[7] Holmøyvik, Michalsen and Mestad (n 4) 18.

the union between Norway and Sweden. The union with Sweden was a personal union, which made the Swedish king also the king of Norway. However, Norway retained its own parliament – Stortinget – its own government, and in June 1815 established its own supreme court as a court of last instance. Before 1814, the court of last instance had been the Danish Supreme Court in Copenhagen. The amendments to the Constitution primarily concerned the personal royal power and foreign policy, which was the King's domain also in the original Eidsvoll Constitution. Therefore, the Eidsvoll Constitution's essence remained intact after the November 1814 amendments.

The early twentieth century witnessed major political developments in Norway, which had a significant impact on constitutional law. An increased dissatisfaction with the union with Sweden led to a growing desire for complete independence, and in June 1905, Norway managed to peacefully dissolve the union and became an independent kingdom and elected a Danish prince as king. Reflecting this political change, Parliament amended the Norwegian Constitution once again. The amendments made in June 1905 reaffirmed Norway's status as a sovereign nation and adjusted various provisions to suit the new political landscape after nearly a century in union with Sweden.

It is common to group the Nordic countries' constitutional systems into a Western part comprising Denmark, Iceland, and Norway, and an Eastern part comprising Finland and Sweden.[8] The East/West distinction is, however, perhaps not as clear as often assumed, at least not by all metrics.[9] The empirical results of this study also challenge the traditional East/West divide. The traditional belief in a constitutional East/West divide still illustrates that the union with Sweden did not deeply affect Norwegian constitutional law, even though the division might not be as fundamental as traditionally believed – a point to which we will return later.

After Norway broke from the union with Sweden, and throughout the rest of the twentieth century, the Constitution was amended now and again, but there were no substantial reforms, and the formal text of the Constitution did not change much. It was not until 1999 that the constitutional landscape changed drastically, when Parliament passed the Human Rights Act.[10] This law, which was passed as an ordinary piece of statutory legislation, which only requires a simple majority in Parliament, incorporated selected human rights conventions into Norwegian law.

This incorporation of international human rights conventions into Norwegian law came five years after Article 110c of the Constitution was passed. Article 110c – which is now part of Article 92 that was amended in 2014 – stated that the government has a duty to respect and secure human rights. However, this was not a

[8] B Thorarensen and H Krunke, 'Introduction' in B Thorarensen and H Krunke (eds), *The Nordic Constitutions: a Comparative and Contextual Study* (Oxford, Hart Publishing, 2018) 3.

[9] ibid 4.

[10] Act Relating to the Strengthening of the Status of Human Rights in Norwegian Law 1999.

substantive right. The provision determined that the legislation of specific human rights should be executed through ordinary laws, a mandate that Parliament fulfilled in 1999 with the adoption of the Human Rights Act. Section 3 of the Human Rights Act states that if there is a conflict, the incorporated human rights conventions shall prevail over other ordinary legislation. This has led most scholars to characterise the incorporated conventions as having semi-constitutional status.[11] This significantly changed the constitutional landscape in Norway. The Human Rights Act is not a formal part of the Norwegian Constitution, but its elevated status has paved the way for a more extensive judicial review, an opportunity the Supreme Court has eagerly seized.[12] This is clearly visible when examining the time distribution of the 40 leading cases, with most of the cases from this millennium.[13]

In addition to influencing Norwegian constitutional law by gaining elevated status in 1999, the human rights conventions truly transformed Norwegian constitutional law in 2014. To celebrate the bicentennial of the Norwegian Constitution,[14] the Constitution underwent a major revision. The revision included the enshrinement of several human rights, inspired by international human rights conventions, into the Constitution and the modernisation of the language. Most notable is the addition of a new chapter on human rights, which was particularly inspired by the European Convention on Human Rights.[15] Following the 2014 amendments, in 2015, an amendment to the Constitution incorporated the courts' judicial review competence into the written Constitution as Article 89. However, this was largely a codification of a constitutional custom that dates back to the early 1800s, but the amendment reinforces the Court's role as the protector of the Norwegian Constitution and as the final interpreter of it. However, the Supreme Court has stated that the new constitutional rights that are based on the ECHR shall be interpreted in accordance with their counterpart in the convention.[16] This illustrates

[11] Currently, five conventions are incorporated by this law: UN Convention on the Rights of the Child 1989; UN Convention on the Elimination of All Forms of Discrimination against Women 1979; UN International Covenant on Economic, Social and Cultural Rights 1966; UN International Covenant on Civil and Political Rights 1966; The European Convention of Human Rights 1950. There are some discussion about the status of these conventions, see J Aall, *Rettsstat og menneskerettigeter* (Bergen, Fagbokforlaget, 2022) 115; E Smith, *Konstitusjonelt Demokrati: Statsforfatningsretten i Prinsipielt og Komparativt Lys* (Oslo, Fagbokforlaget, 2021) 144; JEA Skoghøy, *Tvisteløsning* (Oslo, Universitetsforlaget, 2022) 538; R Aarlie '§ 92', in Mestad and Michalsen (eds), *Grunnloven* (n 4) 898; and JF Bernt, '§ 113' in Mestad and Michalsen (eds), *Grunnloven* (n 4) 1254.

[12] This is illustrated by the increased use of Grand Chamber and plenary compositions after the turn of the millennium, see M Nadim, 'Precedents in the 21st Century' (Oslo, Karnov, 2023) chapter 7.1.1, lovdata.no/pro/#document/KARNOV/karnov-2023-20.

[13] The dataset is published here: K Kelemen, 'Nordic CONREASON kollektion av data om konstitutionellt resonemang i de nordiska högsta domstolarna (Version 1), 15 Maj 2024' (Örebro University, 2024) doi.org/10.60689/zmk7-0z14.

[14] The bicentennial of the Constitution also produced quite extensive research on the Norwegian Constitution, both historical and contemporary. Most notably D Michalsen (ed) 'Nye perspektiver på Grunnloven 1814-2014', which is a six-volume series.

[15] Also, the Constitution was translated to *nynorsk*, another official language in Norway.

[16] See Rt. 2015 p. 93 (Maria) para 57.

how entangled the international human rights conventions and the Norwegian Constitution are.

The 2015 amendment, however, did not include any provision on the level of scrutiny judicial review should have. The new article only stated that 'the Courts have the power and the duty to review whether applying a statutory provision is contrary to the Constitution'.[17] Before 2015, judicial review was a principle not mentioned in the Constitution (N20)[18] – an argument-type that is counted in this project – and the 40 leading cases seem to reflect this. In cases prior to the constitutional amendment in 2015, the Court invoked a principle not mentioned in the constitution in 22 of the 30 cases.[19] In the remaining ten cases decided after the 2015 amendment, the Court invoked principles not mentioned in the Constitution only three times.[20] This suggests that the most common principle not mentioned in the Constitution was, until 2015, judicial review itself.

Even though the Constitution has undergone more than 300 amendments since 1814,[21] the text and structure from 17 May 1814, are still very much present today. Thus, the Constitution is a legal document as well as a national symbol of independence, which perhaps is the reason there has never been a serious attempt to create a new and modern constitution.

As this brief history illustrates, international events have influenced the major amendments to the text of the Norwegian Constitution, sometimes as sources of legal inspiration and sometimes forcefully through international politics. Consequently, international influence has been, and continues to be, significant in Norwegian constitutional law. As we will see, this is also evident in the 40 leading cases included in this study.

B. Institutional and Academic Context

The Norwegian Supreme Court is a court of last instance that decides on all types of cases: criminal, civil, administrative, and constitutional.[22] Norway has no separate administrative or constitutional courts. As of 2025, the Court comprises 19 ordinary justices and a Chief Justice. The current Chief Justice is Toril Marie Øie, who was appointed to the role in 2016 as the first women to hold this position.

[17] The Norwegian Constitution 1814, art 89 (official translation).

[18] The reference to N20 is the variable number. See the Codebook in the Appendix.

[19] All the 22 decisions mention judicial review, which at the time was a principle that was not mentioned in the Constitution. In addition, many of the decisions also refer to other unmentioned principles, such as dualism (in eg, Rt. 1982 p. 421 and Rt. 2000 p. 996), preferred position principle (in eg, Rt. 1996 p. 1415 and Rt. 2007 p. 1281) and interpretation principles (eg, Rt. 2008 p. 1764)

[20] In HR-2016-2554-P (*Holship*), the court refers to 'harmoniserende tolkning i EØS-spørsmål' (harmonising with EEA-law); in HR-2021-417-P *(Acer)*, the Court refers to parts of the preferred position principle; in HR-2021-655-P *(Opinion)* they refer to 'læren om lite inngripende myndighetsoverføring' (the doctrine on small transfer of power).

[21] Mestad, 'Grunnlovshistoria' (n 4) 49.

[22] See art 88 of the Constitution.

Before being appointed as Chief, she served as an ordinary justice on the Court from 2004.

The justices are not specialised in, or assigned to, cases concerning specific areas of law; cases are assigned randomly. The Court employs justices from a variety of legal professions, not only from lower courts or from practicing attorneys but also law professors and lawyers working as prosecutors, in ministries, and elsewhere. Being appointed as a justice on the Supreme Court is associated with high status within the legal profession, although the justices themselves are not commonly known to the general public.

Normally, the justices of the Court rotate between the two five-justice panels, the Appeals Selection Committee, and having an office week. The Appeals Selection Committee, consisting of three justices, acts as the gatekeepers of the Supreme Court. It reviews all appeals and decides whether the Court will hear a case on the merits. The Committee rejects almost 90 per cent of all appeals after a written procedure.[23] Cases that are granted leave to appeal are typically heard by one of the two panels. However, a few times, when the Court finds that the legal questions raised in a case are of great importance, if the Court considers overturning its own precedent, or if a case raises an issue of judicial review, the Court will usually decide to hear the case either in the Grand Chamber, which consists of eleven justices, or *en banc*.[24] All cases granted leave by the Appeals Selection Committee are decided after oral arguments.

The 40 leading cases included in this study span a period during which the Norwegian Supreme Court went through significant institutional changes.[25] First, the procedural rules have steadily strengthened the Court's control over its own docket over this period. Today, the Court has close to full discretionary control over its docket in both civil (including administrative), criminal and constitutional matters.[26] The 2008 civil procedure reform, which granted the Court practically complete autonomy to select its own cases, also introduced a new 'level' within the Court itself: The Grand Chamber. It demands fewer resources than *en banc* proceedings, making it easier to elevate cases above the normal five-justice panels without disrupting the Court's other work.

The second major structural change in the period is that the Court has steadily hired more law clerks, especially during the tenures of Chief Justices Carsten Smith (1991–2002) and Tore Schei (2002–16). There are now more law clerks than

[23] JØ Sunde, *Høgsteretts historie 1965-2015: at dømme i sidste instans* (Bergen, Fagbokforlaget, 2015) 136–43.

[24] Grand Chamber and *en banc* proceedings are commonly referred to as strengthened panels ('forsterket rett' in Norwegian). See Act Relating to the Courts of Justice § 5 (1915).

[25] AW Ghavanini et al., 'Institutions that define the policymaking role of courts: A comparative analysis of the supreme courts of Scandinavia', 23 *International Journal of Constitutional Law* (2023) 770, 774–75.

[26] Nadim, 'Precedents' (n 12) ch 3.1.

justices on the Court,[27] and they carry out a wide range of tasks – assisting both the Appeals Selection Committee in granting leave to appeal and participating in cases decided on the merits in panels.[28]

These two structural changes have influenced the Court's decisions generally,[29] and its decisions on constitutional issues specially. The Court now decides fewer cases on the merits than it did in the 1970s, 1980s, and 1990s, because it had less control over its docket then. The average number of cases decided on the merits in the past two decades has been around 50–60 civil and 50–60 criminal cases per year.[30] The judgments, however, have lengthened, and are referring to a greater variety and more numerous legal sources than in the past.[31] The increased length is, however, not evident in the 40 leading cases selected for this study; they are almost equally long over time (see Figure 1).

Figure 1 Number of words per case over time (estimated LOESS-curve over time including a 95% confidence interval)

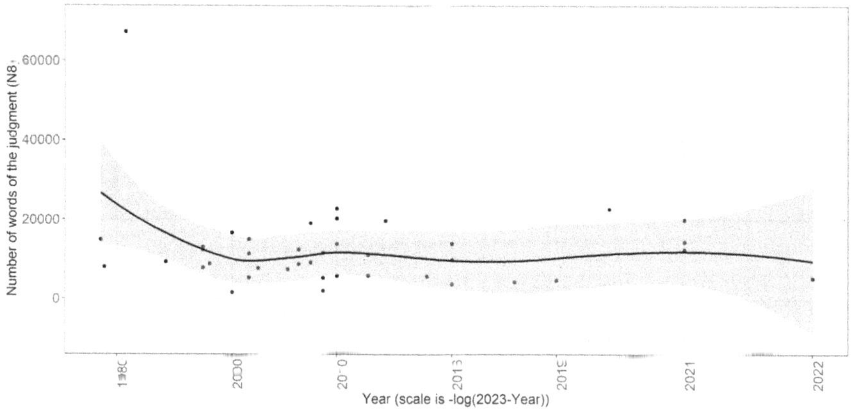

If we look at the portion of the judgments of which the Court's reasoning consists, we see on the other hand an increase very clearly (see Figure 2). This is also in line with the general development of the Court's cases, where we see a decrease of the portion of the judgments that includes the statement of facts and the referral of the parties' arguments and, as a necessity, an increase of the portion consisting of the judges own reasoning.[32]

[27] EN Waltenburg et al., 'Proactive and Powerful: Law Clerks and the Institutionalization of the Norwegian Supreme Court' (2019) 12.
[28] ibid 11.
[29] Nadim (n 12) ch 10.1.
[30] ibid at ch 3.1 and Sunde (n 23) 171.
[31] Nadim (n 12), at ch 10.2.1 and figs 10:9 and 10:14.
[32] ibid ch 10.2.2 and fig 10:17.

Figure 2 Portion of the judges' reasoning over time (estimated LOESS-curve over time including a 95% confidence interval)

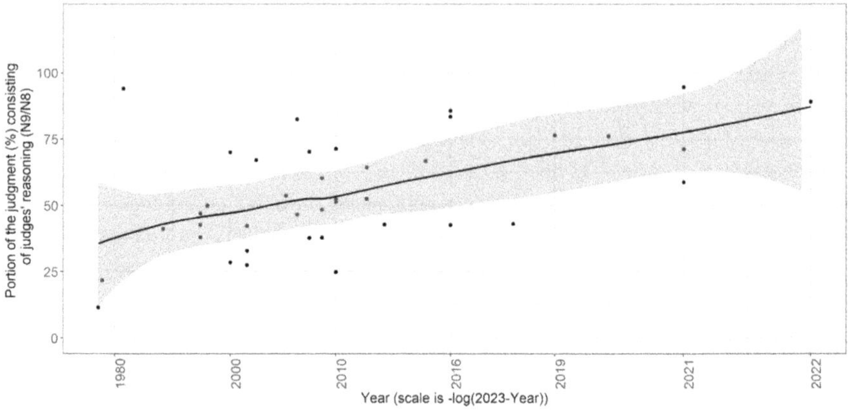

This divergence from the Court's general case law, namely that the landmark cases in this study generally do not increase in length overall, is likely explained by the fact that all but one of the leading cases are heard by either the full court or the special Grand Chamber panel, rather than by five justices in standard panels.[33] Cases elevated above the normal five-justice panels are more homogeneous in terms of length and use of legal sources throughout the entire period, but they have appeared more frequently in the past two decades than before.[34]

The institutional changes of the past three to four decades have given the Court both the time and the resources to focus more on principled questions, such as constitutional questions and judicial review. This is also evident from the fact that the 40 leading cases are mostly recent cases; the median case is from 2009. Moreover, since all judicial review cases, as a main rule, must be elevated to either the Grand Chamber or *en banc*, the increased use of these types of proceedings might also indicate that the Court now handles more cases concerning constitutional issues than it used to, or at least focuses more on these types of issues.[35]

In cases decided on the merits after oral arguments, the civil cases comprise 55 per cent, and the criminal cases 45 per cent. Although the Court does not separate administrative cases from other civil cases, a review of its annual reports since 2013 – when it began categorising cases into specific areas of law – indicates that administrative cases seem to average at around 20 per cent of the total caseload. Thus, a little less than half of the civil cases in an average year are administrative cases. In the landmark cases in this study, however, nine are criminal

[33] The increase in length is not present in these elevated cases, see ibid at s 7.2.1, so this is not surprising.

[34] ibid ch 7.1.1 and fig 7:1.

[35] The Court has always had the possibility to elevate cases to *en banc* proceedings, but it was first written into statutory law in 1926. Since then, the Court has elevated 132 cases to strengthened panels, 56 of which are in this millennium. See Nadim 'Precedents' (n 12) ch 7.1.1 and table 7.1.

cases, 12 are civil cases, and 18 are administrative cases (N7). It is not surprising that the constitutional cases include a larger portion of administrative cases than usual. The Government will most often be the defendant in constitutional litigation, although this is not always the case. In all civil cases concerning judicial review, however, including non-administrative civil cases, the civil procedural rules allow the '[s]tate is entitled to participate in the case to the extent necessary to safeguard the State's interests with regard to the potential conflict of rules'.[36] Thus, the Government appears before the Supreme Court in almost all the 40 leading cases. This procedural rule is unique to Norway among the Nordic countries.

In the period the 40 cases are from, several legal academics were elevated to the Supreme Court bench, most notably Chief Justice Carsten Smith, who was elevated to Chief Justice directly from his position as a law professor at the law faculty at the University of Oslo. Legal academia has had a rather prominent place in the Court's work in general in this period, and thus also in its constitutional reasoning specially. As discussed further below, this might be one of the reasons that legal doctrine often is cited as a legal source in the Court's judgments. Whatever the reason, the relationship between the Court and legal academia, is a symbiotic one. Development of law in general,[37] and constitutional law especially, is oftentimes the result of a dialogue between legal doctrine and the Supreme Court precedent.[38] This back-and-forth between the Court and academia is evident in the material on which this chapter is based and will be further discussed below.

C. Importing Judicial Review

Except for one,[39] all landmark cases included in this study have an element of judicial review (N4). This underscores the important role that judicial review plays in Norwegian constitutional law. In the supreme courts of the other Nordic countries, this seems equally true. No Nordic supreme court has fewer than 70 per cent of judicial review cases, and all but the Finnish Supreme Administrative Court have more than 90 per cent. In this respect, there are no traces of an East/West divide.

In a Norwegian context, however, this has not always been the case and was probably not something that the drafters could have foreseen in 1814. Due to international influence, however, the development of judicial review as part of

[36] Act Relating to Mediation and Procedure in Civil Disputes § 30-13 (2005). Criminal procedure law does not have the same provision, but the Court has allowed the State to participate in criminal cases by analogy from civil procedure, see HR-2021-1107-U.

[37] Two illustrative examples are tort law and civil procedure law.

[38] F Sejersted, 'Det elastiske panser' in E Holmøyvik (ed) *Tolkingar av grunnlava – om forfatningsutviklinga 1814-2014* (Oslo, Pax, 2013) 44.

[39] Only one case is not a judicial review case, and that is an *en banc* judgment on whether the State could participate in a case between two private parties, cf. HR-2000-41-B (*State's Right to Participate*). The case concerned a conflict between Norwegian law and EEA law, in which the Court discusses the principle of dualism, which is a constitutional custom in Norwegian law.

Norwegian constitutional law occurred rapidly.[40] Already on 10 December 1822, the seven-year-old Norwegian Supreme Court decided a case that some scholars argue is the first example of judicial review in Norway – and possibly in Europe.[41] This is remarkably early, and it seems likely that the Norwegian Supreme Court looked to the US Supreme Court's decision in *Marbury v Madison* from 1803 for inspiration already in 1822; the American judgment was at least a clear inspiration to the Court later in the nineteenth century.

In a judgment from 1 November 1866, Chief Justice Lasson wrote an opinion that is clearly modelled on Chief Justice John Marshall's opinion in *Marbury v Madison*.[42] In Lasson's extensive writings on, among other things, constitutional law, he makes several references to American constitutional law. In his work on criminal procedure from 1869, he specifically refers to Justice Joseph Story's *Commentaries on the Constitution of the United States* from 1833, which refers extensively to *Marbury v Madison*.[43] Thus, the ties to American constitutional law seem to have been of great importance to the early development of Norwegian constitutional law, as they had also been for the drafters of the Eidsvoll Constitution in 1814.

Judicial review was highly debated in both politics and legal academia in the nineteenth century. The debate was twofold: It concerned the question of whether judicial review had a basis in the Constitution at all, and if so, how the Court should conduct such a review, especially regarding the level of scrutiny that should apply. Despite the debate over the judicial review competence, the Court continued to strike down statutory laws throughout the nineteenth century. In the late 1800s, there are many examples of judicial review cases, both upholding and striking down statutory laws,[44] and this practice continued into the early 1900s when it reached its peak.

In the years after World War I, the courts' judicial review competence was a highly debated political issue, with voices both in politics and in legal academia contesting the courts' legitimacy in conducting judicial review. This, in addition to the appointment of justices to the Court who were less inclined toward the idea of judicial review, led to examples of judicial review by the Supreme Court becoming rarer. In 1931, the Court's judicial review practice came to a temporary halt. However, its formal competence remained unharmed.

[40] Holmøyvik, Michalsen and Mestad (n 4) 339.

[41] ibid 333. Depending on how they define judicial review, scholars disagree to some extent when the Court first exercised judicial review. The Court itself has stated that it at least started in the 1860s, see HR-2007-1593-P (*Øvre Ullern*). The Court's votes were not public before 1863, so the justices did not write their opinions with the public in mind, which makes deciphering the judgments more difficult in the first 50 years the Court existed.

[42] Holmøyvik, Michalsen and Mestad (n 4) 339.

[43] ibid 340–41.

[44] E Smith, *Høyesterett og folkestyret: prøvingsretten overfor lover* (Oslo, Univsersitetsforlaget, 1993) 163–93 and Holmøyvik, Michalsen and Mestad (n 4) 346–48.

The absence of constitutional review of legislation in the Court's case law lasted almost half a century. In 1975, leading legal scholar Torstein Eckhoff wrote that, notwithstanding the courts' competence to review the constitutionality of laws, he doubted that the courts would ever use that competence again.[45] He was proven wrong quickly thereafter. In January 1976, the Supreme Court decided the *Kløfta* case *en banc*, where a narrow majority (10-7) concluded that the statutory rules regulating compensation for property owners whose land had been expropriated were in violation of the 'right to compensation' clause in Constitution Article 105.[46] This started a new era of judicial review after nearly 50 years of dormancy.[47] This decision marks a new era of judicial review and is the reason for why the chosen landmark cases in this study is from after this shift.

III. Argumentative Patterns

A. Judicial Review

The *Kløfta* judgment is not merely the landmark case that revived judicial review. In its judgment, a unanimous Supreme Court agreed on a doctrine that we might describe as a Norwegian version of the American preferred position principle.[48] However, when reviewing the actual constitutionality, the Court split into five factions. In his opinion, Justice Blom, writing for the majority, stated that the Constitution consisted of three types of constitutional provisions, and that the courts' scrutiny should correspond with the type of constitutional provision with which a law is purportedly in conflict. He categorised the Constitution into three groups:

> [P]rotection of an Individual's personal freedom or safety, ... constitutional provisions that regulate the working methods or mutual competence of the other branches of government, [and] provisions for the protection of economic rights.[49]

The Court added – without much reasoning or with any references to legal sources – that the view Parliament had on the constitutionality of a piece of legislation

[45] T Eckhoff, 'Høyesterett som Grunnlovens vokter' (1976) 10 *Jussens Venner* 1; C Smith, 'Domstolene og rettsutviklingen' (1975) 15 *Lov og Rett* 292.

[46] Rt. 1976 p. 1 (*Kløfta*).

[47] See on the *Kløfta* case in Nadim, 'Precedente' chs 7.1.1 and 7.2.3.

[48] A Tverberg, '§ 89' in Mestad and Michalsen (eds), *Grunnloven* (n 4) 877; GB Nissen, F Hoirthøy and K Gaarder, *Den dømmende makt: domstolene og rettsutviklingen 1814-1964* (Oslo, Universitetsforlaget, 1967); F Backer, 'The Preferred Position Principle i amerikansk og norsk rett' in P Lødrup, S Tjomsland, M Aarbakke and G Aasland (eds), *Rettsteori og rettsliv: festskrift til Carsten Smith til 70-årsdagen 13. juli 2002* (Oslo, Universitetsforlaget, 2002) and Smith, 'Domstolene og rettsutviklingen' (n 45).

[49] Rt. 1976 p 1 (*Kløfta*) 5–6 (author's translation).

should 'clearly' be given 'considerable' weight, and that the Court should be 'careful' not to prefer its own view over that of the legislator.[50]

The Court has reiterated this principle in several leading constitutional cases since then,[51] and it is often regarded as a constitutional custom. However, it has not been codified into the Constitution, making it a principle not mentioned in the Constitution.[52] In the 40 cases in this study, the Court has referred to principles not mentioned in the Constitution (N20) in 25 instances, where almost all references are to this Norwegian version of the preferred position principle and/or judicial review itself.

Thus, the famous *Kløfta* judgment marked a very important shift in the practice of Norwegian constitutional law and may be viewed as the starting point of the modern Supreme Court's constitutional reasoning, and consequently, modern constitutional law. Therefore, all the 40 leading cases in this study are from the period after 1976. The Court's previous constitutional practice, and the constitutional history, is indeed important for the constitutional culture in Norway but is not directly reflected in the quantitative study.

After *Kløfta*, the newly formulated Norwegian preferred position principle had an impact on the Court's judicial review practice, and the Court continued to develop the principle. In particular, the Court further refined its view on the weight to be given to Parliament's own assessment of the constitutionality of the legislation in question, that is, whether the decision on constitutionality is within the legislator's discretion or not. This discussion is present in many (14) of the cases in the study.[53] What is particularly interesting in this regard is that it seems the Court has gradually narrowed the scope of the legislator's discretion by increasingly scrutinising the legislature's evaluation of constitutional questions.[54] By 2010, the legislator's room for discretion was restricted to situations where the Court agreed that Parliament had relied on the correct constitutional norm. The notion of being *careful* of putting its own view over the view of Parliament, was disregarded. In HR-2010-258-P, Justice Utgård, writing for the majority of the Court, stated:

> When the Parliament has conducted a review based on a different norm for constitutional review than the one I believe must be used, it makes it difficult to place emphasis on the actual balancing of interests by the Parliament.[55]

[50] ibid 6.

[51] See, eg, Rt. 1996 p. 1415 *(Borthen)* and Rt. 1996 p 1440 *(Thunheim)*.

[52] See E Smith, 'Konstitusjonelt demokrati' (n 11) 285–86; Tverberg, '§ 89' (n 48) 879.

[53] Counted separately for this chapter.

[54] See Rt. 1976 p 1 *(Kløfta)*, Rt. 1979 p 572 *(Bank Democratisation)*, Rt. 1987 p 80 *(Rønnåsmyra)*, Rt. 1990 p 284 *(Selsbak)*, Rt. 1996 p 1415 *(Borthen)*, Rt. 1996 p 1440 *(Thumheim)*, Rt. 2006 p 293 *(Arve's Driving School)*, Rt. 2007 p 1281 *(Øvre Ullern)*, Rt. 2007 p 1308 *(Sørheim)*, Rt. 2010 p 143 *(Ship Owner Taxation)* and Rt. 2010 p 535 *(The Norwegian Church Endowment)*.

[55] Rt. 2010 p 143 *(Ship Owner Taxation)* para. 172 (author's translation).

In 34 years, the legislature's discretion has narrowed significantly. The Court has shifted from being careful not to elevate its own view of constitutionality over that of the legislature and from ascribing considerable weight to Parliament's own evaluation as a main rule, to ascribing weight to the legislature's view only when the norm for constitutional review that Parliament used is one with which the Court agrees. This development is not evident in the quantitative analysis of the 40 leading cases. It is not measured how much weight the Court has placed on Parliament's own view, only that the Court has stated that Parliament's view is usually relevant. One might expect to see an increase in such outcomes given the evolution of judicial review, but the results do not indicate whether the Court concurs with Parliament on the constitutional norm. However, examining the outcomes of the cases does not reveal a clear trend toward the Court striking down more laws over time.

Even though *Kløfta* marked the beginning of a new era in constitutional practice, the constitutional culture did not change overnight. The development of constitutional law by the courts is a gradual process. For instance, the number of judicial review cases did not surge in the 1970s or the 1980s.[56] The real increase came after international human rights treaties were incorporated into Norwegian law with semi-constitutional status in 1999. Nonetheless, the judicial review mechanism was refined by the Court in *Kløfta*, and the Court seized the opportunity to apply this tool to the newly incorporated human rights.

B. Harmonising with International Law Requirements

Even though Norway ratified all the conventions incorporated by the Human Rights Act long before 1999,[57] the Court did not apply them in their judgments to any meaningful extent.[58] In the 40 leading cases, harmonising with international law requirements (N18) appears as an argument twice as frequently in the cases after 1999 (26 out of 32, which is 81.25 per cent) as in the cases before 1999 (three out of eight, which is 37.5 per cent), which is a significant difference. The Court's constitutional practice was once again affected by international legal ideas. Except for Sweden (41 per cent*),[59] the other Nordic countries (DNK 66 per cent; FIN 74 per cent; ISL 84 per cent) are estimated to be similar to Norway (72 per cent) in terms of using this argument. Again, no clear East/West divide is visible (see Figure 3).

[56] Nadim, 'Precedents' (n 12) ch 7.1.1 and table 7.1.
[57] ECHR in 1954 and ICCPR and ICESCR in 1972.
[58] Nadim, 'Precedents' (n 12) chs 7.2.3 and 7.2.4.
[59] The asterisk marks statistically significant results here and elsewhere.

Figure 3 Harmonising with international law requirements

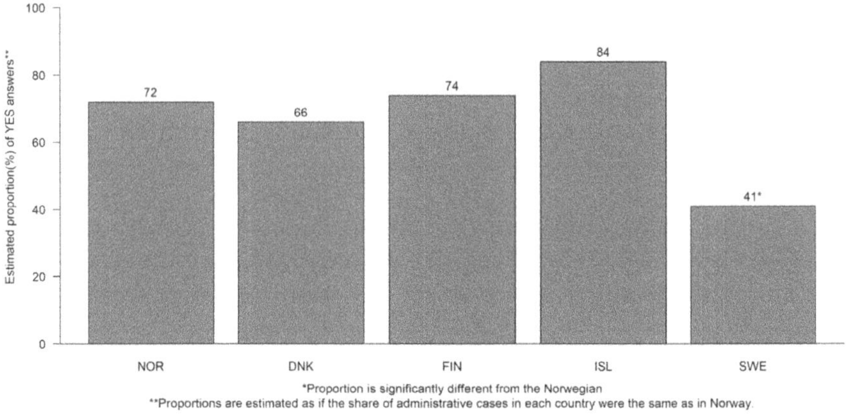

The 40 leading cases in this study also illustrate this international influence by how many of the judgments reference scholarly works on international law (See Figure 4).

Figure 4 Proportion of cases referencing scholarly work on international law

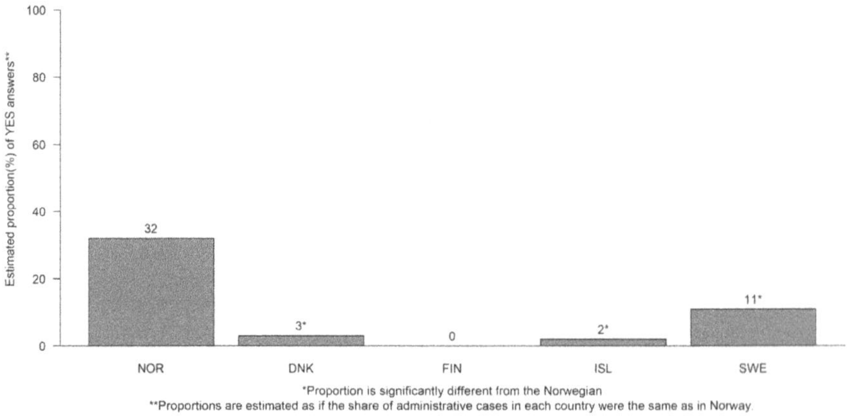

Such references are made in 13 cases, 12 of which are after 1999, and only one before – 38 per cent and 13 per cent respectively, which however is not a significant difference. The Norwegian Supreme Court stands out from its Nordic counterparts, which rarely refer to scholarly work on international law in any period. This is another example of how the traditional East/West divide is not relevant when examining specific aspects of constitutional reasoning.

Most of the time when the Court applies arguments for harmonising with international law, it is aligning with the conventions that Parliament has given semi-constitutional status,[60] and most of the scholarly work cited pertains to the same conventions.[61] This is an illustrative example of a different type of international influence than the American influence on constitutional law, which we see in judicial review, but it is still another example of how Norwegian constitutional law is heavily influenced by external inspiration. The evolution of judicial review and the harmonisation with international human rights conventions also illustrate the Court's role in developing constitutional law, and the interplay between the Court and legal scholars in the field. The Court has always referred to scholarly work in all areas of law.[62] Scholarly work is considered a legitimate source of law, both by the Court and in legal methodology literature,[63] and constitutional law is no exception. This is further evidenced by the 40 leading cases, with 23 (58 per cent) cases referencing scholarly work, including domestic, foreign, comparative, and international sources (N25).

International human rights have also influenced the Court in a broader way, which applies to all types of cases – including constitutional law cases. Over time, the Court has started to write its judgments in a style more akin to that of the European Court of Human Rights (ECtHR).[64] It has become more common for the Court to include a separate section about the law before turning to its specific application.[65] This structure is particularly evident in cases elevated to either the Grand Chamber or *en banc*,[66] which usually involve judicial review and constitutional law issues. Consequently, the writing style of the ECtHR has most significantly impacted how the Court crafts decisions in constitutional law cases. One can argue that the influence of international human rights conventions, particularly the European Convention on Human Rights, which is illustrated by the many instances (29, which is 73 per cent) where the Court applied harmonising with international law requirements as an argument (N18), is an influence that initially affected the substantive constitutional law and subsequently changed the way the Court writes its judgments overall. This influence of constitutional law on other legal fields is perhaps most common in jurisdictions without a separate constitutional court, as is the case in all Nordic countries.

[60] In all instances, the cases including harmonising with international law requirements refer to ratified conventions. However, three cases Rt. 1982 p 241 *(Alta River)*, Rt. 1996 p 1415 *(Borthen)* and Rt. 1997 p 1821 *(Kjuus)* refer to these conventions before they were elevated to semi-constitutional status.

[61] References to scholarly work on international law is almost exclusively literature on the ECHR, and most of the times its Nordic authors.

[62] Nadim, 'Precedents' (n 12) ch 10.2.1 and fig 10:14.

[63] T Eckhoff and JE Helgesen, *Rettskildelære* (Oslo, Universitetsforlaget, 2001); and N Nygaard, *Rettsgrunnlag og standpunkt* (Bergen, Universitetsforlaget, 2004) 105.

[64] HH Fredriksen, 'Bør rettsanvendere flest skrive som Høyesterett?' (2023) 62 *Lov og Rett* 2.

[65] This trend toward more abstract and general judgments is documented extensively in Nadim, 'Precedents' (n 12) ch 10.2.1, and it is happening across all areas of law.

[66] ibid ch 7.1 and fig 7:23.

C. The Back-and-forth between the Court and Academia

Scholarly works have always influenced the Court to a certain extent.[67] Many of the justices have come to the Court from positions as university professors,[68] and many justices publish articles and books on a wide range of topics. The interplay between the Court and academia is also specifically visible in the 40 leading cases. In 23 cases (58 per cent), the Court has referred to scholarly works in one way or another (N25). This includes the 13 instances when references are made to literature on international law mentioned above (see Figure 4). In terms of references to scholarly work, Norway stands out in the Nordic context. It is not as common in the other Nordic countries (see Figure 5). This aspect of constitutional reasoning groups the Nordic countries very differently than the traditional East/West divide.

Figure 5 Proportion of cases in which there is a reference to scholarly work

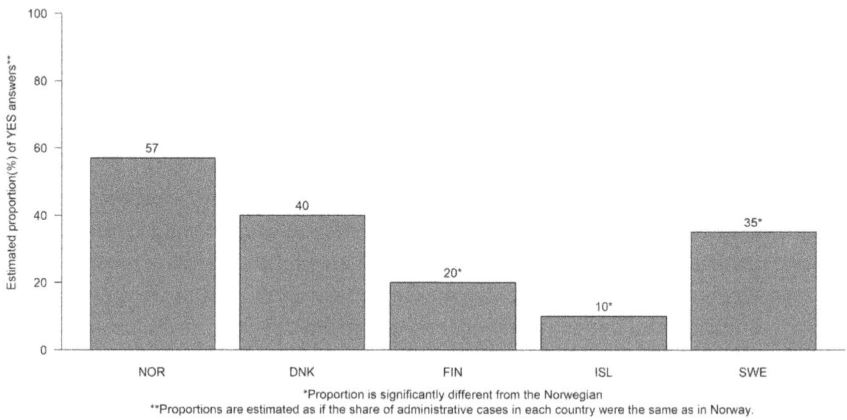

As mentioned, the international influence can also be seen in the Supreme Court's style of writing judgments. However, inspiration is not limited to the ECtHR's way of structuring their judgments; common law courts have also been a clear inspiration for the Court. The Court is not only inspired by specific legal concepts traditionally associated with common law, such as judicial review and the preferred position principle, but common law inspiration is also highly visible in the argumentative style of the Court. Additionally, some Supreme Court justices have explicitly expressed their admiration for common

[67] Legal doctrine is often cited by the Court, see ibid ch 10.2.1 and fig 10:14.

[68] G Grendstad, WR Shaffer and E Waltenburg, *Policy making in an independent judiciary: the Norwegian supreme court* (Bergen, SCPR Press Series, 2015) 91; and GI Hallager, *Norges høiesteret 1815–1915* (Oslo, H. Aschehaug & Company, 1916) 345.

law courts. In 1926, Justice Ferdinand Schjelderup wrote an article titled *The Supreme Court's Position in the Legal Landscape*,[69] in which he states, '[f]or every German judgment, of which one may learn something from, there are ten English judgments, which give true enlightenment'.[70] He viewed German judgments as formalistic and technical, and English decisions as sensible, well-reasoned, and down-to-earth – an example to follow for the Norwegian Supreme Court.

Common law courts, and particularly the US Supreme Court, also inspired Supreme Court Chief Justice Carsten Smith (1991–2002). In 1975, he delivered a speech at the seventh annual judges' conference, while he was a law professor, where he advocated for an American approach to deciding cases in the Supreme Court. Moreover, he promoted a version of the preferred position principle when he was a law professor.[71] In the 1975 speech, his vision was for a Norwegian Supreme Court that controlled its own docket and focused on cases that would have a broad impact. His view was that the Court should not write decisions with the specific conflict in mind, but rather with the aim of developing and clarifying the law – not merely deciding cases but creating precedents. In his speech, Smith frequently referred to the US Supreme Court's way of granting certiorari and writing judgments as a goal to which the Norwegian Supreme Court should aspire. When he became Chief Justice in 1991, he continued to hold this view, and during his tenure as Chief Justice, many significant institutional changes were made to facilitate this view, particularly the two institutional changes regarding law clerks and docket control mentioned above.

D. Argumentative Patterns Inspired by Common Law Courts

The institutional changes explained above, along with the common law influence on both the Court and Norwegian Constitutional Law in general, are visible in the reasoning style of the Court. The justices write personal opinions, frequently including dissents and concurring opinions, which are typical features of common law traditions.[72] In the cases included in this study, the Norwegian Supreme Court Justices write separate opinions to a much greater extent than their Nordic colleagues do (N3, see Figure 6). However, the dissent rate is comparatively low when compared to common law courts.[73] The opinions are written in a pro ct

[69] F Schjelderup, 'Høiesterets plass i retslivet – Bevisumiddelbarheten og den norske ankeordningen av 1925' (1926) *Tidsskrift for Rettsvitenskap* 301.
[70] ibid 305 (author's translation).
[71] Smith, 'Domstolene og rettsutviklingen' (n 45).
[72] A Jakab, A Dyevre and G Itzcovich, 'Conclusion' in A Jakab, A Dyevre and G Itzcovich (eds), *Comparative Constitutional Reasoning* (Cambridge, Cambridge University Press, 2017) 771.
[73] ibid 771, Fig 5.

contra style, using more everyday language and less frequent technical legal jargon, which is also more closely related to common law reasoning.[74]

Figure 6 Separate opinion

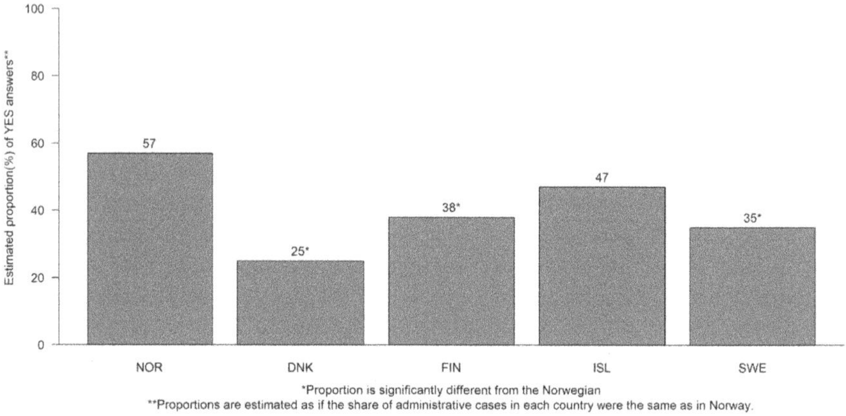

In the 40 leading cases selected, we can see clear specific signs of common law influence. In 36 cases, accounting for 90 per cent, the Court uses precedent-based arguments (N19), which is traditionally seen as a common law feature,[75] even though, for instance, the German Constitutional Court does this routinely.[76] However, the Norwegian Supreme Court clearly stands out from its Nordic counterparts in this respect. This might be attributed to the fact that judicial review itself was based on precedent for a long time, which would explain the high percentage. Nevertheless, the references to precedent include much more than just a reference to the *Kløfta* case for instance to legitimise judicial review. Moreover, the fact that precedents are used also to legitimise the constitutional principle of judicial review underlines that precedents are important and central in Norwegian constitutional law.

Iceland uses precedent-based arguments in about 65 per cent of the cases, which is the second-highest frequency among the Nordic supreme courts. The three other jurisdictions utilise precedents in around 40 per cent of the cases. This is yet another example of how the traditional East/West divide fails to be relevant when examining specific aspects of constitutional reasoning because, in this respect, Denmark is closer to the East-Nordic countries (see Figure 7).

[74] ibid 771.
[75] Jakab, Dyevre and Itzcovich, 'Introduction' (n 2) 14.
[76] German law does not recognise any formal *stare decisis* rule, but this is more complex when it comes to the Constitutional Court itself, see M Hailbronner and S Martini, 'The German Federal Constitutional Court' in A Jakab, A Dyevre and G Itzcovich (eds), *Comparative Constitutional Reasoning* (Cambridge, Cambridge University Press, 2017) 375.

Figure 7 Reference to precedent

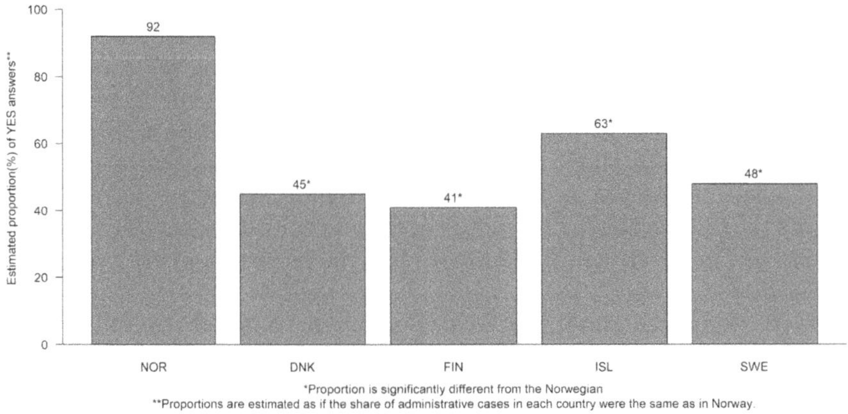

IV. Key Concepts

A. Old Constitutional Text in Need of Constitutional Customs

The Norwegian Constitution is old. Moreover, until 2015, few individual rights were enshrined in the text of the Constitution, and judicial review was not expressly codified. What the Constitution lacked in explicit terms, the Court – and legal scholars – introduced as constitutional custom. The frequent references to customs in the 40 leading cases (N48, 14 instances), as well as the frequent invocation of principles not mentioned in the Constitution (N20, 25 instances), illustrate the shortcomings of the Constitution's text. Judicial review, already discussed as a constitutional custom, was eventually included in the Constitution in 2015. However, there are several other references to custom as well. When a constitutional norm is labelled a custom by the Court, its usually referred to as a long-term established practice. In many instances, precedents from the Court might be used as evidence for a Constitutional custom, but referring to a single precedent is not sufficiently to establish a Constitutional custom unless constitutional practice has followed that precedent for a long time. This illustrates both the close connection between precedents and customs and the differences. When referring to precedent, the Court might also refer to a custom, but it is not a necessity, and vice-versa, when referring to constitutional custom the Court may not have a precedent to refer to – only *inter alia* practice from Parliament. An example of the latter is parliamentarianism.

The original Eidsvoll Constitution established a monarchy and parliament, with a clear concept of the separation of powers. In 1884, a political battle between the Parliament and the Swedish King culminated in an impeachment trial against the King's Council, led by Prime Minister Christian Selmer. The result of the impeachment trial was that parliamentarianism became the de facto form of government and was practised as such in the time after. While it was perhaps constitutionally contentious in 1884, it was nevertheless quickly regarded as a constitutional custom by the beginning of the twentieth century,[77] and remained so until formally codified in the written constitution in 2007 as Article 15, which dictates that the Council of State must resign if the Parliament passes a vote of no confidence.

Furthermore, the principle of legality outside the scope of criminal law was not explicitly part of the Constitution for a long time, until it was incorporated as Article 113 in 2014. This may explain why the 40 leading cases rarely refer to the principle of legality (N31_2). The Court refers to this principle only twice, both times in criminal cases, where the principle of legality has been part of the Constitution since 1814 under Article 96. Another reason may be that the leading constitutional cases typically concern rights other than those protecting individual freedom and security, such as economic rights, which will see in the next section.

B. Economic Rights Over Individual Freedom and Protection

It was mainly in cases concerning economic rights that the Court developed judicial review in the nineteenth century and the Norwegian version of the preferred position principle in the twentieth century.[78] Thus, economic rights cases have had a significant influence on Norwegian constitutional law. This is somewhat visible in the key concepts applied in the 40 leading cases. However, there are not many economic rights cases among the 40 leading cases (only seven). In a Nordic context, the Norwegian Supreme Court, together with the Swedish Supreme Court, refers more often to economic, social, and cultural rights (N50_1) in the leading cases compared to other Nordic supreme courts, although the difference is not significant (see Figure 8). In the Norwegian cases, the references are mostly to economic rights, eg, pension rights. This variable, however, excludes property rights, which in Norwegian Constitutional law have traditionally been used to protect economic rights.[79]

[77] F Sejerstad, '§ 15' in Mestad and Michalsen (eds), *Grunnloven* (n 4) 231, 233–35.

[78] In a recent judgment from the Court *en banc*, HR-2023-2030-P *(Acer II)*, the Court summarised this historical development in paras 110–43.

[79] See eg, Rt. 2007 p 1281 *(Øvre Ullern)* paras 85–97, where the Court discusses the relationship between the two relevant articles of the Constitution.

Figure 8 Proportion of cases in which an economic, social or cultural right is invoked

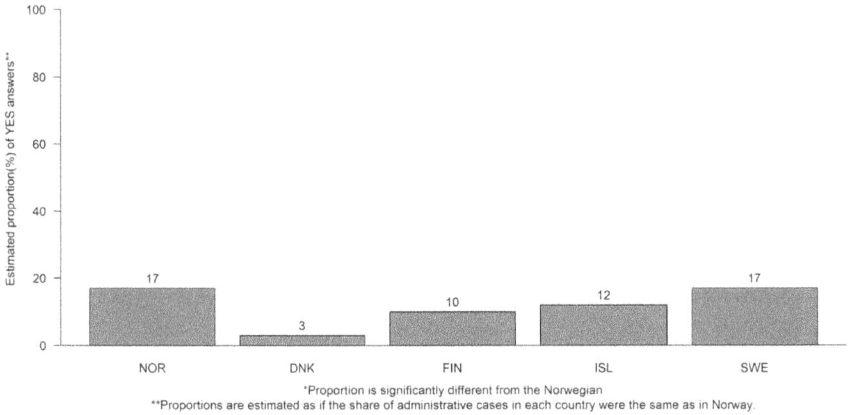

Cases concerning individual freedom and protection are less common and compared to the leading cases from other Nordic courts, the Norwegian Supreme Court stands out. For example, there is only one case where the Norwegian Supreme Court uses freedom of expression and/or freedom of the press as an argument (see Figure 9),[80] while it is somewhat more common in the leading cases from the other Nordic Supreme Courts.

Figure 9 Freedom of expression rights

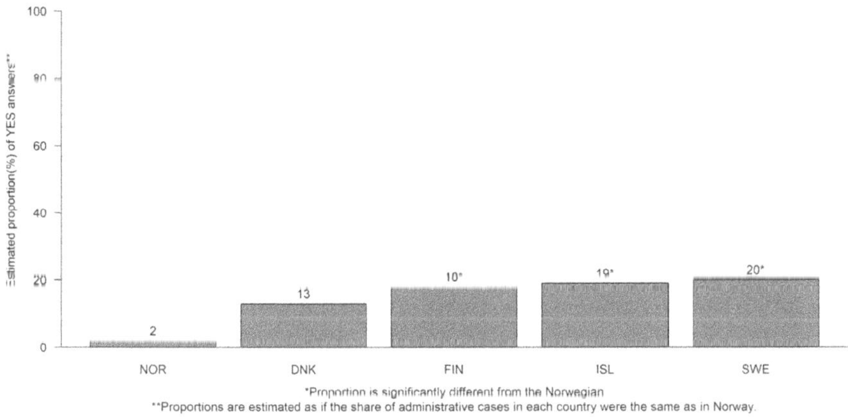

Furthermore, the Norwegian Supreme Court has not applied secularism (N37) as an argument in any of the leading cases. This distinguishes it as the only Supreme

[80] Rt. 1997 p 1281 *(Kjuus).*

Court in the Nordic countries to do so, even though secularism as a constitutional argument is not very common in any of the Nordic courts. The absence of secularism as a constitutional concept perhaps illustrates that questions regarding religion in general, and religious freedom, do not commonly appear in a constitutional context in Norway.[81]

Finally, the Norwegian Supreme Court stands out substantially from its Nordic counterparts when it comes to the use of the principle of legality in the studied cases. As mentioned above, this may be attributed to the fact that the Constitution only included a principle of legality clause applicable to criminal cases until recently, and that so few of the 40 leading cases are criminal cases. When considering other rule of law arguments, such as legal certainty (N31_3),[82] separation of powers (N31_4),[83] access to justice (N31_5),[84] and explicit use of the term 'rule of law' (N31_1)[85] (Norwegian: '*rettsstat*'), the Court does not differ as much from its Nordic counterparts in the studied cases.

C. The Court's Constitutional Role and Separation of Powers

The Court makes reference to three theoretically interlinked concepts several times, which illustrates the Court's awareness of its own constitutional role. In 20 cases, the Court references the separation of powers (N31_4); in 14 cases, it refers to democracy as a concept (N33); and in seven cases, it mentions judicial independence (N32). In 24 cases, the Court refers to at least one of the three concepts, and in three cases all three concepts are mentioned.[86] The Norwegian Supreme Court refers to all three concepts more frequently than its Nordic counterparts, except that the Danish Court refers more often to judicial independence.[87] The frequent use of these concepts may reflect the Court's effort to articulate a precise norm of judicial review. As discussed previously, judicial review has developed through an interplay between the Court and legal academia since the early nineteenth century. In particular, scrutiny levels have been repeatedly discussed after the Court developed the Norwegian version of the preferred position principle. The rationale for letting the scrutiny level depend on the type of constitutional provision claimed to be breached is deeply rooted in ideas of separation of powers, democratic considerations, and an independent judiciary. The emphasis on how

[81] The Constitutional separation between church and state was as late as in 2012, with the amendment of Article 16 of the Constitution. Cases regarding this article are rare, see TB Hjorthaug, '§ 16' in Mestad and Michalsen (eds), *Grunnloven* (n 4).

[82] NOR 34%, DNK 19%; FIN 20%; ISL 9%*; SWE 22%.

[83] NOR 50%, DNK 34%; FIN 46%; ISL 51%; SWE 34%.

[84] NOR 10%, DNK 34%*; FIN 44%*; ISL 5%; SWE 8%.

[85] NOR 24%, DNK 3%*; FIN 9%*; ISL 9%; SWE 5%*.

[86] The combination of separation of powers and democracy appears in ten cases, separation of powers and judicial independence in seven, and democracy and judicial independence in three.

[87] N32: NOR 15%; DNK 24%; FIN 2%*; ISL 7%; SWE 0%* and N33: NOR 35%; DNK 11%*; FIN 19%; ISL 5%*; SWE 9%*.

Parliament has understood the relevant constitutional provision is thoroughly discussed both in constitutional literature and in the Court's case law.[88]

When judicial review was formally inscribed into the written Constitution in 2015, the exact wording did not encompass the classification of different provisions with varying scrutiny levels, nor how the courts should consider Parliament's interpretation of the constitutionality of the challenged legislation during its passage. However, in the preparatory works, Parliament acknowledged the preferred position principle but deemed it unsuitable for codification.[89] Consequently, it remains the Court's responsibility to determine the more precise content of the principle, and Parliament has also given the Court the authority to decide the weight to place on Parliament's own views regarding constitutional questions. Therefore, when reviewing the constitutionality of legislation, the Court must strike a balance among the branches of government, assess how much weight to give the democratically elected Parliament's interpretation of the Constitution, and bear in mind that the judiciary is an independent branch of government. This has probably led to a much more extensive use of the three concepts by the Norwegian Supreme Court than by its Nordic counterparts.

D. The Human Rights Influence – Proportionality and Justice

One very significant event in Norwegian constitutional history is the introduction of human rights into Norwegian constitutional law, as previously discussed. This began with semi-constitutional status within normal legislation in 1999, which then served as an inspiration for an entire human rights catalogue in the Constitution in 2014. The incorporation of human rights has not only changed the substantive constitutional law but also the constitutional culture. In the 40 leading cases, we see clear inspiration from the ECtHR, not only in the style of writing judgments, as discussed earlier, but also in the concepts the Court uses in its constitutional reasoning.

Earlier, we examined how the Court harmonised with international law requirements in almost all cases after 1999 and how it refers to scholarly work on international law quite frequently. Additionally, the Court often applies the proportionality test in the 40 leading cases (N40). Proportionality is not a Norwegian constitutional principle; it has never been part of the Norwegian Constitution,[90] nor has it been considered a constitutional custom as a general principle. However, in 16 of the leading cases, the Court employs the concept, both in relation to the ECHR and as a principle not mentioned in the Constitution. This frequency is not

[88] See references in fns 49 and 55.

[89] Innst. 263 S (2014–15) 11.

[90] In autumn 2023, however, there was a proposal to include the proportionality test in the Constitution. There have been proposals to include a proportionality provision in the Constitution before, but they have not been passed.

remarkably high compared to other Nordic Supreme Courts (see Figure 10),[91] but considering that the principle is not articulated in the text of the Constitution, its use is fairly frequent, which could likely be attributed to the influence of international human rights, and particularly the ECHR.

Figure 10 Proportions of cases invoking the principle of proportionality in a global comparison

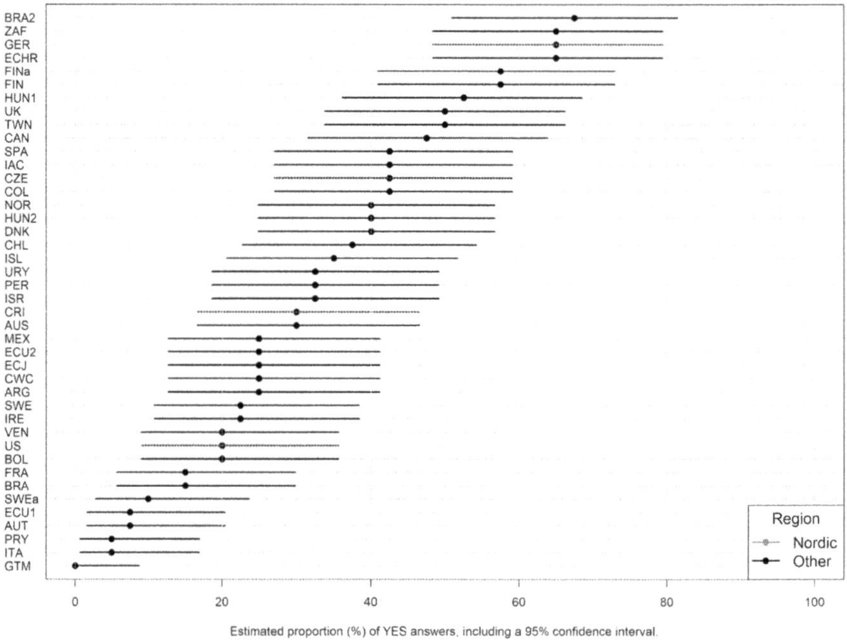

Interestingly, the usage of a proportionality test has not become more frequent after the incorporation of human rights in 1999 compared to the previous period.[92] Therefore, the adoption of the proportionality test as a concept in Norwegian constitutional law may have resulted solely from international influence, rather than formal incorporation. In the eight cases before 1999 included in this study, the principle is invoked five times (which is 62.5 per cent), but not in relation to a discussion on the lawfulness of an infringement of an article in a human rights convention. Instead, it is related to the prohibition against retroactive laws in the Norwegian Constitution (Article 97), which has been a part of the Constitution since 1814.[93] Thus, the proportionality test, as applied by the ECtHR, was likely

[91] NOR 40%; DNK 41%; FIN 58%; ISL 35%; SWE 16%*.
[92] Five of eight cases before 1999, and 11 of 32 after.
[93] See especially Rt. 1996 p 1415 *(Borthen)* and Rt. 1996 p 1440 *(Thumheim)*.

something that the Court found familiar when human rights conventions were incorporated in 1999.

The proportionality test applied by the Court in relation to Article 97 of the Constitution is not exactly the same as the one developed by German courts and adopted by the ECtHR. In cases concerning Article 97, the Court has stated that the proportionality consideration

> includes, among other things, which rights or positions the intervention concerns, the basis the individual or a group has for their expectations, whether the intervention is sudden and significant, and whether the distribution of burdens particularly affects the individual or a group.[94]

This may more closely resemble the concept of justice than a proportionality test according to the ECtHR.[95] When the Court summarises the norm in Article 97, it states that the prohibition against retroactive laws applies only to 'clearly unreasonable or unjust' retroactive laws.[96] Thus, in Norwegian constitutional law, the proportionality principle used before the incorporation of the human rights conventions seems to be closely linked to the concept of justice. Furthermore, in the same cases regarding Article 97, the Court also includes equality as a concept in connection with both proportionality and justice. The three concepts appear to be interlinked in cases concerning Article 97.[97]

Therefore, proportionality seems to embody two distinct concepts in Norwegian constitutional law: both a fairness and equality test for evaluating the constitutionality of retroactive laws under Article 97, and the standard proportionality test used by the ECtHR, which originates from the German courts. The latter is clearly an international influence, but the former seems more deeply rooted in domestic legal tradition.

V. Conclusion

This chapter has highlighted the major international influence on Norwegian constitutional law. We started by laying out a brief overview of Norwegian constitutional history and identifying several points in time when international influences seem to have had an important role in shaping Norwegian constitutional law.

The 10 landmark constitutional cases from 1976 to 2022 also demonstrate the international impact on Norwegian constitutional law. The analysis of the landmark cases has identified patterns and concepts that support the notion that

[94] Rt. 1996 p 1415 *(Borthen)* at 1430 (author's translation).
[95] BM Høgberg, *Forbudet mot tilbakevirkende lover* (Oslo, Universitetsforlaget, 2010) 309–13.
[96] Rt. 1996 p 1415 *(Borthen)* at 1430 and Rt. 1996 p 1440 *(Thumheim)* at 1452 (author's translations).
[97] This is also true in some cases after the incorporation of the Human Rights Conventions regarding art. 97 of the Constitution, see eg, Rt. 2013 p 1345 *(Structural Quotas)* paras 249 and 256.

external sources and ideas shape domestic constitutional practice. The analysis underscores two main findings.

First, international human rights conventions, particularly after their incorporation into Norwegian law through the Human Rights Act of 1999 and subsequent constitutional amendments in 2014, have substantially influenced constitutional reasoning in the Court. The Supreme Court increasingly employs arguments harmonising national law with international law, especially referencing the ECHR. This harmonisation is reflected in both substantive legal principles, such as the adoption of the proportionality test, and structural changes in judgment writing, which now aligns closely with the approach of the European Court of Human Rights.

Second, common law traditions, notably American constitutional practices, have historically and continuously influenced Norwegian constitutional reasoning. This is evident in the judicial review mechanism itself, probably inspired by the landmark US Supreme Court decision *Marbury v Madison*. The Norwegian Supreme Court's use of precedents, separate opinions, and a pro et contra argumentative style further highlights this common law influence.

These findings challenge the notion of a distinct Nordic constitutional law or the notion of an East/West divide in Nordic constitutional law, showing instead a nuanced blend of influences that define Norwegian constitutional law.

7

Constitutional Reasoning in the Swedish Supreme Courts

ÅSA ELMEROT

I. Background and Context

Sweden does not have a specialised constitutional court; instead constitutional review is primarily conducted by the two highest courts – the Supreme Court (*Högsta domstolen*) and the Supreme Administrative Court (*Högsta förvaltningsdomstolen*)[1] – as part of their ordinary judicial functions. Over the years, a wide range of cases have been tried, including several high-profile ones involving Saami rights; the closure of a nuclear power plant; the boundaries of freedom of expression in relation to hate speech targeting homosexuals as well as to manga drawings deemed to constitute child pornography; and the permissibility of double punishment (*ne bis in idem*) in relation to the European Convention on Human Rights (ECHR)[2] and the Charter of Fundamental Rights of the European Union (EU), to mention a few. This chapter examines the constitutional reasoning in a selection of the leading cases from Sweden's two Supreme Courts. The study forms part of the Nordic CONREASON project, which compares constitutional reasoning across the Nordic countries and beyond. Adapting the methodological framework originally developed by the CONREASON project (2011–16)[3] to the Nordic context,[4] we coded 40 cases from each of the Nordic supreme courts. While

[1] The Supreme Administrative Court changed its name from *Regeringsrätten* to *Högsta förvaltningsdomstolen* on 1 January 2011.

[2] Convention for the Protection of Human Rights and Fundamental Freedoms (Rome, 4 November 1950).

[3] A Jakab, A Dyevre and G Itzcovich (eds), *Comparative Constitutional Reasoning* (Cambridge, Cambridge University Press, 2017).

[4] We also adopted additions to the methodology made by another follow-up project to the CONREASON project carried out in Latin America, the CORE Latam Project. The methodology is described in greater detail in ch 2. Our dataset is available at K Kelemen, 'Nordic CONREASON Collection of Data on Constitutional Reasoning in the Nordic Supreme Courts (Version 1)', doi.org/10.60689/zmk7-0z14.

the comparative findings are discussed elsewhere,[5] this chapter focuses specifically on the results pertaining to the Swedish case.

A. The Constitution: History and Tradition

Unlike the other Nordic countries, Sweden does not have a single consolidated written document as its Constitution.[6] Instead, there are four separate enactments, each of which holds the status of fundamental law (*grundlag*): the Instrument of Government (*Regeringsformen*), the Act of Succession (*Successionsordningen*), the Freedom of the Press Act (*Tryckfrihetsförordningen*) and the Fundamental Law on Freedom of Expression (*Yttrandefrihetsgrundlagen*). The Instrument of Government regulates how the state is governed, and also includes a catalogue of fundamental rights and freedoms, making it the document that most closely resembles a traditional Constitution. Although the current Instrument of Government dates from 1974, it builds on a constitutional tradition with its most immediate predecessor from 1809, and roots extending as far back as 1634.[7] The 1974 Instrument of Government has since its adoption undergone several amendments, and a thorough revision was made in 2010. When the 1974 Instrument of Government was adopted, the Act of Succession, regulating the royal succession and dating back to 1810, became the oldest of Sweden's fundamental laws. The Act of Succession seldom receives attention among lawyers, and indeed the fact that the Swedish monarchy today holds merely ceremonial and symbolic functions is evident not from the Act of Succession, but from the Instrument of Government. By contrast, the Freedom of the Press Act holds a special place in Swedish constitutional tradition, with its protection of press freedom, prohibition of censorship and provisions guaranteeing transparency of public documents. The Freedom of the Press Act is from 1949 but trace its history back to 1766.[8] It has also been subject to amendments, and in 2019 it was modernised as to language and structure. While the Freedom of the Press Act regulates the use of the freedom of expression in printed media (essentially books and newspapers), the Fundamental Law on Freedom of Expression regulates the use of the freedom of expression in non-printed media (essentially broadcasted media and certain webpages). The

[5] See ch 8 and K Kelemen et al, 'Constitutional Reasoning in the Nordic Supreme Courts: A Comparative Empirical Analysis' (2025) *International Journal of Constitutional Law* (forthcoming).

[6] Until 2000, also Finland had several separate constitutional enactments, see ch 5 of this volume by M Dahlberg.

[7] I Cameron and T Bull, 'The Evolution and Gestalt of the Swedish Constitution' in A von Bogdandy, P M Huber & S Ragone (eds), *The Max Planck Handbooks in European Public Law, Volume II: Constitutional Foundations* (Oxford, Oxford University Press, 2023) 602; O Peterson, 'Constitutional History' in J Pierre (ed), *The Oxford Handbook of Swedish Politics* (Oxford: Oxford University Press, 2016) 89; B Debaenst, 'Du Gamla, du Nya: 1974 års regeringsform ur ett rättshistoriskt perspektiv' in M Ruotsi, C Taube, A Jonsson Cornell & O Wilske, *Regeringsformen 50 år: 1974-2024* (Uppsala, Iustus, 2024) 43.

[8] Cameron and Bull (n 7) 602.

Fundamental Law on Freedom of Expression entered into force in 1992 and has a structure similar to the Freedom of the Press Act. Together with the Instrument of Government, the Freedom of the Press Act and the Fundamental Law on Freedom of Expression form a framework protecting freedom of expression. When freedom of expression is exercised elsewhere than in the media types covered by these two specialised enactments, it is protected by the Instrument of Government.

The most recent predecessor to the current Instrument of Government was adopted in 1809. It was drafted and enacted during a period of political turmoil and upheaval; the king was deposed and Russian invasion eventually culminated in the loss of Finland. It was influenced by the separation of powers theory, which delineates executive, legislative and judicial power, however it was realised under national conditions.[9] Notably, in the forefront was the protracted power struggle between the Parliament (*Riksdagen*) and the monarchy,[10] and rather than establishing a tripartite separation of powers, it preserved a 'dualism' in which authority was shared between the monarchy and the Parliament.[11] With regard to the judicial branch, in Sweden, the executive and the judiciary were 'systematically interwoven', a feature which was retained in the 1809 Instrument of Government.[12] Rather than giving effort in positioning the judiciary, the focus of the drafters was the relation between the other two branches. The courts had a weak and withdrawn position, and it is telling that in Sweden, the term 'third branch' ('*tredje statsmakten*') in practice came to refer to the media, not the judiciary.[13] Since the adoption of the Instrument of Government of 1809, Sweden has however moved from separation of powers to parliamentarism, with strong emphasis on popular sovereignty.[14]

Although the 1809 Instrument of Government was still in force until the adoption of the 1974 Instrument of Government, the period before its adoption (1922–1974) has by former professor of constitutional law and Justice of the Supreme Court Fredrik Sterzel been coined 'the constitution-less half century' ('*det författningslösa halvseklet*').[15] This is because the written Constitution no longer corresponded with political reality.[16] Several fundamental constitutional changes

[9] F Sterzel, *Författning i utveckling: Tjugo studier kring Sveriges författning* (Uppsala, Iustus, 2009) 16; Cameron and Bull (n 7) 603; O Peterson, 'Constitutional History' (n 7) 94; E Rönström, 'Forskardebatten kring 1809 års regeringsform: till frågan om grundlagens härkomst' (1997) 100(4) *Statsvetenskaplig tidskrift* 118.

[10] Sterzel (n 9) 16; Cameron and Bull (n 7) 614; O Peterson, 'Constitutional History' (n 7) 94.

[11] J Hirschfeldt, 'Domstolarna som statsmakt – några utvecklingslinjer' (2011/2012) 1 *Juridisk Tidskrift* 3, 4.

[12] C Taube, 'En tredje statsmakt? Domstolarna under 1809 års regeringsform' in M Brundin and M Isberg, *Maktbalans och kontrollmakt: 1809 års händelser, idéer och författningsverk i ett tvåhundraårigt perspektiv* (Stockholm, Sveriges riksdag, 2009) 344–45.

[13] Taube (n 12) 347; Hirschfeldt (n 11) 4.

[14] The opening sentence of the Instrument of Government declares that 'all public power proceeds from the people' (Chapter 1, Section 1); See generally Sterzel (n 9) 98–100.

[15] Sterzel (n 9) 19.

[16] Sterzel (n 9) 18; F Sterzel, 'Ett kvartssekel efter "det författningslösa halvseklet": Har Sverige nu en författning?' in E Smith (ed), *Grundlagens makt: konstitutionen som politiskt redskap och som rättslig*

had been implemented, such as general suffrage and parliamentarism, but these were accomplished without major amendments to the constitutional text.[17] With this in mind it is perhaps of no surprise that the 1809 Instrument of Government was not considered relevant, neither in Parliament nor in the courts.[18] However, the so-called 'constitution-less half century' should by no means be understood as a period without rules; rather, those rules were found in constitutional custom.[19] In this context, the 1974 Instrument of Government has been described as reflecting constitutional continuity rather than change, since it was a description of a political reality that had already evolved beyond the then constitutional text in force.[20] A descriptive constitution was also the aim of the drafters, and it is suggested that this is perhaps something fully comprehended only with the 'constitution-less half century' prior to the adoption of the current Instrument of Government in mind.[21]

Additionally, there is the contradiction that, although the 1809 Instrument of Government did not reflect political realities, it was still subject to a considerable amount of amendments, mostly concerning details.[22] This has been described by Fredrik Sterzel through the formulation of the following principle, referred to as the 'minimum principle' ('*minimiprincipen*'), according to which: 'Nothing is too small to justify a constitutional amendment in Sweden, but some matters are too large to be dealt with in the Constitution, and if they cannot be avoided entirely, one should at least address them as little as possible' (author's translation).[23] This tradition has continued under the 1974 Instrument of Government, which has been amended several times but where certain major developments, such as Sweden's accession to the EU, are hardly visible in the constitutional text.[24]

The formal rules for amendments to the fundamental laws definitely facilitate the aim for a constitution kept relevant and up-to-date. Sweden's fundamental laws have, in a comparative Nordic perspective, been characterised as the most 'flexible'.[25] Under the current rules of the Instrument of Government, amendments can be made with relative ease, though this may not remain the case. At present, two decisions of identical wording are required. There is no need for a qualified majority, a simple majority among the present politicians is enough. The second decision, however, may not be taken until a general election has been held, and

norm (Stockholm, SNS förlag, 2002), 77. For an account in English, see O Peterson, 'Constitutional History' (n 7) 94–99.

[17] O Peterson, 'Constitutional History' (n 7) 95.

[18] See on the attitudes towards the 1809 Instrument of Government: Sterzel (n 9) 19, 99.

[19] Sterzel (n 16) 81.

[20] Sterzel (n 9); Cameron and Bull (n 7) 605.

[21] Sterzel (n 9); Cameron and Bull (n 7) 605.

[22] See generally: F Sterzel, 'Författningens föränderlighet: Från grundlagstext till konstitutionell praxis' in M Brundin and M Isberg, *Maktbalans och kontrollmakt: 1809 års händelser, idéer och författningsverk i ett tvåhundraårigt perspektiv* (Stockholm, Sveriges riksdag, 2009) 455.

[23] Sterzel (n 16) 89–90.

[24] ibid 90.

[25] M Suksi, 'Common Roots of Nordic Constitutional Law' in H Krunke and B Thorarensen (eds), *The Nordic Constitutions: A Comparative and Contextual Study* (Oxford, Hart Publishing, 2018) 24.

at least nine months must have passed between the first submission of the matter to the Parliament and the date of the election, unless an exception is granted.[26] Informally, however, as a constitutional custom, major constitutional amendments have been made in consensus.[27] Furthermore, proposed amendments undergo a thorough inquiry and the results are made public.[28] Constitutional changes in modern times are thus debated and there is an expectation that amendments are proposed only when political consensus is reached.

From a comparative perspective, it has been noted that the adoption of the 1974 Instrument of Government was never transformed into a constitutional moment, as for example in Norway.[29] There is no sense of patriotism associated with the Instrument of Government. Rather, it is the Freedom of the Press Act that holds symbolic value for national identity.[30] Since the days of the 1809 Instrument of Government, attitudes toward the Instrument of Government have however changed considerably. Although it has not become a national symbol among the general public, it is no longer challenging to find leading cases that reference the 1974 Instrument of Government in the jurisprudence of both the Supreme Court and the Supreme Administrative Court.[31]

B. Courts and Constitutional Review

Just as the other Nordic countries, Sweden does not have a constitutional court. There is thus not a single court or body, entrusted with the power of constitutional review and interpretation. In Sweden, every court has the power of constitutional review, although only within the context of the actual case before it

[26] The Instrument of Government, Chapter 8, Section 14. See also the Instrument of Government, Chapter 4, Section 7. However, with the emergence of greater threats to democracy and the rule of law than previously foreseen, a recent commission of inquiry has proposed certain changes to this procedure (SOU 2023:12 Förstärkt skydd för demokratin och domstolarnas oberoende). A proposal incorporating these changes has been submitted to Parliament (prop. 2024/25:165 Stärkt skydd för demokratin och domstolarnas oberoende), which has taken the first affirmative decision. If a second affirmative decision is made after the next general election, the process for constitutional amendments will be modified.

[27] Sterzel (n 9) 34–35. See however also: T Bull, 'Institutions and Divisions of Powers' in H Krunke and D Thorarensen (eds), *The Nordic Constitutions. A Comparative and Contextual Study* (Oxford, Hart Publishing, 2018) 51.

[28] On legislative committees within the legislative process in general, see T Bull, 'Judges without a Court – Judicial Preview in Sweden' in T Campbell, K D Ewing and A Tomkins (eds), *The Legal Protection of Human Rights: Sceptical Essays* (Oxford, Oxford University Press, 2011) 393–95.

[29] See generally: Debaenst (n 7) 63–65.

[30] Johan Hirschfeldt, 'Författningens kärnvärden – symbolik, politik och juridik' in K Åhman, *Regeringsformen 40 år 1974–2014* (Uppsala, Iustus, 2014) 33.

[31] For a comprehensive examination of the judgments concerning the Instrument of Government, see M Sunnqvist, *Konstitutionellt kritiskt dömande: Förändringen av nordiska domares attityder under två sekel* (Stockholm, Institutet för rättshistorisk forskning, 2014). See also K Åhman, *Normprövning: domstols kontroll av svensk lags förenlighet med regeringsformen och europarätten 2000–2010* (Stockholm, Norstedts juridik, 2011).

(concrete constitutional review).[32] The uttermost responsibility for review of the constitutionality of legislation is ultimately shared by the two Supreme Courts: the Supreme Court and the Supreme Administrative Court, both of which will be addressed in this chapter. However, constitutional review is decentralised, and also specialised courts, such as the Labour Court (*Arbetsdomstolen*), can rule on constitutional matters, as well as lower courts. Even other public bodies, including administrative authorities, the Government, as well as private entities entrusted with public responsibilities, are entitled to conduct constitutional review.[33] In practice however, such public bodies do not engage in constitutional review to any meaningful extent.[34]

Constitutional review was formally incorporated into the Instrument of Government in 1979, although it had already been recognised in court practice and preparatory works prior to that.[35] Until the revision of the Instrument of Government in 2010, constitutional review of acts by Parliament and the Government was limited to cases where the error was manifest ('*uppenbart*'). The requirement of manifest error ('*uppenbarhetsrekvisitet*') was removed by the 2010 amendments to the Instrument of Government. However, a reminder was inserted in the section on constitutional review, stating that particular consideration should be given to the fact that Parliament is the foremost representative of the people, while also affirming that fundamental law takes precedence over statutory law.[36] The emphasis on Parliament and the principle of popular sovereignty can be seen as reflecting a certain degree of remaining caution with regard to constitutional review.

The Instrument of Government contains few details on the structure of the court system.[37] The Supreme Court and the Supreme Administrative Court are both the highest instances within a three-tier court structure of general courts and administrative courts respectively. Among the Nordic countries, also Finland has administrative courts, whereas Denmark, Iceland and Norway do not. Notably, Swedish administrative courts have a wider scope of judicial review than is common, since they may review not only the legality of decisions, but also their appropriateness.[38] An explanation to this is a distinctive feature in Swedish administrative practice, namely the independence of the administration. Since 1720, Sweden has maintained a separation between the government and the administrative agencies of the state. This construction was retained in the 1809 Instrument of Government as a way to reduce the King's involvement in the daily affairs of

[32] The Instrument of Government, Chapter 11, Section 14.

[33] The Instrument of Government, Chapter 12, Section 10.

[34] H Wenander, 'Förvaltningens lagprövning' (2015) 3 *Förvaltningsrättslig tidskrift* 421.

[35] See, eg, NJA 1964 s 471 and SOU 1963:17 Författningsutredningen, 155–56. J Nergelius, 'Judicial Review in Swedish Law – A Critical Analysis', (2009) 27(2) *Nordic journal of human rights* 142.

[36] The Instrument of Government, Chapter 11, Section 14.

[37] The Instrument of Government, Chapter 11, Section 1.

[38] Cameron and Bull (n 7) 631.

the state.[39] The principle is codified in the 1974 Instrument of Government and explicitly prohibits involvement in administrative decisions concerning the exercise of public authority against an individual or a municipality, or the application of a statutory law.[40] Neither the Government nor the ministers are responsible for administrative decisions in these individual cases, and hence courts are not interfering with political policies when assessing the appropriateness of the decisions.[41]

A key characteristic of Swedish constitutional law is the combined effect of decentralised constitutional review and the structure of the court system, which lacks an apex court or a distinct body with the power to interpret the constitution. Since the early 1970s the two parallel highest instances in Sweden both have as their main task to provide guidance on the application of the law, that is to create precedents (although a weaker form than common law precedents), but within their respective areas of law.[42] At first glance, the jurisdictions of the Supreme Court and the Supreme Administrative Court seem fairly neatly defined, with the Supreme Court deciding on criminal and private law matters and the Supreme Administrative Court deciding on administrative law matters. However, the jurisdiction and responsibility of the courts is not necessarily as clearly divided as this sketch implies. When it comes to constitutional issues, both courts have the competence to provide guidance if the concrete case before them requires constitutional interpretations. Thus, there is not necessarily one and only apex court within the constitutional law area, as the Supreme Court and the Supreme Administrative Court to some extent share competence. It should be noted here that criminal cases concerning freedom of expression are exclusively within the jurisdiction of the Supreme Court, hence we do not have any overlapping responsibilities with regard to constitutional reasoning in this area. Similarly, cases on public access to official documents are exclusively within the jurisdiction of the Supreme Administrative Court. However, without a constitutional court or specially entrusted body, the presence of two parallel courts at the same hierarchical level brings an extra complexity to the question of jurisdiction in constitutional matters, with the potential to affect the reasoning. This could lead to a power struggle between the courts, each considering itself capable of interpreting the constitution. It could also lead to a reluctance to engage in constitutional reasoning, as courts may wish to avoid interpreting constitutional provisions in depth so as not to narrow the room for interpretation available to the other court. Thus, constitutional reasoning could arguably be influenced not only by deference to Parliament, but also by deference to other courts, particularly in a country like Sweden, where there is a strong culture of consensus in constitutional matters.

39 ibid 603 and 631.
40 Instrument of Government, Chapter 12, Section 2.
41 Cameron and Bull (n 7) 631.
42 Code of Judicial Procedure (Rättegångsbalken), Chapter 54, Section 10; Administrative Court Procedure Act (Förvaltningsprocesslagen (1971:291)), Section 36. See also Cameron and Bull (n 7) 601 and 619.

Alternatively, the existence of several courts with overlapping responsibilities in constitutional matters may result in constructive cooperation, where courts draw inspiration from one another to gradually develop a coherent body of constitutional jurisprudence. At times, the question of instituting a constitutional court has been discussed in Sweden, but this topic is not a lively one in the academic and political debate. Something which is, however, discussed is the possibility of merging the two Supreme Courts or enabling and formalising a closer cooperation between them in certain matters.[43] The reasons for enhanced cooperation are not only related to national constitutional matters, but also include arguments related to the ECHR and EU law. Certain steps for greater collaboration between the two Supreme Courts have already been taken, and further developments might be awaited in this regard.[44]

As explained above, constitutional review in Sweden is concrete, meaning that constitutional litigation is intertwined with criminal, private and administrative law cases. There is also a type of abstract constitutional preview, conducted during the legislative process by the Council on Legislation (*Lagrådet*), thus a priori or ex ante. The Council on Legislation scrutinises draft bills which the Government intends to submit to Parliament regarding amongst other issues whether the draft bill is compatible with the rights and freedoms in the Instrument of Government, as well as the rules on delegation of legislative power from the Parliament.[45] The Council on Legislation consists of justices or former justices from the Supreme Court and the Supreme Administrative Court, who serve on the Council for a period of time depending on the workload, after which they return to their regular duties at the court.[46] The views of the Council on Legislation are, however, only advisory and there are examples of Government and Parliament not following the advice given.[47] Additionally, although it is mandatory to request an opinion in certain matters, failing to do so in a given case does not affect the validity of the subsequently enacted law.[48] However, if the legal act in question would later be tried by a court, the courts may of course take the views of the Council on Legislation in consideration when judging on the constitutionality of the act.[49]

[43] See, eg, F Wersäll, Fredrik, 'Ökad domarmakt och makten över domstolarna' (2017) *Svensk juristtidning* 1; J Hirschfeldt, 'En enda högsta domstol: ett första steg?' (2017) *Svensk juristtidning* 257; H Jäderblom, 'Motiverar risken för motstridiga prejudikat en enda prejudikatdomstol?' (2022) *Svensk juristtidning* 547; H Jonsson and T Bull, 'Har Sverige för många domstolar som ska bidra till prejudikatbildningen?' (2022) *Svensk juristtidning* 536.

[44] Code of Judicial Procedure (Rättegångsbalken), Chapter 3, Section 4; Administrative Court Act (lag (1971:289) om allmänna förvaltningsdomstolar), Section 3; SOU 2023:12, 495–510; prop. 2024/25:165.

[45] The Instrument of Government, Chapter 8, Section 21 and Section 22.

[46] The Instrument of Government, Chapter 8, Section 20; Lag (2003:333) om Lagrådet. See also Bull (n 28) 398.

[47] R Lavin, 'Lagrådet och den offentliga rätten 2009–2011' (2012) 2 *Förvaltningsrättslig tidskrift* 149; R Lavin, *Lagrådet och den offentliga rätten 2007–2009* (Uppsala, Iustus, 2009) 113–15; R Lavin, *Lagrådet och den offentliga rätten 1999–2001* (Lund, Juristförlaget, 2001) 155–58.

[48] The Instrument of Government, Chapter 8, Section 21 and Section 22.

[49] Bull (n 28) 407–408; Nergelius (n 35) 143–44.

The role of the Council on Legislation in the legislative process reflects another feature of the Swedish system: the close connection between the justices and the legislative process. For example, one type of legislative committee is a committee of experts, where the Chair may be a justice from any of the Supreme Courts.[50] As for the justices themselves, they have different experiences before being appointed to the Supreme Court or the Supreme Administrative Court. According to the findings of an empirical study on the backgrounds of justices in the two Supreme Courts, the dominant 'type of Justice' in both Supreme Courts since the 1970s has been judges with experience in government ministries, typically combined with judicial experience in a permanent position in a lower court.[51] The study also reveals a continued presence of academics in both Supreme Courts, although not to a degree comparable with the justices having ministerial experience.[52]

C. A Note on the Selection of Cases

The sample comprises the 40 *leading* judgments from each of the Supreme Court and the Supreme Administrative Court. A leading judgment was for the purpose of the study defined as a case that is considered the most well-known or most important within the legal community at large.[53] As possible proxies for the selection we were encouraged to consider cases that are included in textbooks on constitutional law, cases that are frequently cited in scholarly literature, and cases invoked by the analysed court in its own judgments. None of these proxies was however deemed to be decisive on its own.[54] In Sweden, although various compilations of judgments for law students exist in other areas of law, there is no comparable publication in the field of constitutional law, whereby the canon of cases taught at universities could be easily determined. Accordingly, I combined readings of textbooks and scholarly literature (including commentaries) with case law from the courts themselves.[55]

There was no fixed time frame for the case selection; any case that remained relevant today could be included. The selected Swedish cases primarily cover the period from the early 1980s to the early 2020s. There is, however, a notable gap in the sample between the first selected cases (in 1973 for the Supreme Court and in 1974 for the Supreme Administrative Court) and the beginning of the 1980s (in 1981 for the Supreme Court and in 1980 for the Supreme Administrative Court). Frankly, there are few cases from this period that concern the Instrument of Government, and among those that do exist, seemingly few are still considered

[50] Bull (n 28) 393.

[51] J Lindholm, M Derlén and D Naurin, 'The Ideal Justice: Who Are Selected to Serve and What Does It Say about Swedish High Courts' (2022) 135(4) *Tidsskrift for rettsvitenskap* 397, 410.

[52] For a detailed account on the justices' backgrounds, see ibid 418–29.

[53] See ch 1, section 3.

[54] ibid.

[55] The list of selected cases underwent expert review, see ch 1, section 3.

relevant. A comparably large portion of the cases (21 cases from the Supreme Court and 15 cases from the Supreme Administrative Court) stem from the final period of the time span (from 2010–22).

Generally, it seems that the Swedish constitutional scholarly community is less inclined to engage with older cases, particularly if the relevant principles and rules have since been codified. For example, the Supreme Court case that is generally cited as establishing constitutional review has, since its codification in the Instrument of Government in 1979, been taught and cited for purposes of legal history only. As a comparison, the principle that Sweden is a dualist state is not yet codified, and hence the cases establishing this principle[56] are still actively referenced in scholarly literature.

The selected cases could concern any topic. In fact, we were carefully instructed to disregard the issues covered by the cases when preparing the list of leading cases. It was required only that the cases contained *constitutional* reasoning. With the formal definition of Constitution used by the CONREASON project, where a Constitution is 'a norm or a group of norms which are of the highest rank in a legal order in the sense that the validity of all other norms is measured on them',[57] the Swedish Constitution consists of the four fundamental laws (the Instrument of Government, the Act of Succession, the Freedom of the Press Act and the Fundamental Law on Freedom of Expression). Additionally, since a formal definition of the Constitution is the primary criteria for the selection of cases, this excludes cases which do not involve any of the fundamental laws, for example cases where the ECHR and EU law are applied without recourse to a national norm of the highest rank. Although the ECHR is definitely acknowledged as a part of constitutional law, it does not as such have the superior rank conforming to the CONREASON definition of a Constitution. However, cases which concern principles of a constitutional nature, for example principles concerning the relation between national and international law, are nevertheless included in the selection of cases, irrespective of whether they are codified in any of the fundamental laws. In the selected cases we can thus find the principle that Sweden is a dualist state in relation to international conventions, the principle of primacy of EU law, and the principle of treaty-conform construction.[58] Such principles definitely involve both the ECHR and EU law.

Not all four fundamental laws are present to an equal extent in the sample. There are for example only a few cases concerning the Freedom of the Press Act and the Fundamental Law on Freedom of Expression. This is not attributable to a lack of judgments, but to the character of the enactments in question. In addition to constitutional principles, the Freedom of the Press Act and the Fundamental Law on Freedom of Expression both contain provisions which are of administrative,

[56] NJA 1973 s 423; RÅ 1974 ref 61 (RÅ 1974:121).

[57] A Jakab, 'Constitutional Reasoning. A European Perspective on Judicial Reasoning in Constitutional Courts' (2013) 14(8) *German Law Journal* 1215, 1216.

[58] See, eg, NJA 1973 s 423, NJA 1981 s 1205, NJA 2014 s 79 and RÅ 1974 ref 61 (RÅ 1974:121).

criminal and procedural, rather than constitutional, nature.[59] Such criminal law provisions have been referred to as 'constitutionalised criminal law',[60] and something similar could be said regarding the procedural provisions regarding how cases under the Freedom of the Press Act and the Fundamental Law on Freedom of Expression should be adjudicated, as well as the administrative provisions on public access to official documents. Cases which reflect the criminal, procedural and administrative character of the Freedom of the Press Act and the Fundamental Law on Freedom of Expression, rather than touching upon the broader constitutional right to free speech and transparency, are not selected for this study. This choice explains why there are relatively few cases (four out of 40 from the Supreme Court and the Supreme Administrative Court respectively) among the selected cases which concern these two fundamental laws, even though there is a considerable number of cases concerning both enactments in the jurisprudence of the two Supreme Courts at large. This jurisprudence is, however, mainly concerned with constitutionalised details which in other countries would be set out in statutory law. Additionally, although the Act of Succession is a fundamental law, it is invoked only during major events within the royal family, rather than being a subject of constitutional litigation. Concluding, for the purpose of the selection of cases, I have used a formal definition of the Constitution, supplemented by the hereby described delimitations and deviations.

II. Argumentative Patterns

A. Applicability and Deference

This study focuses on constitutional reasoning. Consequently, arguments concerning the interpretation of statutory law are only considered relevant insofar as they contribute to clarify the meaning of the constitutional provisions. This presents a particular challenge in relation to the reasoning of Sweden's two Supreme Courts. For Swedish courts, constitutional arguments may constitute just one aspect of a case, and not always the decisive one. However, the characterisation of the argumentative patterns in our study applies only to the constitutional dimension of the case, and it says nothing about the reasoning in other areas of law present in the case. It is thus important not to draw conclusions regarding the overall reasoning in the selected cases based on the results of this study.

One of the questions addressed in our study is whether courts are inclined to frame a constitutional case in any particular way, for example as a fundamental rights issue or as a matter of competence. But from a Swedish perspective, even before a case is framed as either a competence conflict or a restriction of rights,

[59] H Strömberg and B Lundell, *Sveriges författning*, 23rd edn (Lund, Studentlitteratur, 2019) 14.
[60] Cameron and Bull (n 7) 602.

another question arises: Is the case at all framed as a *constitutional* case? And if so, to what extent is it resolved by *constitutional* provisions? In the Swedish constitutional tradition, the search for applicable provisions to apply in a given case does not necessarily begin with the highest-ranking law, but with the lowest. Constitutional interpretation in Sweden, at least in relation to the Instrument of Government, has been described as 'bottom-up' rather than 'top-down'.[61] Accordingly, when more specific and detailed legal provisions exist, they are applied before broader, more abstract principles, even if those principles are found in higher-ranking legal norms.[62] For comparison, again, the Freedom of the Press Act has traditionally been treated as substantive law and consequently applied in a manner entirely different from the Instrument of Government.[63] Among possible reasons suggested for this difference are the comparably more precise formulations in the Freedom of the Press Act, but also a greater familiarity with the enactment as well as strong political support, including expectations from the press, for its application.[64] Especially, as explained above, during the so-called 'constitution-less half-century', no comparable support existed for the Instrument of Government.[65]

Although Swedish courts nowadays without question demonstrate a greater willingness to apply the Instrument of Government, there are still cases which are solved without excessively delving into constitutional provisions. An example is a case from 2018, concerning a local public order regulation prohibiting begging in public places.[66] In the case, the Supreme Administrative Court avoided addressing whether the prohibition violated freedom of expression protected by the Instrument of Government and the ECHR explicitly. Instead, it limited itself to a general statement that local public order regulations must not conflict with higher-ranking norms or concern matters that are required to be regulated by law, thereby only implicitly suggesting that the measure did not constitute a restriction of a fundamental right.[67] In the end, the Court concluded that the regulation was admissible by applying a statutory law provision according to which public order regulations imposing unwarranted limitations was prohibited, in conjunction with the, albeit constitutional, principle of local self-government, which was used as an argument for deference.

Even when a case prompts the court to consider constitutional provisions, it does not necessarily follow that the issue will be resolved through the application of these provisions. In the study, we measured the use of arguments regarding

[61] Cameron and Bull (n 7) 619.
[62] ibid.
[63] ibid.
[64] ibid.
[65] Sterzel (n 9) 15, 19 and 99.
[66] HFD 2018 ref 75 (not included in the sample).
[67] This is also how the lower courts subsequently interpreted the judgment, stating that although the Supreme Administrative Court did not explicitly express it, it must be assumed to infer that the contested decision did not violate either the Instrument of Government or the ECHR (Kammarrätten i Göteborg, mål 4636-19).

the applicability of the constitution (N14). Such arguments may for example be related to a political question doctrine as well as to matters concerning applicability *ratione materiae.* Arguments classified under *ratione materiae* applicability also encompass instances where the courts assess whether a particular situation constitutes a *restriction* of a constitutional right or if it should instead be regarded as a neutral regulation that does not affect the right in question.

The preparatory works regarding the Instrument of Government from the 1970s present an understanding that not every regulation concerning the use of the fundamental rights and freedoms in the Instrument of Government entails a restriction.[68] A repeatedly cited passage originates from a committee of inquiry on fundamental rights and freedoms.[69] The committee was set up in 1973 to examine how such rights should be protected under the Instrument of Government. In its report, it devoted a section to the issue of restrictions. According to the committee, 'not every negative action taken by public authorities that is prompted by someone exercising a right in a certain way or that compels someone to accept a certain intrusion on their integrity, constitutes a restriction of a fundamental right'.[70] Instead, the 'constitutional protection is primarily directed against actions by public authorities that involve actual physical coercion or the criminalisation of certain acts'.[71] The committee's proposal led to the 1976 reform of the protection of rights and freedoms in the Instrument of Government. In the preparatory works to the 1976 amendments it was stated that 'in general, a regulation constitutes a restriction only if it is explicitly stated or implicitly evident from the regulation that a limitation of a right is intended or forms a natural part of the regulation'.[72] The narrow understanding of what constitutes a restriction presented in the preparatory works has however been subject to critique,[73] and in later preparatory works there are signs of an emerging tendency to also consider the impact ('*effekt*') of specific rules.[74]

Both the determination of whether a matter falls within the scope of a constitutional right and the assessment of whether that right has been restricted can be approached in a deferential way. Examples of such narrow definitions can be found in two cases from the 1980s. In a case from 1986, the Supreme Administrative

[68] Prop. 1975/76:209 Om ändring i regeringsformen, 154; SOU 1975:75 Medborgerliga fri- och rättigheter i regeringsformen, 104.

[69] The committee of inquiry 1973-1975 (*1973 års fri- och rättighetsutredning*, SOU 1975:75).

[70] ibid.

[71] SOU 1975:75, 104 (author's translations).

[72] Prop. 1975/76:209, 154 (author's translation).

[73] I Cameron, 'Vad är en begränsning av en rättighet?' in K Åhman, *Regeringsformen 40 år 1974-2014* (Uppsala, Iustus, 2014) 168–70; K Åhman, '2 kap. RF, Europakonventionen och EU:s stadga om grundläggande rättigheter – en jämförelse' (2016) *Svensk juristtidning* 100 år (festskrift) 460, 469–70; T Bull, *Mötes- och demonstrationsfriheten: en statsrättslig studie av mötes- och demonstrationsfrihetens innehåll och gränser i Sverige, Tyskland och USA* (Uppsala, Iustus, 1997) 424–33; J Nergelius, *Konstitutionellt rättighetsskydd: svensk rätt i ett komparativt perspektiv* (Stockholm, Fritze, 1996) 582–83.

[74] See generally Cameron (n 73) 171–73 and Åhman (n 73) 470–71.

Court rejected the argument that a decision to prohibit street music conflicted with the provisions on freedom of assembly in the Instrument of Government. The Court, combining scope and restriction in a narrow fashion, held that, as it was a decision based on statutory law rules on sanitary nuisance, it did not concern the area protected by the Instrument of Government's regulation of freedom of assembly and hereby it could not be considered a restriction of that right.[75] In a case from 1982, the Supreme Court rejected the argument that freedom of demonstration, protected under the Instrument of Government, would exempt individuals from criminal liability for actions committed during a protest against test drilling for nuclear fuel storage.[76] During the demonstration, the participants had allegedly committed the offence of unlawful dispossession by physically blocking access to the work site with their bodies and refusing to disperse. According to the Supreme Court, the provision in the Criminal Code was not to be regarded as a restriction of the freedom of demonstration. Therefore, the mere fact that an act of unlawful dispossession was committed in connection with the exercise of that freedom did not exempt it from criminal liability. This position has recently received renewed attention amid climate change protests. In a 2023 case, the Supreme Court acknowledged that the criminal offence of unlawful intrusion can, in certain instances, constitute a restriction. However, it was generally considered permissible to penalise unlawful intrusion.[77] The key difference between the two approaches is that when a matter is not classified as a restriction, the procedural safeguards and justification requirements that typically apply to rights restrictions are not triggered. A more nuanced approach was also suggested in the preparatory works to the 2010 amendments to the Instrument of Government. In a section on constitutional review, it was proposed that constitutional review is of particular importance in, for example, the area of fundamental rights and freedoms, whereas a more limited use was considered appropriate in relation to the organisation and function of state bodies. In this regard, it was emphasised that concerning central aspects of the regulation of rights and freedoms in the Instrument of Government, it is 'of particular importance that the rules laid down in the Constitution are given full effect in judicial practice'.[78]

It is generally acknowledged that Swedish courts show deference to the legislator, although the political question is not discussed in terms of a doctrine. Arguments related to a political question doctrine are raised in 13 out of 40 cases from the Supreme Court and in 14 out of 40 cases from the Supreme Administrative Court. Arguments that the issue falls within the discretion of the legislator and hence the law or decision is not to be set aside by reference to the constitution are coded as political question doctrine. Deferential arguments, where it for example

[75] RÅ 1986 ref 108.
[76] NJA 1982 s 621 (one of the cases selected for the study).
[77] NJA 2023 s 1057 (decided after the sample was set).
[78] Prop. 2009/10:80 En reformerad grundlag, 147 (author's translation).

is suggested that it is for the legislator to solve a particular issue, are also coded as a political question doctrine.[79]

In Sweden, whether an issue is political (and therefore not to be decided by the judiciary) can be raised throughout the case instead of being dealt with as a preliminary question. Thus, it may very well be the case that the court first interprets the constitutional provision, and only then assesses whether this interpretation should have any effect in the given case. For instance, in the 1981 case on Saami rights, one Supreme Court justice considered that there existed 'good reasons' to consider that the disputed provisions amounted to unlawful discrimination. However, he concluded that this did not meet the threshold of a 'manifest error' and aligned with the majority (dismissing the Saami claim).[80] Also, arguments related to whether the court should give the legislator a certain leeway (manifest error requirement) are coded as political question considerations. Although the manifest error requirement was abolished in 2010, its underlying principles have necessarily not been abandoned. In a 2022 Supreme Administrative Court case concerning the right to a fair trial, the Court held that, under certain conditions, it may be contrary to the right to a fair trial enshrined in the Instrument of Government, and, if the case concerns civil rights or obligations, the ECHR, for an individual who wins a case against the state to be denied compensation for legal costs. However, the majority adopted a deferential position, concluding that the introduction of a general right for individuals to receive compensation for legal costs in administrative courts raises both principled and practical concerns. These are matters better suited for legislative decision-making, and such a system should therefore not be introduced through case law, unless it is mandated by the right to a fair trial (which the court considered it was not).[81]

Certain types of cases are subject to political question considerations in that they are reviewed in a way that respects political decisions from the outset. This concerns cases where decisions from the government or an administrative authority are appealed to the Supreme Administrative Court in the form of legal review (*rättsprövning*)[82] and decisions of the local self-government which are appealed to administrative courts in the form of municipal review (*laglighetsprövning* or *kommunalbesvär*).[83] Among the selected cases from the Supreme Administrative Court there are eight legal review cases (six against a decision of the government) and five municipal review cases. The municipal review is a review of local self-government decisions, and it is a review of legality, not appropriateness.[84] Similarly,

[79] See the instructions for variable N14 in the Codebook in the Appendix.

[80] Justice Bengtsson, separate opinion in NJA 1981 s 1 (dissent regarding the reasoning, not the result)

[81] HFD 2022 ref 10.

[82] Legal Review of Governmental Decisions Act (Lag (2006:304) om rättsprövning av vissa regeringsbeslut); replacing Legal Review of Administrative Decisions Act (Lag (1988:205) om rättsprövning av vissa förvaltningsbeslut.

[83] Local Government Act (Kommunallagen (2017:725)), Chapter 13.

[84] Local Government Act, Chapter 13, Section 8; prop. 2016/17:171 En ny kommunallag, 252–54.

when it concerns the legal review, the preparatory works are careful to emphasise that the courts in these cases are expected to show deference and refrain from judging on political considerations.[85] Despite this instruction, the Supreme Administrative Court does expound on the meaning of the Constitution in these cases, and it seems that review of legality is thus not in itself an obstacle to explicit constitutional reasoning. For example, a 1999 Supreme Court case on the premature closure of a nuclear power plant is generally considered as one of the leading cases on the principle of proportionality.[86] And in two cases concerning Jehovah's Witnesses' right to state funding, the court expounded not only on consent to medical treatment in relation to children, but also on the right to vote (concluding that it is a right, not a duty).[87]

B. Wording, Preparatory Works, Purpose and Context

The current Instrument of Government from 1974 does not include any provisions on constitutional interpretation. However, its predecessor, the 1809 Instrument of Government, contained a provision (§ 84) stating that the fundamental laws should, in every instance, be applied according to their wording. On the surface, this provision appears to function as a relative straightforward rule on interpretation. However, throughout the years its precise meaning has been the subject of debate and disagreement.[88] For example, when read in the context of constitutional amendments, the provision could instead be interpreted as implying a prohibition against arbitrary changes to the Constitution disguised as explanatory statements or interpretative clarifications, an approach that had regularly been employed until then.[89]

The debate surrounding § 84 was brought up in two committees of inquiry preceding the adoption of the 1974 Instrument of Government,[90] and the existence of the differing interpretations as to its meaning was seemingly among the reasons for not proposing a corresponding provision in the new Instrument of Government.[91] Both committees concluded that the provision was generally cited as supporting evidence for an interpretation already favoured on other grounds. While the 1963 committee argued that this, in itself, cast doubt on the justification for the paragraph, the 1972 committee noted that it was also unclear whether the provision had ever played a meaningful role.[92] It was thus a deliberate choice to not retain the provision in the 1974 Instrument of Government. Stating that no

[85] Prop. 1987/88:69 Om europakonventionen och rätten till domstolsprövning i Sverige, 23–25.
[86] RÅ 1999 ref 76.
[87] HFD 2013 ref 72 (in the sample); HFD 2017 ref 4 (in the sample).
[88] See generally on the debate: Bull (n 73) 238–40.
[89] See Sterzel (n 9) 92–98.
[90] The committee of inquiry 1954–63 (*Författningsutredningen*, SOU 1963:16–19) and the committee of inquiry 1966–72 (*Grundlagberedningen*, SOU 1972:15).
[91] SOU 1963:17, 513; SOU 1972:15 Ny regeringsform–Ny riksdagsordning, 319; see generally: Bull (n 73).
[92] SOU 1963:17, 513; SOU 1972:15, 319.

special rule for the interpretation of the Constitution can or should be established, it was instead emphasised that fundamental laws should 'naturally' be interpreted according to the same principles that apply to the interpretation of laws in general.[93] As the constitutional legislator discontinued further discussion on the issue of constitutional interpretation, the debate on how the fundamental law should be interpreted could continue among legal scholars. Among the interpretative tools suggested we find the ordinary meaning of words, preparatory works and purpose-oriented interpretation, but also systematic considerations.[94]

In our study, we measured the use of the ordinary meaning of words as a type of argument (N16). The ordinary meaning comprises the grammatical-literal interpretation of words or phrases in their everyday or professional meaning. It is noteworthy that the 1974 Instrument of Government was not enacted in isolation, but into an already existing legislative framework. This is relevant also for amendments, and certain words used in the Instrument of Government may have a precise meaning outside the constitutional law context.[95] Arguments which focus on the literal interpretation of the constitutional text is used by the majority of the Supreme Court in nine out of 40 cases and by the majority of the Supreme Administrative Court in seven out of 40 cases. That the wording is not always explicitly interpreted in these grammatical-literal terms does not imply that the Supreme Courts disregard the wording in the majority of the cases. According to the methodology of the study, only explicit use of the ordinary meaning of words is coded for. A more allowing attitude would have led to the argument being coded for in the majority of the selected cases. The wording is typically the point of departure for the constitutional reasoning; however it is not always developed in this grammatical-literal sense, but rather utilised as a stepping stone to the next argument: the preparatory works. After presenting the constitutional provision, the Supreme Courts typically shift focus from the wording to the legislature's intent in relation to the wording. The method of interpretation where the wording is combined with the preparatory works is in legal research referred to as 'strict', as opposed to a 'pragmatic' interpretation, where also practical considerations are of relevance.[96]

As for the intentional argument, references to preparatory works (teleological-historical argument or subjective teleological argument, N23) are explicitly present in about half of the selected cases (the argument is used by the majority of the Supreme Court in 21 out of 40 cases and by the majority of the Supreme Administrative Court in 19 out of 40 cases). The variable is only considered present where there is an explicit reference, either to preparatory works in general or to a particular preparatory work. However, we only measure the arguments which are publicly put forward. Among the selected cases, there is one from each Supreme

[93] SOU 1963:17, 513; SOU 1972:15, 319. Sterzel (n 9) 99.

[94] See generally on the debate: Bull (n 73) 241–50.

[95] G Michanek, 'Markägare – med rätt att döda?' (1995) *Miljörättslig tidskrift*, discussed in Bull (n 73) 247.

[96] H Strömberg, *Normgivningsmakten enligt 1974 års regeringsform*, 3rd edn (Lund, Juristförlaget, 1999) 201.

Court, where it is clear to the informed reader from the formulations used that preparatory works have been consulted, but there is no reference to these works, or to preparatory works in general.[97]

In Sweden, preparatory works are a source of law that is commonly used in relation to statutory interpretation.[98] The tradition of interpreting legislation based on the legislator's intent is longstanding, but it has eventually been supplemented by an emphasis on the wording.[99] In a criminal law context, the Supreme Court has for example emphasised that the will of the legislator cannot extend beyond the wording, to encompass statements in preparatory works that would 'come as a surprise'.[100] While preparatory works are not legally binding, they are nonetheless considered influential in the interpretation of legislation.

The reliance on preparatory works for the interpretation can be explained not only by tradition, but also by their availability and usefulness. To fully appreciate the significance attributed to preparatory works, one needs to contemplate the Swedish legislative procedure. Legislative proposals are investigated and debated, and the government proposals to the Parliament typically include a comprehensive package of reasons for the proposal as well as explanations regarding the proposed legal provisions. A preparatory work may range from different types of inquiries predating the government proposal to the actual proposal sent to the Parliament and the parliamentary committees' comments on the proposal.[101]

A question brought up in the debate on how the constitution should be interpreted is whether the preparatory works should be considered to the same extent in constitutional questions and whether the age of the preparatory works should be taken into account.[102] The strive for consensus present in constitutional amendments may be an additional reason for why the preparatory works should be considered. They are not only available, but also demonstrate the political agreement of the constitutional lawmakers. However, the pursuit of consensus may also lead to preparatory works that are less detailed on sensitive matters, to the point of obscuring rather than clarifying the underlying rationale.[103]

As for the Swedish case, the interesting finding is not that preparatory works are used in the sample, but that they are not used more extensively. A Nordic comparison shows that Finland and Sweden have the highest proportion of references to preparatory works, whereas Denmark and Iceland are in-between and Norway has the comparatively lowest proportion (see Figure 1).

[97] NJA 1982 s 621 and RÅ 2005 ref 39.

[98] A Peczenik and G Bergholtz, 'Statutory interpretation in Sweden' in N MacCormick and R S Summers (eds), *Interpreting statutes: A Comparative Study* (Aldershot, Dartmouth, 1991) 311.

[99] M Sunnqvist, 'Mord, prejudikattolkning och lagtolkning' (2016) *Svensk juristtidning* 541, 449–550.

[100] NJA 2016 s 3 (not in our sample).

[101] H-H Vogel, 'Sources of Swedish Law' in C Wong and M Bogdan (eds), *Swedish Legal System*, 2nd edn (Stockholm, Norstedts juridik, 2022) 28–31.

[102] See generally on the debate: Bull (n 73) 241–50.

[103] For example regarding the instructions on the treatment of the ECHR following its incorporation, see generally J Nergelius, *Svensk statsrätt*, 5th edn (Lund, Studentlitteratur, 2022). The same applies to the government bill on the incorporation of the Convention on the Right of the Child and the interpretative guidance provided therein.

Figure 1 Proportion of cases in which there is reference to preparatory works

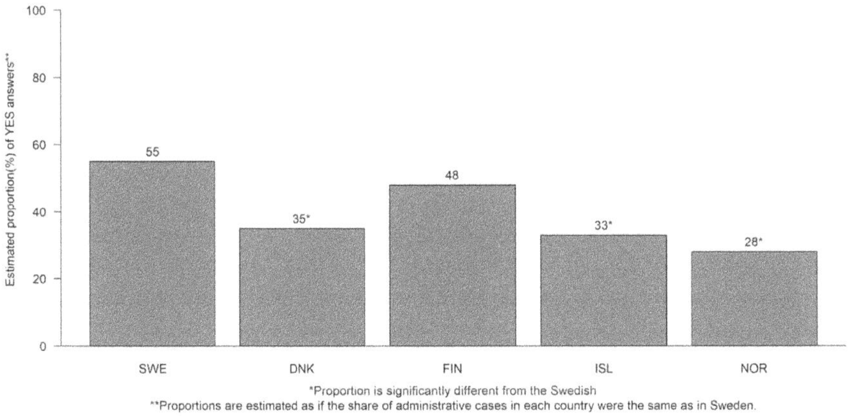

As for Sweden and Finland, it must be noted that the constitutional enactments in both countries are of relatively recent origin.[104] Although the Swedish Instrument of Government was originally enacted in 1974, it underwent revision in 2010, and after the revision it is the preparatory works associated with the revised version that are primarily used.

References to the purpose of the text itself, rather than the purpose of the constitution-makers (teleological-textual argument or objective teleological argument, N22), are comparatively less frequent in the jurisprudence of both Courts (the argument is used by the Supreme Court in eight out of 40 cases and by the Supreme Administrative Court in three out of 40 cases). The difference between the two Supreme Courts might be explained by their different jurisdictions. Criminal law cases including criminal cases concerning freedom of expression belong to the Supreme Court and these cases are also among those where we find examples of reasoning related to purpose (for example in relation to the principle of legality). One possible explanation for the generally low use of teleological-textual arguments is that the preparatory works are so detailed with regard to purpose and legislative intent that there is little else left to be explored. Just as when it concerned the ordinary meaning of words, the Supreme Courts focus on the constitution-maker's understanding of the purpose, instead of elaborating on the purpose which might stem from the text itself.

Finally, on the systematic approach the following can be concluded. Consistent with the study's methodology, the combination of several constitutional provisions, even if they are not explicitly used to interpret one another, is coded as domestic harmonising arguments (N17). About half of the selected Swedish cases (19 out of 40 cases from the Supreme Court and 20 out of 40 cases from the Supreme Administrative Court) contain this type of argument. However, these instances do not necessarily involve a 'true' domestic harmonising argument, where an unclear

[104] See also ch 5, s III(A).

provision is read in conjunction with another provision, and through this operation acquires a certain meaning (systematic interpretation). The Instrument of Government is structured similarly to ordinary legislation, comprising numerous provisions that must be interpreted and applied in conjunction with one another. For example, when assessing the permissibility of restrictions on freedom of expression under the Instrument of Government, one must consider not only the provision defining the scope of the right, but also three additional provisions that collectively outline the conditions under which such restrictions are allowed. Similarly, when addressing delegation of legislative power, a conclusion might require a combination of several provisions in a certain order of application.

A 2005 Supreme Court case can serve as an example of a more elaborated domestic harmonisation.[105] The case in question concerned the permissibility, under the Instrument of Government, of setting out the details of a criminal offence only in a regulation issued by an administrative authority. The Instrument of Government explicitly allows regulations detailing criminal offences to be delegated by the Parliament to the Government, as long as there is a law issued by the Parliament that prescribes the punishment. The regulation in question had, however, been issued by an administrative authority through sub-delegation from the Government. The provision on such sub-delegation in the Instrument of Government contains no limitations as to subject matter: anything can be sub-delegated by the Government, as long as the Government has the power to issue regulations in the first place. Although the sub-delegation in the case thus did not conflict with the wording of the relevant chapter (Chapter 8) in the Instrument of Government, the Supreme Court assessed whether it could still come in conflict with the requirement that restrictions on rights and freedoms must be prescribed by law. The word 'law' in the context of restrictions to fundamental rights and freedoms is limited to statutory law. By interpreting Chapter 2 on fundamental rights and freedoms together with Chapter 8, the Supreme Court concluded that, although sub-delegation of provisions detailing criminal offences punishable by imprisonment was in principle permitted under the rules on delegation in Chapter 8, it followed from a systematic interpretation that sub-delegation to administrative authorities was not allowed as it would represent a significant departure from the principle that criminal provisions involving deprivation of liberty must be enacted by the Parliament.

C. Previous Rulings

Arguments based on previous rulings from the court (N19) are present in all Nordic countries, and Sweden is no exception. A Nordic comparison shows that Norway stands out as the most frequent user of precedent-based arguments. Such arguments are least used in Denmark, Finland, and Sweden, while Iceland shows a greater willingness to refer to previous rulings, although not to the same extent as Norway (see Figure 2).

[105] NJA 2005, s 33. For an earlier example, see RÅ 80 2:69 (Justice Petrén).

Figure 2 Proportion of cases in which there is reference to precedent (N19)

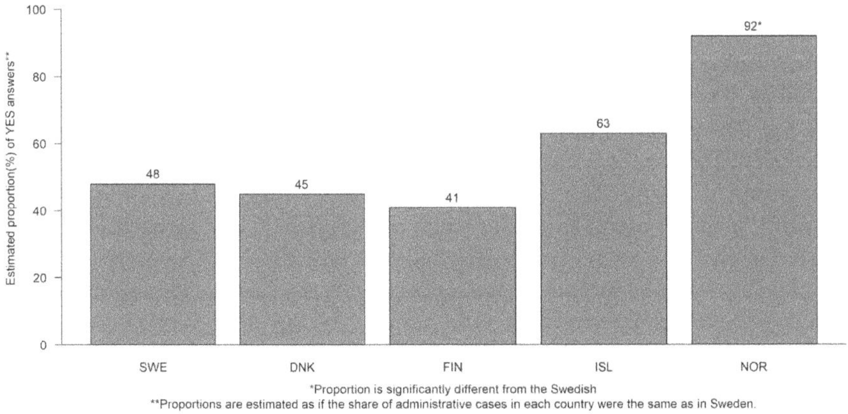

The Swedish Supreme Court refers to previous rulings in 23 of the 40 selected cases. The majority of the cases are from the year of 2005 and onwards. The first two cases in the selection when the Supreme Court used previous rulings regarding the Instrument of Government as an argument are from 2005. There are two outliers from the year of 1985 and 2000 respectively, however they concern not the Instrument of Government, but the Freedom of the Press Act.[106] The Supreme Administrative Court refers to previous rulings in 15 of the 40 selected cases. These cases are more evenly distributed among the selected cases, beginning in 1987.

By precedent-based argument we mean the use of previous judgments of the same court, already resolved, in order to interpret the text of the constitution. In the Swedish case, the two Supreme Courts have for this type of argument been considered as one, meaning that references to cases from either of the courts have been included. As a rule, the Supreme Courts prefer their own case law, although there are instances when they without further ado refer to the case law of the other court. For example, in a 2018 Supreme Court case,[107] concerning proportionality assessment regarding forced land transfer from one property to another, the Supreme Court referred to a 1999 Supreme Administrative Court case[108] regarding property rights and proportionality under the Instrument of Government. And the Supreme Administrative Court in a 2022 case[109] on the issue of reimbursement of legal costs in administrative proceedings in relation to the right to a fair trial in the Instrument of Government[110] referred to Supreme Court case law on the question of costs and expenses.[111] Thus, here we have two examples of provisions in the Instrument of Government being interpreted by both the Supreme Court and

[106] NJA 1985, s 893.
[107] NJA 2018, s 753.
[108] RÅ 1999 ref 76.
[109] HFD 2022 ref 10.
[110] The Instrument of Government, Chapter 2, Section 11.
[111] For example NJA 2015, s 374.

the Supreme Administrative Court. In both cases there is also a notable reliance on the ECHR and the jurisprudence of the European Court of Human Rights (ECtHR).

This type of argument is coded as a binary value, meaning that the dataset does not tell us how many references to previous rulings there are, only that there is at least one. An empirical study of the Supreme Court rulings irrespective of subject matter shows a trend, starting in the late 1980s, towards an increase in references to previous rulings.[112] One reason for this increase, suggested by the authors of the study, is that it marks the point when the Supreme Court's transition from a court of appeal to a court of precedent began to take effect.[113] Our data also show a tendency towards an increase in references to previous rulings, which is consistent with these findings. However, the cases selected for our study were chosen based on their perceived importance, and not in order to be representative over time. Therefore, our study cannot confirm any trends, but it does show that even within our limited sample, we observe the same tendencies noted by other authors.

Something which could also explain the previously rare use of references to previous rulings is the change in the writing style of the courts. Regarding the Supreme Court, this development has been described as a shift from concise and tersely written judgments, where the conclusions are presented as logical deductions from the legal norms, and references to sources are regarded as unnecessary, to more extensive and reasoned decisions that explore and compare alternative solutions.[114] The development is generally considered to have begun in the early 1970s, with its effects becoming evident approximately two decades later.[115] Also this change is attributed to the court's development towards a precedent-creating authority.[116] This tendency is also reflected in our sample of cases, and a similar pattern can be observed in the other Nordic countries.

Since our study focuses on constitutional law, it must also be borne in mind that the current Instrument of Government was adopted in 1974, and its predecessor was rarely applied in court. Consequently, there was a lack of relevant cases to cite. This is reflected in the gap in the sample between the beginning of the 1970s and the beginning of the 1980s, for both courts. With an increasing volume of cases, references to prior rulings have become more frequent, establishing a steady

[112] M Derlén and J Lindholm, 'Judiciell aktivism eller prejudikatbildning? En empirisk granskning av Högsta domstolen' (2016) *Svensk juristtidning* 143, 148–51.

[113] ibid 156–57.

[114] S Strömholm, M Lyles and F Valguarnera, *Rätt, rättskällor och rättstillämpning: en lärobok i allmän rättslära*, 6th edn (Stockholm, Norstedts Juridik, 2020) 397–401; B Bengtsson, 'Högsta domstolens nya skrivsätt' (2012/2013) 3 *Juridisk Tidskrift* 743, 743–74; D Mattsson, 'Reformen år 1971 och en framåtblick' (2022) *Svensk juristtidning* 580, 584–85; G Bergholtz and A Peczenik, 'Precedent in Sweden' in N MacCormick and R S Summers (eds), *Interpreting precedents: A Comparative Study* (Aldershot, Dartmouth, 1997) 293, 295–96.

[115] S Strömholm, M Lyles and F Valguarnera (n 114) 400; Bengtsson (n 114) 743; C Danielsson, 'Utformningen av Högsta domstolens avgöranden nu och då' (2022) *Svensk juristtidning* 513, 516; Derlén and Lindholm (n 112) 151–53.

[116] S Strömholm, M Lyles and F Valguarnera, *Rätt, rättskällor och rättstillämpning*, 400; Derlén and Lindholm (n 112) 151–53.

practice of citation also in constitutional matters. Thus, the growing tendency to reference previous rulings can be reasonably attributed to the increasing number of such rulings and a shift in judicial writing style that allows justices to engage with them more extensively.

D. International Law Harmonisation

Under the notion of harmonisation with international law, we have searched for references to international law, including the ECHR and EU law. Harmonisation is in this case a question of whether the Supreme Courts interpret constitutional law in the light of international law. Using a broad conception of harmonisation, essentially encompassing a general willingness to apply international law in individual cases, we arrive at the following results.

References to the ECHR are present in 23 out of 40 cases from the Supreme Court, but only in nine out of 40 cases from the Supreme Administrative Court. The lower rate of the Supreme Administrative Court can be explained by the fact that it deals with a higher proportion of state organisation cases, which rarely involve considerations of international law. An empirical study on the citations of international law (including not only conventions and treaties but also case law of international courts) in the Supreme Courts of the three Scandinavian countries (Denmark, Sweden, and Norway) concluded that Norway stands out for its significantly higher number of references to international courts compared to its Danish and Swedish counterparts.[117] In our study, Iceland takes the lead, followed by Finland and Norway (see Figure 3).

Figure 3 Proportion of cases in which an international harmonising argument is invoked

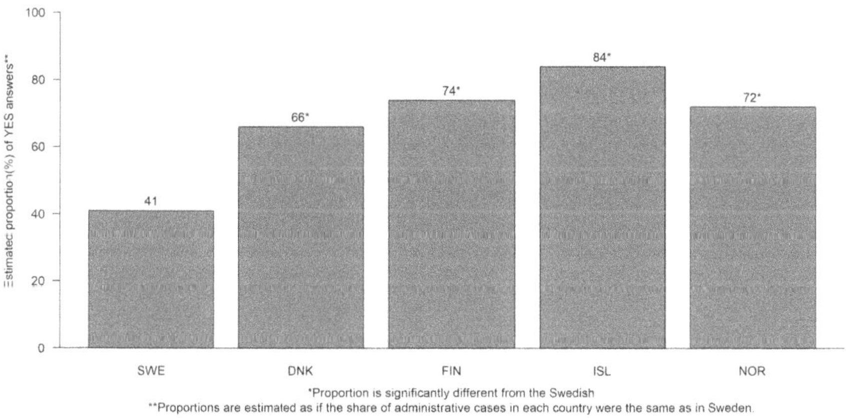

[117] M Wind, 'Do Scandinavians Care about International Law? A Study of Scandinavian Judges' Citation Practice to International Law and Courts' (2016) 85 *Nordic Journal Of International Law* 291.

When it comes to international conventions and national law, Sweden is a dualist state just like the other Nordic countries. This essentially means that an international convention cannot be applied by a national court unless transformed or incorporated into national law.[118] The ECHR was incorporated in 1995 with the status of a statutory law.[119] At the same time, a provision was inserted in the Instrument of Government stating that no act of law or other provision may be adopted which contravenes Sweden's undertakings under the ECHR.[120] This prohibition was inserted to highlight the importance of the ECHR, but it was acknowledged in the preparatory works that the provision as such just reflected the general requirement for the legislature not to issue laws that conflict with any obligations under international law towards other states. According to the preparatory works, the provision is expressly addressed only to the legislature, although it was anticipated that it could also be applied by the courts when exercising constitutional review.[121] The preparatory works are careful to emphasise that the said provision in the Instrument of Government does not change the fact that the incorporation of the ECHR takes place through statutory law. The ECHR is thus 'not given formal status as a fundamental law, nor is any new level created in the hierarchy of norms, between statutory law and the constitution'.[122] However, no other incorporated convention is mentioned in the Instrument of Government the same way as the ECHR, and some authors refer to the ECHR as having a 'semi-constitutional'[123] or a 'quasi-constitutional' status.[124]

Since the ECHR is incorporated at the level of statutory law, the preparatory works suggest solving conflicts by using general principles of interpretation (the principle of treaty-conform construction) and principles of conflict resolution (the principles of *lex superior*, *lex specialis* and *lex posterior*).[125] Additionally, the preparatory works reflect on the response by the Supreme Court during the consultation procedure,[126] suggesting that the special character of the ECHR (as a human

[118] NJA 1973 s 423; RÅ 1974 ref 61 (RÅ 1974:121), both cases selected for the study. See also AD 1972 no. 5; SOU 1974:100 Internationella överenskommelser och svensk rätt, 44-46; O Bring, 'Monism och dualism igår och idag' in R Stern and I Österdahl (eds), *Folkrätten i svensk rätt* (Malmö, Liber, 2012) 16, 28–29; I Cameron and T Bull, 'Sweden' in J Gerards and J Fleuren (eds), *Implementation of the European Convention on Human Rights and of the judgments of the ECtHR in national case-law: A comparative analysis* (Cambridge, Intersentia, 2014) 261, 266–68.

[119] Lag (1994:1219) om den europeiska konventionen angående skydd för de mänskliga rättigheterna och de grundläggande friheterna.

[120] The Instrument of Government, Chapter 2, Section 19.

[121] Prop. 1993/94:117 Inkorporering av Europakonventionen och andra fri- och rättighetsfrågor, 36–37.

[122] ibid (author's translation).

[123] J Husa, 'Nordic Constitutionalism and European Human Rights – Mixing Oil and Water?' (2010) 55 *Scandinavian Studies in Law* 101, 112.

[124] Cameron and Bull (n 118) 266.

[125] Prop. 1993/94:117, 37–38.

[126] During the consultation procedure, relevant authorities express their views on, for example, the conclusions of a commission of inquiry. Accordingly, the Supreme Court and the Supreme Administrative Court may provide opinions in their own capacity, not only through the Council on Legislation.

right convention) implies that as such it ought to carry special weight if there is a conflict with statutory provisions.[127] Although conflicts between the fundamental laws and the ECHR were not anticipated, it is quite clear from the preparatory works that if the ECHR and a provision of a fundamental law conflicts, and this conflict cannot be solved by interpretation, the fundamental law prevails.[128]

When applying a narrow conception of harmonisation, limited to instances where the constitution is interpreted in harmony with international law requirements, a different picture emerges. The results then show that references to the ECHR are present in only five out of 40 cases from the Supreme Court and two out of 40 cases from the Supreme Administrative Court. The degree of openness toward international law thus depends on how harmonisation with international law is defined. With only about a handful cases from the Supreme Courts explicitly harmonising the constitution with international law requirements, Swedish constitutional law represents a quite closed environment. However, cases regarding statutory law in relation to the ECHR (harmonisation or disapplication) are not selected for the study unless they raise issues relating to constitutional provisions or principles. This finding is consequently only relevant in relation to provisions in the fundamental laws.

Comparing the different outcomes regarding references to the ECHR, it can be noted that the Supreme Courts prefer to apply the ECHR and the provisions of the fundamental laws separately, and when doing so the question of harmonisation is not necessarily arising. Thus, such harmonisation is rarely explicitly done, despite the principle of treaty-conform construction pronounced by the Supreme Court in its jurisprudence. Even before the incorporation of the ECHR, the Supreme Court had stated that, as it must be assumed that the Instrument of Government is in line with the ECHR, the ECHR may consequently shed light on the provisions of the Instrument of Government.[129] Among the instances where the reasoning involves actual harmonisation (the narrow conception), we find cases concerning the right to property and the right to fair trial, as well as freedom of movement and deprivation of liberty.[130] It should be noted that the preparatory works address both the right to property and the right to fair trial in relation to the ECHR. Consequently, the Supreme Courts could rely on the preparatory works when allowing the ECHR to influence the corresponding constitutional provisions.[131] Thus, in these cases, harmonisation is carried out on the basis of a solid foundation in the preparatory works.

[127] Prop. 1993/94:117, 38. A nearly identical phrasing was later used in the preparatory works for the incorporation of the Convention on the Rights of the Child (prop. 2017/18:186 Inkorporering av FN:s konvention om barnets rättigheter, 87).

[128] See also RÅ 2006 ref 87.

[129] NJA 1981, s 1205; NJA 1989, s 131.

[130] NJA 2018, s 753 (right to property); NJA 2015, s 374 (right to fair trial); HFD 2017 ref 53 (right to fair trial), NJA 1989, s 131 (freedom of movement and deprivation of liberty).

[131] Prop. 1993/94:117 s 48; prop. 2009/10:80, 159–63.

Among the cases containing references to the ECHR there are also a few references to EU law (present in two out of 40 cases from the Supreme Court and four out of 40 cases from the Supreme Administrative Court). Cases concerning EU law are, however, only selected for this study when they raise issues related to constitutional provisions and principles, thus the figures only show that there are very few such cases among the leading cases selected for the study. References to other sources of international law are equally scarce (present in three out of 40 cases from the Supreme Court and four out of 40 cases from the Supreme Administrative Court.[132]

Among the selected cases, not a single one addresses the question of what constitutes a constitutional text, particularly whether the ECHR is considered part of the Constitution or constitutional law. Although the methodology of the study does not allow for conclusions as to why, it is still feasible to discuss possible reasons. One possible explanation is that the statement in the preparatory works leaves little room for recognising any status other than that of ordinary law. It is also quite clear in Swedish law what counts as the Constitution, and that is the fundamental laws (the Instrument of Government, the Freedom of the Press Act, the Fundamental Law on Freedom of Expression and the Act of Succession). A degree of pragmatism may also be at play. Since the Swedish courts function as Supreme Courts with jurisdiction extending beyond constitutional matters, it is not always necessary to specify whether the rules applied are *constitutional*. The courts can resolve cases using the whole range of legal sources without having to explicitly categorise them. Still even without formal status as a fundamental law, the ECHR has had a profound impact on Swedish law.[133]

E. Foreign Law and Scholarly Work

Our study also measures the use of arguments related to foreign law. Arguments related to foreign case law and legislation (N26), are practically non-existent among the selected cases.[134] The only reference that stems from the Court's reasoning (and not from the parties) is to the German Constitutional Court, concerning non-discrimination in religious matters.[135] Notably, this reference was omitted from a similar passage in a case decided a few years later.[136] That there are also no

[132] For example NJA 2020, s 3.

[133] K Åhman, *Regeringsformen och Europarätten: Hur vissa av regeringsformens bestämmelser och deras tillämpning påverkas av EU-rätten och Europakonventionen* (Stockholm, Norstedts juridik, 2023); Cameron and Bull (n 7) 626; Cameron and Bull (n 118) 261.

[134] Of the three references in the dataset, two originate from arguments made by one of the parties involved, rather than from the court's reasoning, and one is a reference to the German Constitutional Court.

[135] HFD 2013 ref 72.

[136] HFD 2017 ref 4.

references to Nordic sources in the reasoning of the two Courts requires a remark in respect of the tradition of Nordic legislative cooperation.

With varying intensity, Nordic cooperation in legal matters has been conducted since the 1870s and several major legal enactments have been developed in close Nordic cooperation. While the main outcomes of joint legislative projects are found in the area of private law, there has also been cooperation within the field of public law.[137] When adjudicating private law matters, Swedish courts occasionally refer to Nordic legal sources in their reasoning, indicating that such sources are considered at least somewhat relevant in the Swedish legal context.[138] However, no such indications are evident in the selected cases where the subject matter involves constitutional reasoning.

Still, the Nordic perspective is relevant in a Swedish constitutional law context, although this is not necessarily manifested through reasoning in the courts. Inquiries in constitutional law matters include comparative surveys[139] and Nordic experiences have influenced the chapter on the courts and the provision on constitutional review during the 2010 amendments to the Instrument of Government.[140] Nevertheless, there is an absence of references to Nordic case law in the selected cases, something which may be attributed to the lack of such jointly developed legal enactments on the *constitutional* level (since statutory law considerations are not coded for in our study), which would presumably encourage comparative analysis to a greater extent.

We also measured references to scholarly work. Notably, there are also no references to scholarly works on another Nordic system among the selected cases. References to scholarly work on international law are present in eight out of 40 cases from the Supreme Court but only in one out of 40 cases from the Supreme Administrative Court. As for references to literature on international law, a remark can be made. Even though the subject matter of the references concerns the ECHR, the literature referred to is written in Swedish by Swedish authors. Most of these references are to commentaries or scholarly work analysing the case law of the ECtHR.[141] All but one of these references are made between 2005–15. A plausible explanation is that, as long as these sources remained up to date, they

[137] See generally K Korte, 'Om nordiskt lagsamarbete' (1984) *Svensk juristtidning* 700; S Blomstrand, 'Nordic Co-operation on Legislation in the Field of Private Law' (2000) 39 *Scandinavian Studies in Law* 59.

[138] See generally: J Herre, 'Användningen av utländsk rätt i Högsta domstolen på det förmögenhetsrättsliga området' in H Udsen, J Schans Christensen, J Lau Hansen, T Iversen and L Nielsen (eds), *Festskrift til Mads Bryde Andersen* (København, Jurist- og Økonomforbundets Forlag, 2018) 203.

[139] For example, SOU 1993:40 Fri- och rättighetsfrågor; SOU 2008:125 En reformerad grundlag; SOU 2016:19 Barnkonventionen blir svensk lag.

[140] Cameron and Bull (n 7) 615.

[141] Seven cases include references to the same author and title, namely Hans Danelius's commentary on the ECHR: H Danelius, *Mänskliga rättigheter i europeisk praxis: En kommentar till Europakonventionen om de mänskliga rättigheterna*, 5th edn (Stockholm, Norstedts juridik, 2015). Two cases include references to K Åhman, *Egendomsskyddet: Äganderätten enligt artikel 1 första tilläggsprotokollet till den Europeiska konventionen om de mänskliga fri- och rättigheterna* (Uppsala, Iustus, 2000).

provided a convenient means to acquire information about the case law of the ECtHR. It should be remembered in this context that the earlier version of the HUDOC search engine was not as user-friendly as it is today. Notably, however, no English-language literature is consulted. Clearly, there is a preference for sources written in the national language. The reasons for this do not necessarily have to be related to language proficiency. One possible explanation is that the literature authored by Swedish scholars analyses the case law in a way that is more relevant to the national legal context. To refer to literature is however not particularly common even as regards the Swedish system. Among the selected cases from the Supreme Court, there are 15 out of 40 cases with least one reference to scholarly work on the Swedish system and among the selected cases from the Supreme Administrative Court there are eight out of 40 cases.[142]

F. Non-Judicial Bodies and Arguments Beyond the Constitution

Besides previous rulings, the Supreme Courts also refer to non-judicial bodies (N27). The most common references are to the Committee on the Constitution (*Konstitutionsutskottet*), a parliamentary standing committee, and the Council on Legislation. This is an illustration of how constitutional interpretation is conducted not only by the Supreme Court and the Supreme Administrative Court, but by other institutions as well. Both the Committee on the Constitution and the Council on Legislation are key institutions in the legislative process. Although arguments from the Parliamentary Ombudsman (*Justitieombudsmannen*) and the Chancellor of Justice (*Justitiekanslern*) are also of relevance in Swedish constitutional culture, especially where there is a lack of court cases, this is not reflected in the selected cases. Even though the Parliamentary Ombudsman is considered a legal export of Sweden,[143] with decisions that carry significant weight among administrative authorities, there is no established tradition of invoking them in court proceedings.

When constitutional review was formalised, the preparatory works stated that if Parliament had determined that a piece of legislation was compatible with the Constitution, this assessment should be respected as long as it could be considered a possible ('*möjlig*') constitutional interpretation.[144] That is, the courts were implicitly instructed to respect the interpretation of the Parliament. This statement from the preparatory works is referred to in some of the selected cases,

[142] Among these, eight cases, equally divided between the two Supreme Courts, include references to the same author and title, namely a work on legislative power by Håkan Strömberg: H Strömberg, *Normgivningsmakten enligt 1974 års regeringsform*, 3rd edn (Lund, Juristförlaget, 1999).

[143] B Thorarensen, 'Mechanisms for Parliamentary Control of the Executive' in H Krunke and B Thorarensen (eds), *The Nordic Constitutions: A Comparative and Contextual Study* (Oxford, Hart Publishing, 2018) 90.

[144] Konstitutionsutskottets betänkande 1978/79:KU39, 13.

all from before 2010. Constitutional review was until 2010 restricted to cases when the error was manifest. During the 2010 amendments to the Instrument of Government, when the requirement of manifest error was removed, the provision on constitutional review was revised to instead emphasise that particular attention should be paid to the fact that Parliament is the foremost representative of the people ('*folkets främsta företrädare*').[145] According to the preparatory works, this phrasing was intended to serve as a reminder that Parliament is regarded as the primary interpreter of the Constitution.[146] An important body interpreting the Constitution is consequently the Committee on the Constitution.

The Committee on the Constitution scrutinises legislative proposals, and is the primary body through which the Parliament may scrutinise the Government.[147] The Committee on the Constitution consists of politicians, and there is no formal requirement of a legal background.[148] Among the selected cases, the Supreme Court refers to the Committee on the Constitution in three out of 40 cases and the Supreme Administrative Court in six out of 40 cases. If the reference is found in the preparatory works to any of the fundamental laws, this was also coded as subjective teleological argument, since such statements are regarded as preparatory works. Although statements from the Committee on the Constitution do not carry the same weight in Swedish constitutional reasoning as opinions of the Constitutional Law Committee do in Finland,[149] they are still regarded as a relevant source.

Among the selected cases, there are several references to preparatory works of statutory law, in which the Council on Legislation expounds on the meaning of the Instrument of Government (six out of 40 cases from the Supreme Court and five out of 40 cases from the Supreme Administrative Court). The Council on Legislation is not involved in amendments or revisions to the Instrument of Government, though it is involved in matters concerning changes to the Freedom of the Press Act and the Fundamental Law on Freedom of Expression.[150] Thus, it is within the statutory law review process that the Council on Legislation interprets the Instrument of Government. That is, these interpretations are of later origin than the constitutional provisions, and they are not part of the preparatory works to the Instrument of Government. In this study, references to the Council on Legislation's opinions are therefore not coded as references to preparatory works, but only as references to a non-judicial body (N27). This confirms that even

[145] The Instrument of Government, Chapter 11, Section 14.
[146] Prop. 2009/10:80, 148, Konstitutionsutskottets betänkande 2009/10:KU19, 39.
[147] The Instrument of Government, Chapter 13, Section 1. Certain provisions of the Instrument of Government are never adjudicated in court but are instead interpreted by the Committee on the Constitution, for example the provision concerning the relationship between the Government and its administrative authorities (The Instrument of Government, Chapter 12, Section 2).
[148] They however have access to a secretariat for legal advice, see: Bull (n 28) 396–97.
[149] See ch 5, in particular ss II(A) and III(D). See also Bull (n 28).
[150] The Instrument of Government, Chapter 8, Section 20 and Section 21. In the 2025 proposal for constitutional amendments, the Council on Legislation's review is expanded to also include provisions in the Instrument of Government concerning fundamental rights and freedoms (prop. 2024/25:165).

though the opinions of the Council on Legislation are not binding, courts take the views of the Council on Legislation in consideration.

The Supreme Courts also refer to principles and concepts not mentioned in the text of the Constitution. This variable (N20) is present in 16 out of 40 cases from the Supreme Court, and in seven out of 40 cases from the Supreme Administrative Court. When coding for this variable, we included not only principles which are not mentioned at all (such as principles concerning the relation between national and international law, including EU law), but also those principles and concepts that are not explicitly stated, but construed or inferred with the aid of constitutional provisions (such as the requirement that legislation must be generally applicable).[151] However, some form of interpretative effort was required. For example, the principle of proportionality did not qualify as a principle not mentioned in the constitution, as it was considered sufficiently evident in the Instrument of Government.[152] Both Supreme Courts use principles and concepts not mentioned in the text of the constitution, but they differ as to the extent. One possible explanation for this difference is that the Supreme Court's reasoning includes arguments that we have coded as reflecting the *pro homine* principle of interpretation (N28). In the Swedish context, this variable is also coded as a principle not mentioned in the text of the Constitution.

For the purposes of this study, arguments considered examples of *pro homine* reasoning are those asserting that provisions protecting rights and freedoms should be interpreted generously in favour of the individual, and that limitations on such provisions should be interpreted restrictively.[153] This also includes the proposition that the ECHR, as a human rights convention, ought to carry special weight in cases of conflict with national provisions. The last argument was presented as an interpretive tool in the preparatory works on the incorporation of the ECHR.[154] This solution was, in fact, proposed by the Supreme Court during the consultation procedure of the legislative process, so it is perhaps unsurprising that the Court later adopted it as well. While nine out of 40 cases from the Supreme Court contain references coded as the *pro homine* principle, there are no such references found among the selected cases from the Supreme Administrative Court.

Although both analogical reasoning and arguments from silence are accepted methods of legal reasoning in Swedish law, the courts in the selected cases rarely employ either approach. Reasoning in analogical terms is only present in one out of 40 cases from the Supreme Court and two out of 40 cases from the Supreme Administrative Court. Arguments from silence are present only in three out of 40 cases from the Supreme Court and two out of 40 cases from the Supreme Administrative Court. The limited use of analogical reasoning is presumably a

[151] See, eg, RÅ 80 1:92, RÅ 1986 ref 108 and RÅ 1999 ref 76.

[152] See The Instrument of Government, Chapter 2, Section 21. See also The Instrument of Government, Chapter 14, Section 3.

[153] Nordic CONREASON Codebook 1.7, 15.

[154] Prop. 1993/94:117, 38.

consequence of the jurisdiction. For instance, when a case concerns a fundamental right under the Instrument of Government and the court determines that the right is not applicable to the situation at hand, it is often possible to resolve the matter through statutory law without resorting to constitutional analogies. Alternatively, it is since incorporation also possible to rely solely on the ECHR. This contrasts with the Freedom of the Press Act and the Fundamental Law on Freedom of Expression, which limit the possibility of recourse to statutory law once applicable, as they are exclusionary in nature.[155] Moreover, the use of analogical reasoning in relation to the Freedom of the Press Act and the Fundamental Law on Freedom of Expression would depend on the specific subject matter, given the partially criminal law character of these acts.

III. Key Concepts

We also measured the use of different concepts in constitutional reasoning. The selected cases show a low frequency regarding the use of different concepts and an overall low conceptual diversity in the leading constitutional cases of both Supreme Courts. It is remarkably lower in the Supreme Administrative Court than in the Supreme Court, and the Supreme Administrative Court shows the lowest frequency of conceptualisation among all seven Nordic supreme courts (see Figure 4).

Figure 4 Argumentative and conceptual diversity

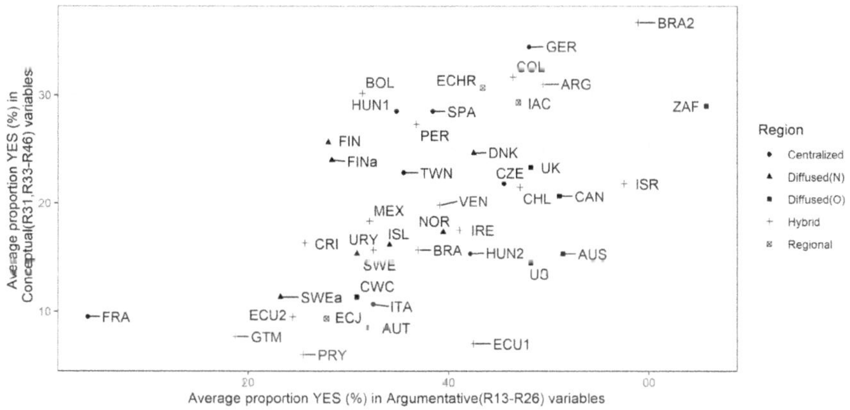

However, it should be noted that certain matters appear less frequently before the supreme courts, and some topics are typically resolved at the statutory level. For

[155] The Freedom of the Press Act, Chapter 1, Section 1, and Chapter 1, Section 9.

example, the key concept of equality (N43) appears less frequently than one might expect, given the emphasis on equality and non-discrimination in Swedish society. The concept of equality is invoked in only four out of 40 cases from the Supreme Court and six out of 40 cases from the Supreme Administrative Court. However, cases concerning equality are not necessarily adjudicated at the constitutional level, as issues such as discrimination in the workplace and education are governed by detailed provisions in statutory law.[156]

Similarly, the key concept of transparency (N51) is notably almost absent from the selected cases, despite Sweden's strong tradition of free speech and public access to official documents. Only two cases out of 40 from the Supreme Court and three cases out of 40 from the Supreme Administrative Court contain references to the concept of transparency. Rather than discussing transparency as a concept, the issue is often not examined beyond the constitutionalised administrative and criminal law in the Freedom of the Press Act and the Fundamental Law on Freedom of Expression. Consequently, such cases have not been included as leading examples of constitutional interpretation for the purposes of this study. Additionally, due to procedural rules, cases concerning public access to official documents can only reach the Supreme Administrative Court when access has been denied, which limits the volume of available cases.[157]

The concept of the rule of law (N31) is present in many of the selected cases, particularly when all of its subcategories are considered. For the purposes of this study, the rule of law was divided into five subcategories: (1) explicit rule of law arguments, (2) the principle of legality, (3) legal certainty, (4) separation of powers and access to justice, and (5) implicit rule of law arguments, which include, for example, the supremacy of the Constitution.[158] Out of all the selected cases, the rule of law is entirely absent in only six Supreme Court cases and ten from the Supreme Administrative Court. While several of the underlying principles are frequently invoked, the rule of law as a general concept is rarely discussed explicitly. Notably, the principle of legality is the most commonly applied subcategory, significantly contributing to the overall frequency of rule of law references in the case material.

As a concept, the rule of law ('*rättsstat*') was not a major topic in Swedish legal discourse until the 1990s. At times, it even carried political connotations, being perceived as opposed to the construction of the welfare state.[159] The principle of legality, however, is not burdened by similar connotations. On the contrary, it is firmly rooted in the Swedish constitutional tradition, and historically even

[156] The Discrimination Act (diskrimineringslag (2008:567)). Additionally, the Equality Ombudsman (*Diskrimineringsombudsmannen*) investigates complaints under the Discrimination Act, something which can result in matters being resolved out of court. Furthermore, certain cases on discrimination belong to the jurisdiction of the Labour Court.

[157] The Public Access to Information and Secrecy Act (Offentlighets- och sekretesslag (2009:400) Chapter 6, Section 7.

[158] See the Codebook in the Appendix.

[159] Sterzel (n 9) 38.

the monarch was bound by the law.[160] The principle of legality is expressed in the current Instrument of Government already in its first provision, according to which all public power is exercised under the law.[161] In the selected cases, however, the principle of legality is primarily expressed through an emphasis on formal requirements enshrined elsewhere in the Instrument of Government. For example, only Parliament may restrict certain rights or regulate specific matters, as indicated by the use of the word 'law' ('*lag*') in the relevant provisions.[162] In this context, 'law' is a formal concept, referring specifically to acts adopted by the Parliament.[163] Drawing on a provision that limits Parliament's ability to make decisions in individual cases, as well as on the preparatory works of the Instrument of Government, the Supreme Administrative Court has interpreted 'law' to require general applicability in order to qualify as such.[164] And the Supreme Court has emphasised that laws must be both accessible and foreseeable.[165]

Proportionality, by contrast, is not a commonly applied concept in the selected cases. While the principle itself is not new to Swedish law, legal scholars have long discussed proportionality as a legal maxim ('*allmän rättsgrundsats*'), even if not always using the precise term 'principle of proportionality'.[166] Since the mid-1990s, the principle of proportionality has experienced a revival, beginning in the case law of the Supreme Administrative Court.[167] Nevertheless, among the selected cases, the principle of proportionality appears in only nine out of 40 cases from the Supreme Court and four out of 40 cases from the Supreme Administrative Court.

IV. Concluding Remarks

This study focuses specifically on constitutional reasoning. Accordingly, arguments relating to the interpretation of statutory law are only considered relevant if they contribute to clarifying the meaning of constitutional provisions. This presents a particular challenge when analysing the reasoning of Sweden's two Supreme Courts, where constitutional arguments may represent only one aspect of a case – and not always the decisive one. Therefore, the findings in this study apply solely to the constitutional dimension of each case and does not reflect the courts' reasoning in other areas of law addressed within the same judgments.

[160] Cameron and Bull (n 7) 603 and 612.
[161] The Instrument of Government, Chapter 1, Section 1.
[162] However, with the exception of the expression 'under the law' ('*under lagarna*') in the Instrument of Government, Chapter 1, Section 1, which has a wider connotation, see Sterzel (n 9) 117–18.
[163] See the Instrument of Government, Chapter 8, Section 1; Sterzel (n 9) 118.
[164] See The Instrument of Government, Chapter 11, Section 4 and RÅ 1999 ref 76.
[165] See NJA 2012, s 400.
[166] Sterzel (n 9) 135–36.
[167] ibid 135.

While constitutional reasoning in Sweden is conducted by two Supreme Courts, the differences in their use of arguments are not overly pronounced and can often be attributed to the different types of cases they handle. In the selected cases, rather than elaborating on the meaning of constitutional provisions beyond the intent of the constitutional legislator, they continue to place significant weight on preparatory works. Thus, both courts primarily rely on traditional sources of Swedish law, and here we include opinions from the Council on Legislation in later legislative proposals where the Council on Legislation interprets the constitutional provisions. Hence, although the two Supreme Courts increasingly reference prior case law, something which can be explained by the transition from courts of appeal to courts of precedent, they continue to draw on preparatory works. For example, in the selected cases, despite the ECHR's significant influence within Swedish constitutional law and law in general, the fundamental laws are not automatically interpreted in accordance with it unless such an interpretation is grounded in the preparatory works.

While constitutional and judicial reforms, along with the influence of international law, such as the ECHR and EU law, have expanded the role of the Swedish judiciary, the emphasis on the Parliament as the primary authority on the Constitution remains a defining feature of Sweden's constitutional culture. In the Swedish context, a 'living constitution' is a Constitution that is continuously modified by the constitutional legislator, rather than one that evolves through judicial interpretation. The Constitution thus never grows old and is consequently accompanied by updated preparatory works, thereby upholding their relevance as authoritative sources in constitutional interpretation. In this regard however, also the justices' backgrounds deserve mention, particularly the predominance of those with ministerial experience, who presumably possess a certain degree of familiarity with this type of legal material. Additionally, the possibility that there is a shared sense of caution and mutual respect between the two Supreme Courts should not be overlooked. This type of deference may lead the courts to avoid interpretations of constitutional provisions that extend beyond what can be safely inferred from traditional sources (such as preparatory works), particularly when such provisions might also fall within the jurisdiction of the other court. Nevertheless, we see that the two Supreme Courts at times draw on each other's case law, and that steps are taken towards closer cooperation also in constitutional matters.

8

Conclusions: Is there a Nordic Constitutional Culture?

KATALIN KELEMEN

I. About Legal and Constitutional Culture

What can constitutional reasoning teach us about a legal culture? In this research, we have been interested in discovering how the Nordic supreme courts justify their decisions in cases that raise important constitutional questions. We began with two fundamental assumptions.[1] First, based on a realist account of judicial decision-making, we acknowledge that judicial decisions are influenced by considerations that are not explicitly included in the written reasoning. Judges are influenced by numerous non-legal factors, including the legal culture in which they were educated. Second, we assume that judges include the reasons they deem legitimate within their legal system and legal culture when writing their decisions. Indeed, as Pierre Legrand put it, culture is 'the framework of intangibles within which an interpretive community operates, which has normative force for this community',[2] referring to 'ways of organising one's place in the moral universe through commitments to standards of reference and rationality'. Our aim has been to explore the 'standards of reference and rationality' of the Nordic countries' constitutional culture.

The concept of legal culture has played a significant role in major debates regarding comparative law and its methodologies.[3] For some, legal culture comprises

[1] See ch 1, s I.

[2] P Legrand, *Fragments on Law-as-Culture* (Deventer, WEJ Tjeenk Willink, 1999) 19, 27.

[3] A competing concept in comparative law literature is that of legal tradition. Comparatists who prefer the term 'legal tradition' to 'legal culture' tend to emphasise how certain legal practices, ways of thinking and institutions are transmitted and preserved through the generations and influence the way we make and apply law in a particular social context. The most well-known representative of this strand of literature is P Glenn, *Legal Traditions of the World*, 5th edn (Oxford, Oxford University Press, 2014). In this study, I avoid using the term 'legal tradition' to ensure terminological clarity and consistency, rather than taking a stance on the competing notions of 'legal tradition' and 'legal culture'. Historical background and continuity are also essential factors in our explanations.

practices, traditions, and professional understandings of lawyers and lawmakers.[4] For others, however, legal culture encompasses much more: it is also concerned with compliance with the law and the general public's attitudes towards it.[5] Since Lawrence Friedman's seminal work published in the 1970s,[6] the former conception has been characterised as 'internal legal culture', while the latter conception has been labelled as 'external legal culture'. In both senses, however, legal culture extends far beyond the 'law in the books' or 'black-letter law' to take into account the 'law in action'. In our project, we have focused more on interpretative practices, traditions and professional understandings, which are at the core of the internal legal culture.

Although we examined judicial decisions and the reasoning in them, which could form the basis of a positivist study of law, comparing this reasoning across different jurisdictions requires a completely different approach. Indeed, all legal scholars who engage in comparisons agree that the legal texts under consideration should be viewed as embedded in a broader cultural context.[7] While they may disagree about the scope of legal culture to be considered and whether to focus on internal or external legal culture – as this also depends on the subject under examination – there is a consensus that a positivist focus on legal rules alone is insufficient. Therefore, we must consider the underlying values or principles of a legal system, as well as unwritten traditions, shared beliefs, common ways of thinking, and professional practices.[8]

Cultural comparatists tend to appreciate the differences in legal experience across different jurisdictions.[9] In contrast, more traditional comparatists embrace the functionalist approach, which focuses on the problems, tasks, or societal needs that law is intended to meet, and attempts to eliminate legal differences between jurisdictions.[10] In our project, we examined five jurisdictions from the same geographical area, Northern Europe, that are traditionally perceived as being very similar to each other. Our cultural, rather than functionalist, approach to comparison has led us to challenge these assumptions rather than accept them, and to avoid taking any similarities for granted. Undoubtedly, the Nordic countries and their

[4] R Cotterrell, 'Comparative law and legal culture' in M Reiman and R Zimmermann (eds), *The Oxford Handbook of Comparative Law*, 2nd edn (Oxford, Oxford University Press, 2019) 710–33, 710–11.

[5] M Siems, *Comparative Law*, 3rd edn (Cambridge, Cambridge University Press, 2022) 175.

[6] L Friedman, *The Legal System. A Social Science Perspective* (New York, Russell Sage Foundation, 1975) 223–67.

[7] Cotterrell (n 4) 711.

[8] ibid.

[9] The most influential proponent of this approach is Pierre Legrand.

[10] The most well-known proponents of this approach were probably Konrad Zweigert and Hein Kötz. See K Zweigert and H Kötz, *An Introduction to Comparative Law*, 3rd edn (tr T Weir, Oxford, Clarendon Press, 1998). However, as Balázs Fekete cautions, the opposition between culturalism and functionalism should not be overstated. Both approaches can be incorporated into the same research project. B Fekete, 'Inconsistencies in the use of legal culture in comparative legal studies' (2018) 25(5) *Maastricht Journal of European and Comparative Law* 551, 553–54.

legal systems have many similarities. This is particularly evident when we compare them to other jurisdictions in Europe and the rest of the world. Our empirical data has also confirmed this, even with a narrow focus on constitutional reasoning in supreme courts.[11] However, the real comparative (and intellectual) endeavour lies in exploring the differences between them. Therefore, a cultural approach to comparison seems to be the right way to go, and it requires that law – in our case judicial decisions – is read in the cultural context that gives it a meaning.

But what exactly is 'constitutional culture'? Is it a subset of legal culture, or is it something distinct from it? Although the literature on constitutional culture is an independent body of scholarship that only refers to the literature on legal culture to a limited extent, there exists a strand of constitutional scholarship that uses the concept as an analytical category to distinguish between different types of constitutional culture. This scholarship considers constitutional culture to be people's ideas, understandings, and attitudes about the constitution and constitutionalism.[12] Our book belongs to this strand of comparative constitutional scholarship, with a specific focus on the ideas, understandings, and attitudes of judges and other legal professionals regarding the constitution and its position among the sources of law, as reflected in the judgments. Consequently, our examination centres on the 'internal constitutional culture' rather than the attitudes of ordinary citizens towards the constitution. We examine this internal constitutional culture narrowly, as our empirical analysis focuses on patterns in constitutional reasoning, while other dimensions of constitutional culture, such as institutional structures, underlying values and ideologies, only serve as explanatory factors.

The importance of legal and constitutional culture is evident in how nearly identical rules or extensive reception of the same rules can lead to completely different outcomes in legal practice.[13] Examining the power of judicial review in the Nordic countries makes it clear that formal legal rules alone cannot explain why this power is used so reluctantly by most Nordic supreme courts. Using anthropological terminology, this can also be viewed in terms of resistance to state law on part of the judges,[14] who are members of a profession embedded in a legal culture that displays a high level of trust in the democratic process and democratic

[11] See Figures 4 and 5 in section 8.2 and accompanying text in ch 2, which show that the Nordic supreme courts, as a group, tend to stand out from the other courts.

[12] T Herklotz, 'Legal Cultures' in R Grote, F Lachenmann and R Wolfrum (eds), *Max Planck Encyclopedia of Comparative Constitutional Law* (Oxford, Oxford University Press, 2013) paras 11–12. Another strand of scholarship views constitutional culture as something that either exists or does not exist in a given society, depending on whether or not citizens regard themselves as bound by their constitution. See, eg, J Mazzone, 'The Creation of a Constitutional Culture' (2005) 40 *Tulsa Law Review* 671.

[13] J Husa, *Introduction to Comparative Law*, 2nd edn (Oxford, Hart, 2023) 5.

[14] This approach is part of the conceptual framework of legal pluralism developed by legal anthropologists. See, eg, J Griffiths, 'The Social Working of Legal Rules' (2003) 35 *Journal of Legal Pluralism and Unofficial Law* 1.

institutions.[15] In this chapter, however, I will use the concept of legal and constitutional culture as the background of law rather than as the interactions surrounding it or the normative universe around it. In other words, I treat legal and constitutional culture as a constellation of extra-legal factors that influence law.[16] The most relevant context for understanding constitutional culture is provided by historical development and the political system.

II. Constitutional Reasoning and the Law's Multiple Levels

A useful lens for reflecting on our findings is provided by the Finnish legal theorist Kaarlo Tuori in his book *Critical Legal Positivism*.[17] He approached the law from the perspective that it operates on multiple levels, with legal culture representing the intermediate level. The first level is the surface level, where legal change is an everyday phenomenon, occurring through mechanisms such as legislative changes. The most important legal practices in modern society – law-making, adjudication, and legal science – primarily manifest at this surface level. Key elements at this level include statutes and regulations, court decisions, and the contributions of legal science.[18]

Beyond the surface level, however, the law also encompasses deeper layers that both create preconditions for and impose constraints on the material at the surface level. In their professional activities, legal actors often draw on their knowledge of the sub-surface levels, although they rarely articulate this knowledge in a discursive form.[19] There are two sub-surface levels: legal culture and the deep structure of law. The level of legal culture is characterised by a slower pace of change. At this level, legal argumentation and ideologies about the relationship between the legislature and courts are formulated. Tuori describes legal culture as a domain of primarily practical knowledge, thus he employs this concept in the sense of internal legal culture. For example, when a judge applies a statutory norm, they rely on their understanding of legal culture, even if this knowledge is not necessarily explicitly articulated. For Tuori, the elements of legal culture encompass the doctrine of sources of law, general legal doctrines, and methods of legal interpretation and argumentation, which form the precise focus of this book.[20]

[15] M Lundström, 'Value Relativism, Procedural Democracy and Opinion Representation – Reflections on Three Conceptual Underpinnings of Swedish Anti-Constitutionalism' (2009) 27 *Nordic Journal of Human Rights* 242; Jaakko Husa, 'Constitutional Mentality' in P Letto-Vanamo, D Tamm and BOG Mortensen (eds), *Nordic Law in European Context*, vol 73 (Cham, Springer, 2019).

[16] Fekete (n 10) 555–57.

[17] K Tuori, *Critical Legal Positivism* (Abingdon and New York, Routledge, 2016). See also K Tuori, *Rättens nivåer och dimensioner* (Helsinki, Helsingfors universitet, 2022), DOI 10.31885/9789515179296.

[18] Tuori, *Critical Legal Positivism* (n 17) 154–61.

[19] ibid 150–51.

[20] ibid 167.

The third level of law is the deep structure of law, where change occurs at the slowest pace. This level reflects the core values inherent in the legal system, such as human rights, the rule of law, and democracy. Tuori characterises the deep structure as the deepest and most sedimented layer of law.[21] He also emphasises that what matters is not the exact number of levels of law we identify but rather the recognition that law extends beyond its visible surface and that law should not be reduced to normative materials like individual regulations and courts decisions. It is also open to debate which elements belong to each level.[22]

Understanding law as comprising these different levels helps explain why the doctrine of sources of law and the influence of Scandinavian Legal Realism remain deeply embedded in judicial reasoning in the Nordic countries. This layered approach also clarifies why there are no drastic changes in constitutional interpretation, even as the surface level of law has been radically transformed by Europeanisation and globalisation. While court decisions, as linguistically formulated norms, clearly belong to the surface level of the law,[23] constitutional reasoning operates at all levels. First, it is part of the surface level, as interpretative legal dogmatics are an integral part of legal scholarship.[24] Second, constitutional reasoning is embedded in legal culture, which assigns specific roles to the courts, the legislature, and legal science through the doctrine of sources of law and ideologies about the relationship between the legislature and courts. Common law countries typically emphasise the role of courts, while civil law countries, to which Nordic legal systems are definitely closer, place more emphasis on the legislature.[25] The doctrine of sources of law 'serves as the intra-legal guide for assessing the weight to be accorded to the interventions of the various participants in the continuing debate about the contents of the legal order'.[26] However, constitutional reasoning can also be considered part of the deep structure of law. Basic legal categories and concepts are part of this deep structure, and the fact that three research projects applying the same methodology to different courts worldwide could share a list of key constitutional concepts demonstrates that this deep structure transcends legal cultures. These basic legal categories enable legal thinking and argumentation itself.[27]

In summary, our approach to studying constitutional reasoning has been to cut through the law's multiple levels. We examined the texts of judicial decisions, which belong to the surface level, focusing on the legal argumentation and conceptualisation contained within them that already reveal the underlying legal culture. In particular, we examined the conceptualisation present in judicial decisions by

[21] ibid 183–91.
[22] ibid 154.
[23] ibid.
[24] ibid 155.
[25] ibid 156.
[26] ibid 157.
[27] ibid 187.

measuring the use of key constitutional concepts in them, which form part of a legal system's core values and therefore represent the deep structure of the law.

III. About Nordic Legal and Constitutional Culture

From a historical perspective, concerns about the creation of a Nordic legal culture emerged as late as the second half of the nineteenth century, when the Nordic Meetings for Lawyers were initiated and institutionalised.[28] Before that, the Nordic countries had not exhibited significant similarities in their political histories. There were no shared political institutions, no common legal language or legal procedures. However, the notion of a Nordic legal culture had evolved into an established fact by the interwar period, due to the intensive legislative cooperation between the Nordic countries,[29] which produced a series of common Nordic legislation since 1880.[30]

Without going into much detail about the historical development of the Nordic countries' political systems, we can point out that, largely due to the geographical reality of vast forested territories that were difficult to control, a model of cooperation with the local peasantry and their popular assemblies developed. This model differed from both continental European and English feudalism and laid the foundation for Nordic legal culture.[31] Despite the substantial knowledge and influence of Roman and canon law in the Middle Ages, the cooperative model of governance resulted in an early emphasis on legislated law, a long tradition of lay participation in courts and the use of vernacular languages for legal purposes.[32]

With regard to Nordic constitutional culture in particular, Jaakko Husa – one of the scholars who has devoted the most attention to the subject – identifies the following common elements: a parliamentary system combining separation of powers and consensual democracy, cautious systems of judicial review, respect for the will of the legislature, the political question doctrine employed by the courts, the absence of separate constitutional courts, a combination of written and unwritten rules and principles, strong elements of constitutionalism, and a pragmatic and practical legal style.[33]

The last one of these general features commonly associated with the Nordic legal and constitutional culture, pragmatism, provides a valuable perspective for

[28] In 1872. JØ Sunde, 'The History of Nordic Legal Culture and Court Culture: The Story of What Should not Have Been, but Still Came to Be' in L Ervo, P Letto-Vanamo and A Nylund (eds), *Rethinking Nordic Courts* (Cham, Springer, 2021) 49, 62.

[29] ibid 50.

[30] ibid 62.

[31] ibid 56.

[32] ibid 57–59.

[33] J Husa, 'Nordic Constitutionalism and European Human Rights – Mixing Oil and Water?' (2010) 55 *Scandinavian Studies in Law* 101, 109–10.

understanding constitutional reasoning. According to the Norwegian scholar Sverre Blandhol, legal pragmatism is an approach to law that can be broken down into ten components: anti-fundamentalism, anti-formalism, rhetorical understanding of language, problem orientation, experience orientation, consequence orientation, moderate scepticism, pluralism, contextualism, and style.[34] In essence, legal pragmatism rejects the pursuit of absolute certainty of knowledge derived from general principles, as well as the notion that a formal logical system can be constructed with the necessary degree of linguistic coherence and precision. This means that lawyers are not expected to establish a perfect correspondence between legal concepts and reality.[35] Pragmatism encourages lawyers to focus on solving practical problems and considers law as a continuous process, to be developed by trial and error, rather than a closed and complete system. In Blandhol's scheme, pluralism means that pragmatists are open to a multitude of arguments and do not exclude some of them a priori simply because they do not align perfectly with a general principle or absolute formula. It promotes a type of communication that is rich in metaphors and does not adhere to fixed argumentative rules.[36] The historical roots of the very pronounced pragmatic tendencies of the Nordic legal systems can be traced back to the remarkable continuity of the development of legislation from the Middle Ages, the problem-oriented attitude of Nordic legal scholars between the eighteenth and nineteenth centuries, which was suspicious towards the *Begriffsjurisprudenz* of the German tradition, and the rise of Scandinavian legal realism.[37]

This pragmatic attitude permeates court practice and judicial reasoning in many ways. First, the deferential attitude of Nordic judges towards the legislature can be partly explained by pragmatism, given that it is also a consequence of the practical availability of a large body of high-quality preparatory works.[38] Nordic legislation is generally simple and general in nature, with the necessary details for its application found in the legislative materials.[39] The lack of interest in theory is also reflected in the simplicity of judicial argumentation, which usually avoids complex language and only states what is necessary to explain how the court reached its decision.

In our research, we measured the conceptual and argumentative diversity of the cases in our sample by considering the average number of argument types and

[34] S Blandhol, *Nordisk Rettspragmatisme – Savigny, Ørsted Og Schweigaard Om Vitenskap Og Metode* (Copenhagen, DJØF, 2005).

[35] K Kelemen and F Valguarnera, 'Legal Pragmatism: A Comparison with the Nordic Legal Method' (2025) *Italian Law Journal* (forthcoming).

[36] Blandhol (n 34).

[37] For a detailed historical account see Kelemen and Valguarnera (n 35).

[38] Uwe Kischel, *Comparative Law* (Oxford, Oxford University Press, 2019) 560–61.

[39] ibid 561. As Kischel observed, 'Scandinavian lawyers clearly do not care much about the precise theoretical classification of legislative materials, legal practice, and legal doctrine as a source of law, so long as it is clear *that* they are used in practice, and *how* they are used in practice'.

key concepts (see Figure 1). Our empirical observations confirm that, globally, the Nordic supreme courts draw on a more restrictive repertoire of arguments and concepts than most other supreme and constitutional courts worldwide, although this is more evident in relation to concepts than argument types. This seems to confirm Jaakko Husa's observation that, in the Nordic tradition, 'the nature of argumentation is not so "heavy" as in Germanic law, nor so cryptic as in French law, and to some extent there is a casuistic nature'.[40]

Figure 1 Argumentative and conceptual diversity of supreme and constitutional courts in their leading constitutional cases[41]

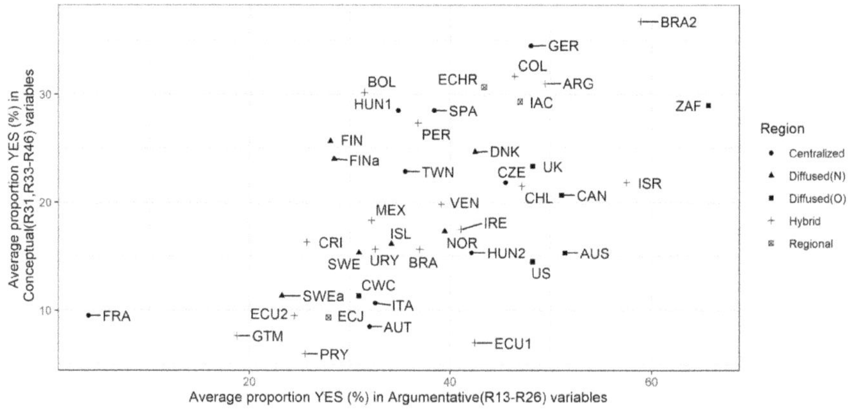

In particular, Sweden's two supreme courts stand out for exhibiting significantly lower diversity in argumentation and conceptualisation than their Nordic counterparts, although the Icelandic Supreme Court is in a similar position. Unlike the decisions of other Nordic supreme courts, Swedish supreme court judgments do not include the text of the lower court decisions. We therefore tested whether considering including these decisions in the analysis would change the position of Swedish Supreme Court (HD) in this scheme.[42] The result is that there is no significant change in position. The Swedish Supreme Court is slightly ahead of the Icelandic Supreme Court in terms of argumentative diversity, while conceptual diversity remains unchanged (see Figure 2).

[40] Husa (n 33) 110. This observation is also cited and discussed by Maija Dahlberg in ch 5, s II(B).

[41] In these figures, 'SWEa' stands for the Swedish Administrative Supreme Court, and 'FINa' stands for the Finnish Administrative Supreme Court. The shapes of the dots represent the various systems of judicial review, distinguishing between the diffused model (which further distinguishes Nordic courts from those in other countries that follow the same model), the centralised model, hybrid systems, and regional courts. See ch 2, s III(C) and VIII(A).

[42] Thus, we coded all 40 cases from the Swedish Supreme Court (HD) twice: once without and once with the lower courts' decision. All other findings are based on the first coding, which did not take into account the lower courts' reasoning. We did not perform this test for the Swedish Administrative Supreme Court (HFD).

Figure 2 Argumentative and conceptual diversity of supreme and constitutional courts in their leading constitutional cases, including the reasoning of lower courts in relation to the Swedish Supreme Court (SWE)

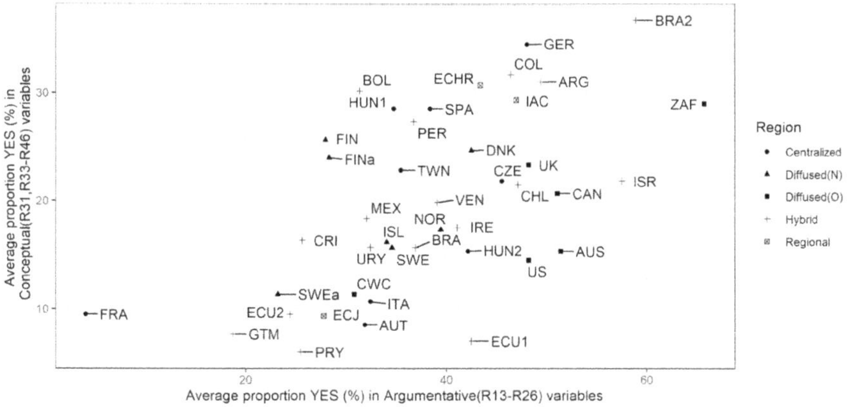

The argumentative diversity of the Norwegian and Danish Supreme Courts is significantly higher than that of the other Nordic supreme courts. Interestingly, however, the Norwegian Supreme Court exhibits significantly lower conceptual diversity than the Finnish and Danish Supreme Courts. In light of this diverse picture, we are led to question whether there is a distinct Nordic style of constitutional reasoning.

IV. A Nordic Style of Constitutional Reasoning?

In our project, we aimed to empirically examine the extent to which commonly accepted assumptions in legal scholarship are true in relation to constitutional reasoning. Thanks to the data being gathered using the same methodological and conceptual framework as two other projects, the conditions for comparisons to those from 33 other courts around the world, including supreme, constitutional and regional courts, were good.[43] We applied principle component analysis on the argumentative and conceptual variables, separately and simultaneously.[44] Although there is variation among the Nordic courts when it comes to argumentation, they seem to take a fringe position globally (see Figure 3).[45] Albeit small (but intact when the third component is also included) a statistically significant East-West division is discerned among the Nordic courts.

[43] See ch 1, s III, and ch 2, ss III and VIII.
[44] For an explanation of this type of statistical analysis see ch 2, s VIII(B)(ii).
[45] No clear interpretation of any extracted component was found. However, for 17 argumentative variables, the two (three) first components accounted for as much as 42% (51%) of the variation.

Figure 3 Courts' scores on the first and second principal component, extracted from variables on argument types (R12–R26, R29)

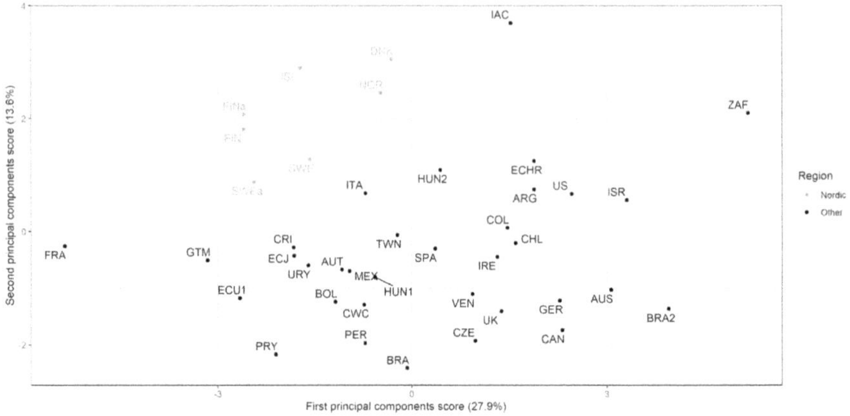

The variation between the Nordic courts becomes more apparent when focusing on the use of key concepts than when focusing on argumentation (see Figure 4).

Figure 4 Courts' scores on the first and second principal component, extracted from variables on conceptualisation (R31, R33–R46)

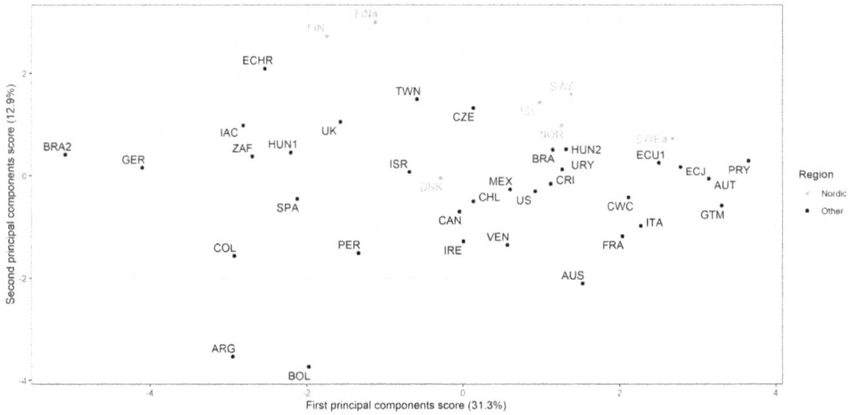

However, with regard to key concepts, one has to be cautious with drawing far-fetching conclusions from these findings as they are heavily influenced by the constitutional texts and the historical circumstances under which the leading constitutional cases arose. For example, the Danish sample of leading constitutional cases includes the famous *Maastricht*, *Lisbon* and *Ajos* judgments, which concern constitutional questions related to Denmark's EU membership. This explains the more frequent use of concepts such as sovereignty, state form and form of government than in the other Nordic countries.[46] Therefore, when it comes

[46] See ch 3.

to conceptualisation, a similar Nordic fringe position is less visible.[47] Although Iceland and Norway are closer to Denmark, Finland and Sweden are quite far apart, so it is difficult to identify an East-West division.

While Finland's position close to the European Convention of Human Rights (ECHR) might not be surprising, given that the Finnish Constitution is relatively new and the rights catalogue is essentially modelled on the ECHR, it is also unexpected, since the role of Finnish courts in constitutional questions has traditionally been considered entirely secondary.[48] While the constitutional jurisprudence of the other Nordic countries has also been heavily influenced by the ECHR and Strasbourg case-law, this influence has become particularly apparent since the 1990s. Our sample from these countries also includes cases that were decided prior to the incorporation of the ECHR into domestic law.[49]

When considering the first components extracted simultaneously from all (32) argumentative and conceptual variables, the outcome aligns with the previous results, although a slightly smaller share of the total variation is explained.[50] This suggests that, in spite of the within-Nordic variation, when considering argumentation and conceptualisation together, the Nordic courts appear to occupy an area of their own in terms of constitutional reasoning globally (see Figure 5).

Figure 5 Courts' scores on the first and second principal component, extracted from variables on argument types and key concepts (R12–R26, R29, R31, R33–R46)

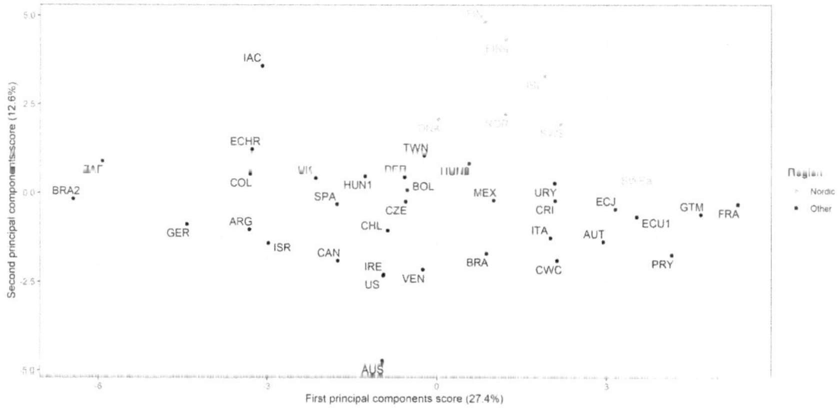

Thus, in essence, our empirical data seems to suggest that a Nordic style of constitutional reasoning exists. An even more pressing question is, however: what are the defining characteristics of this Nordic style?

[47] Although it is somewhat reinforced when the third component is included.

[48] See ch 5.

[49] The oldest Finnish decision in our sample is from 2000 (Decision KKO 2000:28 of the ordinary Supreme Court). The period before 1995 accounted for 26.5% of the non-Finnish cases in our sample (53 out of 200 cases).

[50] 24%, 11%, and 8% respectively. See ch 2, s VIII(B)(ii).

V. The Europeanisation of Constitutional Reasoning

A recurring theme of Nordic constitutionalism that is often used to explain the findings of our research is the idea of 'progressive subordination' of the Nordic legal systems to both branches of European law (European Union law and the ECHR) since the 1990s.[51] According to the narrative, this led to a stronger emphasis on human rights and general principles, and a departure from the approach dictated by Scandinavian legal realism, which is sceptical of abstract concepts and the power of judicial review. This development presented Nordic courts with a challenge to the dualist doctrine on the relationship between international law and domestic law, as illustrated by the Icelandic Supreme Court's struggle to maintain coherent jurisprudence in this area, as explained by Haukur Logi Karlsson in his chapter.[52]

This transformative development is not unique to the Nordic countries. Talk of constitutional pluralism[53] or multilevel constitutionalism[54] is commonplace in European legal scholarship. As Maija Dahlberg points out in her chapter on the Finnish supreme courts, 'it is no longer possible or even meaningful to distinguish between constitutional, European, and international systems for the protection of human rights'.[55] The proportion of cases dealing with fundamental rights issues was higher in the Nordic supreme courts than in most other courts around the world, with the exception of the Swedish Supreme Administrative Court (see Figure 6).

This finding confirms that the power of judicial review is exercised primarily in fundamental rights matters, demonstrating the limited competence and persisting reluctance of the Nordic courts to engage in constitutional questions related to state organisation. Indeed, we can also see a statistically significant difference in the proportion of cases dealing with matters of state organisation and lawmaking power[56] between the Nordic countries and other systems with a decentralised or hyrbid model of judicial review (see Figure 7).[57] Our data shows that the Nordic supreme courts deal with matters relating to state organisation and lawmaking even less frequently than ordinary supreme courts in other parts of the world.

[51] See ch 1, s II(D).

[52] See ch 4, s IV.

[53] M Avbelj and J Komarek (eds), *Constitutional Pluralism in the European Union and Beyond* (Oxford and Portland, Hart Publishing, 2012); K Jaklic, *Constitutional Pluralism in the EU* (Oxford, Oxford University Press, 2013).

[54] See, eg, I Pernice, 'Multilevel Constitutionalism and the Crisis of Democracy in Europe' (2015) 11 *European Constitutional Law Review* 541.

[55] See ch 5, s III(C).

[56] Including questions relating to the principle of legality and the delegation of legislation.

[57] The vertical line represents the odds ratio of the Nordic countries.

Figure 6 Proportion of cases in which the court decided a constitutional question related to fundamental rights

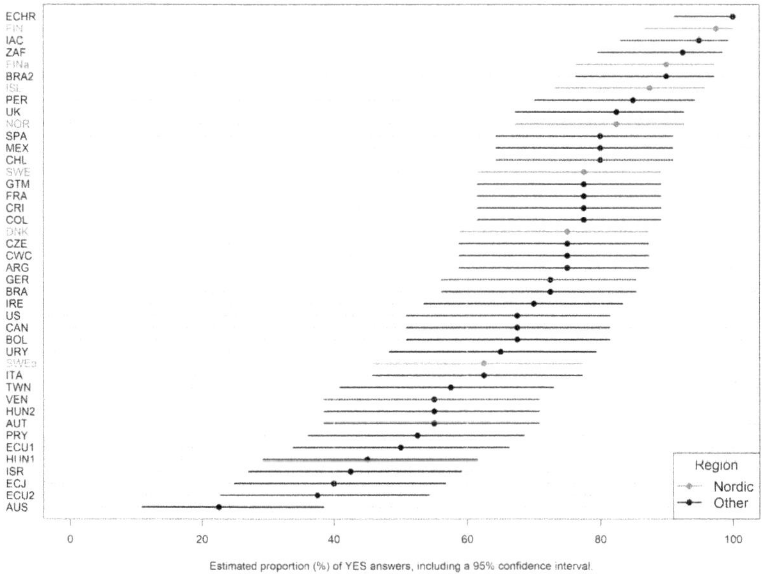

Figure 7 Cases in which the court decided a constitutional question related to state organisation and lawmaking power (odds ratios and 95% confidence intervals relative to Nordic (reference line at 1))

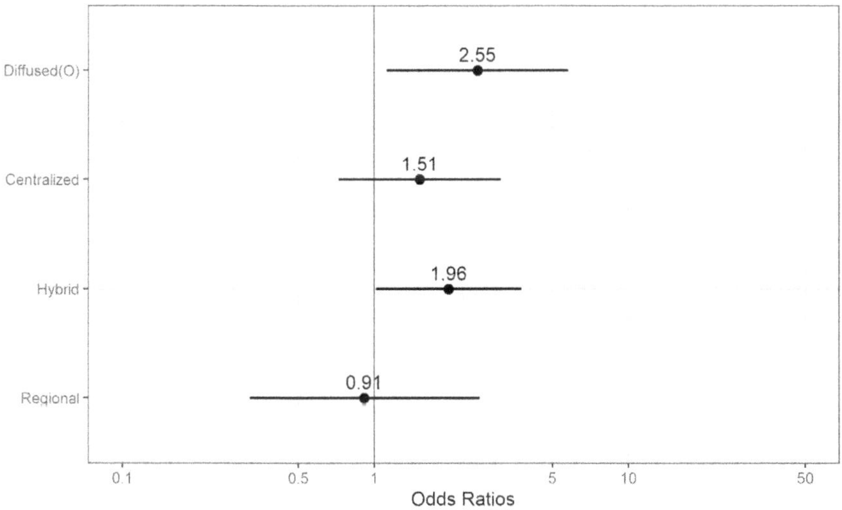

Thus, our data suggests that the transformative effect of Europeanisation is most evident in fundamental rights adjudication in the Nordic countries. While this development undoubtedly brings the Nordic countries closer together, contributing to the emergence of a Nordic style of constitutional reasoning, it also brings them closer to other European countries, fostering convergence at a continental level. As the Nordic countries are part of the wider European phenomenon of constitutional pluralism, also known as multilevel constitutionalism, it is becoming increasingly difficult to identify the Nordic-specific features of constitutional reasoning. However, we have attempted to do this in our research and identified a few common traits that distinguish the Nordic countries from the other European systems.

VI. The Nordic-specific Traits of Constitutional Reasoning

While quantitative data can give us an indication of certain features that seem to characterise the practice of the Nordic supreme courts to a greater or lesser extent than that of other courts, it alone is insufficient to capture Nordic-specific traits of constitutional reasoning. It must be considered alongside the constitutional history of these countries and the substance of the cases included in the sample. The texts of the judgments alone do not provide a complete picture. For this reason, all of the authors had to consult additional materials, primarily scholarly literature on constitutional history and case law, to interpret the data.

For example, our Danish authors, Helle Krunke and Mikael Kenno Fogde, made use of a special type of additional material to gain a better understanding of the reasoning of the Danish Supreme Court in three of its 40 leading cases: they examined the deliberation protocols.[58] This allowed them to take a look behind the curtains and discover that, for example, deliberation protocols from previous cases are often used by judges as valuable material when deciding a case. As these deliberation protocols are not considered to be sources of law,[59] they are not referenced in the judgments and were not included in our variables. This highlights the limitations of relying solely on a quantitative approach, or on the texts of judgments for that matter.

Given this premise, the quantitative data still offers valuable information on how judges choose to frame their decisions. As mentioned before, we can assume that judges include the reasons they deem legitimate within their legal system and legal culture when writing their decisions. Therefore, the arguments

[58] See ch 3, s I.

[59] Although researchers can request access to these protocols after 20 years, they are not made available to the general public. This practice is therefore also problematic from the point of view of legal certainty and the rule of law. See ch 3, s II.

and concepts that appear in the judgments can be examined as 'standards of reference and rationality'.[60]

Using the quantitative data as a starting point, we can see that when the Nordic supreme courts are compared with other courts around the world that were analysed using the same methodology, a few general features, argument types, and key concepts emerge that appear to exhibit similar proportions in the Nordic countries, while most other (non-Nordic) supreme and constitutional courts that have been examined show different proportions. These include

- the relatively low proportion of cases that contain at least one separate (dissenting or concurring) opinion,[61]
- the low proportion of cases in which the courts found the challenged act or decision to be unconstitutional,[62]
- the high proportion of cases dealing with constitutional questions relating to fundamental rights,[63]
- the rare use of arguments from silence,[64]
- the relatively high proportion of cases in which subjective teleological reasoning is used,[65]
- the high proportion of cases in which the principle of the rule of law is invoked, either explicitly or implicitly,[66]
- the low proportion of cases in the concept of human dignity is invoked.[67]

Given the strong Europeanisation of constitutional reasoning discussed above, it is worth examining the stance of other European courts in relation to these variables. Are the Nordic supreme courts closer to each other than to other European courts? Examining the data suggests that the answer is affirmative. In relation to these seven variables, more significant variation is evident among the other examined European courts, including both domestic and regional courts.[68] For example, as regards the use of separate opinions, some European

[60] See n 2 and accompanying text.

[61] Variable N3/R3. All Nordic supreme courts are within the range of 25–57.5%. If we exclude the Norwegian and Icelandic Supreme Courts, the range is between 25% (DNK) and 37.5% (SWE, FIN and FINa).

[62] Variable N4/R4. All Nordic supreme courts are within the range of 25–55%.

[63] Variable N5/R5. All Nordic supreme courts are within the range of 62.5–97.5%.

[64] Variable N21/R21. All Nordic supreme courts are within the range of 0–7.5%.

[65] Variable N23/R23. All Nordic supreme courts are within the range of 27.5–55%.

[66] Variable N31/R31. All Nordic supreme courts are within the range of 72.5–97.5%.

[67] Variable N42/R42. All Nordic supreme courts are within the range of 0–7.5%. In global comparison, the South African Constitutional Court exhibits the highest proportion (67.5%).

[68] These include 11 courts: the Austrian Constitutional Court, the Constitutional Court of the Czech Republic, the European Court of Human Rights, the European Court of Justice, the French Constitutional Council, the German Federal Constitutional Court, the Constitutional Court of Hungary (measured separately for the period 1990–2010 [HUN1] and period 2012–2013 [HUN2]), the Supreme Court of Ireland, the Constitutional Court of Italy, the Spanish Constitutional Court, and the Supreme Court (House of Lords) of the United Kingdom.

constitutional courts (namely the French, the Austrian and the Italian courts) do not even allow separate opinions to be published.[69] The extent to which separate opinions are used varies significantly among those European courts that allow them, while the Nordic supreme courts all exhibit a relatively low proportion (see Figure 8).

Figure 8 Proportion of leading constitutional cases that contain at least one separate (dissenting or concurring) opinion in a global comparison[70]

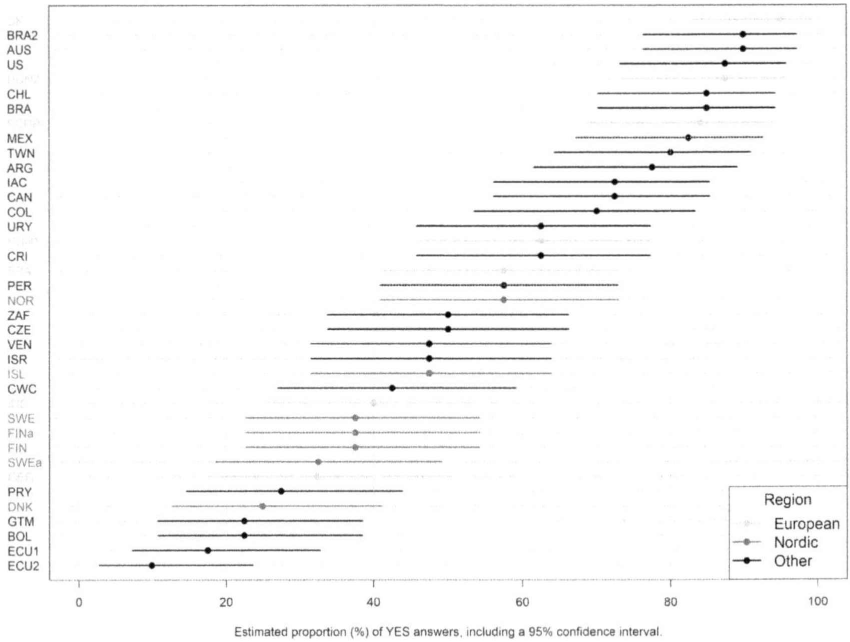

With regard to the principle of the rule of law, the seven Nordic supreme courts exhibit by far the highest proportions among the 18 European courts examined.[71] This is, however, also the most commonly used key constitutional concept globally.[72] Other, substantive concepts, such as equality, free speech and

[69] I analysed and compared the use of separate opinions in European constitutional courts in detail in a previous monograph: K Kelemen, *Judicial Dissent in European Constitutional Courts: A Comparative and Legal Perspective* (Abingdon, Routledge, 2018).

[70] This figure only contains those courts that allow the publication of separate opinions.

[71] Immediately below the Nordic supreme courts, we find the Hungarian Constitutional Court (period 1990–2010) and the Constitutional Court of the Czech Republic. Perhaps unsurprisingly, these are the two formerly socialist countries analysed in the parent project. See also A Jakab and J Fröhlich, 'The Hungarian Constitutional Court' in A Jakab, A Dyevre and G Itzcovich (eds), *Comparative Constitutional Reasoning* (Cambridge, Cambridge University Press, 2017) 394, 432.

[72] A Jakab, A Dyevre and G Itzcovich, 'Conclusion' in A Jakab, A Dyevre and G Itzcovich (eds), *Comparative Constitutional Reasoning* (Cambridge, Cambridge University Press, 2017) 761, 764.

privacy, seem to be more contingent on the subject matter and facts of the specific case. This can also be explained by the formal and issue-independent nature of the rule of law principle, which makes it relevant in virtually any constitutional case.[73] Indeed, even in Tuori's scheme of levels of the law, the rule of law belongs to the deepest layer, the deep structure of the law, as a core value inherent in the system.[74] However, it is not unique to the Nordic legal systems, even though this concept is invoked more frequently in Nordic constitutional reasoning than elsewhere. There are a few European courts among the examined ones that use the rule of law principle rarely. These include the Austrian Constitutional Court, which adopts a formalistic approach to the rule of law, and began to rely on this principle in its reasoning from the 1990s only;[75] the Italian Constitutional Court, which displays low conceptual variety in general;[76] and, unsurprisingly, the French Constitutional Council, which is known for its very terse reasoning style, and did not use the concept in any of its leading cases, either explicitly or implicitly.

Unlike in the other two projects, we also measured which components of the (thick conception of) the rule of law appeared in the reasoning. While we cannot compare this finding with those of the non-Nordic courts, it is still a relevant result that the 'rule of law' is mentioned explicitly in only a small proportion of these cases. The Nordic supreme courts far more commonly invoke the associated principles, primarily the principles of legality and separation of powers. However, we classified any discussion on the relationship between the branches of government and expressions of deference to the legislature as a 'separation of powers argument'. Thus, the relatively high proportion of cases (32.5–52.5 per cent) that rely on this specific component of the rule of law in all seven Nordic supreme courts confirms that a deferential attitude towards the legislature is a shared characteristic of Nordic constitutional reasoning.

The low proportion of leading cases in which the courts found the challenged act or decision to be unconstitutional and the relatively high proportion of cases in which subjective teleological reasoning is used in all seven Nordic supreme courts also indicate this. A well-known feature of Nordic legal culture is that courts tend to rely on preparatory works,[77] which are the main vehicle for subjective teleological reasoning. We wanted to test to what extent this holds true for constitutional interpretation. We found that, with the exception of the

[73] Followed by the principle of proportionality, which is also a formal and issue-independent principle in fundamental rights cases. See ibid.

[74] See s II above.

[75] K Lachmayer, 'The Austrian Constitutional Court' in A Jakab, A Dyevre and G Itzcovich (eds), *Comparative Constitutional Reasoning* (Cambridge, Cambridge University Press, 2017) 75, 79 and 91.

[76] Moreover, the principle of the rule of law is not explicitly mentioned in the text of the Italian Constitution, neither as '*stato di diritto*' nor as principle of legality (*principio di legalità*). See T Groppi and I Spigno, 'The Constitutional Court of Italy' in A Jakab, A Dyevre and G Itzcovich (eds), *Comparative Constitutional Reasoning* (Cambridge, Cambridge University Press, 2017) 516, 553–55.

[77] See, eg, Kischel (n 38) 560–61.

German Federal Constitutional Court and the Irish Supreme Court, all the other European courts examined make use of this type of reasoning to a lesser extent than the Nordic supreme courts (see Figure 9). These proportions would be even higher if we were to measure the extent to which this type of argument is used in statutory interpretation.

Figure 9 The proportions of leading constitutional cases in which subjective teleological reasoning is used for constitutional interpretation, in a global comparison

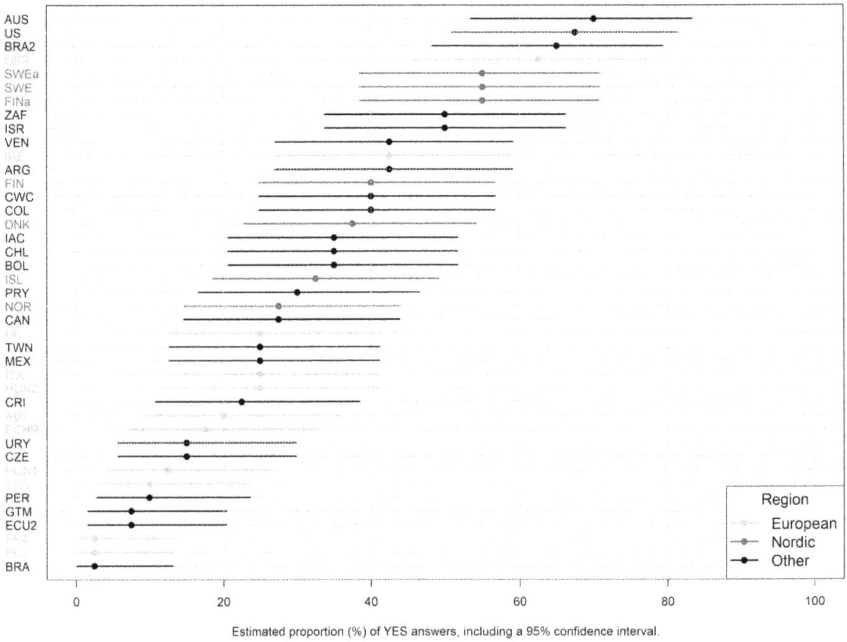

Subjective teleological reasoning used in constitutional interpretation is based on different premises to those used in statutory interpretation. This is because both Nordic and other European constitutions have significant historical differences. They greatly vary in age and in the historical circumstances in which they were adopted.[78] In the Nordic context, constitutions are considered to have strong democratic legitimacy because they are adopted and amended by the legislature through a special procedure.[79] Consequently, their preparatory works serve as a legitimate basis for their interpretation. The preparatory works of the Nordic

[78] See Table 1 in ch 1, s II(A).

[79] See T Bull, 'Institutions and Division of Powers' in H Krunke and B Thorarensen (eds), *The Nordic Constitutions: A Comparative and Contextual Study* (Oxford, Hart Publishing, 2018) 43, 53. This special procedure is sometimes accompanied by other demands, such as a popular vote in Denmark (see Article 88 of the Danish Constitution).

constitutions are also not significantly different from those of ordinary legislation, except for the oldest provisions, for which there are typically few or scattered materials.

In addition to the seven variables examined above that reveal common Nordic features, there are many more argument types and key concepts in which six Nordic supreme courts appear to occupy a similar position when compared globally, with only one deviating from the others (see Table 1).

Table 1 Variables for which one of the seven Nordic supreme courts' estimated proportion deviates from the other Nordic courts in a global comparison

Variable	Proportions of Nordic courts in global comparison	Range of Nordic courts	Nordic deviant	Proportion of Nordic deviant
N14 Cases that consider the applicability of the constitution to the case at hand	Average proportion	30–57.5%	Danish Supreme Court[80]	95%
N15 Cases in which analogical reasoning is used	Low proportion	0–7.5%	Danish Supreme Court[81]	37.5%
N16 Cases in which literal interpretation is used	Low proportion	5–25%	Norwegian Supreme Court	42.5%
N18 Cases in which international harmonising argument is used	High proportion	55–85%	Swedish Supreme Administrative Court[82]	27.5%
N19 Cases in which an argument is based on precedent	Low proportion	22.5–65%	Norwegian Supreme Court	92.5%

(continued)

[80] As Helle Krunke and Mikael Kenno Fogde explain in their chapter, this may reflect the practice that the state attorney or both parties alerted the Supreme Court to the fact that it is overall reluctant to thoroughly review the constitutionality of legislation. See ch 3, s II.

[81] In their chapter, Helle Krunke and Mikael Kenno Fogde explain that this type of argument is usually introduced by the parties, who argue about how to interpret the old Danish Constitution in modern-day society. See ch 3, s III.

[82] In her chapter, Åsa Elmerot suggests that this may be because the Supreme Administrative Court deals with a high proportion of cases relating to state organisation and legality matters and there are fewer fundamental rights cases in its sample. See ch 7, s II(D). Interestingly, this does not apply to the Finnish Supreme Administrative Court, which deals with fundamental rights issues in 90% of its leading constitutional cases, and indeed invoke international law in 62.5% of the cases.

Table 1 ***(Continued)***

Variable	**Proportions of Nordic courts in global comparison**	**Range of Nordic courts**	**Nordic deviant**	**Proportion of Nordic deviant**
N22 Cases in which objective teleological reasoning is used	Low proportion	7.5–25%	Danish Supreme Court[83]	55%
N33 Cases in which the concept of democracy is invoked	Low proportion	5–20%	Norwegian Supreme Court[84]	35%
N34 Cases in which the concept of sovereignty is invoked	Low proportion	0–5%	Danish Supreme Court[85]	17.5%
N35 Cases that invoke arguments related to the form of the state	No such cases.	0%	Danish Supreme Court[86]	7.5%

As already mentioned before, which key concepts tend to be used in the leading constitutional cases is heavily influenced by the content of the constitutional texts and the historical circumstances under which those cases arose. However, given this premise, compared to other countries of the world included, Table 1 shows that the commonalities of the Nordic countries tend to demonstrate a lower frequency of various types of arguments and key concepts. The only exception is the use of arguments based on international law in constitutional reasoning, which corroborates the prevailing narrative in literature that constitutional law in the Nordic countries has progressively become subordinate to European law over the last few decades.

As we explained in the first chapter of this book, all Nordic countries are perceived as dualist systems.[87] However, the status of international law is rather complex and lacks detailed regulation in the domestic constitutions.

[83] See ch 3, s III.

[84] As Morten Nadim explains in his chapter, this concept is often invoked in combination with the principle of separation of powers and judicial independence. See ch 6, s IV(C).

[85] As Helle Krunke and Mikael Kenno Fogde explain in their chapter, this depends on the fact that several Danish landmark judgments are related to Denmark's EU membership. See ch 3, s III.

[86] See also ch 3, s III.

[87] See ch 1, s II(D).

Unsurprisingly, Nordic judges seem to take a pragmatic approach to this issue. Although we found a comparatively high proportion of leading constitutional cases that employ international harmonising arguments, a closer look at the judgments reveals that Nordic judges tend not to discuss the status of international law, preferring to simply apply its norms directly. In other words, they do not elaborate on the status of international law in the hierarchy of sources. This also confirms what previous research has already showed: that Nordic courts typically demonstrate a parallel use of the constitution and international human rights treaties, rather than a full harmonisation.[88] Clearly distinguishing constitutional reasoning from statutory reasoning in fundamental rights matters has also been challenging, because much of the concretisation and regulation of fundamental rights takes place in the form of parliamentary legislation.[89]

Interestingly, such high proportions of international harmonising arguments are typically observed in countries that adopt a monist approach to international law. In his chapter on the Icelandic Supreme Court, Haukur Logi Karlsson presented the tension between a dualist approach and monist tendencies in the case-law.[90] Indeed, among the domestic courts examined globally, the Icelandic Supreme Court exhibits the highest proportion, together with the Finnish Supreme Court. It is also the only one among the Nordic supreme courts that discusses whether the ECHR is considered to be part of the domestic constitution in a meaningful number of cases.[91]

Table 1 also shows that, in an intra-Nordic comparison, the Danish and Norwegian Supreme Courts account for most of all the deviations. Although we cannot draw too far-fetching conclusions from this observation, it does make us wonder whether it shows, to some extent, the existence of an East-West divide. As mentioned earlier, the principal component analysis of the argumentative variables also seems to suggest this. Indeed, six of the nine variables in Table 1 are argumentative variables (ie, measuring the presence of certain types of arguments). Thus, we can detect some measure of an East-West divide in relation to argumentation, but not conceptualisation, between the Nordic countries.

[88] T Ojanen, 'Human Rights in the Nordic Constitutions and the Impact of International Obligations' in H Krunke and B Thorarensen (eds), *The Nordic Constitutions: A Comparative and Contextual Study* (Oxford, Hart Publishing, 2018) 133, 157.

[89] ibid 144.

[90] See ch 4, s IV.

[91] We measured this using variable N13 (see the Codebook in the Appendix), for which we established our own subcategories that had not been applied in the other two projects. Therefore, we cannot compare these findings with those from non-Nordic courts. Apart from one Danish case, this type of argument did not appear in any of the other Nordic supreme courts. In addition, none of the 160 Finnish and Swedish cases included in the sample used arguments establishing or discussing the text of the constitution in any of the three subcategories of this variable. These subcategories distinguished between arguments that discussed whether the ECHR, other sources of written law, or a tradition or custom were considered part of the constitution.

VII. Final Thoughts

As several scholars have observed, the case of the Nordic countries demonstrates that strong democracies and the rule of law can coexist with weak constitutions and a weak power of judicial review.[92] The Nordic countries consistently top rankings measuring the state of democracy and the rule of law.[93] At the same time, as our study also demonstrated, Nordic courts rarely strike down legislation as unconstitutional. They prefer to rely on international human rights instruments instead of their domestic catalogues of constitutional rights. They also avoid taking a stance on the status of international law in relation to the domestic constitution. Moreover, they rely on the legislature's preparatory materials when interpreting constitutional provisions and tend to defer to the will of legislature in general.

However, we also demonstrated that the Nordic supreme courts exhibit significant diversity in many other respects, and an East-West divide can be detected in relation to their argumentative patterns. In particular, the supreme courts of the two Eastern Scandinavian countries, Sweden and Finland, exhibit a lower argumentative diversity, ie. they rely on a less diverse repertoire of arguments than the supreme courts of Denmark, Iceland, and Norway. However, in some respects, the Swedish and Finnish supreme courts, somewhat unexpectedly, seem to be far from each other. The Finnish courts invoke international law more often, use key constitutional concepts and non-legal arguments more frequently. They also reference the Parliament's Constitutional Law Committee more often.

Overall, our book shows that while the Nordic supreme courts share several distinctive traits, such as pragmatism, a deferential approach to the legislature, and extensive use of international human rights instruments, their constitutional reasoning is far from uniform. The data reveal both commonalities and significant internal variation. This suggests that what may be called a 'Nordic constitutional culture' is less a single, coherent model than a spectrum of shared practices shaped by history, institutional setting, and Europeanisation. The book therefore reframes the idea of Nordic exceptionalism: rather than a monolithic style of constitutional reasoning, there exists a family resemblance of approaches that together illustrate how strong democracies can operate with relatively weak constitutions and limited judicial review.

As discussed in this book, when trying to adapt the CONREASON methodology to the Nordic context, we faced several challenges. First of all, we learned that

[92] See, eg, R Hirschl, 'The Nordic Counternarrative: Democracy, Human Development, and Judicial Review' (2011) 9 *International Journal of Constitutional Law* 449; M Zamboni, 'The Role of the Constitution in Sweden: Addressing its Patchy Legal Legitimacy and the (Half-Way) Transition from Political to Legal Constitutionalism' (2025) 19 *ICL Journal* 47.

[93] See, eg, the World Justice Project's Rule of Law Index, worldjusticeproject.org/rule-of-law-index/, which however does not include Iceland.

examining court practice alone would not provide a comprehensive understanding of Nordic constitutional reasoning. In a context where most constitutional discourse takes place outside the courtroom, primarily in parliaments, other public bodies, and academic circles, one cannot draw far-fetching conclusions about constitutional reasoning based solely on court practice. Norway might be an exception, but we were interested in understanding the Nordic countries as a group, which are often perceived as, and presented as, homogeneous. As our data also showed, they are not. However, this does not exclude the existence of certain common traits.

The question of whether a distinct Nordic constitutional culture exists is an even more ambitious endeavour – arguably too ambitious for any single research project. Nonetheless, we aspire for our study to make a meaningful contribution to that broader investigation. Therefore, our findings should be read in conjunction with other comparative studies on shared institutional structures and common underlying values in the Nordic countries. We expect this comparative analysis of constitutional reasoning in the Nordic supreme courts to enrich debates on Nordic constitutional culture, providing an empirical foundation for many of its elements.

Appendix

Nordic CONREASON Project Codebook[1]

The questions used in our project are marked by an N. After that number, between brackets, you will find the number of the same question in the CONREASON Project and in the CORE Latam Project, where applicable. During the duration of the project, this codebook was adjusted and updated seven times.[2]

We would like to minimise missing values (or 'not applicable', N/A values). We would like to have uniform data (with two exceptions: 'not applicable' is used for N4, if – because of the nature of the procedure – it does not make sense to inquire what the case disposition was, ie whether the state won or not, and N17, if the domestic constitution is not applied in the case). Beyond that, the questions are 'is there an argument of type-x in this judgment?', and the answer is either YES or NO (whether the NO can be explained by the fact that it was not even possible to have such an argument for some reason, can be explained in the report itself, but in the coding we just want a YES or NO). Otherwise, we might run into very difficult problems of deciding whether we deal with a NO or with a N/A.

In the case of **binary variables** (approximately half of the variables, 27 out of 53), there is only one column, in which you have to write either YES or NO (except for N4, where 'N/A' and blank box are also an option, and N17, where 'N/A' is the third option). In the case of **categorical variables**, you will find as many columns as different YES options. There is no separate column for NO. If all boxes are left blank for that variable, it will be equivalent to a NO.[3] While the coder is instructed to write a number in the box for the categorical variables, in the final dataset these are converted to YES or NO. There are, however, three categorical variables where you must choose at least one of the options. These are N5 (general topic), N7 (type

[1] Version 1.7, last modified on 7 February 2024. This appendix is a reformatted version of the codebook available at K Kelemen, Nordic CONREASON Collection of Data on Constitutional Reasoning in the Nordic Supreme Courts (Version 1), doi.org/10.60689/zmk7-0z14. In the online version, Variables and instructions that come from the CORE Latam Project but were not, or not explicitly, included in the CONREASON Project are highlighted in green. New questions, changes or additional explanations specific to the Nordic CONREASON Project are highlighted in blue (so these were not included in either the CONREASON or the CORE Latam Project).

[2] For details on the additions and corrections see the online version published together with the dataset.

[3] This is the case for 14 categorical variables: N3, N13, N14, N16, N18, N23, N24, N25, N26, N31, N34, N41, N45, and N50.

of dispute), N11 (panel formation). For these three variables, leaving all boxes blank is not an option.

The analysis always concerns the whole judgment, not only the majority opinion (the only exception is N52). The main question for this project is not what is in the 'winning arguments', but which arguments are accepted as legitimate arguments by the argumentative culture of the given (supreme or constitutional) court, ie. what may be used as an argument. And this takes into account the separate opinions as well. This means that we also count arguments and concepts contained in quoted sources, including the parties' arguments, as these arguments are also indirectly legitimised by the court. This also means that even arguments and concepts used by the lower courts (if included in judgment) are to be coded. The Swedish cases are planned to be coded both with and without the lower courts' decision so that we can evaluate the latters' impact on constitutional reasoning.

Please use the technique of taking **side notes** whenever the instructions ask you to do so.[4] By side note we mean a separate file (either in Word or in Excel format), where you annotate in which cases you found that given characteristic that we are not able to measure in the coding.

1. Variables Related to the Characteristics of the Case

N1 (Q1/Q1): Reference of the decision

Please give the official reference of the decision in original language.

N2 (Q2/Q2): Year

Specify the year in which the decision was delivered.

N3 (Q3/Q3): Dissenting or concurring opinions in the case

Please indicate the type(s) of separate opinion attached to the judgment by writing the relevant **number(s)** in the relevant column(s) (ie. write '1' in column P3_1, '2' in column P3_2, etc.). If a certain type of separate opinion is *not* present in the judgment, leave the box in that column blank. If there are no separate opinions at all, please leave all columns blank.

1) Dissenting on the constitutional issue
2) Dissenting on other issues
3) Parallel concurring opinion on the constitutional issue

[4] You find such instructions for variables N25 and N28, and as a general instruction for all variables related to conceptualisation (see section 3).

4) Parallel concurring opinion on other issues
5) Supplementary concurring opinion related to the constitutional issue
6) Supplementary concurring opinion related to other issues[5]

The same separate opinion be counted both as a dissent and as a concurrence if the dissent and the concurrence concern different constitutional issues. Definition of parallel concurring opinion: the judge offers an alternative reasoning, so s/he agrees with the outcome but not with the reasoning. Definition of supplementary concurring opinion: the judge offers additional arguments supporting the same outcome, while not questioning the reasons offered by the majority. If the opinion is parallel concurring, it cannot be supplementary on the same constitutional issue at the same time.

In the dataset the following aggregations of the subcategories are also included as separate variables: N3_135 (separate opinions related to the constitutional issue), N3_246 (separate opinions on other issues), N_12 (dissenting opinions), N_34 (parallel concurring opinions), N_56 (supplementary concurring opinions).

N4 (Q4/Q4): Case disposition / Outcome of the constitutional issue

Please indicate whether the court found (at least partially) against the law/decision/act (of the government) challenged (YES or NO). If the judgment prescribes a binding interpretation (of a statute or of the Constitution), then the box should be left blank. If the court established an 'unconstitutional omission' (if that is possible in your legal order), then it counts as a YES. Admissibility decisions can also be categorised as YES (admissibility granted) or a NO (admissibility denied). If the case is only about interim relief, then an interim relief against the law/decision/act also qualifies as a YES.

In the case of a supreme court, such as the Nordic courts analysed here, it is important to distinguish between the disposition of a case and the decisions on a constitutional issue. The fact that an appellant wins a constitutional argument does not necessarily mean that the appeal is upheld, since the constitutional issue might have been only one aspect of a complex case. Therefore, in line with the UK Chapter of the CONREASON Project, in the Nordic jurisdictions we take into consideration how the court decided the constitutional issue, not how it disposed of the case.[6]

This variable may also be 'not applicable' if the legal dispute took place between private individuals or organisations. In such case you must write N/A in the box. However, not all civil cases qualify automatically as N/A. If the court exercises

[5] 'Parallel concurring opinion' and 'supplementary concurring opinion' are the terms used in the UK Chapter, so for the sake of coherence and clarity we employ these terms. See T Gyorfi, 'The Supreme Court (House of Lords) of the United Kingdom' in A Jakab, A Dyevre and G Itzcovich (eds), *Comparative Constitutional Reasoning* (Cambridge, Cambridge University Press, 2017) 713.
[6] ibid 692.

judicial review of legislative or executive acts, then it is to be marked either as YES or NO. N/A is to be marked in the case of horizontal application of the constitution, procedural issues or general principles.

Summing it up, there are four options as an answer to this question:

- YES
- NO
- N/A
- leaving the box blank

N5 (Q5/Q5): General topic

Please specify: (F) Fundamental rights, (S) State Organisation, (P) Procedural, Due Process aspect, or (O) Other. When the issue is characterised as pertaining to the separation of powers or federalism, it is to be coded as (S). Other rule of law or legality matters do not belong to this category and should be coded as 'Other' (N5_O).[7] The (P) option means that the court, instead of examining the constitutional question on the merits, decides on procedural grounds (for example, declares the petition inadmissible). When the due process of the main procedure before the lower court is the constitutional question, it does not count as (P) but as (F). You can also indicate a combination of the general topics if there were several in one single judgment. Write the relevant **letter(s)** in the relevant box(es).

N6 (Q6/Q6): Concrete issue

Please characterise the issue at hand, using your own words. More than one issue may be entered. Write words and short expressions rather than full sentences in this box, at a reasonable level of abstraction (not too specific and detailed).

N7 (–): Type of dispute

Please indicate under which jurisdiction the case was decided by the court, by writing the relevant **letter (only one)** in the relevant box, and leave the other boxes blank:

C) Civil case
P) Criminal case
A) Administrative case or a case against the executive branch
O) Other

N8 (–/Q8): Length of the judgment

Please indicate the number of words of the judgment, also considering the separate opinions. Only the following parts are to be *excluded* from the word count: the

[7] See A Jakab, A Dyevre and G Itzcovich, 'Conclusion' in A Jakab, A Dyevre and G Itzcovich (eds), *Comparative Constitutional Reasoning* (Cambridge, Cambridge University Press, 2017) 784.

summary, keywords and references listed before or after the text of the judgments. The lower court's decision is to be taken into account in the word count even if it takes the form of a separate attachment to the judgment.[8]

N9 (–/–): Length of the majority reasoning

Please indicate the number of words of the court's reasoning in the judgment, including the case disposition. Please disregard the statement of the case (facts, sources of law, procedural history and the parties' arguments) when counting the number of words. As a rule of thumb, the majority reasoning begins where the court begins to talk about law and discusses the legal questions raised in the case.

In the dataset a separate variable (N9_8) has been created to indicate the proportion between the total length of the judgment and the length of the majority reasoning (see column DQ).

N10 (–/–): Voting result

Please indicate how many members of the decision-making panel voted for and against the judgment, by indicating the number of judges in favour first. For example, if 3 judges voted for and 2 judges voted against the judgment, write '3-2' in the box. If all five judges voted for the judgment, write '5-0' in the box.

In the dataset the variable N10_un is added as a binary variable (see column DP) indicating whether the decision has been unanimous (YES or NO).

N11 (–/–): Panel formation

Please write the letter (O) if the case was decided by an ordinary panel or the letter (S) if it was decided by a strengthened panel (eg Grand Chamber or plenary session) in the relevant column. Leave the box in the other column blank.

2. Variables Related to the Arguments Used in the Case

You should only consider *constitutional* interpretation. If a case brought before the supreme court deals exclusively with the interpretation of ordinary legislation, then these arguments are not relevant – or, at least, not directly relevant – for this Project. As regards the interpretation of a statute in the light of the constitution, we are only interested in arguments establishing the meaning of the constitution, as opposed to how these arguments bear on the meaning of ordinary legislation.

Please try to classify the arguments as one from our list. If – despite your efforts – it does not seem possible, then there is a special box in the table (N28), and you

[8] The Swedish cases have, however, been coded both with and without the lower courts' decisions.

can explain in your report (the qualitative analysis) why it did not fit into any of our categories.

Please mark also those judgments with a YES where a certain argument was considered but eventually rejected (eg, if the opinion distinguishes the case at hand from former precedents, it does count as an 'argument from precedent'). However, do not mark YES if the argument type is rejected altogether as irrelevant or inappropriate (eg, the argument 'we do not consider here moral arguments because it is a court of law' does not count as a non-legal argument).

You should equally consider majority and minority (dissenting or concurring) opinions: it does not matter whether the argument turned up in the majority or in the minority opinion. We only consider whether a type of argument came up in the reasoning, not how many times it did. Because of repetitions and half-repetitions, it would be difficult and very time-consuming to quantify the frequency within the judgments.

If we consider an argument as borderline between two types of arguments, then we shall make a mark for both categories. If a judgment quoted an argument from another judgment, then the quoted argument also qualified on its own (and not just as a 'precedent-argument').

Simple affirmations, declarations, or the recalling of factual circumstances, as well as mere citations of laws or the constitution, are not considered as reasoning without answering why that information or detail supports the opinion. In order to be able to call a set of propositions an argument, it needs to contain an inference, a sort of logical connection that binds the premise to the conclusion with a normative force. For instance, pseudo arguments are assertions that could appear as arguments at first sight, but after a more careful analysis, they do not contain the necessary normative connection between the mentioned assertions. Furthermore, there are deceptive arguments, that refers to the intentional use of fallacies, such as appeal to emotions, arguments *ad hominem* or distractions from the substance of the issue at hand.[9] These distinctions and definitions are also relevant in relation to the second-last variable (N52).

If the ECHR has a constitutional or semi-constitutional status in your jurisdiction, please take into consideration the special instructions concerning variables N13 (establishing or discussing the text of the constitution), N17 (domestic harmonising argument), N18 (harmonising with international law), N20 (invoking a concept or principle not mentioned in the constitution), and N23 (historical teleological argument).

N12 (Q7/Q9): Structure of argument

Please specify if you identify: (C) a 'one-line conclusive argument', (L) 'parallel conclusive arguments', or (D) 'parallel, individually inconclusive, but

[9] CORE Latam Project Guide, pp. 4–5 (on file with the authors).

together conclusive arguments', and write the relevant **letter** in the relevant column.

- (C) (1) 'one-line conclusive argument': We mean a self-standing structure, in which every premise is presented as a necessary component of the argument.
- (L) (2) 'parallel conclusive argument': We mean a cumulative parallel structure, in which distinct, autonomous considerations lead to the same conclusion.
- (D) (3) 'parallel, individually inconclusive, but together conclusive arguments': The various considerations brought up by the opinion are neither presented as necessary nor as sufficient to entail the conclusion, but as elements bearing, at least, some relevance for the issue at hand.

The three types of structure are in a more or less relationship as to their structural clarity, ie. the 'one-line conclusive arguments' is the clearest structure and the 'parallel, individually inconclusive, but together conclusive arguments' is the most opaque one.[10] The structure of a judgment that contains only one argument (or which just simply states the interpretation without explaining why the court chose it) is a (C) (1).

Every judgment is one analytical unit, regardless the presence of separate opinions and the number of constitutional questions decided in it. If both (C) (1) and (L) (2) structures are present in the same judgment, then mark it as (L) (2). If you notice a (D) (3) structure, then mark the judgment with (D) (3) even if there are also (C) (1) and (L) (2) structures. This also applies to the opinion of the lower courts cited in or attached to the supreme court's decision.[11]

The analysis shall focus on the reasoning that is related to the constitutional issue, as opposed to the reasoning of the whole opinion. It can happen that the constitutional reasoning is built on a 'one-line conclusive argument', but the judge also supports the conclusion of the decision by another, non-constitutional argument. For the purpose of this analysis, this additional argument does not make the structure of the argument 'parallel conclusive', since the additional argument is not related to the constitutional issue. On the other hand, when the judge's position on the constitutional issue is based on a 'one-line conclusive argument', but an intermediary step in the reasoning is supported by parallel arguments (either individually conclusive or not), the structure is to be coded as a parallel argument.[12]

If there is no constitutional argument in the judgment, for example because the court only interprets a statute in conformity with the constitution without interpreting the constitution or because there is no logical link between the invoked constitutional provisions and the court's conclusion, leave all boxes blank.

[10] A Jakab, A Dyevre and G Itzcovich, 'CONREASON – The Comparative Constitutional Reasoning Project. Methodological Dilemmas and Project Design' (2015) *MTA Law Working Papers* 2015/9, 13, real.mtak.hu/36806/1/2015_09_jakab.pdf.

[11] The Swedish cases are, however, coded both with and without the lower courts' decision.

[12] This explanation is from Gyorfi (n 5) 692–93.

N13 (Q8/Q10): Establishing or discussing the text of the constitution

Please indicate whether the opinion explicitly discusses what counts as constitutional text. Establishing the text is different from establishing the content of the constitution. The latter refers to the meaning and interpretation of what is already identified as a *constitutional* text. Prior to that is the question of what counts as a constitutional text. This is the question the present category is intended to capture. It includes all segments of an opinion in which the constitutional status of legal sources is considered (eg, what is considered to be a standard of review). These arguments usually emerge when it is not clear whether a norm is part of the supreme law of the land, ie if it is recognised as a constitutional text or not. In the Nordic context it may also include discussions on whether or not a constitutional custom or tradition counts as constitutional text and whether the ECHR is considered part of the constitution in the broad sense. At the same time, if it is taken for granted by the court that the ECHR has a constitutional or semi-constitutional status, and the issue is not being explicitly discussed, (1) is *not* to be marked.

If there is no such discussion in the reasoning, leave all columns blank. If there is, please indicate which type of discussion can be found in the reasoning by writing the corresponding **number(s)** in the relevant box(es):

1) Discussing whether the ECHR is considered part of the national constitution / constitutional law;
2) Discussing whether other sources of written law, which are not incorporated into the constitution, are considered part of the constitution / constitutional law;
3) Discussing whether a tradition or custom is considered to be part of the constitution / constitutional law.

N14 (Q9/Q11): Is the applicability of constitutional law discussed?

Please indicate whether the opinion explicitly considers whether constitutional law can be applied by the Court to the case at hand (eg, because/despite political question doctrine). Does the opinion consider the applicability of constitutional law to the case at hand? This question may notably arise in connection with political question doctrines and state of emergency situations or, in EU member states, in relation to the primacy of EU law over domestic constitutional law, or when the court holds that the case is not governed by the constitution, but by some other legal source. Deferential arguments, stating that no constitutional answer can be found to the question, should also be noted here. This category covers considerations as to the applicability *ratione materiae* of the constitution, the binding force, as well as to the enforceability and justiciability of the constitution. Illustrations are statements such as 'the case at hand has no constitutional relevance', 'the case falls within the discretion of the legislator [or other non-judicial institution]', 'a Constitution has to bind all state organs', etc. Using the doctrine of conventionality control or concepts like the margin of appreciation would fall under this category as well. If the court finds that constitutional law is not applicable to the case at hand, the judgment can be included in the list of landmark cases only if the court states this explicitly in its reasoning.

If there is no such discussion in the reasoning, please leave all columns blank. If there is, please indicate which kind of discussion can be found in the reasoning by writing the corresponding **number(s)** in the relevant box(es):

1) Political question doctrine
2) Other questions of applicability *ratione materiae*
3) State of emergency situations
4) Primacy of EU law
5) Other

N15 (Q10/Q12): Analogy

Please indicate (YES or NO) whether the opinion features any instance(s) of analogical reasoning. For the purposes of our research, analogy is an argument that is presented as filling a gap (lacuna) in the constitution and is used to solve a case that is not explicitly regulated by the constitution by using a constitutional provision that regulates similar cases, or by using similar institutions or principles from other fields of jurisprudence. If the court categorically says that "analogy as such is always an invalid argument" then you should *not* count it. But if the court simply rejects the use of analogy in a certain case without rejecting the genre of this argument in general, then you should count it.

N16 (Q11/Q13): Ordinary meaning of words

Please indicate whether the opinion explicitly considers the ordinary meaning of the text of the constitution. By ordinary meaning of words, we refer to the grammatical-literal interpretation of the words/phrases/articles of the constitution, following its everyday or professional meaning.

If there is no explicit reference to the ordinary meaning of the text of the constitution in the reasoning, please leave both columns blank. If there is, please indicate where that reference can be found by writing the corresponding **number(s)** in the relevant box(es):

1) in the majority opinion,
2) in a separate (dissenting or concurring) opinion.

N17 (Q12/Q14): Domestic harmonising arguments

Please indicate whether the opinion seeks to conciliate different constitutional requirements with one another. In case harmonising involves international law, or sources of international law that were incorporated into national law, it should be categorised under N18 (with the separation of N17 and N18, we aim at acquiring information also about the openness towards international law). Please do not consider interpretation of statutes in light of the constitution, as that is not about the interpretation of the constitution but about the interpretation of statutes which we are not dealing with. This method refers to those types of arguments that interpret different articles, sections or provisions of the same constitution in harmony with each other. It can also be called 'integrative' method or 'systematic interpretation'. If the national constitution is a fragmented constitution, it also includes arguments that seek to conciliate the provisions of the central constitutional document (eg, the Instrument of Government) with provisions contained in other fundamental laws. Contrary to N20 (concept or principle not mentioned in the text of the constitution), this argument is always based on the text of the constitution.

If the opinion does not apply the domestic constitution at all, please write N/A (not applicable) in the box. This will be the case when the reasoning only relies on the ECHR or on general constitutional principles.

N18 (Q13/Q15): Harmonising with international law requirements

Please indicate whether the opinion seeks to interpret constitutional law in light of international law (including EU law and the ECHR).

If there is no such argument in the reasoning, please leave all columns blank. If there is, please indicate which kind of source the court seeks to harmonise the constitution with, by writing the corresponding **number(s)** in the relevant box(es):

1) EU law / EEA law (including CJEU / EFTA Court case-law);
2) ECHR[13] (including ECtHR case-law);
3) Other binding sources of international law (eg, the ICCPR);
4) Sources of international soft law (eg, an opinion of the Venice Commission).

If the ECHR is considered to have a constitutional or semi-constitutional status in your jurisdiction, and it is being harmonised with another international human rights treaty, this variable is to be marked both as (2) and (3), even if the domestic constitution is not invoked. In this way we acquire more accurate information about the openness towards the different sources of international law.

N19 (Q14/Q16): Precedent-based arguments

Please indicate (YES or NO) whether the opinion considers previous rulings of the court. Please also mark it with YES if the court distinguished the present case from the former one, and therefore they did not apply it. A precedent-based argument means the use of previous judgments or preliminary rulings of the same court,

[13] In CORE Latam, the first option is reference to international legal instruments from the Inter-American system, while we consider the two European systems (EU/EEA and ECHR) separately. We can still collapse the data on (1) and (2) later in order to compare the frequency of references to regional instruments in Latin-America and Northern Europe.

already resolved, in order to interpret the text of the constitution. Only those precedents count that are relevant to the constitutional question and the constitutional reasoning.

N20 (Q15/Q17): Invoking a concept or principle not mentioned in the text of the constitution

Please indicate YES or NO. The application of concepts and principles (including different constitutional tests for fundamental rights restrictions) developed by courts or by legal scholars.

Examples of such concepts and principles: (1) overarching constitutional principles, whose legal status does not derive from any specific enactment, but rather from the fact that they serve to rationalise and justify legal rules and legal institutions (such as separation of powers, rule of law or parliamentary sovereignty); (2) doctrinal categories that are recurrently used to structure the argument of the court, such as proportionality, if not specifically mentioned in the constitution.[14]

If you consider the ECHR to be part of the constitution, then concepts that are explicitly mentioned in the ECHR (including its Preamble) cannot be counted here.

This variable does not cover the implicit use of concepts or principles that are mentioned in the text of the constitution.

N21 (Q16/Q18): Argument from silence

Please indicate (YES or NO) whether the opinion considers argument from silence. An argument from silence (*argumentum ex silentio*) is based on the omission or lack of expressive reference to something in the constitution.

N22 (Q17/Q19): Teleological (textual) arguments

Please indicate (YES or NO) whether the opinion invokes or considers the supposed purpose of the constitutional text or part thereof. This kind of teleological argument (often called 'objective teleological argument', because it refers to the purpose or the aim of the provision in question that has expressive textual basis in the constitution) refers to the purpose of the text rather than to the purpose of its authors. Consequently, references to preparatory works are not to be marked here, but under N23.

N23 (Q18/Q20): Teleological (historical-intentional) arguments

Please indicate whether the opinion invokes or considers the purpose of the constitution-makers. This type of teleological argument (often called 'subjective teleological argument') equates the purpose of a constitutional provision with the

[14] These examples are from Gyorfi (n 5) 699.

purpose pursued by the constitution-makers. It may take the form of a reference to the travaux préparatoires. These may also include expert opinions by scholars that were taken into account during the constitution-making process. (In such case it is only to be coded here, and not under N25).

If there is no such argument in the reasoning, please leave both columns blank. If there is, please indicate where that argument can be found by writing the corresponding **number(s)** in the relevant box(es):

1) in the majority opinion,
2) in a separate (dissenting or concurring) opinion.

If the ECHR is considered to have constitutional or semi-constitutional status in your jurisdiction, references to the preparatory work of the incorporation of the ECHR are not to be counted here if the argument is about the purpose of the incorporation of the ECHR and not about the purpose of the ECHR itself.

N24 (Q19/Q21): Non-legal arguments

Please indicate (YES or NO) whether the opinion explicitly considers economic, sociological, moral/religious or scientific/medical arguments. The present project does not want to contribute to the endless debate about the concept of law, so we are using a rather practical and simple test on what counts as 'non legal'. For the purposes of the present research, non-legal arguments are explicitly moral/religious, economic, sociological and scientific/medical arguments (ie, arguments that are explicitly grounded on considerations external to the law) about the interpretation of the constitution.

There is a significant degree of overlap between legal and other forms of discourse. This fact is particularly evident in the realm of constitutional law and with terms such as 'sovereignty', 'human dignity', 'democracy', etc. Generally speaking, though, the fact that an expression is also used in moral or political discourse does not automatically make it non-legal. Though explicit mention in the constitutional text is not a necessary condition for legalness, it should in principle be sufficient. So, if a specific constitutional rule mentions 'public morality' or 'budgetary stability' then the explanation of these concepts is legal. Also, the explanation of the facts of a case does not qualify as a non-legal argument: we are looking only for arguments which justify a certain interpretation of a constitutional rule.

We also remind you that the court should not be regarded as having recourse to a non-legal argument when a non-legal argument is rejected as invalid, irrelevant or inappropriate. If, for example, the court observes 'we do not consider here moral arguments because it is a court of law', this does not count as a non-legal argument.

The proportionality analysis is an interesting issue because it explicitly requires courts to balance rights against public morals or safety, etc. We would still suggest that this should not be categorised as a non-legal argument. Because if we say that this is a non-legal argument, we will end up including too much in the 'non-legal' category. Similarly, many constitutions explicitly refer to public morals and safety and health or 'human dignity' and therefore require the courts to interpret them and protect them. But again, if we included these concepts which are commonly contained in written constitutions, the category of non-legal arguments would become too broad, and it would be misleading.

The relationship with teleological reasoning is also an interesting issue, because the purpose of a norm is usually a non-legal purpose. If the court refers to a non-legal purpose of the norm that it interprets, then it is to be coded as a teleological argument (N22 or N23, depending on if it is only based on the text or on the intent of the constitution-maker), and not to be marked here. On the other hand, if the court argues that this norm is to be interpreted in a given way because this and that non-legal reason, then it is a non-legal argument and to be marked here. In any case, we either mark teleological argument or non-legal argument, not both at the same time (in relation to the same argument).

If there is no such argument in the reasoning, please leave all columns blank. If there is, please indicate which kind of non-legal argument(s) the reasoning invokes or considers, by writing the corresponding **number(s)** in the relevant box(es):

1) economic argument,
2) sociological argument,
3) moral/religious argument,
4) scientific/medical argument.[15]

N25 (Q20/Q22): Reference to scholarly work

Please indicate (YES or NO) whether the opinion explicitly mentions academic literature. Unnamed, generic references to the 'dominant doctrine', 'authoritative doctrine', etc, should also be qualified as references to scholarly works. On the other hand, the use of concepts and theories known to have scholarly origins should not count as "references to scholarly works" if no explicit references to legal scholarship are made. Nuances in the use of scholarly arguments that are not captured by the Table can, and should, be discussed in your written report (the qualitative analysis).

Since the CORE Latam project (unlike the parent project) instructed the coders to mark this variable only in case of a direct reference, and not in case of a reference

[15] Non-legal arguments were categorised in a different way in the UK chapter: (1) policy arguments, (2) principles of political philosophy, (3) empirical assumptions, (4) positive morality arguments. See Gyorfi (n 5) 703–704. Example of empirical assumption: the significance of the dress code in Muslim society. Example of positive morality argument: the increased social acceptance of different sexual orientations.

contained in a citation, if the reference is contained in a citation, please take a side note, but still mark it under N25.

In the UK Chapter, also references to non-legal academic literature were included here (eg, literature on the historical or socio-economic context).[16] The authors of the US Chapter, on the other hand, did not include references to scholarly work aiming at establishing empirical rather than legal propositions.[17] In the Nordic CONREASON Project we choose the second option, so only references to legal scholarship are to be marked under this variable. If the judgment refers to other (non-legal) research, it may be marked as N24 (a non-legal argument).

If there is no such reference in the reasoning, please leave all columns blank. If there is, please indicate the legal system object of the referenced scholarly work by writing the corresponding **number(s)** in the relevant box(es):

1) Scholarly work on the domestic legal system,
2) Scholarly work on another Nordic legal system,
3) Scholarly work on international law,
4) Scholarly work on a foreign legal system, including comparative works.

When marking (2), (3) or (4), please take a side note on the country of affiliation of the author(s).

A scholar's expert opinion given in the context of the drafting or amending of the constitution (for example in the form of a memorandum) is not to be counted here but under N23.

In the dataset the following aggregations of the subcategories are also included as separate variables: N25_13 (scholarly work on domestic and international law), N25_24 (scholarly work on foreign law).

N26 (Q21/Q23): Reference to foreign legal material

Please indicate YES or NO. A vague reference to 'foreign laws' or an expression such as 'after having analysed the results of comparative law' does qualify as a comparative law argument in the Excel Table. By contrast, simply quoting a foreign concept (even if it is used in a foreign language, eg German words like *Drittwirkung*) should not count as a reference to foreign law. By referring to foreign law, we allude to arguments that explicitly invoke or consider foreign legal sources (foreign countries' legal norms, foreign courts' sentences or the 'results of comparative law', meaning the experience of foreign legal institutions).

Nuances in the use of both foreign law arguments that are not captured by the Table can, and should, be discussed in your written report.

[16] ibid 704.
[17] ibid 744.

If there is no such reference in the reasoning, please leave all columns blank. If there is, please indicate the geographical origin and the type of the referenced legal material by writing the corresponding **number(s)** in the relevant box(es):

1) Nordic case-law,
2) Nordic legislation or other written source of law,
3) Non-Nordic case-law,
4) Non-Nordic legislation or other written source of law.[18]

If the reference to foreign law is part of a historical account aiming to explain the origin of a constitutional provision and not to interpret the constitutional provision in question, it is a part of subjective teleological reasoning (N23) and not to be marked here.

In the dataset the following aggregations of the subcategories are also included as separate variables: N26_12 (Nordic law), N26_34 (non-Nordic law), N26_13 (case-law), N26_24 (legislation or other written source of law).

N27 (–/–): Reference to a non-judicial body's opinion

Please indicate (YES or NO) whether the judgment explicitly refers to the opinions of a domestic non-judicial body on a constitutional matter. This includes, in particular but not exclusively, references to the opinions of the Law Council (*Lagrådet*) in Sweden and the Constitutional Committee in Finland.

N28 (–/Q24): Pro homine or pro persona principles

Please indicate (YES or NO) whether the judicial opinion explicitly uses *pro homine* or *pro persona* principles of interpretation. This is an interpretative principle the aim of which is to maximise the protection of human rights and, at the same time, minimalise restrictions pertaining to them. It has an interpretative aspect and an aspect of application of the law. The first means an extensive interpretation or a restrictive interpretation depending on which one is more in favour of the effective protection of rights, while the other aspect means the preference of norms that are more favourable to the effective protection of human rights.

Thus, the application of this principle includes restrictive interpretations of limitations on rights. On the other hand, it does *not* include the constitutional-friendly or constitutional-rights-friendly interpretation of ordinary legislation (*verfassungskonforme Auslegung*), if the argument does not contribute to establish the meaning of the constitution. In other words, it is to be marked as YES when the constitutional right is being interpreted, not the statute.

[18] In the CORE Latam project, the two options were (1) foreign laws from Latin American countries, (2) foreign laws from other regions, therefore our data obtained from (1)+(2) is comparable with their (1), and our (3)+(4) with their (2).

At the same time, the use of this principle has to be explicit at least to some extent. Even if it is not named, it should still be discussed in some form (for example, when the court claims that is chooses a certain interpretation in order to ensure the effective protection of a right).

If you mark YES for this variable, please take a side note on how explicitly and in which form this principle is applied.

N29 (Q22/Q25): Other types of argument or method

Please indicate YES or NO. Including references to domestic legal history, if you cannot qualify it as some kind of teleological argument.

Other arguments included in the UK Chapter: deference (to the other branches of government)[19] and arguments from actual political practice (especially in relation to the limits of prerogative powers).

N30 (–/–): Incomplete constitutional arguments

Please indicate (YES or NO) whether the judgment contains any incomplete constitutional argument. By incomplete argument we mean that the court identifies the legal basis (typically: a constitutional provision) on which it bases its finding but does not draw a logical inference from it that would create a clear and logical connection between the legal basis and the finding. In other words, it states that the finding is based on a given provision, but it does not explain why, so it is not possible to identify a method of interpretation on which the argument is based, not even in the form of reference to a secondary legal authority.

3. Variables Related to Conceptualisation

The CORE Latam project instructed the coders that it is not enough that a key concept is mentioned in the reasoning, but it has to be used in the framework of an argument or in the context of substantial analysis.[20]

In the Nordic context, we also count concepts that are applied in the judgment implicitly.[21] We also created a separate variable to measure the extent to which the courts use concepts and principles implicitly (N53). However, even in the case of implicit use of a concept or principle, so when the court does not name the concept or principle itself, it has to be clear to an informed reader to which concept or

[19] See Gyorfi (n 5) 707–708. Please note that we code deferential arguments under the 'rule of law' variable (as a 'separation of powers' argument = N31_4).

[20] See the Results of the July 4th, 2019 CORE Project Meeting, 4 (on file with the authors).

[21] The arguments (variables N13–N30), on the other hand, have to be used explicitly in the judgment.

principle the court refers exactly.[22] Therefore, every time you mark a concept or principle as present in the judgment under the following variables (N31–N51), please take a side note on whether that concept or principle was mentioned explicitly (ie. named by the court) or implicitly (in a way that is clear to an informed reader to which concept or principle the court refers to exactly). An even simpler way to do it can be to write the value ('YES' in the case of a binary variable or a number or letter in the case of a categorical variable) in red colour in the Excel file when the given concept or principle is only used implicitly in the judgment. This will also help you to choose the value for the last variable (N53).

N31 (Q23/Q26): The rule of law invoked as an argument

Please indicate whether the opinion invokes the rule of law or a similar concept. This refers to the rule of law (or similar concept, such as *rättsstat* in Swedish) and includes principles the concept is generally taken to imply: the separation of powers, the supremacy of the constitution, access to justice, principle of legality (*legalitetsprincipen*) and legal certainty (if these are considered to be part of the rule of law in the legal order you are analysing).

If there is no such concept invoked in the reasoning, please leave all columns blank. If there is, please indicate which concept is invoked, by writing the corresponding **number(s)** in the relevant box(es):

1) Explicit rule of law argument / *rättsstat*
2) Principle of legality / *legalitetsprincipen*
3) Legal certainty / *rättssäkerhet*
4) Separation of powers / *maktfördelning*
5) Access to justice
6) Other implicit rule of law argument

Mark (1) if the court uses the exact term 'rule of law' (in the respective language).

By principle of legality, we mean that if the legislature intends to interfere with fundamental rights or principles, it must express that intention by clear and unambiguous language, and that certain matters are to be regulated by law according to the constitution. In criminal law, it means that no one shall be held guilty of any criminal offence which did not constitute a criminal offence by the law when it was committed (*nullum crimen, nulla poena sine lege* principle).

[22] Note that many concepts and principles are already defined broadly in the codebook. We tried to solve this problem by creating subcategories for some of these variables: rule of law (N31), sovereignty (N34), nation (N38), core content of rights or competences (N41), freedom of expression (N45), and economic, social, cultural and environmental rights (N50). There are, however, many of the remaining binary variables that are still defined broadly. An implicit use means that the court does not explicitly name any of the subcategories or related concepts mentioned in the Codebook but can still be clearly qualified as such.

When used in the specific context of criminal law, it is also to be coded under N44. The 'being provided by law' requirement of the proportionality test is *not* to be counted here but only under N40.

By legal certainty, we mean both the law's internal consistency and its predictability.

By separation of powers, we mean the separation between the executive, legislative and judicial powers. Discussing the relationship between any two of the three branches may fall under this category. Explicit deference of the judges towards the legislature is also to be included here. If you marked N14_1 (political question doctrine), you also have to mark N31_4.

By access to justice, we mean access to courts and any discussion of this problem. Discussions on the right of appeal are, however, not to be coded here but under N44 (basic procedural rights), unless in the context of the national constitutional tradition the right of appeal is enshrined in the constitution and perceived as part of access to justice.

Mark (6) if the court uses the concept of rule of law implicitly, while none of the other four values are applicable (for example when the supremacy of the constitution is invoked). Even in this case, it has to be clear to an informed reader that the court meant to refer to the rule of law, so use this option parsimoniously.

N32 (-/Q27): Judicial independence

Please indicate (YES or NO) whether the reasoning expressively invokes the concept of judicial independence (*domstolarnas och domarnas oberoende* in Swedish). The concept of judicial independence means that no other state function can interfere with the judicial branch, as it shall enjoy independence from the interventions of the other branches. The judges while interpreting and applying the laws shall only be subjected to the constitution and the laws. Judicial independence has a structural aspect, according to which the judicial branch shall have an independent organisation, and a financial one, which refers to the budgetary independence that this branch shall enjoy. If you mark this variable as YES, you should also mark N31_4 (separation of powers).

Arguments on judicial deference to the legislature or to the executive are not to be included here but under N31_4 (separation of powers). If the judgment invokes the concept of impartiality of judges, it is not to be marked here but under N44 (basic procedural rights).

N33 (Q24/Q28): Democracy

Please indicate (YES or NO) whether the opinion invokes democracy. Reference to the concept of democracy may also come in the form of phrases such as 'sovereignty of the people' (*folksuveränitetsprincipen* in Swedish) or 'government of the people'. It also includes references to instruments of direct democracy (referendum, popular initiative), but not references to local democracy, which are considered under the concept of federalism (N39).

Following the conceptualisation offered by Dahl (1971), a substantive perspective of democracy categorises political regimes in relation to the outcomes that they generate. A minimalist, or procedural, perspective of democracy refers to political regimes in relation to their institutions and procedures. In this regard, democracy can be conceptualised and measured into two dimensions: (1) contestation or the extent to which the demos are free to create political organisations in order to channel the social demands into decision-making process; and (2) inclusion or the degree of participation in the democratic process.

This variable is not to be marked if the term 'democracy' is only invoked as part of the necessity clause of the proportionality principle ('necessary in democratic society').

N34 (Q25/Q29): Sovereignty

Please indicate whether the opinion invokes sovereignty. According to the Westphalia Pax, sovereignty means state authority (Krasner 2001). Following Thomas Hobbes, sovereignty relapses on the ultimate decision unit. Sovereignty within a state comprises a permanent population, a geographically defined territory, and a government with the capacity to establish (cooperative) relations with other sovereign states.

This variable includes references to the concept of state, statehood, international independence, and parliamentary sovereignty.[23] References to popular sovereignty (*folksuveränitet*), on the other hand, are to be considered under the 'democracy' variable (N33), not here.

If there is no such concept invoked in the reasoning, please leave all columns blank. If there is, please indicate which version of the concept is invoked, by writing the corresponding **number(s)** in the relevant box(es):

1) external sovereignty (eg, state sovereignty),
2) internal sovereignty (eg, parliamentary sovereignty).

N35 (Q26/Q30): State form

Please indicate (YES or NO) whether the opinion invokes arguments related to the form of the state (republic, monarchy).

N36 (Q27/Q31): Government form / Government system by procedural structure

Please indicate (YES or NO) whether the opinion invokes arguments related to the government form (parliamentary, presidential).

[23] 'Parliamentary sovereignty' was coded under this variable for the UK. See Gyorfi (n 5) 715.

N37 (Q28/Q33): Secularism

Please indicate (YES or NO) whether the opinion invokes arguments related to the separation of state and religion. This includes references to 'secularism', the separation of church and state and state neutrality in religious affairs (or the 'laic state'). Freedom of religion is also included here.[24]

N38 (Q29/Q34): Nation

Please indicate whether the opinion invokes the concept of nation (*folk* in Swedish). By the term of nation, we refer to the concept of nation-state (*nationalstat* in Swedish), which is a sovereign territory whereby the vast majority of inhabitants shares a similar culture and identity. We also mean to include the competing notions of nation, such as 'plurinationality'. It includes both civic and ethnic definitions of the concept (or a mixture of these) and references to ethnic minorities.

If there is no such concept invoked in the reasoning, please leave all columns blank. If there is, please indicate in which form this concept is invoked, by writing the corresponding **number(s)** in the relevant box(es):

1) the nation-state or national identity,
2) nationality (in the sense of national citizenship),
3) a national or ethnic minority.

N39 (Q30/Q32): Federalism / Government system by power structure

Please indicate (YES or NO) whether the opinion invokes federalism (including 'regionalism', 'autonomous regions', 'devolution', 'autonomy of local governments', 'subsidiarity').

N40 (Q31/Q35): Proportionality

Please indicate (YES or NO) whether the opinion considers proportionality or similar means-end test. Proportionality is a legal construct used to adjudicate human rights disputes, ie to resolve collisions between colliding values and rights. There are different versions of the test, but usually the model includes the following steps: legitimate aim, suitability of the aim, suitability of the restriction, proportionality of the restriction. We mean to include all versions of the test, from plain 'balancing' and 'scrutiny' until the most elaborated tests. An argument about whether a restriction is provided by law does not, in itself, qualify as a proportionality argument, but some kind of balancing has to take place or be at least taken into consideration.

[24] See the Results of the June 11–12, 2020 CORE Project Meeting, 4 (on file with the authors).

N41 (Q32/Q36): Core of constitutional rights or competences

Please indicate whether the opinion considers doctrines referring to the core content (*Wesensgehalt*) of either fundamental rights or of competences. Please write (1) if the opinion considers the core content of a right. The legal construct of 'core content of rights' refers to the unchangeable or inviolable essential origin of fundamental and human rights. Please write (2) if the opinion considers the core content of a competence. If there is no such doctrine mentioned in the opinion, please leave both columns blank.

N42 (Q33/Q37): Human dignity

Please indicate (YES or NO) whether the opinion explicitly invokes the concept of human dignity. According to Steinmann (2016), 'human dignity' is a contested concept. At the ontological level, the author defined 'human dignity' as a value or a right, directly associated with the unique qualities of every individual and the recognition of the second-generation social and economic human rights.

N43 (Q34/Q38): Equality

Please indicate (YES or NO) whether the opinion invokes equality (*jämställdhet, jämlikhet* in Swedish). This includes references to non-discrimination. By the concept of equality, we mean both general legal and political equality, in which all citizens in a given state are of equal standing before the law, and the equal treatment in terms of (human) rights (prohibition of unjustified discrimination).

N44 (Q35/Q39): Basic procedural rights

Please indicate (YES or NO) whether the opinion invokes basic procedural rights. This includes references to procedural due process, right to effective judicial review, adversarial principle, rights of the defence, right to be heard, *ne bis in idem*, principle of the legality of criminal offences and penalties, presumption of innocence, but excludes references to the constitutional requirements of the legislative and constitution-making process and parliamentary procedures.

N45 (Q36/Q40): Freedom of expression

Please indicate whether the opinion invokes freedom of expression rights. This includes reference to freedom of speech and freedom of the press. Please write (1) if the opinion invokes freedom of expression or freedom of speech, while write (2) if it invokes freedom of the press in the relevant column. If none of these freedoms is mentioned in the reasoning, please leave both columns blank.

N46 (Q37/Q41): Privacy rights

Please indicate (YES or NO) whether the opinion invokes the right to privacy or the right to respect for private and family life. This includes references to data protection and copyrights.

3.1. Additional Key Concepts from the CORE Latam Project

N47 (Q43): Justice

Please indicate (YES or NO) whether the opinion invokes or considers the concept of justice. We consider here the material concept of justice (both in the corrective and distributive sense). Justice has three basic elements: it is interpersonal, meaning that it can only exist in relation to another person(s); it involves a duty, meaning there is something that is owed to another person; and it implies equality, meaning an equilibrium or balance in relation to what is owed. This also includes references to reasonableness (*rimlighet* in Swedish).

N48 (Q44): Custom

Please indicate (YES or NO) whether the opinion invokes or considers the concept of custom (*sedvana, sedvanerätt* in Swedish). Custom refers to the legal tradition on a national level, either with or without an explicit mention of a concrete source from the domestic legal history. On a high level of generality, references to the 'constitutional tradition', 'customs of law' or the like should be included in this category. It applies only if one cannot qualify it as subjective teleological argument. It also includes references to local traditions, eg Sami customs. If you marked N13_3 (discussing whether a tradition or custom is part of the constitution/ constitutional law), you should write YES here too.

N49 (Q45): Family

Please indicate (YES or NO) whether the opinion invokes or considers the concept of family. References to family in general, or specifically to the social, legal and cultural aspects, conditions or values of family shall be considered here.

N50 (Q47): Economic, social, cultural and environmental rights

Please indicate whether the opinion invokes or considers second- or third-generation rights. Write (1) if the opinion invokes or considers economic, social and/or cultural rights, while write (2) if it invokes or considers environmental rights in the relevant column. If none of these rights is invoked or considered in the reasoning, please leave both columns blank. The right to property is not to be marked under this variable.

3.2. Additional Key Concept only in the Nordic CONREASON Project

N51: Transparency

Please indicate (YES or NO) whether the opinion invokes or considers the concept of transparency. This also includes references to access to public documents.

4. Conclusive Measurement Variables

N52 (–/Q50): The overall weight of the arguments

This variable refers to the ratio between those arguments that were mentioned but not taken into consideration and those that in fact contributed to the conclusion of the issue at hand (ie, the disposition of the case). Please check (M) (1) if the majority of the arguments mentioned in the opinion were ratio decidendi or obiter dictum arguments. Please check (E) (2) if the proportion between the ratio decidendi and obiter dictum arguments on the one hand, and the decorative, rhetorical or deceptive use of arguments, on the other hand, were practically equal. Please check (R) (3) if in the majority the opinion used rhetorical or deceptive arguments.

This variable is coded on the basis of the majority opinion, so not taking into account separate opinions, because it aims to discover to what extent do the arguments used by the court actually determine the outcome of the case.

If there is no constitutional argument in the judgment, for example because the court only interprets a statute in conformity with the constitution without interpreting the constitution or because there is no logical link between the invoked constitutional provisions and the court's conclusion, leave all boxes blank.

N53 (–/–): Implicit use of concepts

This variable refers to the ratio between implicit and explicit use of concepts and principles, concerning the concepts and principles coded under variables N31–N51. Please check (E) if the <u>majority</u> of the concepts and principles are mentioned in the opinion <u>explicitly</u>. Please check (P) if the proportion between the explicit and implicit use of concepts and principles were <u>practically equal</u>. Please check (I) if in the <u>majority</u> the opinion used concepts and principles <u>implicitly</u>. Please check (O) if the opinion <u>only</u> invoked concepts or principles <u>implicitly</u>, and none of them was named explicitly.

If there are no constitutional concepts or principles used by the court at all in relation to the interpretation of the constitution, leave all boxes blank.

Complete List of Cases Used in the Nordic CONREASON Project

Danish Supreme Court

U1921.148H	1920
U01921.644H	1921
U1925.277H	1925
U1935.1H	1934
U1941.1070/2H	1941
U1967.22H	1966
U1971.299H	1971
U1972.903H	1972
U1980.1037/2H	1980
U1986.898/3H	1986
U1993.757H	1993
U1994.29H	1994
U1994.536H	1994
U1996.1300H	1996
U1997.1157H	1997
U1999.360H	1998
U1998.800H	1998
U1999.1798H	1999
U1999.841H	1999
U2004.382H	2003
U2004.2661H	2004
U2006.1539H	2006
2006.770H	2005
U2008.378H	2007
U2008.671H	2007
U2008.2394H	2008

U2010.1035H	2010
U2010.1547H	2010
U2011.1365H	2011
U2012.1761H	2012
U2013.2696H	2013
U2013.3328H	2013
U2013.1451H	2013
U2017.824H	2016
U2017.1795H	2017
U2018.1690H	2018
U2018.1460H	2018
U2021.1893H	2021
U2021.4999H	2021
U2022.3378H	2022

Finnish Supreme Court

KKO 2000:28	2000
KKO 2002:116	2002
KKO 2003:107	2003
KKO 2004:26	2004
KKO 2004:62	2004
KKO 2005:82	2005
KKO 2006:71	2006
KKO 2007:36	2007
KKO 2008:83	2008
KKO 2008:93	2008
KKO 2008:24	2008
KKO 2008:10	2008
KKO 2009:80	2009
KKO 2009:84	2009
KKO 2009:27	2009
KKO 2010:74	2010
KKO 2010:39	2010
KKO 2010:88	2010

KKO 2011:43	2011
KKO 2011:38	2011
KKO 2012:11	2012
KKO 2012:81	2012
KKO 2012:95	2012
KKO 2012:58	2012
KKO 2012:52	2012
KKO 2014:13	2014
KKO 2014:14	2014
KKO 2014:35	2014
KKO 2014:93	2014
KKO 2014:67	2014
KKO 2015:14	2015
KKO 2015:92	2015
KKO 2016:20	2016
KKO 2020:68	2020
KKO 2021:42	2021
KKO 2021:88	2021
KKO 2022:25	2022
KKO 2022:26	2022
KKO 2022:1	2022
KKO 2022:8	2022

Finnish Supreme Administrative Court

KHO 2005:50	2005
KHO 2005:43	2005
KHO 2006:58	2006
KHO 2007:77	2007
KHO 2008:25	2008
KHO 2009:15	2009
KHO 2009:93	2009
KHO 2009:82	2009
KHO 2011:107	2011
KHO 2011:39	2011

KHO 2011:56	2011
KHO 2012:75	2012
KHO 2012:53	2012
KHO 2012:63	2012
KHO 2013:136	2013
KHO 2013:142	2013
KHO 2014:1	2014
KHO 2014:126	2014
KHO 2014:98	2014
KHO 2014:57	2014
KHO 2015:38	2015
KHO 2016:180	2016
KHO 2016:187	2016
KHO 2016:33	2016
KHO 2016:96	2016
KHO 2017:151	2017
KHO 2018:85	2018
KHO 2018:171	2018
KHO 2018:112	2018
KHO 2019:8	2019
KHO 2020:87	2020
KHO 2020:97	2020
KHO 2020:44	2020
KHO 2021:140	2021
KHO 2021:162	2021
KHO 2021:152	2021
KHO 2021:83	2021
KHO 2021:1	2021
KHO 2022:63	2022
KHO 2022:62	2022

Icelandic Supreme Court

118/1942 Hrafnkatla	1943
159/1968 Læknatal	1968

23/1974 Hundahald	1975
16/1983 Spegilsmálið	1984
81/1983 Kjarnfóðurgjald	1985
239/1987 Framamál	1988
120/1989 Hrd 1990 bls 2	1990
252/1989 Áfengiskaup dómara	1989
31/1990 Hæfi héraðsdómara	1990
129/1991 Afnám launahækkana	1992
124/1993 Leigubílstjóramál	1993
103/1994 Dómarafulltrúi	1995
110/1995 Samherjamál	1996
342/1995 Skipstjórnarábyrgð	1995
145/1998 Veiðileyfamál	1998
177/1998 Blindur nemandi	1999
64/1999 Landbúnaðargjöld	1999
65/1999 Good morning America	1999
12/2000 Vatneyrarmál	2000
15/2000 Stjörnugrís	2000
125/2000 Öryrkjadómur	2000
419/2000 Faðerni	2000
167/2002 Réttur til verkfalls	2002
549/2002 Öryrkjadómur II	2003
220/2005 Tóbaksauglýsingar	2006
278/2006 Bubbi fallinn	2007
92/2007 Þagnarréttur í samkeppnismálum	2007
491/2007 Áfengisauglýsingabann	2008
371/2010 Tvöföld refsing í skattamálum	2010
340/2011 Neyðarlög – meðalhóf	2011
37/2014 Ragnar Hall og Gestur Jónsson	2014
214/2014 Egill Einarsson	2014
10/2018 Frumskipun Landsréttar	2018

12/2018 Beiðni um enduruptöku (sterkt tvíeðli)	2019
9/2020 Réttarmorð	2021
26/2020 Endurskoðunarvald dómstóla í samkeppnismálum	2021
31/2020 – Ummæli eiginmanns dómara	2020
34/2020 Milliliðalaus sönnunarfærsla (veikt tvíeðli)	2021
52/2021 Lágmarksframfærsla frá TR	2022

Norwegian Supreme Court

Rt-1976-1	1976
Rt-1977-24	1977
Rt-1982-241	1982
Rt-1990-284	1990
Rt-1996-521	1996
Rt-1996-1415	1996
Rt-1996-1440	1996
Rt-1997-1821	1997
HR-2000-41-B	2000
Rt-2000-996	2000
Rt-2002-509	2002
Rt-2002-557	2002
Rt-2002-497	2002
Rt-2003-359	2003
Rt-2006-293	2006
Rt-2007-1281	2007
Rt-2007-1308	2007
Rt-2008-1409	2008
Rt-2008-1764	2008
Rt-2009-1118	2009
Rt-2009-1412	2009
Rt-2009-1423	2009

Rt-2010-143	2010
Rt-2010-535	2010
Rt-2010-1170	2010
Rt-2010-1445	2010
Rt-2012-519	2012
Rt-2012-2039	2012
Rt-2013-1345	2013
Rt-2015-421	2015
HR-2016-225-S	2016
HR-2016-304-S	2016
HR-2016-2554-P	2016
HR-2018-865-S	2018
HR-2019-2301-A	2019
HR-2020-2472-P	2020
HR-2021-417-P	2021
HR-2021-1975-S	2021
HR-2021-655-P	2021
HR-2022-863-A	2022

Swedish Supreme Court

NJA 1973 s. 423	1973
NJA 1981 s. 1 (Skattefjällsdomen)	1981
NJA 1981 s. 1205	1981
NJA 1982 s. 621	1982
NJA 1984 s. 648 (Bostadsbidraget)	1984
NJA 1985 s. 893 (Manifestetmålet)	1985
NJA 1986 s. 489 (Laboratorieassistentens blodprovstagning)	1986
NJA 1987 s. 198 (Löntagarfonderna)	1987
NJA 1989 s. 131	1989
NJA 1996 s. 370 (Gränsälvskommissionen)	1996

NJA 1996 s. 577 (De otillåtna märkena)	1996
NJA 2000 s. 132	2000
NJA 2000 s. 355	2000
NJA 2005 s. 33 (Blankettstraffbudet och Skogsstyrelsens föreskrifter)	2005
NJA 2005 s. 805 ("Predikan i Borgholm" eller "Pastor Green-fallet")	2005
NJA 2006 s. 467 (Flygbladen på skolan)	2006
NJA 2007 s. 695	2007
NJA 2007 s. 918	2007
NJA 2008 s. 567	2008
NJA 2012 s. 105 (Arbetarskyddsstyrelsens föreskrifter)	2012
NJA 2012 s. 342	2012
NJA 2012 s. 400 (Mangamålet)	2012
NJA 2013 s. 350	2013
NJA 2013 s. 502 (Juniavgörandet)	2013
NJA 2014 s. 79	2014
NJA 2014 s. 323 (Medborgarskapet I)	2014
NJA 2014 s. 332	2014
NJA 2015 s. 45	2015
NJA 2015 s. 298	2015
NJA 2015 s. 374 (RF och rättegångskostnaderna)	2015
NJA 2015 s. 631	2015
NJA 2015 s. 899	2015
NJA 2016 s. 1165	2016
NJA 2017 s. 157 (Laserpekaren II)	2017
NJA 2018 s. 103 (Medborgarskapet II)	2018
NJA 2018 s. 743 (Den korta remisstiden)	2018
NJA 2018 s. 753 (Parkfastigheten)	2018
NJA 2019 s. 577 (Laserpekaren II)	2019

NJA 2020 s. 3 (Girjasdomen)	2020
NJA 2021 s. 498 (Filmen från Christchurch)	2021

Swedish Supreme Administrative Court

RÅ 1974 ref 61 (RÅ 1974:121)	1974
RÅ 80 1:92 (Lex Kockum)	1980
RÅ 80 2:69	1980
RÅ 81 2:15	1981
RÅ 81 2:25	1981
RÅ 83 2:32	1983
RÅ 83 2:5	1983
RÅ 84 2:52	1984
RÅ 1986 ref. 108 (Gatumusikanterna i Gamla stan)	1986
RÅ 1987 ref. 21	1987
RÅ 1991 ref. 21	1991
RÅ 1991 ref. 87	1991
RÅ 1992 ref. 10	1992
RÅ 1993 ref. 10	1993
RÅ 1993 ref. 79	1993
RÅ 1995 ref. 4	1995
RÅ 1996 ref. 5	1996
RÅ 1996 ref. 28	1996
RÅ 1997 ref. 50	1997
RÅ 1999 ref. 76 (Barsebäcksmålet)	1999
RÅ 2000 ref. 19	2000
RÅ 2002 ref. 8	2002
RÅ 2005 ref. 39	2005
RÅ 2006 ref. 73	2006
RÅ 2006 ref. 87	2006
HFD 2011 ref. 10	2011
HFD 2013 ref. 30	2013
HFD 2013 ref. 37	2013

HFD 2013 ref. 72	2013
HFD 2014 ref. 28	2014
HFD 2015 ref. 45	2015
HFD 2015 ref. 51	2015
HFD 2016 ref. 44	2016
HFD 2016 ref. 59	2016
HFD 2017 ref. 4	2017
HFD 2017 ref. 22	2017
HFD 2017 ref. 53	2017
HFD 2018 ref. 7	2018
HFD 2021 ref. 43	2021
HFD 2022 ref. 10	2022

INDEX

NB–locators in **bold** indicate information in tables and those in *italics* indicate information in figures

access to justice, 12, 182, 225, 226
  Denmark, 69
  Norway, 146
administrative courts, 24
  Finland, 101, 114–18
  Sweden, 157, 162, 165–66, 173, 181–83
administrative decisions:
  Denmark, 55–56, 68
  Sweden, 156–57
applicability of constitutional law, 48, 162–63, **203,** 216–17
argumentation, 2, 17, 21, 28, 188–89
  European Court of Human Rights, 108–9, 112, 120–21, 122
  Finland, 105, 116, 119, 122–23
  Iceland, 90–91
  Nordic style, 102–3, 189–90, 191–92, 193–95, 205
***Ástráðsson* case (I),** 80, 86
Australia, 17, 123
autonomous regions, 228
autonomy of local governments, 228

basic procedural rights, 226, 229
binding precedent doctrine:
  Finland, 106–8
  Iceland, 83
  see also precedent-based argument

Canada, 122–23
Caribbean Commonwealth, 25
Charter of Fundamental Rights of the EU (CFREU), 115–16, 151
civil law tradition, 106–7, 189
codification of judicial review:
  Norway, 147
  Sweden, 6, 7, 160
common law tradition, 106–7, 140–2, 150, 189
Conceptualist School (*Begriffsjurisprudenz*), 4–5, 191
concurring opinions, 20, 66–67, 73, 141, 199–200, *200,* 210–11, 214, 217, 220
CONREASON project, 1–2, 3–4, 16–21, 23, 33–34, 46, 209–10
  aim of project, 24
  background, 24
  bivariate correlations, 28
  cases used, **233–42**
  categorisations of legal systems, 27
  comparisons of categories
    administrative and non-administrative cases, 36
    between Nordic and international countries/courts, 37–46
    between Nordic countries/courts, 36–37
    within Nordic countries/courts, 35
  data collection, 24–25
    court and country indicators, 26
    external datasets, links with, 27–28
  degree of linear association between variables, 34–35
  descriptives, 29–30
  design of project, 24–25
    case selection, 25–26
    consensus and inter-coder reliability, 25–26
    court and country indicators, 26
    expert opinion, use of, 25–26
  inferential claims, 30–31, *32, 33*
  Nordic and international countries/courts compared, 37–38
    aggregated court level, 38–46
    canonical correlations, 40
    cluster analysis, 43–44
    difference in means, 45–46
    dimensionality of data, 40–43
    discriminatory power, 44–45
    multiple factor analysis, 40–43
    pairwise correlations, 39–40
  relationships between variables, 34–35

trends over time, 29
univariate distributions, 28
variable coding, **47–50**
arguments used, 213–24
characteristics of case, 210–13
conceptualisation, 224–31
conclusive measurement variables, 231
consensual democracy, 190
see also democracy
constitutional amendments:
Denmark, 52
Iceland, 92, 93
Norway, 126–27, 128–29, 150
Sweden, 11, 22, 152–56, 166, 177, 178–80
travaux préparatoires, 163–64, 166, 168
constitutional culture, 2, 22, 190–93, 206–7
collective Nordic culture, 8, 22, 185–88, 190–91, 206–7
Finland, 22, 98, 104, 119
CLC and non-judicial ex ante review, 112–14
Iceland, 89, 104
Norway, 104, 136–37, 147
Sweden, 22, 98, 104, 178, 184
constitutional interpretation, 9, 11
Denmark, 56, 62, 72
Finland, 103, 120–21
ECHR-related arguments, 108–12
national parliaments, respect for, 104–6
political question doctrine, 104
precedent, 106–8
references to non-judicial bodies, 112–14
Iceland, 91–92
non-judicial bodies, 8–9
Sweden, 11, 166–67
ordinary meaning of words, 167, 169–70
pro homine principle, 180–81
purpose-oriented interpretation, 169–70
systematic considerations, 170–71
travaux préparatoires, 167–69
constitutional origins, 9–10
Iceland, 76–77
WWII, 77–78
Norway, 126–27
Sweden, 152–55
constitutional pluralism, 109, 196, 198
constitutional reasoning, 2–3, 5, 8, 18–19
Finland, 99–101, 121–23
Nordic-specific constitutional reasoning, 198–205
Sweden, 161–62, 181, 183–84
equality principle, 181–82
legality, 182–83
non-discrimination principle, 182
proportionality, 183
rule of law, 182–83
transparency principle, 182
constitutional rights, 206, 223–24, 229
Denmark, 65–66
Finland, 99, 103–4, 107, 109–12, 114, 121, 121–22, 123
Norway, 128
Sweden, 161, 163–64
constitutional supremacy, 182, 225, 226
constitutionalism, 5, 187, 190, 196–98
Finland, 112, 121–23
legislature-centred approach, 9–12
court systems, 38
Finland, 101, 118
Iceland, 81
Sweden, 155–59
constitutionality of legislation, 53–54
Denmark, 7, 49, 53–55, 65–66, 71–72
Finland, 6
Norway, 10, 147
Sweden, 155–56
CORE Latam Project, 17, 25, 209, 221–22, 224, 230
criminal law, 225–26
Finland, 116
Iceland, 88
Norway, 144
Sweden, 160–61, 168–69, 180–81, 182
custom, 16, 216, 230
Finland, 101–2
Iceland, 82, 93–94, 95–96
Norway, 128, 136, 143–44, 147–48
Sweden, 154–55

democracy principle, 2, 4, **20**, 187–88, 189, 206, 220, 226–27
consensual democracy, 190
Denmark, 52–53, 56, 58, 70, 73
Finland, 102, 105, 107–8
Norway, 146, **204**
deference to the legislature, 10–11, 15, 190, 191, 201, 206, 224, 226
Denmark, 73
Finland, 97, 104–6, 121–22
Iceland, 88, 95
Norway, 137
Sweden, 157, 161–66, 184
Denmark, 51–52
concept of core content, 65–66
Constitution

amendments, 52
constitutional principles, 53–54
constitutionality of legislation, 53–54
democracy principle, 56–57
equality principle, 59–60
EU law, relationship with, 63
human rights, 52
Iceland compared, 65–66
justice versus law, 58
legal reasoning, 58–59, 73
legality principle, 57–58
review of administrative decisions, 55–56
separation of powers, 53
deference to the legislature, 73
democracy, 55–56, 58, 70, 73
dissenting opinions, 66–67
foreign case law, 60, 73, 176, 222–23
judicial independence doctrine, 53, 58, 64, 69–*70*
judicial review, 7, **7**
Kompetenz-Kompetenz doctrine, 63
length of the judgments, 66
Maastricht formality judgment, 51–52, 71
Maastricht reality judgment, 51–52, 63, 71
manifest error requirement, 10–11, 51, 53, 73
national identity, 70–71
Norwegian law, influence of, 63–64
rule of law (*retsstat* and *retssikkerhed*), 67–68, 73
access to justice, 69
judicial independence, 69
legal certainty, 69, 73
legality principle, 68
separation of powers, 69
state sovereignty concept, 64, 73
supremacy of EU law, 63
Supreme Court as a third state power, 71–72
teleological arguments, 61–63, 72
travaux préparatoires, 56, 62, 71, 71
Tvind judgment, 3, 7, **7**, 51–52, 53, 59–60, 63, 69, 71–72
devolution, 228
dissenting opinions, 20, 199, *200*, 210–11, 214
Denmark, 66–67, 73
Iceland, 80
Norway, 141, *142*, 150
Sweden, 165
diversity:
argumentative diversity, *181*, 191–93, *192*, 206
conceptual diversity, 181, *181*, 191–93, *192*
dualist approach to international law, 2, 12–13, 204–5
EEA law, 14
EU law, 14
Iceland, 75, 82–83, 84–87, 95, 196
Norway, 129, 133
Sweden, 153, 160, 173–74

East-West division among the constitutional systems, 63–64, 127, 133, 137–38, 140, 142, 150, 193–95, 205, 206
Eckhoff, Torstein, 5, 135
economic, social, cultural and environmental rights, 144, 225, 230
effective protection doctrine, 223–24
Finland, 111–12
equality principle, 20, 36, 200–1, 229
Denmark, 59–60, 67
Iceland, 92–93
Norway, 149
Sweden, 181–82
EU law, 13–15
Denmark, relationship with, 63, 70
Finland, 100, 103, 110, 115–16
Norway, 107–8
primacy of EU law, 160, 216, 217
Sweden, 158, 160–61, 184
European Convention on Human Rights (ECHR), 12–13, 16, 27, 42, 195, 196, 216–20
Denmark, 52
Finland, 99, 108–12, 195
Iceland, 75, 78, 82–87, 94–95, 205
Norway, 128–29, 139
Sweden, 2–3, 151, 173, 176, 180, 184
European Court of Human Rights (ECtHR), 12–13, 27
Denmark, 68–69
Finland, 103, *108*, 109–10, 111, 112, 115, 122–23
proportionality principle, 120–21
harmonisation of constitutions with ECtHR case law, 218
Iceland
Ástráðsson v Iceland, 80, 86
interpretation, 83, 91
precedents, 83, 85–87
Norway, 139, 140, 147
proportionality, 148–49
Sweden, 171–72, 177–78

European Economic Area (EEA), 13–15
  harmonisation of constitutions with EEA case law, 218
  Iceland, 75, 78, 82, 95–96
European Free Trade Area (EFTA), 13–15
  harmonisation of constitutions with EFTA case law, 218
  Iceland, 78
Europeanisation, 22, 103, 189, 196–98, 199–200, 206

family, 230
  right to respect for private and family life, 230
federalism, 102, 212, 226, 228
Finland, 97–98, 118–19
  binding precedent doctrine, 106–8
  Constitution, 98–99
  constitutional interpretation, 120–21
  constitutional reasoning, 99–101, 121–23
  democracy, 105, 107
  European Convention on Human Rights, 99, 108–12
  effective protection doctrine, 111–12
  EU law, 99
  fundamental rights doctrine, 107
  human rights obligations, 107–8
  judicial reasoning, 101–2
  judicial review, 5–6, **7**, 107
  legality, 119–20
  manifest error requirement, 10–11
  NATO membership, 98
  non-judicial ex ante review, 112–13, 121–22
  political question doctrine, 104
  pro homine principle, 110–11
  proportionality, 120–21
  sources of law doctrine, 101–2, 105–6
  style of legal argumentation, 102–3
    Supreme Court, 103–4
  Supreme Court, 103–4
    reference to Constitutional Law Committee, 117, 122
    reference to ECHR, 114–15
    reference to EU law, 115–16
    reference to precedents, 117–18
foreign law, 222–23
  Denmark, 60, 63
  Iceland, 78, 91, 95
  Sweden, 176–78
freedom of expression, 20, 36, 229
  Denmark, 58
  Norway, 145–46
  Sweden, 151, 152–53, 157, 160–61, 162, 169–70, 176, 179, 181, 182

government form, 20, 64, 102
  parliamentary government, 98, 190, 227
  presidential government, 98, 227

harmonising arguments:
  domestic harmonising arguments, 16, 169–70, 217–18
  harmonising with international law requirements, 16, **20**, 83–84, 85, 139, 150, 173–76, **203**, 205, 218
Historical School, 4–5
Hobbes, Thomas, 227
human dignity, 20, 52–53, 199, 220–21, 229
human rights:
  Denmark, 52, 72
  Iceland, 65, 83, 86, 88
  Finland, 107–8, 109, 112, 114
  Norway, 108, 127–28
    justice, 149
    proportionality, 147–49
  Sweden, 184
  see also Charter of Fundamental Rights of the EU; European Convention on Human Rights; European Court of Human Rights

Iceland:
  constitutional interpretation, 91–92
  constitutional origins, 76–77
    WWII, 77–78
  criminal law cases, 88
  customary law, 94
  Denmark compared, 65–66, 91–92
  dualist reasoning modality, 82–83, 84–86
  European Convention on Human Rights, 75, 82–87, 94–95
  EEA Agreement, 75
  European Free Trade Area, 78
  equality principle, 92–93
  harmonisation, 83–84
  human rights, 65, 83, 88
  International Covenant on Civil and Political Rights, 78
  International Covenant on Economic, Social and Cultural Rights, 78
  international law, relationship with, 82–83, 88–89
  judicial review, 6, **7**

judicial style of reasoning, 88, 95
majority reasoning
legal academia, 80–81
legal argumentation and appropriate material, 89–91
legal formalism, 91
legal positivism, 91
monist reasoning modality, 84, 85
NATO membership, 77–78
private law cases, 88
proportionality principle, 93
public law cases, 88
sovereignty, 95–96
Supreme Court, 78–79
appointment of judges, 80
case load, 79–80, 87–88
case management, 79–80
institutional reforms, 79
Inter-American Court of Human Rights (IACtHR), 25, 27, 218
International Covenant on Civil and Political Rights (ICCPR), 78, 128, 137, 218
International Covenant on Economic, Social and Cultural Rights (ICESCR), 78, 218
international law harmonisation, 16, **20**, **203**, 205, 218
Finland, 103, 110
Iceland, 83–84, 85
Norway, 137–39, 150
Sweden, 173–76

judicial independence doctrine, 10, **49**, 226
Denmark, 53, 58, 64, 69, *70*
Finland, 101
Norway, 146–47
Sweden, 156–57
judicial reasoning, 2, 189, 191–92
Denmark, 51–52, 57, 59–60, 62–63, 72
Finland, 101–2
Iceland, 87–94, 95
judicial review:
legal basis of (constitutional) judicial review, 5–7, **7**
manifest error requirement, 10–11, 156, 165, 178–79
manifest unconstitutionality requirement, 10–11
weak-form review, as, 9–10, 12, 122–23, 206
justice versus law, 58, 230

***Kløfta* case (N),** 6, 11, 135–37, 142
***Kompetenz-Kompetenz* doctrine:**
Denmark, 63

Latin America, 17, 25, 58, 110, *110*
see also CORE Latam project
law of obligations:
Denmark, 59, 61
legal academia:
see also legal scholarship
Iceland, 80–81
Norway, 133, 134, 140, 146
legal certainty, 225–26
Denmark, 56, 60, 67–68, 69, 73
Norway, 146
Sweden, 182
legal culture, 19, 22
collective Nordic culture, 185–88, 190–91
constitutional reasoning, 188–89
Denmark, 63–64, 66–67, 80–81
Finland, 22, 97–98, 107, 112, 119
travaux préparatoires, 201–2
legal formalism, 4–5, 201
Finland, 102–3
Iceland, 91
Norway, 141, 190–91
Sweden, 158
legal positivism, 4, 186
Finland, 102–3, 119
Iceland, 91
legal realism:
American legal realism compared, 4
legal formalism, relationship with, 4–5
Scandinavian legal realism, 4, 12, 189, 191, 196
legal reasoning:
constitutional reasoning, *see* constitutional reasoning
judicial reasoning, *see* judicial reasoning
legal scholarship, 189, 196, 219, 221–22
Denmark, 58, 63
Finland, 100, 107, 109–10
Iceland, 80–81, 89–91
justice versus law, 58
Norway, 133, 134, 138–39, 140, 146, 147, 190–91
Sweden, 177–78
legality principle, 201, 212, 225–26, 229
Denmark, 57–58, 64, 68, 69
Finland, 119–20
Norway, 144, 146
Sweden, 156–57, 165–66, 169, 182–83

legislature and legislative process, 8, 15
Denmark, 56
Finland, 97, 103, 104, 112, 122
Iceland, 76, 90–91
Norway, 136–37
Sweden, 153, 158–59, 168, 170, 174, 178
legislature-centred approach to constitutionalism, 9–12
Lundstedt, Vilhelm, 4

***Maastricht formality* judgment (DK),** 51–52, 59–60, 64, 71
***Maastricht reality* judgment (DK),** 51–52, 57, 63, 71
majority reasoning, 3, 26, 66–67, 73, 87, 213
manifest error requirement, 10–11, 156, 165, 179
***Marbury v Madison* (US),** 133–34, 150
monist reasoning modality:
Iceland, 82, 84, 85, 205
Montesquieu, Charles Louis de Secondat, 10
morality and law, 4, 185, 220
multilevel constitutionalism, 196, 198

nation and nation-state, 12, 59, 70, 127, 228
national identity, 228
Denmark, 59, 70–71
Sweden, 155
NATO:
Finland, 98
Iceland, 77–78
natural law, 4, 91
***ne bis in idem* principle,** 151, 229
New Zealand, 123
non-discrimination principle, 229
Swedish, 176–77, 181–82
non-judicial bodies:
constitutional interpretation, 8–9, 223
Sweden, 178–81
ex ante review
Finland, 112–13, 117, 121–22
preparatory works, 8–9
non-legal arguments, 20, 214, 220–21, 222
Finland, 102, 206
Nordic context, specificities of, 4, 15–16, 216–17, 224–25
judicial review, 5–7
role of non-judicial bodies, 8–9
legislature-centred approach, 9–12
position of international law, 12–15
Nordic legislative cooperation, 177, 190

Norway, 125–26, 149–50
common law courts, inspiration from, 140–1–43
constitutional history, 126–27
Denmark, influence on, 63–64
economic rights, 144
individual freedom and protection, relationship with, 145–46
European Convention on Human Rights, 128–29
harmonising with international law requirements, 137–39, 147–48
international human rights, 127–28
justice, 149
proportionality, 147–49
judicial review, 6, **7**, 129, 133–35, 135–367
legal scholarship, 140–41
precedent, *143*
constitutional custom, 143–44
preferred position principle, 11
separation of powers, 146–47
Supreme Court, 129–30, 140–41
law clerks, 130–31
cases decided on the merits, 130–33
***nullum crimen, nulla poena sine lege* principle,** 225–26

ordinary meaning of words, 217
Denmark, 55
Sweden, 167, 169

parliamentary committees, 6, 8
Finland, Constitutional Law Committee, 107, 114
Sweden, Konstitutionsutskottet, 6, 11, 168, 178
parliamentary ombudsman, 8
Sweden, 178
parliamentary supremacy/sovereignty, 226–27
Denmark, 64
Finland, 98, 99, 104
Sweden, 98, 104, 182, 225
pluralism, 109, 190–91, 196, 198
political question doctrine, 106, 190, 216–17, 226
Finland, 104
Sweden, 162–63, 164–66
politics and law, 1, 4, 113, 129, 134–35
popular sovereignty, 5, 8, 227
Finland, 104
Sweden, 153, 156

pragmatism:
Finland, 102–3, 122
Nordic interpretation, 102, 102–3, 206
European Convention on Human Rights, 122
freedom of expression, 176
legal and constitutional culture, 190–91
pluralism, 191, 204–5
preparatory works, 167, 191
Sweden, 167, 176
precedent-based argument, 218–19
Finland, 122
Iceland, 142
Sweden, 170–73
preferred position principle, 11, 135–36, 140–41, 144, 146–47
preparatory works, *see* ***travaux préparatoires***
privacy rights, 93, 200–1, 230
private law:
Finland, 105
Iceland, 78–79, 88
Sweden, 157, 177
pro homine **principle of interpretation,** 223–24
Finland, *110*, 110–11, 122
Sweden, 180
proportionality principle, 2, **20**, 219, 220–21, 225–26, 227, 228
Finland, 120–21, 122
Iceland, 93
Norway, 147–49, 150
Sweden, 166, 171, 180, 183
public law:
Finland, 116
Iceland, 78–79, 88
Sweden, 157–58, 177

regionalism, 228
respect for the will of the legislature, *see* **deference to the legislature**
Ross, Alf, 4, 56
rule of law, 2, **20**, 189, 200–1, 206, 212, 219, 225–26
constitutional reasoning, 182–83
Denmark, 52–53, *57*, 60, 67–71, 73
Finland, 114
Norway, 146
Sweden, 182–83

scholarly work, **20**, 221–22
Denmark, 60, 63
Iceland, 89–91
Norway, 138–39, 140–41, 147
Sweden, 177–78
secularism, 145–46, 228
separation of powers doctrine, 3, 10, 190, 201, 212, 219, 225–26
Denmark, 53, 58, 67, 68–69
Finland, 102, 104, 107
Norway, 144, 146–47
Sweden, 153, 182
sources of law doctrine, 8, 187, 188–89, 213
Denmark, 198
Finland, 101–2, 105–6, 119
sovereignty, 4–5, 8, **20**, 194, **204**, 219, 220, 226–27
Denmark, 64, 73, 74, 194
Finland, 104
Iceland, 77, 78, 95–96
Sweden, 153, 156
standards of reference and rationality, 185, 198–99
state form, 227
Denmark, 64, 194
Finland, 102
state sovereignty concept, *see* **sovereignty**
subsidiarity, 228
supremacy of constitutions, 182, 226
supremacy of EU law, 14, 63
see also EU law, primacy of EU law
supremacy of EEA law, 13–14
Supreme Court as a third state power, 71–72
Sweden, 151–52
case selection, 159–61
constitutional history, 152–55
constitutional interpretation, 166–67
ordinary meaning of words, 167, 169–70
pro homine principle, 180–81
purpose-oriented interpretation, 169–70
systematic considerations, 170–71
travaux préparatoires, 167–69
constitutional reasoning, 161–62, 181, 183–84
equality principle, 181–82
legality, 182–83
non-discrimination principle, 182
proportionality, 183
rule of law, 182–83
transparency principle, 182
constitutional review, 155–59
court system, 156–57
courts, 155–59
deference to the legislator, 161–66
EU law, 184

European Convention on Human Rights, 160, 162, 165, 168, 172, 173–76, 177, 180–81, 184
foreign law, 176–77
international law harmonisation, 173–76
judicial review, 6–7, **7**
codification, 11
manifest error requirement, 10–11
non-judicial bodies, reference to, 178–81
precedent-based argument, 170–73
preparatory works, 6, 11–12, 156, 163–64, 166–70, 174–76, 178–80, 183, 184
scholarly work, 177–78

teleological reasoning, 2, **20**, 221, 224
Denmark, 61–63, 72
Finland, 105–6
Iceland, 91–92
Sweden, 167–68, 169, 179
teleological (historical-intentional)/ subjective teleological arguments, 91–92, 167–68, 179, 199, 201–2, 214, 219–20, 223, 230
teleological (textual)/objective teleological argument, 169, **204**, 219
transparency, 20, 231
Denmark, 60, 73
Sweden, 152, 161, 182
travaux préparatoires, 8–9, 191, 201–3, 219–20
Denmark, 56–57, 62, 71, 74
Finland, 98, 99, 102, 105–6, 111, 121–22
Iceland, 83, 90–91, 95
Norway, 147
Sweden, 6, 11–12, 156, 163–64, 166–70, 174–76, 178–80, 183, 184
Tuorli, Kaarlo, 188–90
***Tvind* judgment (DK),** 3, 7, **7**, 51–52, 53, 59–60, 63, 69, 71–72
type of dispute, 20, 212

United States, 17, 134, 135, 139, 141, 150
US Supreme Court, 134, 141, 150
unwritten rules and principles, 2, 186, 190
Denmark, 59–60, 67
Finland, 101
Iceland, 82

written rules and principles, 9, 15–16, 185, 190, 216, 220–21, 223
Denmark, 57, 67
Finland, 101–2, 103
Iceland, 83, 93–94, 96
Norway, 126, 128, 130
Sweden, 144, 147, 152, 153–54, 172, 177–78

www.ingramcontent.com/pod-product-compliance
Ingram Content Group UK Ltd.
Pitfield, Milton Keynes, MK11 3LW, UK
UKHW020804290926
15470UKWH00003B/942

9 781509 991549